SIMON & SCHUSTER

New York London Toronto Sydney Tokyo Singapore

Out of Thin Air

THE BRIEF WONDERFUL LIFE OF NETWORK NEWS

REUVEN FRANK

Simon & Schuster
Simon & Schuster Building
Rockefeller Center
1230 Avenue of the Americas
New York, New York 10020

Designed by Levavi & Levavi
Manufactured in the United States of America

1 2 3 4 5 6 7 8 9 10

Library of Congress Cataloging in Publication data
Frank, Reuven, date.
Out of thin air : the brief
wonderful life of
network news / Reuven Frank.
p. cm.
1. NBC News—History.   2. Television broadcasting of news—United States.
3. Journalists—United States—Biography.   4. Journalism—Social aspects—
United States.   5. Press and politics—United States.   6. United States—
Politics and government—1945—I. Title.
PN4888.T4F68 1991
384.55'06'573—dc20
91-12876
CIP
ISBN 0-671-67758-6

This book is
for Bernice.

1

Television news began with the 1948 political conventions. The networks themselves were only seven weeks old, having been born on May 1 when AT&T inaugurated regular, commercial intercity transmission of television pictures. Suddenly, owning the expensive novelty called a television set had a redeeming purpose. Born at the conventions, network news departments came to be defined by their convention coverage. Newspeople relished the status they attained within their networks at convention time, and individuals were judged by how well they had done or might be expected to do. Above all, whoever was his network's visible face at the conventions became its symbol, its standard-bearer for four more years—Douglas Edwards, John Cameron Swayze, Walter Cronkite, Chet Huntley, David Brinkley. All this lasted perhaps two decades, a long time in television.

Four television networks were launched that May 1, three by the established radio networks ABC, CBS, and NBC, and one, DuMont, by a maker of television receivers. (NBC was also a subsidiary of a major manufacturer of TV sets, the Radio Corporation of America.) At the time, AT&T's "coaxial cable" reached only nine cities, from Boston in the north to Richmond, Va. in the south. In those cities, seventeen stations would carry the convention pictures, every moment of everything that happened, plus hours of nothing happening at all.

Radio had never tried such "gavel-to-gavel" coverage. With profitable programs already in place, it didn't need the conventions. But for the new television networks, still unsure of what they were doing or how they were going to pay for it with so few advertisers, it was a windfall. While politicians innocently filled hours of broadcast time, New York managers could save money by turning off lights, locking studios, and sending home (unpaid) actors, musicians, and comedians—in 1948, it was the answer to an accountant's dream.

For the week of the Republican convention alone, one network's television coverage was forty hours longer than its radio coverage, and a new medium brought a new audience to the drama of the roll call of the states, first brought to the country by radio in 1924.

Whatever the year, whichever the party, the uninflected, unaccented loud reading of four syllables across a crowded hall would announce the time of collective decision.

"A-la-ba-ma." Americans heard that sound for the first time in 1924, the longest convention in history, when it took 103 roll-call votes until a candidate got the two-thirds vote that the Democrats required for nomination. The nominee was soon forgotten, but for years Americans could still hear the lead-off state voting 101 times for its favorite son: "A - la - ba - ma."

"Alabama casts twenty-four votes for Oscar W. Underwood."

Yet in 1948, network executives were reluctant. To them, the conventions were a nuisance, not an opportunity. Without enough experienced technicians to man the cameras, lights, and control rooms, they believed that instead of being an accountant's dream, costs would far exceed income. But the manufacturers believed that convention coverage would sell TV sets, and with manufacturers owning two of the networks, NBC and DuMont, live coverage was inevitable.

The political parties definitely wanted live coverage. They had picked Philadelphia because it was on the coaxial cable, with access to whatever television there was. When the Democratic National Committee met to hear the proposals of the cities vying to be host, there was the usual talk about transportation and hotel rooms, and how much tangible help—that is, cash—a city would kick in. When the manager of WFIL-TV, Philadelphia, explained what the coaxial cable was, and pointed out that a third of America, 168 electoral votes' worth, would be "within reach" of a television set, San Francisco, which had more hotel rooms, withdrew its bid.

Doing business under federal license, the networks could hardly ignore the implied invitation. The two major party conventions would include every official, every legislator, every regulator who could shape a radio or television company's right to exist. In network contacts with politicians in Philadelphia's restaurants and hotels, no one said a word about licensing—but no one forgot about it either.

The 1948 conventions were the last held in a hall that was not air-conditioned. Early TV cameras needed floods of artificial light, and it was a hot July even for Philadelphia. All live pictures from inside the convention hall came from pooled cameras—otherwise each network would have invaded the hall with its own cameras, its own lights. But television showed, and newspapers wrote about, sweat darkening the delegates' light-colored, summer-weight suits and adding a glow to the faces of their wives.

In addition to the pool pictures, each network had a broadcasting room inside the "headquarters hotel," the Bellevue-Stratford, and interview studios within the convention hall building. And television mobile units, each the size of a cross-country moving van, were diverted from covering baseball games in cities like New York and Chicago and sent lumbering through the streets of Philadelphia.

There were fewer than 150 million Americans that year. Chicago was still the country's second largest city, and Philadelphia the third.

Of the eighteen cities in the United States with television stations, only nine were along the coaxial cable and could telecast the live coverage. NBC's coverage was seen in seven of the nine, DuMont's reached four, and ABC and CBS each had three affiliates carrying the live picture. The stations in the other cities received their coverage via the U.S. mails. A day or so later, the postman brought a much-edited kinescope, a film of a television picture, of what had gone on the day before.

Afterward, the networks would boast that 10 million Americans along the coaxial cable had seen at least part of the coverage. That figure was printed in newspapers and periodicals and then, typically, one source quoted another, which led to another, and suddenly a press release became Truth. But as of June 15, less than a month before the first convention, only 314,000 American homes in the eighteen cities with stations on the air had television receivers, and there were only 40,000 more in "bars and other public places." For 10 million Americans to have seen at least some part of the coverage is just not possible. But it is the record, the permanent, ineradicable record.

That summer, everyone who streamed into Philadelphia—politicians and reporters, candidates and managers—had an acute sense of the history they would make. To both Republicans and Democrats that year, whether Roosevelt's coalition would survive and what would be the shape of postwar America were the consuming questions. Television's presence was noted and generally welcomed, but it was interesting only as a novelty. That television would itself be history, that it would even *shape* history, was yet to be understood.

The Republican convention began on Monday, June 21. All the previous week, the networks had been broadcasting whatever they could to whip up interest, to teach themselves how to do this new thing, to keep busy. There was much made of the various "firsts"—the first live broadcast from the Senate Office Building, the first from a campaign headquarters. And during the conventions there were more "firsts": the first press conference to be carried on live television; the first time a President was seen on live television getting on a train in one city and off in another. NBC's television broadcast logs for those days read like a baby book: the first step, the first tooth, the first word.

The networks were groping for what constituted television coverage of a convention. The idea of chasing news with a live camera was still to be born. The "first televised press conference," which Governor Thomas E. Dewey of New York held on the second afternoon of the Republican convention, was part of the swift flow of the news rather than the kind of formalized set pieces most of the candidates had offered the preceding weekend. Television's presence was simply a conditioned response to a real problem that needed solving. When word came of the press conference, a journalist trained in print mused that he would normally send a reporter and a photographer and wondered if he could send a camera unit. He could, and they did. Then, having done it once, they did it again. And again.

The event that triggered this novel response came out of the dominant political news of the winter and spring. The two main political questions that year were whether the Democrats would find someone to replace the unpopular Harry Truman, and who, among Dewey, Senator Robert Taft of Ohio, and Harold Stassen, the former boy governor of Minnesota, would win the Republican nomination. Both questions were still unanswered when the parties assembled in Philadelphia. In those days, such things were still decided at political conventions. In other words, there was news. Covering news live was seen to be possible. Sometimes cameras were manhandled into place in time, but usually reporters learned the news and then talked about it on camera. By seeking news beyond the confines of the published schedule, television proved itself more than a toy, more than a show. Newspapers wrote about it; people talked about it.

The events themselves have faded into footnotes, but as part of the history of television, they play higher on the page. Dewey's Tuesday press conference was in effect a claim of victory. He had won a large, key delegation from a "favorite son" and wanted not only to announce it and to boast of it but to use it to sustain his momentum, so that the victory he claimed could become a reality.

The press conference followed a night of maneuvering and arm-twisting and a morning of rumors and denials. When it was scheduled, those at NBC television headquarters who have since come to be called producers and executive producers, asked, "Could cameras get there and be set up in time?" The technical manager in charge of cameras said, "Perhaps." They were. No other television network thought to be there and radio arrived late. So when the Dewey bandwagon started rolling toward the nomination, the moment was seen on NBC television.

At each network, the stars of radio news, all widely known to the public by name and voice, resisted assignment to the television coverage, though some did occasional duty, a few minutes each day, as a favor to some executive. ABC shifted reporters and commentators back and forth. Martin Agronsky and H. R. Baukhage were among those describing the proceedings in both of ABC's media, in a staff led by Elmer Davis, whom many of us considered the best broadcast journalist ever. In ABC's television interview studio at the Bellevue-Stratford, a feature reporter, Walter Kiernan, filled the longueurs by chatting with hot-dog sellers, bellhops, pretty girls.

At the two senior networks, remarkably parallel stories were unfolding. The key job, "anchoring" the convention coverage, fell to men of lesser status. At NBC, John Cameron Swayze no longer had serious radio assignments; instead, he was employed almost exclusively in narrating the house "newsreel" and filling in on special or trial television broadcasts. The same was true of Douglas Edwards at CBS. But their work at the conventions—identifying delegates, summarizing speeches, explaining arcane procedures—endowed them with a sort of fame in the cities of the Northeast. Their small audience included executives of broadcasting companies, advertising agencies, big manufacturing companies, as well as lawyers, dentists, and others of the well-to-do. With that constituency, Swayze and Edwards each succeeded to the evening newscast when his network got around to starting one. For years after, old-timers in broadcasting newsrooms would regale the young with the story of two virtual failures too low in the pecking order to refuse to work for television, which made them rich and famous.

Edward R. Murrow, by far the most eminent and recognized among the CBS news staff, elected not to anchor its television coverage, but he did agree to help out. Having agreed to help a little, he ended up doing a great deal, sitting on one side of Edwards while the intellectual Quincy Howe sat on the other, offering his comments and information for almost all of the endless hours of the conventions. Murrow's work drew praise from Jack Gould of the *The New York Times*. "Straight adult reporting seasoned with real humor," said Gould. "Some of Mr. Murrow's quips were far and away the most amusing words heard all week in Philadelphia"—a pleasant notice in refreshing contrast with some of the later Murrow iconography. But CBS leadership, always so proud of Murrow and of everything it did in news, did not find its television convention coverage worth mentioning in the company's next annual report to shareholders.

What happened at CBS and ABC television those weeks was what could be expected; their staffs of journalists, most of them with radio experience, some trained only in print, scrambled to adjust to unfamiliar devices while teaching themselves to report on television, to mind the unfamiliar picture, to wonder what interested the audience. In contrast, the National Broadcasting Company, biggest and richest in radio and about to become the same in television, abdicated control of its most important TV journalistic undertaking of the year to an outsider. In an arrangement unknown in American broadcasting before or since, editorial control was actually assumed by an advertiser, a sponsor, the way they did with soap operas.

True, the sponsor was *Life* magazine, itself a journalistic enterprise of stature and good name, but NBC News was not "solely responsible" for most of what it telecast as news. This strange arrangement violated all the rules.

It all started when *Life*'s publisher, Andrew R. Heiskell, approached NBC to suggest buying sponsorship of the conventions. His approach was hesitant and tentative, and he was astonished when the network grabbed at the idea. As the day approached, he decided it would be wise if he went to Philadelphia to see that "*Life* was getting its money's worth." Some of his colleagues had scoffed at the folly of his expenditure, and he was worried that they might be right. Exactly how much money changed hands is uncertain. Later, trying to remember back forty years, Heiskell thought he had paid $250,000. At the time, however, John Crosby wrote in the *New York Herald Tribune*, "*Life* paid $150,000 to N.B.C. (exclusive of costs) for the combined *Life*-N.B.C. television broadcasts," calling it "one of the more expensive promotion stunts of our time." Regardless what he paid, Heiskell reaped his "money's worth" in coverage, gavel-to-gavel and beyond, of the Republican and Democratic national conventions, special programs on the two weekend days preceding each, a wrap-up every morning of the previous day's activities, and a special summary after each convention. On the other hand, *Life*'s commercial messages were seen in only a few cities, and on very few sets.

Heiskell learned what he had bought when he got to Philadelphia, three days before the first gavel sounded. The chief of the NBC technical crew asked him what he wanted done next.

"What do you want to do?" he asked.

"What do you mean?" Heiskell asked.

"Well, aren't you running this?"

It defies belief. Equipment and people, journalists and technicians, had been assembled from NBC's stations in New York, Washington, Cleveland, and Chicago, and others were hired locally, all to cover the Republican National Convention, about to start in a matter of days. But no one had been put in charge of what the people and the equipment were to do, when they were to do it, or for how long!

Heiskell took over without asking anyone—someone had to. He allocated editing and supervisory jobs to reporters he had brought with him from *Life* and other Time, Inc., magazines. They ran the coverage until the Democrats' last gavel sounded, four weeks later. It was sudden and unplanned, which may be why there was no outcry inside or outside NBC about a sponsor in editorial control of the year's biggest news coverage. Thus, four years later, NBC would still have had no one with experience in running the television coverage of a convention.

Asked long after why he believed *Life* could reap "good promotion" over a network of no more than seven stations, Heiskell explained that he had hoped all the newspaper reporters gathered in Philadelphia would notice television and write about it. In this way *Life* would get good promotion. Whatever else can be said about what happened, Heiskell confounded the skeptics by getting exactly what he was looking for. Newspapers wrote a lot about television, the new toy, and almost always mentioned *Life* magazine when they did.

By that time, Heiskell was too busy running NBC's coverage to pay attention. He decided what stories would be covered and by whom. He deployed equipment when technicians told him it was available. He had an interview waiting to replace every speech if it grew dull. He presided over editorial meetings every night from about eleven until three the next morning, plotting what to do the next day. As *Life*'s publisher, Heiskell had enough clout to keep the Bellevue-Stratford kitchens open at night to feed his exhausted, famished editorial board. He had a wonderful time.

Long before he found editorial control in his lap, Heiskell had thought the *Life* image would be enhanced if some of the interviewing in the NBC television broadcast were done by *Life* and *Time* reporters. The appropriate editors, all old friends and colleagues, willingly lent him a few reporters. (To those editors it meant having more experienced hands on the scene, available to them but charged to someone else's budget.) Heiskell thought then, and later, that they were humoring him—"If Heiskell wants to do this crazy thing," he imagined them saying—and that no one expected anything useful to come out of his experiment. Some of his borrowed journalists became editors and producers; the rest chased news and talked to the cameras.

In the Time, Inc., way, Heiskell also brought to Philadelphia a small contingent of researchers, "usually bright young women assigned as gofers to get this senator or that governor or delegate" to where they were going to be interviewed. All in all, *Life* made a substantial commitment in its search for a little bit of newspaper promotion.

How could NBC have abdicated control? Intentionally by the NBC executives who made the deal with *Life*? By default because those who mattered were involved in the weightier, more profitable matters of radio? Above all, where were NBC's lawyers? Nothing happens in broadcasting without lawyers. Decades later, looking for answers, I could find no one still alive who had taken part in the deal for NBC. There is no way to know why the oldest, richest network agreed to share its moment with *Life*'s "promotion" scheme.

Here, however, is a guess: Managers of the network saw television coverage of the conventions as a nuisance while the bosses up at RCA thought it would sell television sets. *Life* could sell sets as well as anyone. No one could quarrel about their professional credentials, and NBC would have to make fewer demands on a technical staff that

had no experience in live television coverage and was already stretched too thin to satisfy the higher priority of radio. Thus, management delegated its worries. Chance, in the form of Andrew R. Heiskell, brought the perfect solution to the insoluble problem. It was done very informally. "I'm not sure we even wrote a piece of paper," Heiskell said later.

During the conventions, Niles Trammell, president of NBC, dropped by the television control room at about seven o'clock every evening—"to pat our heads," Heiskell remembered. NBC vice president William F. Brooks, the head of news, came by even less frequently. Other than those two, "the big honchos at NBC had nothing to do with anything." As for Henry Luce, editor of *Life*, the man who thought it up, who owned it, who was its supervising presence, he had very little interest in television. He showed up often at the *Time and Life* newsroom, but only once at the NBC television control center presided over by Heiskell and his associates. He might be paying for it, but he had no interest in how it worked.

There were even a dozen or so people from Young & Rubicam, *Life*'s advertising agency. They presumably knew all about television production. David Levy came as a Y&R staff television producer with many nonfiction credits, including *We, the People*, an early hit of radio nonfiction entertainment. Levy later wrote: "Our people dreamed up special events, persuaded delegates to come onto the shows we created, actually produced much of the material. . . . The whole project served as a commercial for *Life*. LIFE-NBC was on the cameras and on the microphones, but NBC personnel wore NBC/LIFE. (I know; I made up the design of the badges and the markings.)"

However the arrangement rankles in principle, Heiskell, and his colleagues from *Life* and *Time*, saw to it that NBC included more news in its coverage than any other network. Furthermore, although the proceedings were interrupted far less often than in future years, it began here, irritating politicians and causing debate on why television was there. The intent was to cover news, whatever news there was, and if there was none in the selection of the committee to escort the permanent chairman of the convention to the podium that evening, or in Mrs. D. Risely Cox singing "Oh, What a Beautiful Morning," the networks would switch to something else.

What politicians considered interruptions was journalism to the newspeople from NBC and the magazines. They filled otherwise dull or empty time with remote broadcasts of panels and discussions, man-in-the-street interviews, and a dizzying array of special features. Each morning that week, Alex Dreier, a well-known news broadcaster from NBC's Central Division, was seen being shaved in the barbershop of the Bellevue-Stratford Hotel as he told Alfonse, the barber, what to expect from that day's sessions and answered Alfonse's questions about points of parliamentary procedure. Alfonse added his own opinions and commentary. Late Monday afternoon, while the convention was still in recess, Sally Kirkland, *Life*'s fashion editor, and Nancy Osgoode of NBC's Washington news staff, chatted for fifteen minutes about ladies' hats seen at the convention. A four-foot lady elephant, hired to promote the Taft candidacy, made frequent appearances on all the networks when the Taft candidacy was being discussed. There were also serious, sometimes news-making, sometimes substantive interviews, and there were times when no one could think of anything better to fill the passing minutes than to have reporters talk to each other.

Much of this took place in Room 22, NBC's principal television studio in the convention hall building. Room 22 was very high up and well back of the hall, and delegates had to climb up narrow metal stairways, brushing bright summer suits against grease spots, to arrive sweaty and out of breath; but all invitations were cheerfully accepted. The name—it was not its room number—had a nice resonant quality for television, which the people from *Time* and *Life*, curiously, appreciated quicker than those from NBC. One of the *Life* contingent picked it when he saw Ben Grauer, a key member of NBC's reporting staff, buying Max Factor Number 22 facial makeup to hide his heavy beard from the television camera. In his best basso vibrato, an announcer would intone, "This is *Appointment in Room 22* . . . on-the-spot reports with the people who today [pause] make *history*! . . . As part of their coverage of the Republican National Convention, *Life* magazine and the National Broadcasting Company are honored to present. . . ."

Room 22 was in fact a suite of three rooms. One, long and narrow, served as the control room, with monitors, scopes, and other paraphernalia on rickety wooden boxes rising from an equally rickety table made of boards laid across sawhorses. A larger one was the workroom, where scripts were written, meetings were held, and editorial decisions were made. It also served as the "green room," where guests awaited their turn at live broadcast or tarried on their way out.

The third room, the studio, was about twelve feet square. Reachable only through the workroom, it was large enough to have two large sets: one was just a desk and some chairs on a raised platform; the other, to the left, along the wall, had a permanent scenic flat before which people could sit and discuss major issues. This position could appear to be somewhere else. Someone at the anchor desk would say, "We switch now to NBC-*Life* headquarters for women." The "switch" was merely to the other camera, pointing to the wall to the left of the desk before which some women delegates were seated ready to be on television. It was glamorous, but it was also physically taxing. Whenever Room 22 was ready to go on the air, on went the huge, hot, blinding lights demanded by the primitive cameras of the time. Only cameramen could work in their undershirts.

There was an air of joy and uplift among the assembled Republicans, delegates, elected officials, and hangers-on alike. The end of the long drought of jobs and power was in sight, a drought that had begun sixteen years before when Franklin Roosevelt had demolished Herbert Hoover. Now, after a Depression and a War and a Return Home, the Democrats were through. Everyone knew it, the Democrats no less than the Republicans. Monday night, Clare Boothe Luce brought the convention to its feet when she gleefully described the Democrats as sundered into "a Jim Crow wing led by lynch-loving Bourbons, a Moscow wing masterminded by Stalin's Mortimer Snerd, Henry Wallace . . . and a Pendergast wing run by the wampum-and-boodle boys . . . who gave us Harry Truman."

(Wallace had been Roosevelt's secretary of agriculture, then his third-term vice president. He was dumped for Truman when Roosevelt ran the fourth time, and Truman succeeded when Roosevelt died. Wallace became secretary of commerce, then was fired for criticizing U.S. policy in the budding Cold War. The American Left started gathering around him as a possible third-party "peace" candidate. Thomas Pendergast was the Missouri Democratic party "boss" who had helped Truman in his early career. Joseph Stalin was the general secretary of the Communist Party of the Soviet Union [CPSU]. Mortimer Snerd was the second most popular dummy employed by ventriloquist Edgar Bergen.)

The convention sessions followed one another, as did the interviews in Room 22; the tonsorial activities of Alfonse, the barber; and the inexorable movement of the Dewey juggernaut toward the nomination. On Wednesday, starting at 10:00 P.M. and lasting until after 4:00 Thursday morning, twelve candidates were offered in nomination, but unless Taft and Stassen could get their people to unite to stop Dewey, the nomination was his. They could not. Thursday, June 24, the balloting started at 2:36 P.M. NBC, the technological leader in the industry, was following the race with a felt board, the kind designed to brighten the lives of kindergarten children, to which adhered little figures with sandpaper backing. The figures were moved by hand to show who was ahead. The delegate totals, as they accumulated through the roll call, were rung up on a cash register whose numbers were superimposed over the picture of the convention as it went through the process.

"A - la - ba - ma . . ."

It was almost five o'clock before the second ballot ended. Dewey was thirty-three votes short of his majority. In Room 22, Swayze reported that if it went past a second ballot, the stop-Dewey coalition would form. Connecticut and others wanted to switch to Dewey to put him over, but after a ballot is official no changes are allowed. The coalition moved to recess. It was carried by voice vote. NBC switched back to New York for *Howdy Doody*, a profitable program for children, which was broadcast throughout the conventions—a matter of priorities. While *Howdy Doody* was on, Taft tried one more time; he telephoned Stassen and asked him to withdraw. Stassen refused. It was all over. When coverage resumed, the third ballot was no more than a formality. Dewey's nomination was unanimous.

A violent electrical storm struck Philadelphia that Thursday evening. On the roof of the convention hall, Clarence Thoman, chief engineer of the NBC affiliated station in Philadelphia, WPTZ, made a heroic name for himself during the storm by hanging on to antennas and keeping them in place on the roof while the television broadcasts continued. In the hall, one delegation after another joined the Dewey bandwagon. In Room 22, Swayze and Grauer explained the parliamentary necessity of having a vote if it was going to be unanimous. Before 9:00 P.M., *Time* reporter Sidney Olson told Room 22 of the beautiful rainbow outside. At 9:00, the audience saw it for itself as the program switched to the pool camera at the Bellevue-Stratford Hotel. The cameras showed Dewey riding off in his limousine to the convention hall, toward the rainbow, into a horizon of black clouds moving rapidly away, leaving the deep blue of a late June dusk.

The Democrats gathered in the same Philadelphia convention hall on Monday, July 12, to nominate Harry Truman. It was a gloomy, sodden occasion. No one believed Harry Truman could win except Harry Truman, and he was back in Washington.

On television, everything—the mood, the pace, the story—changed. All the rage that builds up in the middle ranks of a party long in power spilled out on the streets, in the hotels, and in the convention hall of Philadelphia—and on television. Fewer people came, and they spent less. Shopkeepers and cabdrivers grumbled. Everybody was upset about something. All of them had learned about television from watching the Republican convention and needed no coaxing to appear. They all took their cases to the lights and the cameras.

Each newsmaker and attention-seeker followed the pretty young *Life* researcher up the steel stairs to Room 22, submitted to makeup without complaining, and, barely containing impatience, answered the questions that skillfully or clumsily brought out the news story of the day.

On the Saturday before the convention, Jacob Arvey, head of the Democratic party in Chicago, national organizer of Democratic Eisenhower-for-President clubs for the past year, brought his case to Room 22. Eisenhower had, the day before, finally made a statement so unequivocal about his unavailability for the Democratic nomination that even Arvey had to accept it. James Bell of *Life* and Morgan Beatty of NBC asked Arvey, What next? He was not sure. But he was not sure *on television*.

On Sunday, the day before the convention opened, the focus shifted to the Southerners and their grievances. A mobile unit was at the Benjamin Franklin Hotel where Southern delegations were caucusing and grieving. They demanded a civil rights plank for the platform that would reflect "pure Americanism." Then, in Room 22, a Mississippi mayor forecast doom for the Democratic ticket, a Mississippi editor said Truman must step aside, and Mrs. Julius Talmadge, cousin by marriage to Georgia's nationally known ex-governor, Eugene Talmadge, expounded on the importance of states' rights to women, all in the same half hour. *Life* was covering on television as *Life* always covered in the magazine: close-ups, close-ups, and more close-ups, and as much editing as the copy could stand. On television it translated into "pace" and the audience was swept along by the velocity, which on television often passes for content.

Between the sessions on that first day the program switched to the White House press room, where a half dozen reporters, some from

NBC, some from print, talked about what the President and the White House staff were doing while the convention was going on. The logs noted "the first television program from the Press Room of the White House." Ninety minutes later, the convention still in recess, Heiskell and James asked for and got cameras in New York and Washington as well as Philadelphia. First the cameras showed what was happening in the streets, Broad and Chestnut in Philadelphia, Sixth Avenue and 50th Street (outside the NBC studios) in New York, and Pennsylvania Avenue in Washington, using the cameras still at the White House from the preceding special program. Hey, this was fun! In the three cities, leading Democrats talked about election prospects and the rest of the platform—agriculture and foreign policy—while NBC reporters said what an unusual television program this was, three cities tied together by miles of coaxial cable and split-second coordination. In the control rooms, *Time* people and NBC people were ecstatic. The NBC log noted, of course, "First time for a round-robin program in television."

After Senator Alben W. Barkley of Kentucky took over the convention's temporary chairmanship with a stem-winder of a speech, there came an address by Mrs. India Edwards, executive director of the Democratic party's women's division. Her subject was inflation, more on the mind of voters at home than anything that seized and deadlocked the convention in Philadelphia. Mrs. Edwards knew about television, knew that people in their homes could see her. So instead of merely telling them, she showed them.

She took helium-filled balloons out of a hat box and let them rise to the ceiling of the hall to show what would happen to prices if evil Republicans took over. She brought with her a little girl named Sally Zimmerman and cited the cost of every article of clothing Sally wore—all the fault of Republican majorities in both houses of Congress. From a shopping bag she took a carton of milk and a steak, which she waved at the approving delegates.

Don Hewitt, later founder and executive producer of *60 Minutes*, was an associate director in the CBS television control room. When he saw Mrs. Edwards leave the steak and the milk carton on the podium, he raced down the narrow stairs from the CBS studio, past the guards, into the hall, and up onto the platform, where he dashed to the podium, grabbed the steak and the milk, and ran back so Edward R. Murrow could wave them at the audience a second time. NBC, not for the last time, had been too clever for its own good. Before

India Edwards had even finished her speech, they had cut away to Room 22 for an exclusive interview with Senator Barkley. But Barkley would not comment on the only matter of news that came up, the clear lead his keynote speech had given him for the nomination for vice president. While NBC had Barkley ducking questions, the others were showing Mrs. Edwards releasing balloons, waving steaks, and clucking over the prices parents had to pay to clothe a little girl.

The party platform, the heart of the fight that was tearing the Democratic party apart, was scheduled for presentation Tuesday, the next day. For the first time in its young life, television would be present at a watershed event in history. The party's factions could not agree on a compromise position on civil rights, and the presentation of the platform was delayed a day. All day Tuesday and all that night, the arguing, the conciliating, the posturing, and the dealing continued. As power brokers moved from room to room, there was nothing to report from the convention floor, and Room 22 got only rumors— and empty time to fill.

Then the television audience saw a historical event unfold spontaneously before its eyes, two days of conflict and resolution that changed the course of the country, the struggle to commit one of America's two major parties to redress by law the disabilities that enshackled Negro Americans. In one form or another, the issue was to dominate American society for the rest of the century, but never was the issue so clear as it was at that convention, or seen so clearly as by the people who saw it covered live on television.

The first sign that news had started coming over the dam was the appearance in Room 22 of Hubert H. Humphrey, mayor of Minneapolis and candidate for the U.S. Senate. Despite his misgivings that it would damage his chances for election, he had allowed his friends among the party liberals to draft him to lead the fight for a strong civil rights plank. The next day his leadership would make him a national figure, a role he would keep until he died. The convention's evening session opened with memorials, to Franklin Roosevelt, to the war dead. There were eulogies. A bugler played "Taps." The music included "A Mighty Fortress" and "My Buddy." It was very hot in the hall. The cameras panned faces of bored and worried delegates. Many held cardboard fans that they fluttered, looking on television like a wheatfield, across which, according to one account, "photographers' bulbs flashed like heat lightning."

Then the cameras showed a Negro delegate appearing, unannounced, on the platform. George Vaughn of Missouri, one of the few black delegates—the Democratic convention boasted hardly more than the Republican—wanted the convention to refuse to seat the Mississippi delegation, who had announced in advance that they would walk out if a strong civil rights plank were adopted. By two voice votes, one of them into microphones ordered closed by the chair, his motion was rejected. The hall erupted in disorder while inexperienced cameramen and directors tried to follow the action jumping back and forth across the convention floor. The big-city, big-state delegations opposed to seating Mississippi attacked the chair. The convention was now a day behind schedule, with the bosses still unable to find a civil rights compromise around which the factions could unite. Delegates were told to reconvene at 11:00 the next morning to stay in session until the platform, the nominations for President, the seconding, and the voting was done on Wednesday, July 14.

That next day's coverage lasted fifteen continuous hours. At noon, while Alfonse the barber was shaving Alex Dreier, Mrs. Emma Guffey Miller sent sealed cardboard cartons of white doves into the convention hall. Mrs. Miller, national committeewoman for Pennsylvania and sister of the former senator whose name was on the federal law governing coal mine safety, had been deputized by the florists of Philadelphia to release the doves when the party's nominee, President Truman, appeared before the convention to accept its nomination. But before that could happen, platform and controversy were still to be faced. Attempts at a compromise went on out of camera range all that afternoon, but the issue was also being fought out in public on television. The platform was moved at 2:30, with a strong statement supporting civil rights modified by a bow to constitutional propriety, to satisfy Southerners who insisted the Constitution left such matters to the states alone. Even so, three Southern amendments were offered to specify that civil rights were for the states to decide. Then Andrew J. Biemiller, former congressman from Wisconsin, moved the liberals' stronger plank, adding to the party platform a list of what the next Congress must do.

Television stayed with the debate. Southern speakers, led by Texas's former governor Dan Moody, tried to convince the delegates that a states' rights statement was only logical, only their due. Hubert Humphrey mounted the podium. His earnest, homely face sweated in the television lights as his passionate argument, in his clipped, Midwestern syllables, was carried across the hall and to almost every radio and television set in the United States. "There are those who say to you, we are rushing this issue of civil rights," he said with the cadence and voice that would become familiar to all Americans. "I say we are a hundred and seventy-two years late. There are those who say this issue of civil rights is an infringement of states' rights. The time has arrived for the Democratic party to get out of the shadow of states' rights and walk forthrightly into the bright sunshine of human rights."

When Humphrey finished, suddenly and thereafter a national figure, Illinois led an unexpected, spontaneous ten-minute demonstration in the aisles. The Texas amendment was defeated on a roll-call vote. The two other Southern amendments went down to voice votes. The Biemiller amendment was last; the clerk called the roll. When the roll reached "Illinois, sixty votes," it was bedlam. All of Illinois's votes had gone for the amendment. One after the other, in the middle of the alphabet, the Northern states cast unanimous votes. The amendment to the platform carried, 651½ votes to 582½. The time was 4:37 P.M. Alabama waved for recognition. Sam Rayburn, the convention's permanent chairman, ignored them. A voice vote approved the amended platform and he recessed the convention until evening. The next order of business would be the presidential nomination.

NBC filled the recess with films and interviews. No Howdy Doody today. At 6:45 P.M., NBC switched to Washington; David Brinkley was heard describing the picture of Union Station, the arrival of the presidential car, and the President with his wife and daughter walking to the train and boarding. Over pictures of the exterior of the train, White House correspondent Frank Bourgholtzer was heard from inside the train describing people sitting down. At 7:00, the train was seen leaving Union Station, and then the cameras showed the Baltimore & Ohio Station in Philadelphia where the presidential train would arrive. NBC-*Life* was ready. In the background, the flashing lights of a motorcycle escort could be seen vibrating in the gloom.

At 8:02, the clerk called the roll of the states for the purpose of nominating a candidate for President of the United States.

"A - la - ba - ma."

Handy Ellis, the Alabama chairman, said Alabama's Democratic presidential electors had been instructed "never to cast their vote for a Republican, never to cast their vote for Harry Truman, and never to cast their vote for any candidate with a civil rights program such as adopted by this convention. "We bid you good-bye," he said. With that, he and twelve of Alabama's twenty-six delegates marched out of the hall. All of Mississippi's twenty-three delegates followed. It was 8:10.

From NBC, from *Life*, from Young & Rubicam, the young *Life* researchers descended on the defecting delegates as they left the hall. They were invited to Room 22 and almost all came. While Grauer interviewed them, Swayze tried to keep track of the convention. By prearrangement, and on cue (a hand signal from an assistant director), the delegates unpinned their credentials and threw them onto the scarred, cigarette-burned desk. Then, on another cue, they did it again. One Alabama delegate was openly weeping. Another delegate explained, "He's leaving home." It was in every way a "staged event." Another first? The staged tossing of credentials was soon the talk of the Philadelphia news corps. A joke? A scandal? Or just good gossip?

Less than half an hour later, Phil M. Donnelly, the governor of Missouri, rose to nominate Harry Truman, whose train was at that moment approaching Philadelphia. NBC's picture cut back and forth between the nomination and the arriving train. Truman, listening to the radio broadcast, stayed aboard until Governor Donnelly was finished. Now the picture alternated between the President on the station platform and the (organized) demonstration on the convention floor. At 9:40, the Truman family boarded a limousine; the demonstration continued as the car disappeared in a celebration of flashing lights and howling sirens; back to the demonstration in the aisles of the convention hall. In the control room, handshakes. *Life* loved NBC; NBC loved *Life*; the delegates loved Harry Truman—or so they told themselves. (Some of the demonstrators' signs read, "I'm Just Mild About Harry.") Chairman Rayburn could not control the delegates or stop the demonstration. Finally, at one minute after ten, he made the band stop playing and the demonstrators took their seats.

Candidate after candidate was nominated and seconded, five in all, but it seemed like more. Back to Room 22 for an "exclusive" with Clark Clifford, the President's counsel. The President, said Clifford, recognized that half a million sets (!) would be tuned into his acceptance speech. It was Clifford who had told Truman he should not read a written speech but speak from notes, looking directly into the camera—and at the people.

The nominating and seconding ended just before midnight. The nomination took only one ballot. Before 1:00 A.M., Truman had won the nomination with 947½ votes to 263 for Senator Richard Russell of Georgia. The leftover half-vote had gone to Paul McNutt. At 1:30

A.M., Senator Ablen Barkley was declared by acclamation to be the party's nominee for vice president. Ten minutes later, Harry Truman walked up to the podium. He had spent hours in a hot, airless, concrete-floored room waiting for the call to appear. As the band struck up "Hail to the Chief," he strode forward to accept his party's nomination for President, for the first time in his own right.

"Plump, powdered and behatted," as *Time* described her, Emma Guffey Miller stepped forward for her moment in history. Her doves had been in their boxes for more than twelve hours in the heat that came from the live television lights and from too many bodies using up too little air. When the boxes were opened only some of the doves were still alive. Those survivors were crammed into a huge floral replica of the Liberty Bell, a gift of the allied florists of Philadelphia. Mrs. Miller bustled to the podium to present the tribute to the President.

The doves, exhausted but freed, flew around the platform amid ducking party dignitaries. Many came to rest on top of the standing fans, each eight feet high, there to compensate a little for the heat of the television lights. Others wheeled over the hall dropping their waste. One fan was near the podium, and the Honorable Sam Rayburn of Texas, House Minority Leader, later the outstanding House Speaker of the second half-century, was in its direct line. He caught a dove in his hands and threw it into the crowd. All along the East Coast on television, across the whole country by radio, Rayburn was heard to growl: "Get these goddam pigeons out of here!" Politics and television had truly met.

If nothing else, the incident woke the convention. It was almost two in the morning, but a week's gloom had vanished from the convention hall. Who knew how many were still at their television sets at that hour? (At every convention over the years to come, we would always be astonished to learn how many.) Truman spoke from his notes into the camera. His head was up, and his forearms chopped down as his flat, Missouri syllables shot across the hall. "Senator Barkley and I will win this election and make these Republicans like it. Don't you forget it." Cheers. Never were farmers as prosperous as now, "and if they don't do their duty by the Democratic party, they're the most ungrateful people in the world." Cheers. "And I'll say to labor just what I've said to the farmers."

A voice in the back called out, "Give 'em hell, Harry!" and it became the theme of the campaign.

The convention adjourned at 2:31 A.M. and in the Bellevue-

Stratford, the newspeople gathered and, until dawn, talked out their exhaustion, their excitement, their letdown. They drank a little and someone rounded up some food. As happens at these times, groups drifted back and forth sampling the other fellow's whiskey. Murrow and some others from CBS turned up at the NBC party. Robert Trout, long a stalwart of CBS news broadcasting but for that year only NBC's principal radio broadcaster for the conventions, met Murrow at the door and took him to meet Heiskell.

They had no sooner shaken hands than Murrow rounded on Heiskell for betraying the integrity of news, for staging an event, for threatening the future of this new and promising medium of journalism. Trout, who had known Murrow a long time, had never heard him like that. Heiskell, staggered by this barrage, took a while to realize that the objection was to the tossed credentials, which he viewed as a fuss over nothing. The confrontation itself, however, is interesting. One of the founders of *Life* magazine and one of the outstanding reporters in the history of radio each brought to television a different vocabulary. Heiskell had been in news all his professional life; Murrow had come to it late, after what was essentially an academic career, a far cry from going out with a still photographer on a news assignment. It was a conflict between two of the great names of mid-century American journalism that was not—and still hasn't been—resolved.

Nine days later, on a weekend, the Progressive party met in the same hall to nominate Henry Wallace for President. *Life* let NBC handle this one alone, and the Progressives got no subvention from the city of Philadelphia, as had the two traditional parties. The Left called the Progressive party into being to take votes away from Harry Truman, who everyone knew was going to lose anyway, and then fight the political establishment for control of the Democratic party. This same purpose had brought six thousand states' rights Democrats to Birmingham, Alabama, the previous weekend. But Birmingham was not on the coaxial cable, so the fiery speeches and the nomination of Governors Strom Thurmond and Fielding Wright was covered only in print and on the radio, while the Progressives were covered gavel to gavel.

Ahead was the most remarkable national political campaign of this century, as Truman confounded both the polls and the pundits to win a surprise victory. Along with his astonishing upset, Truman's unrelenting campaign has passed into legend. But almost none of the election campaign got on television, his or Dewey's: a few film clips in newscasts, some speeches carried by individual stations as (local) paid political advertising, but little more. It was by the convention coverage that network television, tiny audience and all, had proved it could record and report serious news.

A few weeks after the 1948 conventions, Niles Trammell offered to put Heiskell in charge of all of NBC's television programming. He turned it down. David Sarnoff would be his boss and Robert Sarnoff (David's oldest son) would be an NBC vice president reporting to him; it was no place to be. The job went, in time, to Pat Weaver, an advertising agency executive, and Heiskell returned to the world of magazines. Looking back, he would recall what an adventure it was rather than the mark he had left. Perhaps it would have gotten there anyway, television not only showing what happened as it was happening but trying to explain why. Or even showing what someone important did not want shown.

Before they started, *Motion Picture Herald*, a trade newspaper, had predicted that the 1948 conventions would do for television what the 1924 conventions did for radio, when Alabama cast its twenty-four votes for Oscar Underwood.

Born in 1948, television news went on to cover party conventions with increasing intensity, even after they had lost their role in the political process. Since television news is always a part of the history it covers, it was outstandingly part of history when the conventions' stage was taken over in the sixties by Vietnam and civil rights, the two wrenching dramas of America in the second half of the twentieth century. Then, gradually, conventions ceased to matter. But even after the music stopped, television kept on dancing. The networks could not stop covering the now meaningless conventions.

2

After the conventions, the people from *Life* and *Time* returned to their offices, their meetings, and their haberdashers, and few of them had any truck with television news again. The people from the networks went back to their newsrooms and bureaus, the lucky majority to the ample and welcome bosom of radio news, a handful to create television news, too busy with each day's needs to know that that was what they were doing. Between the 1948 conventions, when television was a novelty, and the 1952 conventions, when it was the most important medium of coverage, they stumbled along, devising ways of presenting news and methods of using pictures as news that have become standard, accepted American fare. All were arrived at by trial and error. In those four years, also, television moved toward becoming a universal American presence. More and more cities had stations; more and more homes had receivers; more and more Americans paid heed. During those four years, TV became the country's most important advertising vehicle. It was not yet the most important channel of information, but it was getting there rapidly.

I arrived at NBC in 1950, halfway through those four formative years. There had already been time for precedent. ("That is not how we do things," someone would say, but when I did it anyway no one complained; if it worked, it, too, became "how we do things.")

In early August 1950, on an impulse, I joined NBC News as something called a "news writer." At the time, I was night city editor of the *Newark Evening News*, the premier newspaper of New Jersey, circulation a quarter million. Even if night city editor of an afternoon paper sounds more impressive than it is, I was, three years out of school, one step up the ladder, known to my superiors, set—I thought—for life at one of those pillars of the American press that last forever. (Fifteen years later, after two ownership changes, the *Newark Evening News* died at the hands of television, assassin of afternoon newspapers.)

Then Gerald Green called. A classmate and friend, later a successful novelist, Green had been less lucky than I in his first job out of school. His was with International News Service (INS), least of the three wire services, where he worked nights stealing and rewriting foreign dispatches from places where INS had no one of its own. When NBC offered a way out he seized it, to the ridicule of all us old friends who mocked news on television as a bastard thing, a blot on the sacred banner we had set out to show around the world. When he called me to ask if I would consider working in television news, I, of course, said no.

Green is a bad-tempered man. He was offended that I turned him down without even pretending to need time to think about it. What was so grand about me, he asked, working nights, sleeping days—if the baby let me? The least I could do, he said, out of courtesy to him if nothing else, was to come by and look. That seemed reasonable, so I did.

We met where he worked, the eleven-story building of Pathé Film laboratories on the corner of Park Avenue and East 106th Street, looking down on the tracks of the New York Central. NBC had rented space there for its national and its local New York TV news so it could get exposed newsfilm to the lab quickly. There were newsrooms and film-editing rooms and three studios—a little one and a big one for news, and a third for live dramas that could not be accommodated "downtown" in Rockefeller Center. Two theatrical newsreels and the processing laboratories themselves took up the rest of the building.

Green took me to a lower floor, to a room that looked to me like a movie theater, with 150 empty seats. On a full-sized theater screen were moving pictures—*in negative*. The only sounds were the whirring of a projector behind the back wall and the whispering of two men sitting behind a long counter at the rear of the theater. This was a screening room, I was told. One of the men was a news writer, the other a film editor. The film was from Berlin, Russians on one side and all us good guys on the other.

Despite the picture being in negative, it was easy to tell Soviet uniforms from American, and even French and British. The news writer was saying things to the film editor like: "Open with a shot of the crowd for about seven seconds. Then a couple of scenes of the jeep driving up, then the general gets out for about five. . . ." I thought, What a wonderful way to live!

I tried it for two weeks, writing a little of this and a little of that. Following newsreel practice, after a piece of newsfilm was cut to a usable length, perhaps forty-five seconds, I got a "spot sheet" describing the scenes with each scene's length in feet. For 35mm film, which rolls at ninety feet a minute, three feet equals two seconds, but one was not to think that way. Length was a measure of time; one foot equaled two words, except that the first foot of any sequence would merit only one word. And writing too short was better than writing too long. Like all newsreel writers, I was to write in the present tense. After two weeks of writing sports stories, ladies' fashion stories, and even some minor news stories, I was ready to take the job. I gave the *Newark Evening News* two weeks' notice. So, for two more weeks, I worked at 106th Street until afternoon, took the subway to Pennsylvania Station and the railroad to Newark, and worked there until midnight.

Only on the day I said I was ready to take the job did I ask the man who interviewed me how much it paid.

"One hundred dollars a week," he said.

"I'm already making a hundred a week," I told him. (I lied. As night city editor of New Jersey's most important newspaper I was paid $90 a week. The *Newark News* was not a union shop.)

"Okay," he said. "One hundred and ten."

I asked another question: "Why me? All you know is I'm Green's friend and I type faster. NBC is a worldwide news organization. Why didn't you get someone from radio news downtown?"

"Well, to be honest, nobody down there who is worth a damn thinks this is going to last. They hate it."

And that is how I got into television.

By August 1950, both CBS and NBC each had regular network

television "newscasts" weekday evenings, summaries of the day's news modeled on the networks' radio newscasts, which had been so important during and after World War II. It was my good fortune to arrive early in the process of television news finding its way in the new medium. Some of the news reported was shown on film; more of the day's news was reported, but the newsfilm itself was of earlier events. Only in the biggest American cities could newsfilm get on the air the same day, and foreign news certainly couldn't in those days before communications satellites. Nevertheless, the booming introduction to NBC's newscast promised "Today's news today!"

Newscasts from NBC and CBS had grown out of their successful coverage of the 1948 conventions. CBS had taken the plunge first, late in 1948, with Douglas Edwards as its newscaster. Early in 1949, the advertising agency for Camel cigarettes went shopping for a television newscast. Camel cigarettes, already sponsoring on NBC a nightly wrap-up of news highlights—film only, some of it quite old, without live elements like a newscaster or maps—wanted to be known for presenting news on television more seriously, which its marketers said would appeal to people who smoked. The two networks competed vigorously for this plum, making any promise that seemed helpful. NBC won. John Cameron Swayze was picked as the newscaster.

Now both senior networks had daily national newscasts, and their contrasts reflected the fundamental differences between the two organizations. The CBS staff modeled television news on radio news, the same structure for writers and editors, the same standards, purposes, and emphasis on words. On camera were lesser lights of that distinguished and garlanded staff, Edwards, Winston Burdette, Larry Le-Sueur. After a few unsatisfactory attempts, CBS News gave up its own national and world newsfilm organization and hired a syndicated service called Telenews to supply film from faraway places. CBS gradually hired its own crews to supplement this service, especially with sound film of press conferences, hearings, and major speeches. But what they got from Telenews was the basis of what they showed each night.

At NBC, the term *newsreel* was not a figure of speech but an accurate description of a fact of life. NBC's radio news broadcasters and writers superciliously avoided television except when ordered. Meanwhile, NBC's management, which was barely committed to television and less to news, had tried to put news on television by hiring one of the theater newsreel companies to do it for them, but the newsreel companies, each a tiny part of a large motion picture production organization, turned them down. So they hired an out-of-work newsreel executive to set up a department. He in turn hired out-of-work newsreel cameramen. The stories they covered were newsreel stories—Miss America, ice-cream-eating contests, press agents' schemes, movie openings, women's fashions, spring training, girls on water skis.

NBC's news cameramen filmed as though for theaters, on 35mm film. Their basic tool was the Eyemo, a hand-held camera powered, like a child's toy car, by a clockwork motor wound between scenes by a large key on the camera's side. It made one minute and ten seconds of picture before it had to be reloaded. It took us several years to realize that the 16mm film used by CBS and almost everyone else was lighter, more flexible, and cheaper—and not only the film but also all the associated equipment, the cameras, editing tables, and processors. Such film was also more practical for recording sound, which was becoming more and more important as we tried harder and harder to cover news. In those days, NBC's news film was silent; crews shot almost no sound, not statements, not interviews, not even ambient noise. Someone had, in fact, bought sound cameras; huge contraptions intended for cavalry charges and torrid love scenes. But these were rarely used other than for fashion shows. Gerry Green once suggested sending a sound camera to a New York longshoremen strike. Cameramen and editors laughed off his suggestion. Imagine that: Sound at a newsreel story!

At NBC, only Washington filmed sound; Washington stories were all talk, anyway. Our bureau in Washington equipped itself with the early 16mm sound cameras that were being developed for this new television business, and they had to send the film to a nonunion laboratory for processing. Otherwise, NBC's newsfilm was mute, shown against background music chosen from a mood music record library for which we bought rights by the year. (Even here, real music from real records was forbidden to us under the rules.)

There was precious little show business glamour on 106th Street. The only places for lunch were a grimy lunchroom in the building's basement, a Prohibition-era Irish bar on Lexington Avenue, or some family restaurants in the Italian enclave still holding out farther up First and Second avenues. Some days, lunch meant a cab ride downtown, usually shared among four. (Cabs came infrequently to East 106th Street. From time to time, some well-known actor would step out of one on the way to rehearsing *Armstrong Circle Theater* in the big studio on the third floor. Once, in a cab that had brought Raymond

Massey, we found a penny on the floor. "How nice," someone said. "He left his picture.")

Camel and its agency insisted NBC hire Clarence Thoman from WPTZ, Philadelphia. Thoman, the broadcast engineer who had kept the antennas from flying off the convention hall roof during the rainstorm, was knowledgeable and ingenious about live television equipment, but he had no experience in news. Camel said openly that NBC had no one they would trust to do their program. Hiring Thoman was a condition of sale; it was met.

Camel also assumed the right to pick the name, *Camel News Caravan*. They honestly believed that years of radio big band music had engraved the words *Camel Caravan* on the public's mind. When Camel cigarettes transmogrified from Glen Gray and his Casa Loma Orchestra on radio to John Cameron Swayze and the news on television, no one presumed to ask what was a news caravan. What Camel wanted Camel got—because they paid so much, because they might have gone to CBS, and especially because they dealt with NBC's salesmen and managers, who were paid to sell and manage.

The money from Camel cigarettes supported the entire national and worldwide structure of NBC Television News—salaries, equipment, bureau rents, and overseas allowances to educate reporters' children, with enough left over to allow for some other programs, local news, talk, a weekly program aimed awkwardly and self-consciously at high school students, a sports newsreel Friday nights in summer when Gillette razors did not sponsor boxing. Even when there were other paying advertisers, Camel paid for the infrastructure that made their programs possible.

One reason Camel picked NBC was that we emphasized pictures more than CBS, and one reason we continued to do this was that Camel wanted them. As a result, the organization to provide pictures grew rapidly. NBC owned television stations in New York, Washington, Chicago, Los Angeles, and Cleveland. Network and local news were not yet differentiated organizationally, and their local newsrooms were still part of NBC News, which gave us five network news bureaus. We had a staff cameraman in Florida for girls on beaches, for baseball and other sports, and, as an afterthought, for hurricanes; another in Dallas; and, in most cities, stringers—paid by the assignment or the day, or by the used foot of film when something they shot on their own was used. Some of the stringers worked for others as well, usually newsreels, who needed them only a few times a year. Our enterprising

Kentucky stringer fixed six Eyemo cameras and some lights to a steel bar controlling them by a single switch. On the rare occasion when something newsreel-worthy happened on his turf, he pointed his steel bar, his lights, and all six cameras, and sold the same film to five newsreels and NBC. He became a legend.

Theater newsreels were "made up" on Mondays and Thursdays, and all free film was released then, even government film. That meant the Defense Department's combat reports from Korea were available to television only on Mondays and Thursdays. It also meant that press agents for corporations with something filmable held back their announcements for Mondays and Thursdays. When Boeing rolled out its first civilian jetliner, the 707, the film was held back for a Thursday. I was then writing the *News Caravan,* and I refused to observe the condition. When Boeing insisted, I said I would not use the film at all. "You can't do that!" they said. I could. Newsreels were not in the news business; I was. I relented when they promised not to do it again, but my point was made and holding back film to favor newsreels soon stopped. From being taken for granted, we became the wooed. Slowly the newsreels died away. It was not a big event in American journalism because they had never realized their potential.

We got our foreign film from many sources. Central to our supply was our exclusive mutual exchange with the BBC. We alone in the United States could have everything of theirs and they were entitled to everything of ours. Oral tradition had it that David Sarnoff, founder of both RCA and NBC, had arranged this during World War II while in London serving on Eisenhower's staff. If that is how it happened, "the General"—as everyone called him because of a brigadier's star he got when he left the army—got us the best newsfilm coverage in the world. Copies of the edited film used on BBC television news and sometimes prints of the unedited reels—rushes—of timely stories were flown to us daily. It was a treasure trove.

Besides the BBC, we had exchanges with European newsreels, primarily French and Italian. In the previous decade, millions of young Americans in uniform had been to Europe; tens of millions back home had learned all the strange-sounding place names from newspapers and their internal complexities from the reports of what happened after the war ended. The politics and economics of Western Europe became, for a few years, American concerns. A new French prime minister was a story; an Italian interior minister who sent jeep-mounted troops against Communist demonstrators, Tito's break with

Stalin, all these were news to a newly sophisticated America in the days of the gathering Cold War. George Bidault and Maurice Thorez, Alcide de Gasperi and Palmiro Togliatti became names in the American media, cover stories of the newsmagazines. We also looked to these foreign newsreels for funny pieces: cute stories, weird inventions, crying babies. If the information sheets or translated scripts that came with the film were inadequate, we made it up.

All networks received free a weekly newsreel called *Welt im Film*, produced in West Germany by the U.S. State Department for showing in West German movie houses as part of the mission to teach democracy. Its prime topic was the Cold War. Americans became familiar with Konrad Adenauer and Ludwig Erhard and Franz-Josef Strauss, the heroic Kurt Schumacher and the burly Ernst Reuter. I learned from my predecessor to open the script for some inexplicable sporting event with, "For the first time under the Allied occupation, a centuries-old tradition is revived . . ." whether it be stomping grapes along the Mosel or the old ladies' hundred-meter dash in Hannover. But it was mostly news, ideally recent but usable either way because seeing it was different even if you knew about it. We assumed everyone who watched us had read a newspaper that day, or heard some radio, but *seeing* it was different, which made it worthwhile. If journalism is more than "information retrieval," television news is more than just words.

As audiences grew, so did the price NBC charged Camel. We could afford to expand our own staff coverage nationally and abroad. Our foreign film staff began to build. Radio correspondents in the traditional centers reluctantly agreed to look for cameramen to shoot events. Knowing little and caring less, they often hired incompetents. To a radio correspondent, newsfilm usually meant a picture of him talking. There were transoceanic recriminations, but in time trial and error gave us film bureaus in London, Paris, Rome, Tokyo, a stable stringer in Tel Aviv, and lesser presences elsewhere. We were especially fortunate in West Germany and Korea, the two most important news locations of the Cold War, the dominant story of the time. In many ways, the Cold War shaped television news, and television news helped shape the Cold War.

West Berlin was the unmatched news center, the constant source of television pictures, and we had them. Gary Stindt had arrived in Berlin after VE-Day as an air force newsreel cameraman and had taken his discharge there. In a Rhineland pawnshop, he had traded PX cigarettes for two 300mm lenses—very long lenses indeed—and set himself up as a stringer for any American newsreel that wanted coverage. Once he had two signed up, he married a local beauty whose blond hair and perfect cheekbones had graced a *Life* magazine feature about Germany rebuilding. In those years, a breed of American journalist, no less a conqueror than the troops he came with, could set up shop in a vanquished capital, Tokyo or Berlin, smoking tax-free cigars and eating in subsidized correspondents' clubs. These journalists owed more to Joel McCrea, who starred in the movie, "Foreign Correspondent," than to Walter Lippmann. They would send back pictures or dispatches about rising from the ashes or, conversely, the rebirth of militarism or, later, the fight to keep out the Stalinist hordes—the big stories of the time in all the American media.

Stindt was by any measure one of that group, but the unlikeliest. He was the ultimate German burgher. He had been born in Berlin to a father who was a newsreel cameraman of some prominence and a mother who was Jewish. The father's connections kept his mother out of the camps, but the young boy was sent to relatives in New Jersey for safekeeping. Pearl Harbor found him learning the still photographer's trade at the United Press in New York. He enlisted in the U.S. Army Air Corps, where he learned how to make movies, from training films to combat action. From the Signal Corps training center in Long Island City to the linkup with the Russians at the Elbe, he did what Air Corps cameramen did, things like filming into a plane in flight while strapped to a wing. He had left Germany a frightened teenager; he came back a victor.

With television, Stindt became a stringer for NBC. Then, in 1951, at about the time I started writing the *News Caravan*, he was elevated to staff and told to set up a bureau. A couple of cameramen in Berlin, another in Munich, stringers in every major city, contacts with Austria, then Poland, increasingly in Eastern Europe, a cameraman here, a broadcasting executive there, a visit to a national television service about to be inaugurated—and soon he had sources of film all the way to Turkey.

In truth, Stindt was an indifferent cameraman. But he was a born journalist, smelling out and chasing stories, overcoming his shyness to bully the great and powerful for a news item, enjoying the company of newspeople more than that of news makers. Lucius Clay and John McCloy and Willy Brandt and Franz-Josef Strauss were in his book, but so was the Pan Am traffic manager in Frankfurt. Stindt was not only a creature of his time, he was a creature of television. He knew better than anyone that film did not matter unless it got there. The Pan Am traffic manager in Frankfurt would meet a plane bringing our film from anywhere and get it off as fast as possible on the next plane to New York: Pan Am's, TWA's, Lufthansa's, or whoever's. Details like this governed our lives. A half-hour's difference in Frankfurt could mean losing a day in showing the news film in the United States. Gary Stindt's looseleaf phone book got us pictures of goose-stepping Red Army honor guards, meetings of something called the *komman-datura*, a place called Checkpoint Charlie, and news from Poland and Czechoslovakia and even farther.

The we/they world of the Cold War became the ideal archive film: DC-3s landing every thirty seconds, unloading coal and bread, with crewmen tossing candy bars into the outstretched hands of children. Those images made their way to the TV screen and, above all, to newsfilm libraries, to be extracted and replayed, burning themselves into our memories. They are still being used forty years later.

Korea, by contrast, was the Cold War grown hot. The war was idealized as monolithic, expansionist, Stalinist communism crossing one frontier too many, with young Americans in uniform mobilized to redraw the line. Film from Korea followed close upon the live coverage of the 1948 conventions that brought television its first rec-ognition for bringing news. In retrospect, the Cold War in Europe, the hot war in Korea, and infant television news were made for each other.

Korea was a vague ancillary responsibility of the Tokyo bureau. Like most American news organizations, NBC had a Tokyo bureau headed by an experienced correspondent who had arrived with Gen. Douglas MacArthur after reporting a great deal of the Pacific War, island by island. For the victors and those who accompanied them, Tokyo was a bed of luxury. Also, MacArthur was always news, conquered Japan was always news, and even the emperor was news, so reporters in Tokyo enjoyed the benign attention of home offices.

The NBC bureau chief made the customary obeisance to the new medium by hiring an American newsreel cameraman who had arrived in Tokyo with the troops and remained in the conquered capital. Like his colleagues, he had known the monotony, danger, and discomfort of the vast reaches of the Pacific war, and filming news for television seemed a reasonable way to settle down while the better part of most days was spent developing paying sidelines. After wars come the spoils of war, and it is easy to feel superior if you have not been through it. Nor could we find it in our hearts to fault him. After North Korean troops crossed the 48th parallel on June 25, 1950, he said that all the money in New York would not get him to Korea to cover the fighting. He hadn't followed MacArthur to Tokyo for yet more war. He would hire someone else for that.

The bureau chief first hired Japanese and Koreans, but the U.S. Army in those early days of defeat and retreat would not let them near the action, nor did they film very well when they could. NBC News and the other networks were thrown on the Defense Department's newsreel ration of battle footage every Monday and Thursday. Some of it was remarkably good, some less good, but all of it was processed, printed, and edited by the Army Signal Corps. It came to us days after the events, and we could never be sure what had been left out.

Early in July, less than a month after the North Korean invasion, the twin sons of a United Press still photographer appeared at the office of NBC's chief Washington newsfilm cameraman and applied for jobs covering the fighting. Still in their early twenties, they had had experience only in taking still photographs. They practiced using a hand-held 16mm silent camera for two or three days and then went to Korea. They came back heroes, Charles and Eugene Jones, the Jones boys. They had boundless energy and wanted only to be where there was action, shooting, war. Their filming was raw, much of it useless, but they were uninhibited about shooting dozens of rolls. Out of an hour of raw film an editor might get a minute of the fighting, but the minute was real combat.

It was the best battle footage available to any American audience. The idea of two young men in that exotic place had a special appeal to newspaper readers—and to NBC's tireless press agents. The first few months of the war in Korea were a bad time for the United States and its young troops, and this heightened the appeal of the twins risking their lives to show America what was going on. Few paused to give credit to the news writer—not I—who pored over each day's interminable film shipment, sometimes running it back and forth dozens of times looking for a coherent narrative that was governed by its own logic and gave a sense as well of the difficult fighting, the constant pressure, the retreat to the Pusan perimeter.

Gene and Charley were Americans, the same age as the soldiers fighting, and were given access everywhere. Reports reached New York that they were not above staging an incident, hyping a drama, but they denied it. At times, a streak of poetry showed in their work, a rabbit running through a field of fire, pigs rooting in the dirt floor of a burned-out hut. It was the kind of thing old newsreel hands never gave you, but the Jones boys were too young to know what was not done. It was instilled in old newsreel hands that film costs money, and they were judged by how little they used, how well they made every exposed foot count. The Jones boys never learned that either.

The success and fame of the Jones twins were the success and fame of the *News Caravan*, which developed an audience of extraordinary size for those days. There were weeks when more people watched the *News Caravan* than Milton Berle, the quintessential "hit" of early television. Their coverage helped push the Defense Department (DoD) to release its own film almost daily rather than just on Mondays and Thursdays, thereby making even more film available for the television audience. DoD film reports became longer and better; its editors left more in for release. Then the services even began to compete among themselves. Months later, when I became the writer for the *News Caravan*, some of the best newsfilm of all time was coming free from government sources. The films by U.S. Marine combat cameramen of the frozen retreat from Chosin Reservoir stands as some of the most graphic, wrenching, courageous combat footage ever made. The Jones twins had no part in that filming—they had, in fact, left Korea by then—but they may ultimately deserve credit for getting it released to the public.

Years later, when Vietnam was being touted as the "first living room war," I would mention the footage I saw every day from Korea, not just the stuff from the Jones boys but also the handout films of frozen marines retreating down the snowy mountainside from Chosin, knitted scarves around their faces under their helmets, hollow eyes and bearded cheeks showing through, rags over their combat boots to keep in a little body heat. Nobody would remember later, but in millions of living rooms those pictures were seen night after night after night.

In the fall of 1950, with victory imminent for the American forces racing north through North Korea, I suggested that someone should be preparing some kind of special program, titled, perhaps, *Victory in Korea*. My boss said it was an excellent idea and told me to do it. I didn't know how, but no one else had the time, and I could learn as I went along. For two months I was thrust into close contact with those who know film best, the film editors. They showed me how film could satisfy whatever I wanted of it, so long as I knew what I wanted. All this took place lunch hours, evenings, and weekends, because no one was available to relieve me of what I was already doing.

Miles of the Jones twins' film and at least as much from the Defense Department, foreign sources, and amateurs, all were matched to a chronology I had cobbled together from newspaper clippings: the initial shock, the collapse of the South Korean army, MacArthur in command, falling back to the Pusan perimeter, "space for time," two armies and a million civilians hemmed into four thousand square miles. Then, in the face of despair and defeat, the amphibious leapfrog, MacArthur's landing at Inchon, cutting off the North Korean rear and slicing across the peninsula.

There was no deadline yet there was a deadline. Reports from the battlefront were more and more optimistic; pictures came daily showing North Korean soldiers marching in to surrender and North Korean villages welcoming American GI's, just as they had five years ago. From when we were finished until there was a print ready for broadcast would take more time than I had expected. It was time to hurry, there was still the final editing of a half hour of film, the writing of the final script, the new experience of a "recording studio" where announcers read script I had written to go with the pictures, the story of invasion, almost defeat, then triumph. The recording, the "mixing" of narration, and the adding of music and battle noises took two days, with me watching details, learning. In the afternoon of the second day, November 26, 1950, with film reaching heroic climax, words and music soaring together, someone found we were missing an "effects loop" of some kind. An assistant was sent from midtown Manhattan to 106th Street while we busied ourselves with small matters. He came back with the loop, and with a shred of AP copy someone had sent me: The Chinese had crossed the Yalu River into Korea and were marching south. There would be no victory in Korea.

My half-hour program, my first magnum opus for television, would never be seen. But I had learned to cut film, and I had learned I liked it. No one taught me my new trade: It was too new a trade to have teachers. Other than instructions on how many words fit into, or over, one foot of 35mm film, I was learning as I went. Watching film editors, and listening to their rationalizations and their lore, I saw how they juxtaposed pictures, an essential step to learning film narrative. In film-editing rooms, places I have always enjoyed most, I learned the processes, the challenges, and the exhilaration when an intractable and disconnected record could be wrestled into an interesting story. That provided an experience even writing a successful script could not surpass. Others prefer the solitary act of writing, or the complications of filming in the field, but the place I felt most fulfilled was the room where film was cut.

I was becoming a partisan of television. There were special problems to using pictures to report news, few of which were yet solved and some of which would remain forever unsolved, but there were also special attractions. Working with pictures challenged the whole intellect. There have been several studious accounts of television news and how it felt its way in those early days, written mostly by students who inquired into it rather than craftsmen who had worked there. At least one important study stated that those first newscasts were "no more than" a newscaster interspersed with pictures. It is logical that people who write the words consider them more important than pictures, but perhaps not when the words are about television.

Pictures *are* the point of television reporting. Television enables the audience to see things happen, and that is what newspapers and magazines and radio cannot duplicate, while all use basically the same words. More and more, then and since, television news would be graded on the words it used rather than the pictures it showed. The early pictures were primitive, but we got better; late, but we got faster; meager, but we got more and more. Academics and savants have spent too little time charting that progression and too much time with the words of the newscasters, judging them sometimes by the furniture they sit among, the paint on the wall behind them, or how their teeth register on the chroma scale. The pictures they "introduced," which took harder physical work and more acquired skill, and more risk, were taken for granted.

My first exposure to working with pictures in this way, and the first time I started thinking these kinds of thoughts, was during the time I spent with *Victory in Korea*. Some time after that instructive experience, the writer of the *Camel News Caravan*, who held a reserve commission, was called up to help win the war in Korea, and I was asked to replace him. I became the *News Caravan* "writer"—the only one—the best job in the place.

My first day in the new job was St. Patrick's Day, 1951. My first decision was not to use any film of New York's St. Patrick's Day parade, which had been on all the channels all day, and which I did not consider news. The film assignment man came out of his back office fuming. Four of his six cameramen had been out all day filming the parade. "We have always used the parade!" he shouted at me.

He had come from newsreels, not from news. He would say, "You can't miss with kids or dogs." The managers we worked for allowed him to influence the choice of stories on the *News Caravan*, already a major source of information for many Americans, and he saw my decision as an effrontery and a challenge. But I found such "news" embarrassing. As we were becoming more important, as more people were watching, we had to grow up. I soon set out to eliminate all newsreel leftovers. I won some; I lost some. For example, I stopped the use of foreign newsreel clips of professional wrestling, always good for a belly laugh. But I lost on showing on Monday film of a Saturday football game as well as film on ladies' fashions. In both cases, I was told "someone at the agency" liked them. As to the fashion films, inquiry revealed that the "someone at the agency" was someone's wife.

A bright and pretty secretary who dressed well had been exalted to the position of news writer to write two fashion scripts a week, about a hundred seconds. But she had never learned to write, so I had to write those scripts while she stood behind my shoulder telling me what was new about this skirt or those culottes. It was harmless enough, but we had only thirteen minutes a night for the news.

We also had certain prohibitions. We must never show a "No Smoking" sign. We must never show a live camel, a smelly, ugly beast, quite unlike a Camel cigarette, which the commercials described as "smooth-tasting" and recommended by "most doctors." Nor might we ever show anyone smoking a cigar. The best-known person then alive was Winston Churchill: wartime prime minister, architect of victory, emperor of spoken English, Book-of-the-Month Club best-seller, even more popular with Americans than at home—and constantly in the news where his famous and beloved face always had a cigar in it!

I felt it was a cause: The rule must be changed. The people I worked for were doubtful—even frightened. As I went higher, the going got tougher. Winning Camel cigarettes to sponsor NBC's news in the face of CBS's competition had been a coup. Also, Camel paid the bills for just about everything NBC did in the name of television news, including the salaries of the people who worked on other programs as well as the management's. Was it really so important? With reservation and trepidation, they let me make the approach. It was surprisingly easy. Of course I could show Churchill with a cigar. But I got no more than a specific waiver; the rule still held. No one else. Not even Groucho Marx.

These were nuisances, not burdens. When it came to what I would consider news itself, I was never told to use a story, or not to, or how to. There was no interference with news, not in an editorial sense, not from the sponsor or the agency or the NBC business department. I speak only for myself, but I wonder how many print journalists can claim the same thing.

The daily functioning of the *News Caravan* was a simple business. We were all feeling our way together. Some of the structure of radio news, both in the getting and the presenting, was assumed in television, although not as much at NBC as at CBS. Mostly, we figured out what to do when the time came for something to be done. Early as it was, there was a great deal at stake, in money, in prestige, even (to be sententious) in public responsibility, and it is astonishing how we were allowed to do as we pleased. When Woolworth heiress Barbara Hutton had a world-watched romance with a Dominican playboy named Porfirio Rubirosa, we played it as a soap opera, opening with organ music and a plummy voice inviting us to the latest adventures of Babs and Porfirio; we edited the film in a story about the French dodging taxes to the rhythms and words of Eartha Kitt singing, "C'est Si Bon." Nobody we worked for said, "Hey, that was great!," nor did they say, "Don't ever do that again."

Our superiors—executives and managers miles away in Rockefeller Center—never interfered. Decisions were made by the director and me. No one else would, so we had to. The job of our "director," I should explain, was not the same as it was for those directing entertainment programs like the live dramas so prominent at the time, but they belonged to the same union. News department directors were skilled at using live cameras at sporting and other unrehearsed events, like political conventions and Washington occasions. Most were self-taught, and for that matter self-declared. A news writer I knew once said, "I can do that," and thereafter did: it paid better. (To further the confusion, a "news director" is something else again. He or she runs a news department, usually at a station, demonstrably the least secure job in all television.)

Network programs, from newscasts to *Hamlet*, usually used three live cameras. Our three were pointed at Swayze, so when he was on camera more than ten seconds, he could look to another camera to vary the picture. The cameras also took pictures of cards with white letters on black background, which were then inserted over film to show where an event took place or to identify a speaker. We also had a title card that said: A CAMEL NEWS CARAVAN EXCLUSIVE. And another that said: ANOTHER CAMEL NEWS CARAVAN EXCLUSIVE. I once suggested: STILL ANOTHER CAMEL NEWS CARAVAN EXCLUSIVE.

In newsreel fashion, film scripts were read by anonymous announcers who stood at a microphone in the back of the studio. To coordinate the words of a film's narration with the scenes they were supposed to match, I would tap the announcer on the shoulder and he would read until the next cue. Swayze talked when I pressed a button in a contraption I wore in a shoulder harness. This flashed a light behind what looked like books on his desk but was actually a box over which dust jackets had been pasted. The director would say, "Cue John," and I would press the button that switched on his light. Then Swayze would read a news item that would lead into the next piece of film, and I would hear in my headset the director in the control room ordering the film to roll. When it showed up on the monitor, I would tap the shoulder of the next reader.

Only in our out-of-town reports did we have reporters covering events and talking over pictures of the events they themselves had covered. Besides our own reporter in Washington, with his report or two each night, we liked to originate in cities along the closed loop that AT&T provided for television distribution around the country, called the "round-robin." NBC did this notably more often than CBS, as it had in radio news, largely because NBC was part of RCA, where the orientation was to machines and engineering, so even NBC's program executives were curious about how things worked. (This skill in switching around the country, and the promise to do a lot of it, had helped to get the Camel sponsorship.)

We switched mostly to stations in Chicago, Cleveland, or Philadelphia, where local news staff was considered NBC News staff, people who knew us and knew what we wanted. At first they offered news stories, then, increasingly, we assigned them news to cover. There were times we even had to tell them what was news in their city before asking them to cover it for us. For example, whenever the North Koreans released an American prisoner of war, we had someone search out and talk to his family. To cover a minor economic recession, we initiated a roundup of local conditions and responses, switching live from city to city during the program—videotape had not yet been invented. Omaha, Oklahoma City, and Kansas City soon signed on, usually through the initiative of the local news director, who liked being on the network showcase; then Atlanta and Charleston.

The poorest local news departments were in stations owned by newspapers. Not all newspaper-owned stations had bad news departments, but those that did were terrible. In 1952, the station owned by the *San Francisco Chronicle* had no news department at all. We—the *News Caravan*—were all their on-the-air news, except when someone read a local bulletin behind a slide.

Then there was the national coverage of the kidnapping of Bobby Greenlease in Kansas City. The story was so well covered that when the child's body was found in St. Louis, the front page of one New York tabloid read only: "The Boy Is Dead." That morning, I was in the office early and heard the AP bulletin bell for the discovery of the body. Almost at once there was a telephone call from the newsroom of the St. Louis station, owned by the *Post-Dispatch*, proud paper of the Pulitzers. I took the call confident that I was about to be offered film of the discovery of the body and the capture of the two kidnappers. But the man on the other end had no idea what I was talking about. It was from me that he learned the boy's body had been found and the kidnappers caught. He was amazed.

I had him go to the *Post-Dispatch* city desk while I held the phone. He came back confirming that the Greenlease boy's body had been found and two people were being charged. I then asked him please to send a camera to where the body was found, another to where the suspects were being held, and, if he had a third, maybe the morgue. I would call later about their report for that night's *News Caravan*.

Only then did I venture: "By the way, why did you call?"

"We have some film of last night's Veiled Prophet's Ball," he said, "and we were hoping to make the *News Caravan*."

The Bobby Greenlease kidnapping was one of those news stories that involve the American public for weeks. The kidnappers were tried in Kansas City, where we were well-served by Randall Jessee, news director of the *Kansas City Star* station (no rule is absolute). This was long before cameras were allowed in courtrooms, so the only film we could expect would be of lawyers going up and down the courthouse steps, and the accused barely seen inside fast-moving cars. Jessee suggested a courtroom artist, like the ones newspapers used. He had a friend in mind, Thomas Hart Benton.

Thus, NBC television news covered the trial of Bobby Greenlease's kidnappers with Thomas Hart Benton's courtroom drawings. Benton kept them.

. . .

Late in 1951, CBS started a weekly program series called *See It Now*, presided over by the most highly regarded broadcast journalist of the time, Edward R. Murrow. At first, each program included more than one topic, few if any dealing with breaking news or was assembled under deadline pressure, and usually but not invariably of seriousness and substance. Stories ran much longer than they could on the evening news programs, if they would be used at all. In other words, Murrow and his producer, Fred W. Friendly, presented what would later be called a "magazine" news program. They brought to it style, a substantial budget, curiosity, professional ethics, and personal concern. Although audiences were not large, the kind of people advertisers were then calling "influential" were impressed, as were those who wrote about television in newspapers. From time to time, *See It Now* devoted its entire hour to one topic. Those programs were very effective and stirred up the most talk. At NBC, executives were asking why we weren't doing things like that. A new question was heard in the corridors of 30 Rockefeller Plaza: "Who is, where is, our answer to Murrow?"

This went on for several years. The question was put to the managers of the news department when they met with their superiors. It reached the newspapers, as such things must, with references to a putative search, with the fatuous phrase itself seeing print, "NBC's answer to Murrow . . ."

The people who ran NBC enjoyed telling us that although our news programs were successful enough in ratings, revenue, and other crass criteria, they had no stature, that what we were doing was far short of television's noble potentials. This was particularly the refrain of Pat Weaver, NBC's vice president for television programs, a powerful position in those days when a network had only one president. Among other things, the programs vice president controlled time on the air, the only thing that matters in broadcasting.

Pat Weaver—Sylvester L. Weaver, Jr.—earned his place in television's pantheon with his talent for innovation combined with a commitment to upper-middle-class taste. He had the educated amateur's conviction that news should enlighten and uplift. The idea that news results from the combined energies of a lot of craftsmen working at their craft was not only strange to him but repugnant. News was science; news was frontiersmanship; news was pursuing new developments in art and culture. Above all, news was teaching; news was making people better. Once, during the controversial peacetime draft, an old associate of his produced a telling half-hour profile of a young, blue-collar Philadelphian drafted for the army, showing his last week as a civilian. Weaver told him, "I don't much care for people stories."

Weaver's most lasting contribution to America and the world was morning television. *Today* was his idea. At the time, almost everybody thought it was a dumb idea. No one would turn on a TV set in the morning, when normal people were preparing for work, for school, for the day, they said. This attitude continued after the program went on the air and for a year or so beyond, to Weaver's chagrin and the frustration of the people who worked on the program. Weaver had thought that he could win the audience over from radio, which could enter every room with news and gossip and enlightenment in a way television as yet could not.

He laid out his thoughts and dreams and requirements for *Today* in a series of memoranda, including a famous one where he adjured everyone involved to "have fun with the stuff." News coverage would show headlines of newspapers from around the country and have the principal "communicator"—Weaver's word, and one of which he was proud—seen on the phone as he talked to someone in a foreign news bureau. It seemed to me and others a crabbed use of the medium's potential to show miscellaneous front pages and the back of a man talking on the telephone. Nowhere in his long treatment of what he wanted *Today* to be did he deal with the prospect, much less the advantages, of using television to show news events taking place.

Like a lot of broadcasting executives from outside journalism, Weaver thought news was what you read in *The New York Times*, and broadcasting's role was to discuss and explain it. His favorite suggestion was to equip a moving van with live cameras and, for an event of great importance, drive it up to some leader's house and ask him what he thought of it. His usual example was Sam Rayburn. If anyone suggested Sam Rayburn might be too busy or unwilling to talk to a television camera, he considered that typical NBC News negativism. So, on *Today*'s very first day, the live cameras of a television mobile unit caught Adm. William Fechteler, chief of naval operations. The admiral had not been warned he would be on television; in fact, the unit was there hoping to catch anybody who would be news, with no specific news in mind. Surely there was news to be had if you lay in wait for people arriving for work at the Pentagon, the most powerful building in the world!

The hapless reporter asked the admiral, "How's the Navy going these days?"

"It was all right last night when I left it," said Fechteler, and he walked into the building.

End of news.

Today was launched early in 1952, a program of the entertainment department with news provided by NBC News on the hour and half hour including newsfilm. Gerald Green was head of the news part of *Today* with the title of managing editor, a term later used to emolliate anchormen. *See It Now* and *Today*, starting within months of each other, were both part of the growing reach of television and television news, its expanding importance and self-importance. These were new forms, neither resembled anything on radio.

Today did poorly at first, carried by few stations and watched by few people, bringing in less than it cost. The traditional histories insist this turned around when the reporters and communicators were joined by a chimpanzee named J. Fred Muggs. It is true ratings and revenue jumped around the time Muggs arrived. But something else happened at the same time: The news professionals on the *Today* staff stopped reading Pat Weaver's memos. They went back to presenting news as they always had, with a slight bias to what was heard over what was seen, like a radio program, because people do not watch at that hour as much as they listen.

It also took time for Americans to accept the idea of watching television in the morning. It had never been done. It had never been possible. A program like *Today* is a habit, and habits are neither changed nor formed by the dreams or fiats of executives. Whatever the cause, *Today* went suddenly from disaster to affluence.

As for the evening newscast, Weaver made little secret of his low opinion of John Swayze. Like many, he gave Swayze too little credit for professional experience in news. Swayze had started as a newspaper reporter in Kansas City and, as happened often in the days before the wire services would sell to broadcasting, he learned the uses of the microphone by originating a daily newscast for a local radio station from the newspaper's city room. He had gone to NBC, worked his way up to news director of NBC's West Coast regional network, and then became a full-time news broadcaster. To Weaver this was merely experience in a profession he did not quite accept. Weaver did not like Swayze or NBC News—and which was the chicken and which the egg was his secret. He tried several times to hire reporters whose bylines he had read in the The New York Times, portly men in vests with mushy speech patterns who could not say "Howdy" in fewer than a thousand words. Three decades later, long-retired and pursuing other interests, Weaver dropped by my office for a friendly chat about bygone days. I asked him if he ever realized how his widely trumpeted low opinion of what we did destroyed morale in the news department. No, he had not thought of that.

"But you must admit," he added, "you never had anyone worth a damn." Many years later, and he still wouldn't let go.

By the time *Today* was being planned we had grown to eight television news writers in New York, some in daily work on the *News Caravan*, a couple doing local New York news programs and a syndicated newsfilm service for stations; two writers on the weekly sports newsreel; and one writer on *Watch the World*, a weekly half hour with Swayze, again behind his desk, introducing topics of supposed interest to high school students. (This was said to be General Sarnoff's favorite program. Despite a wooden, patronizing style, it won many awards with stories like the endless painting of the George Washington Bridge—as soon as one painting was finished it was time to start again at the other end. It once did a report on how neckties are made, and another on the fresh-flower market. From then on, Swayze did the *News Caravan* wearing a new necktie every day with a fresh flower in his lapel.)

The arrival of *Today* more than doubled the number of news writers, and the newcomers immediately joined our efforts for a union contract. The search started late in 1951, but was deferred when some old-timers said NBC might pay a Christmas bonus. (It didn't.) I wonder what paltry sum could have prevented, or at least delayed, having to pay a union wage to television news writers. With the obvious jokes about NBC standing for No Bonus Christmas, we organized early in 1952 under the aegis of the Television Writers' Group of the Authors' League and advised the company we wanted to negotiate a contract. Since I wrote the *News Caravan*, which paid all the bills, they made me shop steward, believing a threat from me to "down tools" would be taken more seriously than if it had come from any of them.

The negotiations were long and dull. After a lot of nonsense, the company offered us the radio writers' union contract. Declaring passionately that if we wanted the radio writers' contract we would have applied to be radio writers, I led a walkout. The executive secretary stayed behind, saying to the company, "Now, you've done it."

Management was truly worried. They did not understand what we did or how we did it, nor did they care so long as we did it. It seemed to work, and they did not want to disturb it. After two weeks, we came back to "the table" to get not all we wanted but enough. The basic pay was $165 a week, plus extra fees for those who wrote fully sponsored network programs, the last remnants of the silly and degrading "talent fee" system whereby "creative" people were paid more not for harder or more original work but for network programs that had commercials in them.

Having a union contract made us feel more professional, more grown-up. Besides, most of us were scheduled to go to Chicago for the two national political conventions of 1952, which would have been awkward without a contract. The Radio Writers' Guild, sticking on points we had given up, had already failed to negotiate a contract, and a strike had been announced. If they went to Chicago it would be at their own expense, to picket. I had tried to explain to one of them that when an important and interesting event is being covered live, a network does not need writers. Television or radio, live broadcasting writes itself. We did not part friends.

To celebrate the extension of the live television network to the West Coast, Swayze and I were to spend the week before the 1952 conventions in California broadcasting the *News Caravan* from Los Angeles for three days and then from San Francisco for two. Negotiations for the writers' contract were not wrapped up until late in the afternoon of the day I was to leave. Our general secretary, Evelyn Burkey, had put her face in the face of NBC's chief negotiator and said, "Frank doesn't get on a plane until we have a contract."

I left that evening. It was before passenger jets, or even nonstop flights to California. Between dozes, it occurred to me that if I had stayed with the *Newark News* I might indeed by then have progressed to being sent to Chicago to cover the conventions, but I liked it better this way. Television mattered more.

3

There was something about Chicago that loved conventions. From the first convention in 1831 until the disorders of 1968, one out of every three national political conventions met there. Several times both major parties met there, as they did in 1952.

The stockyards had moved away by then, leaving only acres of empty pens and here and there a ramshackle slaughterhouse that still hung on. The Stockyard Inn still stood, a good place for steaks, and the International Amphitheater still housed cattle shows as well as political conventions. The other theater of political activity was along South Michigan at Balboa with the Conrad Hilton Hotel on one corner and the Blackstone on the other. Parties and candidates set up headquarters in the Hilton; politicians with clout booked into the Blackstone. Talk in lobbies and bars reflected the Republicans' belief that 1952 was their year.

The billboard facing South Michigan Avenue from across the Chicago River declared Dad's Root Beer's benign interest by saluting the two dads contending for the Republican nomination: Senator Robert A. Taft of Ohio, a president's son, a traditional, Midwestern Republican making his last attempt at the office he had once seemed born to; and General of the Army Dwight D. Eisenhower in his first try for elective office, no longer misperceived as savior of Democratic liberals but champion of the Republicanism of New England, the Atlantic seaboard, and downtown New York. High above the turmoil of movers, shakers, and camp followers, the two bald heads looked so alike that only Taft's rimless glasses distinguished them. The billboard made no unseemly claim that either man endorsed Dad's Root Beer, only that these were indeed eminent dads in a nation of dads.

The weather was unusually pleasant that first week of July, the week before the Republican convention. While the two smiling countenances—Taft's and Eisenhower's—looked down on crowds milling happily on Michigan Avenue, upstairs in the public rooms of the Conrad Hilton the Republican National Committee and the convention's credentials committee met to decide the course of the party and the election. In the streets there was the usual jollity of out-of-towners rubbing elbows with locals, scrubbed-faced middle-class kids of junior high school age exploring for souvenirs, and the three layers of politics (the hobbyists, the activists, and the professionals) picking up acquaintances where they had left off four years before . . . "And this is his charming wife."

There were two new elements in Michigan Avenue that week preceding the convention: live television cameras and picket signs. TV's mobile units, parked in the side streets and in back of the hotels with cables snaking to cameras on the various floors of the Conrad Hilton, spied out the latest news, the smallest detail. A camera or two were spared for outdoor pictures to set the scene as each program began, particularly on Sunday afternoon, the day before the convention opened, when each network presented a "special" program replete with film of past conventions, interviews with the mighty, picture essays about what was ordinary and what was naughty about Chicago, a century of newsroom clichés, and (still a novelty) reporters reporting live from the very streets of the city.

One was talking away when a hand moved into camera view thrusting a bottle of Coca-Cola into his. On live television, there was nothing he could do. But before he had finished talking, another hand removed the bottle of Coca-Cola and replaced it with a bottle of Pepsi-Cola. The 1952 conventions were the stage of bitter battles in the war between the colas. Coca-Cola, moving swiftly, had secured exclusive rights inside the International Amphitheater. Pepsi-Cola riposted with thirty-five coolers in the Conrad Hilton Hotel, attended by eighteen off-duty airline stewardesses, who gave away ten thousand bottles each day.

Pepsi-Cola used stewardesses because all available models in Chicago, a major advertising center, had been hired by the Taft campaign, which named them "Belles for Bob," dressed them in cheerleader costumes bedecked with Taft signs and buttons, and told them to cluster at any live television camera. Taft's managers said openly that their aim was to "overwhelm" the TV picture on all three networks. The incongruity of the models' flashing teeth and aggressive busts representing bald, bespectacled, austere, intellectual Bob Taft was overridden by hunger for television exposure—by whatever means. If Coca-Cola and Pepsi-Cola could do it, so could Republican conservatism.

Television was beginning to dominate political decisions. Old hands were learning, new ones growing up conditioned to know, that no decision is judged solely on its merits. First you asked how it will look on television. The Taft managers not only wanted television to show pretty girls with Taft buttons, they also tried to hide from television their decisions about credentials—that is, the crucial decisions being reached upstairs while the crowds caromed off each other in the street below. For the Republicans in 1952, the big issue would be credentials, who were the delegates and who the impostors. Once that was settled, all else would be formality, even the nomination.

Television was a novelty in 1948; in 1952, it was a fact. People in broadcasting favored no faction, sought no personal nonjournalistic gain, but their insistence on access to news may well have upset strategies. About 17 million homes had receivers that year. Sixty-four cities in thirty-eight states carried NBC's live coverage. Department store advertising trumpeted: "Get a TV set! See the conventions!" Newspapers reported this would be the biggest undertaking in television history. Since it was so short a history, this was a small boast, but no one realized such things at the time.

For a third of a million 1952 dollars, the hall had been air-conditioned. A press release estimated that 12,000 bodies in that hall in that city in that month would generate 6.6 million BTUs of heat an hour, equal to burning 46 gallons of oil or 530 pounds of coal or 6,600 cubic feet of natural gas. What the press release did not say was more to the point: Delegates would be spared being seen on television with dark patches under their arms, and speakers at the rostrum would not be exposed in the nation's living rooms with sweat dripping from their noses. The air-conditioning was considered important enough to post guards in case of sabotage.

The sponsors, appropriately, were makers of TV sets, although they also had other appliances to push. CBS was "brought to you" by Westinghouse, represented on camera by Betty Furness, making hers a household name. Philco was the NBC sponsor, and Admiral was ABC's. Jay Jackson, Philco's announcer, opened every night of the convention itself solemnly stating that Philco's sponsorship did not constitute an endorsement of its products by the Republican National Convention.

Other set manufacturers also benefited as the prospect and then the fact of live convention coverage caused a surge in the sale of sets. We kept hearing that when politicians called home to ask, "How did I look?" or merely "Did you see me?," they often learned that the local dealer had run out of receivers. This was especially true of small-and mid-sized cities without large manufacturers' distribution centers. Crosley, a smaller manufacturer, placed a quarter-page ad in *The New York Times*:

> This year, you won't just read what a candidate says; you'll look him straight in the eye when he says it. You'll judge his intelligence, his physical and intellectual vigor—and whether he can "take it" under pressure. . . . This year, television assumes a new and profound role in your life—and in the life of America. See and know the man you vote for. Take a good long look. . . . Don't vote 'til you see the whites of their eyes.

In this atmosphere, Taft did not stand a chance. In a foretaste of many future battles, it was not the people in television who defeated Taft, but the presence of cameras.

Seven delegations were contested, primarily in the South and the border states, with seventy-two contested delegates, the margin of victory. Taft's organization controlled not only the credentials committee but the Republican National Committee itself. It might have won the nomination, and the election had it not banned television from committee meetings. This action became the story—on television—for the whole week before the convention as the credentials committee continued to meet behind closed doors. Television is good at showing closed doors. Whenever a committee member left the room, he was waylaid by cameras and asked what was going on. It was the only way to get the news, and it dramatized that the meeting was closed to television.

The Taft leadership soon realized how they were "playing" on camera. A representative finally confronted the NBC cameras and insisted that it was not Taft who had objected to live coverage of the commitee meeting. It must have been some other fellow. Guy George Gabrielson, the national chairman, also sought out the camera to deny guilt; he was really for television, not against it.

The mountains kept coming to Mohammed. The Eisenhower people smelled blood. They also came to the cameras, proclaiming they favored television, they loved it, they wanted it, and that barring it was an outrage, a denial of the American way. First came Congressman (later Senator) Hugh Scott of Pennsylvania: "By a single word, Taft could let you in." Then Senator Henry Cabot Lodge, the Eisenhower campaign's convention manager, added a few strong patrician words. Then more Taft delegates sought out the limelight to say that they, too, favored live television. By Tuesday, everybody was in favor of live television, but it was still banned from the meeting. Inside, the first contested delegation, Florida, was considered, and the vote gave the state to Taft.

Georgia went to Taft on Wednesday, Louisiana on Thursday. Meanwhile, the Republican National Committee, fifty-two men and fifty-two women, had moved into the room that had been vacated by the credentials committee and promptly barred television there, too; so there were now two closed doors. The meetings were not closed to the press, only to cameras. Reporters, even television reporters, might sit and observe and report—but no pictures. Would the maneuverings have *looked* too raw, or were the Taft people unaware that in politics, even more than in the rest of American life, the Age of Television had arrived?

Taft's juggernaut plunged ahead to hollow victory and ultimate defeat. After the credentials committee and the Republican National Committee reviewed the contests for delegates, almost all the decisions were in favor of the Taft delegates. With nine declared candidates, no one had expected a first-ballot choice, but the early weight of the voting seemed to be going to Taft. Still, Eisenhower's organizers never seriously feared being beaten. They planned to go over the heads of the committees to the delegates. Senator Lodge told an interviewer they were counting on the committees being overturned because of what had been seen on television. And that is exactly what happened, although what had been seen on television was closed doors. They were, however, the symbol of television being barred.

During that preconvention week, all the networks interrupted program schedules of sleepy summer weekdays, and none more than NBC, to show that highly technical fight over who might sit on the convention floor the coming Monday. Barred from where the news was, NBC put on a special program Sunday night about the news story of the week: the fight over the largest contested delegation, Texas. Since the committee's debates could not be shown, six Texans were recruited, three from each side, to make their cases in a studio, to claim legitimacy, cry fraud, call each other names, shout when shouted at, and predict victory. Every television program or news bulletin included a prominent statement about the barring of the cameras, and each was a blow at Taft's candidacy.

On the second day of the convention—too late—the Taft forces surrendered. Live television was allowed in the meeting rooms of both the credentials committee and the national committee. Television had won its victory. It was a victory, especially, for Bill McAndrew, the new boss of NBC News, who had been drafted from a station executive's job in Washington less than a year before to try to make one organization out of NBC's radio news and television news. The 1952 conventions were his first big challenge. McAndrew pushed company brass for more special news programs, more interruptions of the entertainment schedule, and more time on the air. A solid, old-fashioned, print-trained journalist and an astute judge of realities, McAndrew understood better than most that in broadcasting status is measured by time on the air. During the week before the convention, he took every minute he could.

He expanded *Meet the Press*, the original and prototypical newsmaker interview, to an hour, and had its brigade of reporters question leadership figures all week under different program titles, a half hour here, an hour there, sometimes a mere fifteen minutes. He even achieved the ideal special broadcast: He interrupted an interruption. It was Monday morning, and he had broken into the entertainment schedule for an interview with Speaker of the House Joseph Martin, the convention's permanent chairman. As Martin was making the usual politician's noises denying that the party was hopelessly divided, Martha Rountree interrupted to switch to the LaSalle Street Station where Herbert Hoover, the only living ex-President, was arriving by train from California. (Hoover didn't say much, so they switched back to Martin.)

During convention week, McAndrew launched *Convention Call*, in which viewers called in to ask NBC reporters to explain what was happening, especially rules of procedure. Although television had shown in 1948 that it could cover conventions, the 1952 conventions were the first most Americans had seen. They were apparently entranced. A torrent of calls from viewers all over the United States overloaded telephone company switchboards. After a day, Illinois Bell refused any more calls, and we had to ask viewers to send their questions by telegram. *Convention Call* was broadcast at least twice a day that week, before sessions and when they were in recess. There were more questions than the reporters could handle.

Meanwhile, every time a live camera showed up in a vulnerable place, usually a street corner, someone would appear waving a sign that said: ABC-CBS-NBC/RADIO WRITERS GUILD/ON STRIKE. Entrances to hotels and the amphitheater were also being picketed. When I arrived in Chicago from California on Saturday evening, my colleagues were waiting nervously for their shop steward. It was not that they wanted to honor the radio writers' picket lines, but they "felt funny" about it. They wanted me to tell them what to do. We had warned the radio writers that if they went on strike for clauses we had consciously given up in our own negotiations, we would not honor their picket lines. If those clauses had been good enough to strike for, we would have done so ourselves. It was not quite labor solidarity, but beyond refusing, if asked, to do struck work, I could see no obligation on us.

I told them I was going to work; they could do as they liked. That ended it. To quiet their rumbling stomachs, I telephoned the appropriate NBC vice president, who had never heard of me, offering my good offices as an intermediary, which sounded even stuffier to me at the time I said it than it does now writing it. I made another call to Evelyn Burkey, the executive secretary of the Television Writers' Group, in the New York offices of the Authors' League, and told her I saw no reason to observe the lines and I was sorry her counterparts were making nasty noises at her.

On television, the convention sessions settled into a pattern. The anchorman, rarely seen, spoke continually over a picture of the proceedings, identifying who was making the speech or the objection, describing what was about to happen, explaining the complexities and the details that were not apparent to the eye. CBS's anchorman was the virtually unknown Walter Cronkite, who had signed on with CBS in its Washington bureau only two years before. A journalist since his college days, Cronkite had covered Eisenhower and his headquarters throughout the war in Europe. Working with him were such old hands as Murrow, Charles Collingwood, and Eric Sevareid.

NBC had gone outside its organization for the television anchorman to work beside H. V. Kaltenborn, Morgan Beatty, and Richard Harkness. Bill Henry was already past sixty. Since leaving college, he had been a fixture at the *Los Angeles Times* as reporter, sports editor, war correspondent, Washington bureau chief, and now columnist. Broadcasting had become an additional profession, supplying him with recognition and avocation. He was good at it, both as a reporter and as a newscaster, but it never became his prime occupation. To broadcasting, he brought a pleasant voice, a California speech pattern, and a writer's way with words and sentences. He had covered his first convention as a newspaper reporter in 1928, as a radio broadcaster in 1940. He knew everybody in government and most of them liked him. He was that kind of man.

The position of network news anchorman had not yet been exalted to Joseph of the Dreams, and Henry shared his seat with others, and even surrendered it for special programs, committee hearings, and news interruptions. His job was to be the man back at headquarters. He sat in a tiny studio in the network work space on the second floor of the convention hall with one of his daughters, who kept his files, and an NBC director who was his link to the control room. He watched the action on television, along with the audience, and talked over the picture. Part wise man and part traffic cop, Henry filled the slow periods with bits of news and information, alerting the viewers to upcoming reports.

At CBS, Cronkite, doing roughly the same thing, had the advantage of a production staff that was better at it. They consciously gave him center stage and drew attention to him. The CBS producers developed what was for that time an ingenious procedure, putting Cronkite's face in a corner of the picture of the proceedings, the relative size of a postage stamp. As a technical achievement, it was simple and unsophisticated, but no one had done it that way before, and it helped make Cronkite famous. There was no thought of doing the same with Bill Henry, even if our people could figure out how to, because he was not truly one of ours.

Between the Republican and Democratic conventions, when the newspapers were trying to appreciate the awesome phenomenon of people in their living rooms watching news, the two anchormen were asked what they had learned. Characteristically, and significantly, Henry thought he had said too much while Cronkite said he had not explained enough. Henry said the people in the control booth were always asking him to say more, which he considered "a terrible hang-over from radio." It is true that everyone in authority in the NBC control room had at least twenty years' experience, most of it in radio. But at CBS, where the same condition obtained, they tried to get Cronkite to say less. Cronkite wanted to pass on to viewers the kind of information that NBC's Bill McAndrew had arranged for by broad-casting *Convention Call*. It can be assumed that both control rooms were trying to achieve the same proportion of anchortalk. The differ-ence was in the receiving ears. The basic question seems to have been how often the same question need be answered to enable the audience to follow what was going on, or, conversely, how smart is the audience? Henry thought it was smarter than Cronkite did.

Cronkite got the CBS brass to consider putting an "average man" beside him in his little studio to watch the convention with him on the TV monitor. This "average man" would ask Cronkite to enlighten him whenever he did not understand what was going on. Cronkite would explain, to him and to all the millions out there. Cronkite later told the *The New York Times* that the plan was dropped because, supposedly, no one knew where to find an average man. Whoever vetoed the idea did Cronkite the greatest favor of his career.

Bill Henry and Walter Cronkite were heard, and seen, in cities in the East and the Midwest. West of Omaha, the telephone company provided only one channel that could carry television pictures, and the networks had to share it. In fact, the trip Swayze and I took to California the week before the Republican convention was a way of marking the debut of the *Camel News Caravan* as the first truly trans-continental television news program. Each night's program was re-corded at the time of broadcast—7:45 P.M. in the East, 4:45 P.M. along the Pacific. In those days before videotape, the recording was a shaky, smeary picture on 16mm film, which was particularly bad when the recording was of other film, which meant all newsfilm. Called a kine-scope after the tiny, high-intensity TV tube that shone the image on the film, this film would be transmitted along the West Coast, from Seattle to San Diego, at 7:45 Pacific time. A newscaster and—if pos-sible—new film, would stand by in Los Angeles ready to jump in with fast-breaking news that had taken place in the three hours since the original broadcast, or with items of special regional interest.

NBC was the first to do this. But since networks broadcast the news at different hours, we could all do this without interfering with each other. However, when it came to convention coverage, all three networks would obviously be carrying it at the same time. With only one television line, they could show only the three-network pool pictures. Therefore, whichever network a Western viewer watched, he saw only the proceedings in the hall, nothing else (no interviews, no Bill Henry or Walter Cronkite, no switches to train stations or headquarters hotels). Over the pool pictures, each network added its own sound. So those from Denver westward watching NBC saw what was happening in the convention hall and heard (but did not see) David Brinkley, who was sharing the anchor chore with someone from NBC's Chicago news bureau.

Meanwhile, NBC was showing off its new technical advance: a small, hand-held, live-television camera with its own transmitting capacity so it would not have to be connected anywhere by wire. It could roam the floor of the convention showing delegates reacting to speakers and even join a wireless microphone for interviews. After many meetings in the NBC publicity offices, the miraculous device was dubbed the "walkie-lookie." But some unsung newspaper writer preferred "creepie-peepie," and from the moment he first used it the camera had no other name. The vaguely naughty implication of the nickname sat poorly with high officers of both NBC and RCA, but "creepie-peepie" stuck. Unfortunately, the "creepie-peepie" did not always work, and since there was only one, it wasn't all that useful.

The committee sessions went over into the convention week, and television alternated between them, now that the committee was open to cameras. NBC skipped the convention Tuesday afternoon to show the annual All-Star baseball game—when that contract had been signed, no one had thought to check to see if the game conflicted with the conventions—and Tuesday night, Herbert Hoover spoke. On Wednesday, the convention began in earnest. The credentials committee, now before live cameras, had that morning approved one delegation out of seven for Eisenhower. But Wednesday night the convention reversed its credentials committee and the party's national committee to seat the Eisenhower delegation from Georgia. In 1952, any delegate could ask that his delegation be polled. For the first time, it was polled on live television. The voting was slow, and the procedure cumbersome. The delegate demanding the poll often did so for a petty or frivolous reason. J. Leonard Reinsch, arrangements manager for the Democrats, whose convention would follow the Republicans into the amphitheater, watched in a hotel room with a few assistants. What they saw led them to find a way to avoid polling delegations on camera, but it was too late to make any changes before 1956.

The kind of conflict that made national political conventions interesting to watch broke out when the last Taft speaker ascended the platform during the Georgia debate. Senator Everett M. Dirksen of Illinois was a stocky man with a large, rubbery face under a shock of unruly, curly graying hair. His voice was low, like the sustained notes of a cello, his sentences rounded, and his cadences measured. He was popular in his party, willing to go anywhere to speak to the faithful, and it was those he had helped whom he called on as he spoke.

Dirksen asked delegates not to expose their party to obloquy by contradicting its national committee and rejecting its credentials committee, which had favored the Taft slate. He appealed to New England, where he had often dined, and to New Jersey, whose calls for help he had never spurned. He pleaded with Pennsylvania:

"Don't press this too tightly upon the Republican party," he asked them. "Search your hearts."

Then he turned his body to face New York.

"To my friends from New York," he said. His tone was smooth and intimate. The rostrum looked almost directly down on the New York delegation. On the left aisle, the speaker's right, sat the governor, Thomas E. Dewey, twice the Eastern faction's choice, and twice the party's candidate—against Roosevelt in 1944 and Truman in 1948. Now he was the commander of Eisenhower's disciplined, modern election machine. Dirksen extended his right arm, raised his forearm, pointed his little finger, the immortal Dirksenian pinkie, at Dewey. His soothing resonances, loud enough to fill the hall but mellow enough to charm a rabbit, rose suddenly to anger:

"We followed you before, and you took us down the road to defeat!"

The hall erupted in cheers and boos, shouts and insults. Banners waved, fists shook, everyone stood. Midwestern conservatives, tasting the gall of Taft's impending defeat, howled their anger and frustration. The band played unheard as the picture showed Dewey seated, his neat mustache and his overbite making him seem, as always, to be chortling. The challenge to him was direct, the insult personal. It was his fault the Republicans were out of power and jobs! Now, with victory in sight, would he deny the heartland its due, old Republicanism its victory, he who had achieved the impossible by losing to Truman four years before?

The galleries took up the shouting. The cameras showed a still photographer knocked down in the crush of angry people. The chairman banged his gavel, pleading for clear aisles, threatening to eject visitors while Dirksen stood at the podium, his head turning from side to side, his eyes smiling, and Dewey sat in his chair, the camera coming back to him, in profile, his mouth partly open, his cheeks shiny, saying nothing. It was twenty-three minutes before Dirksen could deliver his last paragraph, an anticlimax. A Wisconsin delegate was shown being taken out on a stretcher.

The response supporting the Eisenhower delegates from Georgia was only a formality. The issue had been decided and everyone knew it. We had time for a commercial.

The roll call was held up by factions demanding delegations be polled, a delegation at a time, a delegate at a time. Tension alternated with boredom and impatience. Finally, the Eisenhower delegation was seated, 607 to 531. It was almost two in the morning, Central time, before all the votes had been taken and the session adjourned. Every contest had gone to the Eisenhower organization. They no longer looked like the underdog; they no longer claimed to be the underdog. They were, perhaps, the first dog who understood television. Eisenhower was nominated on the first ballot, and his choice for vice president, California's junior senator, Richard M. Nixon, was named by acclamation.

Throughout the convention, I had the best seat in the house. My job in Chicago was what it was in New York, to write the *Camel News Caravan*. We had a studio in the convention hall from which to broadcast, bigger than Bill Henry's little booth, a few film cameramen assigned to us to do convention sidebar stories, and world news back in New York. Instead of highly paid announcers, David Brinkley read film scripts when tapped on the shoulder. Since he was the *News Caravan*'s Washington reporter, we had worked together by telephone; this was the first time we had met. Each evening, at seven Chicago time, after the program ended, I would find a sandwich and a free Coke and spend the rest of the night in the control room. I sat where I could, usually the step between the control room's two levels, staying out of people's way, watching.

It was a wonderful place to see what was happening in the convention, but it was also the best place to watch how a convention was covered. It was all centered in this dark little room, to which all the pictures, telephone lines, and microphone feeds led. Sitting there I was open to a dozen sources. I would look at pictures from the pool or our own cameras and wonder why the director or the producers did not use them on the air. But I was there on sufferance and knew enough to keep my thoughts to myself—especially the one that we were doing a mediocre job. I sampled the various news sources and learned that the best information came through the earphone when the knob was at "NBC Radio." As I listened, I watched a dozen live pictures at once. For me, it was like bathing in news. I never again enjoyed a convention as much; but then, I never again saw a convention for the first time.

When the Republicans went home, so did most of the journalists. Although there was only one week between the two conventions, an unusually short time, few wanted to hang around Chicago. The producer of the *News Caravan* did. I learned later that his budget was greatly helped by closing the New York studio for a month and putting Swayze in a cheaper studio at the NBC facility in Chicago's Merchandise Mart. It was for that reason that he stayed in Chicago for the week, as did Swayze, and Brinkley, and the director, and I. It was a dull week, but we made our way through it while the rest of NBC News went back to New York to join those who had stayed behind without convention assignments.

Those back in New York were observing the Radio Writers' Guild picket lines. Presumably, so would those returning home from Chicago. There were secret exceptions; the man who wrote the scripts for the weekly Gillette sports newsreel—Look Sharp! Feel Sharp! Be Sharp!—carried his portable from New Jersey to a tavern at 107th Street and Lexington Avenue. He passed the finished scripts, one at a time, out the back door. Receiving the scripts was Julian Goodman, the manager of the Washington bureau, who had been pressed into service for the duration of the strike and was the (nonunion) writer of record. Goodman later became my boss, as president and then chairman of NBC. It became one of my fonder imaginings to picture him gingerly approaching the East 107th Street entrance of Farrell's Bar & Grill to wait in the rain for the door to open and a mysterious hand to thrust a few pages of script at him.

To us, the strike was primarily a nuisance. Those back in New York, uncomfortable and puzzled, took to calling me in Chicago: I really must honor the picket line, because without the *News Caravan* other action against the company was piddling. Finally, reluctantly, I agreed. It was the opposite of muscle tactics; it was the tyranny of weakness. People needed help and I seemed to be the one denying it. I told those who called, and then the executive secretary and the Chicago representative of the radio writers, that I would observe a picket line if there was one. Someone in the proper place with a proper sign would have to bar my entrance, to proclaim a dispute in progress. After all, I was not on strike; I was refusing to cross someone else's picket line, presumably out of fear of violence, which the law allowed, and not out of solidarity, which the law forbade.

The Chicago representative agreed. He informed me that one striking radio writer had stayed behind for just this contingency, someone from ABC, a native of Chicago who had moved in with his mother. He would call me. That was Tuesday.

Wednesday morning I arrived at the Merchandise Mart, a building occupying a full block with entrances on all four streets, where NBC occupied two floors. I walked twice around the block, past every entrance; I was unpicketed. I stood in a corridor reading the paper, then made my round again. No one. I went up to the newsroom to begin the day's work.

Shortly before noon I received a call.

"This is your picket," a voice whispered.

I had not thought of him as mine. "Where are you?" I asked.

"Downstairs."

I found him in the coffee shop, at a far table, a slight, youngish, baldish man with a file folder under one arm. I could see no picket sign. "Where's your picket sign?"

He held out the legal-sized manila folder with the top facing me and furtively separated the two leaves, like someone in a Peter Arno cartoon offering, "Feelthy pictures, m'soo?" On the inside of the folder, hand-printed, in two-colored pencil, I could read: ABC/CBS/NBC—RADIO WRITERS' GUILD—ON STRIKE. No one had thought to leave behind a real sign. I accepted being duly picketed and ordered coffee. As we drank, I laid out rules: I would not work that day, but if they wanted me to stay out tomorrow, it was up to him to be at the building picketing by nine o'clock. We chose the entrance and exchanged telephone numbers. I went back up to the newsroom.

In proper form, I told the producer that because of a labor dispute that threatened my health and safety I was returning to my hotel.

Brinkley could write the news scripts since he belonged to a different union. Somebody said lunch, but it was too early, and besides, that would be fraternizing. Bravely humming "Joe Hill," I headed for the cab stand and a lazy afternoon. It turned out to be a short one. At five o'clock the executive secretary called from New York to tell me that the strike had been settled. Unfortunately, it was not my single-handed achievement. It was settled while the picket and I were having coffee, but it had taken a few hours to ratify. When we hung up, I telephoned the picket not to come tomorrow since his strike had ended. His mother said he was at the beach.

Interestingly, the incident made me a little less junior. For a while afterward, in the RCA Building in New York, I was known to some as the one with his own personal picket. The graphics department worked up a pleasant little cartoon which went up on my wall. Years later, sitting on the founding committee of the Writers' Guild of America, I had a radio writer throw up to me that in 1952 I had not honored their picket line. Indeed I had, I answered, in my own good time.

The Democrats came to Chicago determined to learn from the Republican errors they had so avidly followed on television. The party chairman, Frank McKinney, announced that the "party of the people" would hold no secret sessions; all committee meetings would be open to television. The shadow of 1948 lay over everything—the conflict, the bitterness, the riven party. Television was more central to the Democratic convention than it had been to the Republican in important ways. Indeed, television had thrust the country into the year of politics that spring with the New Hampshire primary, when the junior senator from Tennessee, Estes Kefauver of the coonskin cap, had defeated a local politician widely accepted as a "stalking horse" or surrogate candidate for the President, Harry Truman.

It was the first primary ever to get television coverage. The networks chased the candidates around the state in a way that seemed minimal a few years later, but it was the biggest such effort to that time. Although Republican candidates also met in the primary, and Eisenhower won an anticipated victory, the race among the Democrats had received the most attention. Kefauver went from New Hampshire to Wisconsin, and from Wisconsin to South Dakota, network television on his heels at every step, reporting him in news programs every evening. And when Truman withdrew himself from nomination, that speech, too, was on television.

Kefauver was heavily covered because he was popular, which itself was a product of the television coverage of his committee's hearings into the workings of organized crime. Those hearings glued hundreds of thousands if not millions to their sets for days, watching a parade of felons and racketeers, shady politicians and crooked cops. Few indictments came out of the hearings; organized crime was not disorganized. But Estes Kefauver, who had reached the Senate by fighting the Memphis political machine of Edward H. "Boss" Crump, emerged as a crusading knight in armor. More liberal than his reputation, and hiding a keen intellect behind country-boy speech, he arrived at the convention with more committed delegates than any other candidate for President, delegates he had won in the primaries. But primaries were still a rarity, and "a lot" of delegates was less than a majority. The combined party leadership could deny him the nomination. And it did.

The leadership's candidate was Governor Adlai Stevenson of Illinois, who said he did not want the nomination, and there was every indication he meant it. Col. Jacob Arvey, Chicago's Democratic boss and a party power, wanted Stevenson to be the candidate. So did Harry Truman—he detested Kefauver as a spoiler of good Democratic organizations. Truman was himself an accredited member of the Missouri delegation, but for the first few days he stayed in the White House watching the proceedings on television. In Chicago, Kansas City councilman Thomas Gavin, Truman's alternate, refused to tell reporters how he had been instructed to vote.

Monday morning, July 21, delegates and alternates found cards on their seats reading, "Watch yourself—you may be on television." They were asked not to read newspapers, or yawn, or wear flashy jewelry. Nose-picking was not specifically enjoined, but the warning broadly hinted that television was an all-seeing eye. There might even be lip-readers out there!

Learning from NBC Radio, NBC's television reporters roamed the floor with portable microphones interviewing delegates. It was an improvised and disorganized way of getting to where the news was—on the floor among the delegates—but without portable cameras, the picture distracted from the interest. The only picture available to use with the reporting came from the television pool, which did or did not show from far away the reporter talking to someone in a crowd. With three networks and some independent stations all relying on the pool pictures, its producers and directors dared not favor us with the picture we needed.

Most of a long, dreary Monday session was spent on a battle over a loyalty oath, not quite as strong as 1948's but enough to set Southern teeth on edge. After the adjournment, after the delegates had given way to the sweepers, Robert C. Doyle, the organizer, executive producer, and principal director of the television pool, went to the floor to help set up cameras. Among a small cluster of idle onlookers he saw Jake Arvey.

"Hey, did you see any of that?" he asked.

Arvey replied that he had.

"That was really great television," said Doyle.

Arvey was noncommittal. Doyle continued, "People are really getting an insight into how this works."

"Yes, perhaps," said Arvey. "How many people do you think were watching?"

"Millions," said Doyle. "Fifty million, maybe eighty." (In fact, he had no idea, but he had to say something.)

Arvey shook his head. "We can't do this any more," he said. "It's not good for politicians to be seen fighting."

On Thursday, July 24, the gavel sounded shortly after noon, Chicago time. Before it did, Bill Henry announced that NBC News's live television coverage of the 1952 conventions now totaled one hundred hours. He did not mention the All-Star game. After the gavel came the roll call of the states for the purpose of placing in nomination. Each candidate was allowed less hijinks time than at former Democratic conventions, but there were so many candidates! After eleven hours the convention was just winding up placing the ninth name in nomination. Mixed in with the music and the snake dances and the streamers were points of order and fierce, impassioned debates about the right to vote of delegates who had not signed a loyalty oath.

The cameras switched to outside the International Amphitheater, where people with tickets to the evening session were pushing and shoving, trying to get in. Their tickets were useless. There was no evening session. This was still the afternoon session, called to order at noon.

Back inside, Senator Paul Douglas of Illinois moved for adjournment. Douglas was floor manager for the Kefauver campaign, which realized it needed extra time to knit together an anti-Stevenson coalition. The cameras showed Douglas below Chairman Rayburn's lectern shouting, "Mr. Chairman! . . . Mr. Chairman! . . ." his face darkening, his voice hoarse, his frustration patent; finally Rayburn recognized him. At the back of the hall, Douglas's daughter was watching, afraid her father would suffer a heart attack. "Oh, Daddy, don't," she muttered to herself. "Oh, Daddy, don't." It was now midnight.

The party nabobs refused adjournment, and the debate on who might vote was resumed. As it does once every four years, it seemed that Democrats had never hated each other as they did at that moment. Some wastepaper caught fire; a delegate who was a fireman seized a microphone and successfully exhorted everyone to avoid panic; the fire was put out. On television it was drama threatening to tip over into tragedy; in the next day's newspapers it was barely a paragraph. At two in the morning, fifteen hours after it was called to order, the longest continuous session in the history of political conventions was adjourned. Delegates were told to be back in nine hours to choose their candidate for President—one day late.

Before the delegates were seated the next morning, an NBC executive tricked David Brinkley into a small studio on the second floor where, seen live across the entire network, he was shown film of his wife and, for the first time, saw his son, born Tuesday in a Washington hospital. Brinkley, a private man, swallowed his embarrassment and kept his smile on for the camera. (Twenty-eight years later, that boy won a Pulitzer Prize for his reporting from Cambodia.)

It took three ballots to nominate Adlai Stevenson, the last time any party nomination would go to more than one ballot. A new era had opened in the land, and like most new eras it was hardly recognized for what it was, an era of live television coverage, whenever there was access, whenever the event was so definite that it could be covered. Few yet appreciated (and many still don't), the differences between live television and regular television news coverage. The latter is disciplined, edited, traditional. It has unique capacities but shares the imperatives, verbal tradition, and sense of craft of news coverage in all media. Live coverage is unique to television. Radio live coverage, the only sort that is remotely comparable, is the sound of a human standing in the presence of what is taking place and describing it. The sounds of the event are never enough by themselves. The picture of an event often is.

Live coverage is more than pointing the cameras and standing back. Sporting events are the simplest form of live coverage. The event is predictable; the outcome is not. Yet only for the aficionado can sports be satisfactorily covered by cameras and noise alone. The same with news events. From the beginning, from 1952, the argument has raged. Newspaper writers wanted less talk, or no talk at all. If the proceedings were complicated, too bad; if they were dull, so be it.

Seeing the Korean War on the *Camel News Caravan* got Americans to accept that television was more than vaudeville, Milton Berle and Ed Sullivan, wrestling and baseball, *Dragnet* and *Howdy Doody*. Network live coverage of the 1952 conventions had them watching history while it was happening. The presidential campaign that followed, however, elicited no special effort from television news. There were reporters and cameramen where candidates spoke and met voters. Film was shipped to be transmitted for inclusion into evening news programs, processed, edited, scripted, and the script then spoken over the film as part of the regular news presentation. The wire services did it. The newspapers did it. The television networks did it. They did not do enough of it, but they did it.

From then on, increasingly, people in television news grew uncomfortable about what exactly their job was during presidential campaigns. They covered them as important news events, but they felt, and were told, that was too little. What appeared on regular news programs was never enough for shadings and subtleties, issues and principles. Sunday interview programs, appearances on morning programs—did they count as part of the coverage? When debates arrived, were they part of television news or of television the medium? In time, the principal topic of political coverage on television would be television, an amusing anomaly for outsiders, a bed of nails for those inside.

The 1952 conventions made television a necessity in the American home and gave it respect and status. If nothing else, sales of television sets showed this to be true. Exploring space would provide major occasions for live coverage; so would civil rights marches, parades of heroes, in time even courtroom trials, but not most breaking news events, the daily bread of news. Live coverage works only if there are physical boundaries. This is not an ethical rule but a practical one. There can be no live coverage from a battlefield, surely not from a battle at sea. When Americas Cup races are shown on live television, there is in the picture itself no sense of contest, only in the accompanying talk; the viewer cannot tell who is winning or by how much. Live coverage must be able to encompass an event.

Meeting these criteria, live coverage of the 1952 conventions gave Americans history and drama at the same time, a sense of being present at something both interesting and important. Four years old, American network television entered American society. It was not noticed as such; there were no learned analyses—yet.

Meanwhile, the Dad's Root Beer billboard at the S-curve on Chicago's Lake Shore Drive, was being steadily modified as the political year played itself out. After the Republicans left town, Taft and Eisenhower were painted out to make room for Stevenson and Kefauver. Once the Democrats had nominated their candidate, Kefauver's picture was erased and one of Eisenhower put up to face the one of Stevenson. The challenging message was: "Which Dad Are You For?"

After the election, Eisenhower's picture was kept, but Stevenson's was replaced in turn by a picture of a bottle of Dad's Root Beer, with the legend: "Two party favorites." At this, Dad's received a White House letter asking that, with no slight intended to the root beer, the sign come down because it might be construed as an endorsement. Dad's participation in the political process had ended.

4

NBC News returned from Chicago reasonably well satisfied with itself. In less than a year, Bill McAndrew had made it an organization capable of covering the 1952 conventions respectably, if not with distinction. The production deficiencies obvious to some of us were not McAndrew's prime interest; he wanted to get on with expanding news coverage, consolidating the organization, and bringing news on television closer to his very traditional view of what news should be in whatever medium. But soon Pat Weaver's irritation with NBC News began to show, and for the next few years it darkened the atmosphere and sometimes distorted what we were trying to do. We did not yet know that all this time relations between Weaver and Sarnoff had been deteriorating, and Pat may unknowingly have been taking it out on us—on McAndrew, mostly.

In these formative years we were feeling our way to what came to be called documentaries and magazine programs. Now that we seemed to be in control of daily news presentation, with the hugely successful *News Caravan* in the evenings and *Today* settled down in the mornings, the feeling was growing that we could be doing more. New ways of presenting news had to be found. We had to overcome the obstacle of NBC News and NBC management often working at cross purposes while *See It Now* on CBS was becoming better and stronger and being recognized as major American journalism.

Although he took little part in the clog dance about "our answer to Murrow," Weaver kept at McAndrew about something he called "feature news." At the time, the low status of news at NBC was reflected in the fact that news, that is McAndrew, reported to X who reported to Y who reported to Pat Weaver. For example, the protocol for interrupting a program with a news bulletin was so rigid that by the time we got the okay, the bulletin might no longer be news. And almost every time they met, Weaver asked why McAndrew wasn't pestering him for more time for "feature news." McAndrew would ask for specific examples: "What sort of thing did you have in mind, Pat?"

"Oh, please. I shouldn't have to tell you, of all people, what news is."

And McAndrew would then walk back to his office, bent slightly forward, his feet shuffling, the way he did when the world got to be too much and the inmates threatened to take over the asylum. He called in Green and me, and we would brood together. To us, coming out of daily print journalism, "features" meant news out of the mainstream, human interest, or humor, or foibles, the kind of news that plays below the middle of the page, usually two columns wide under an italic headline. We would search newspapers and wires for "features" about children and animals, someone who had invented a new dance step, the last doctor who made house calls, and the like—"cat in a tree" stories, we called them. We were puzzled that such stuff could interest the great Weaver, who boasted he had won ballet its biggest audience in history with a single network performance and had invited Albert Einstein to come on NBC to explain the theory of relativity. We would assemble a list of "features," which McAndrew would give to Weaver at their next meeting. Weaver would read it and toss it back with a wearied, "No, that's not what I meant." After the scene played several times, the badgering stopped, but McAndrew knew in his heart he stood poorly with his boss, and he did not know why. This went on for months.

A few years later, sitting in a suburban movie theater with my wife, I read the opening words on the screen, "An RKO Theater Feature Presentation," and I suddenly realized what Weaver had been after. "Feature." Not short subject. Not cartoon. Not what newspaper people called a "feature story" but what movie people called "a *full-length feature*"—in fact, "An NBC News Feature Presentation." Weaver wanted documentaries but did not know how to say it! And we, frustrated at not doing documentaries, could not divine what he had in mind. By the time I understood, Weaver had long since left NBC, documentaries were an accepted part of what we did, and network news had achieved status and recognition both inside the networks and in the country. On Monday morning I told McAndrew I had found the key to the mystery. He just smiled; to him it no longer mattered, but I felt as though I had deciphered the Rosetta stone.

While we were looking for "features" for Weaver, CBS's *See It Now* was developing strongly. Faithfully watched by the kind of people whose approval means prestige, it nevertheless disturbed few of the anointed in its first couple of years. For the first months, necessarily, they reported a lot on the presidential year and its politics, but they found many of their stories abroad, making tangible such places as Germany, South Africa, and Israel.

Like every such program for the next forty years and beyond, *See It Now* tried to enrapture the audience with the magic its professionals found in the liveness of live television. One such report showed a new thing called a computer. In two-way live sound and picture communication with Edward R. Murrow, an operator showed what the computer could do, ending by programming its beeps to sound out a Christmas carol. *See It Now* was not all portentous. But to the audience Murrow meant portent, the planes of his face, the resonance of his baritone, the way he intoned his invariable closing, "Good night and good luck," implying, "You'll probably need it."

From the (envious) NBC newsroom came:

> "No one's brow furrows
> Like Edward R. Murrow's."

Murrow's increasing impact on America was derived, to a considerable degree, from his personality, though not entirely. There was also the way CBS supported his undertakings. I believe that at NBC, which tried to hire him at least once, Murrow would have achieved far less, just as I believe he would have been less successful as a tenor. Finally, there was, from the very first day, a symbiosis between the infant television, born when the Berlin airlift was less than a month old, and the Cold War, which Murrow and *See It Now* used to good effect.

Because early television needed things to show, and because the Cold War gave it point and drama, there was in those days a lot of live coverage of United Nations debates, such as that of the Security

Council during the crisis over the Soviet incursion into northern Iran and the Council and the General Assembly uniting the world against the invasion of South Korea. Sir Gladwyn Jebb and Andrei Gromyko became stars and a veto was more dramatic than a soap opera. When the General Assembly, waiting for its headquarters to be built, held its annual meeting in Paris, the Ford Foundation paid NBC for a special program every night for all those weeks, film flown back daily to be narrated by historian Arthur Schlesinger, Jr. Again, the feeling was that regular news coverage was not enough. Additional programs were needed to explain things better.

Newscasts were being criticized as inadequate, and live coverage, in many ways perfect television, left journalism prey to manipulation by those who controlled the events being covered. It was also a Cold War story when Senator Joseph McCarthy of Wisconsin won instant, permanent fame pursuing the Communist conspiracy he said was at the heart of U.S. government. His stage was the Senate hearing room, and his hearings were open to television. He not only found no Communists; he slowed down those who might. But it was theater, and the cavalier disregard of rights, and even lives, behind the shield of senatorial immunity was ignored by most of the audience and added to the drama for others.

Just as McCarthy's hearings were open to live television, so were those of various other committees of the House and Senate that elected to look into matters of subversion and security, and they are remembered as McCarthy's although they were not. It became rather a jumble. The coverage was extensive, if not always live, all echoing the other media at a time when many major newspapers felt they had to have in-house journalists who specialized in the evils of communism, like Frederick Woltman of Scripps-Howard or Victor Riesel of the *New York Post*. It became a special "beat" among a newspaper's other special beats like medicine, architecture, or the Mafia, and was vigorously promoted. Among those seized by a common urge to root out subversion, a few of the legislators and their staffs probably felt they were protecting their country. But I also remember Roy Cohn's mother calling Bill McAndrew every day there was a hearing to ask if Roy would be "on the television" that night.

The Cold War concern with security and secrecy, grounded in an atmosphere of international danger, fanned by demagogues and fed by fear, was duly reported as news. The reporting was not submissive, but it was deadpan, because that is how twentieth-century American journalists report important matters. Demagogues learned to manipulate reporting so that when a senator or anyone else who was libel-proof made an outrageous charge, the fact that he made the charge was the news, but reporting that news gave currency to the charge. Casual viewers or readers might easily accept as fact the substance of the charge, often a malicious lie. It took American journalists a long time to recognize this trap and look for a way to avoid it. One way would have been for reporters themselves to look into the charges and report their findings. But they never had the time. Murrow had not only the time but the guts.

Late in 1953, Murrow broadcast the first of several programs that promoted him from the history of journalism to the history of the United States. A U.S. Air Force lieutenant had been discharged as a security risk because his Serbian immigrant father might have Communist sympathies. A *See It Now* special program about the case drew enough public attention so that the secretary of the air force reviewed and then rescinded the dismissal. The audience got to see the machinery and machinations that went into such cases, into the much reported but little appreciated hunt for subversives, "security risks," and other proclaimed threats to the Republic.

A program a few weeks later also responded to the atmosphere of the time. It dealt with the refusal of an American Legion post in Indianapolis to rent its hall to the local American Civil Liberties Union. Then, in March 1954, *See It Now* presented its famous half hour about McCarthy. Some have seen this program as the catalyst in McCarthy's downfall. Some who came later suggest that McCarthy was already falling and it made no difference. The argument is scholastic: CBS did it—*See It Now* did it—no one else.

CBS gave McCarthy airtime to answer Murrow. Speaking alone into a camera was a new context for him, and he was not very effective. He went back to his more accustomed activities, but, in time, Eisenhower had had enough. McCarthy tried to use his biggest weapon, the hearings of his committee, to bully the U.S. Army on behalf of a young staff assistant who had been drafted. McCarthy dragged the secretary of the army himself before the live cameras, and it was finally too much. The Senate rose up against McCarthy, and President Eisenhower came out from behind his neutrality. It was no longer enough that McCarthy helped Republicans get elected. A Senate committee formally, and on live television, examined his fitness to serve; he was censured, and became a spent force.

In the spring of 1955, *See It Now* lost its sponsor, Alcoa, and its regular spot in prime time, although everyone denied the reasons were political. For the next three years it was a series of occasional documentaries. At NBC, meanwhile, the chivvying about finding the "answer to Murrow" died down because that kind of journalism was seen to mean trouble, or because boredom set in, or both. During *See It Now*'s three years of regular weekly broadcasts, from 1952 until it lost its sponsorship and its regular slot in 1955, NBC broadcast very few special news programs.

In all of 1952, except for programs that were part of the coverage of a presidential election year, the only NBC program that might be considered special was a live tour of the White House. President Truman showed NBC's correspondent Frank Bourgholtzer through the historic rooms and played "The Missouri Waltz" for him. Truman had already announced he would not stand for reelection, and he was relaxed and charming as he guided the audience through the historic rooms. Truman and Bourgholtzer were friendlier and more comfortable with each other on live television than Mrs. John F. Kennedy and Charles Collingwood were on film a decade later, yet the historic quality of the earlier program has generally gone unnoted. As George Raft's manager said to him in a movie in which he played a solo dancer, "A gal gives them something to look at."

The following year, the pressure inside the news division, incorporating management's embarrassment in the face of *See It Now*, the professionals' need to go beyond the fifteen-minute nightly newscast, and, no doubt, individual envy and ego, became too big to ignore. Three major news events in 1953 moved NBC management to give us airtime for special programs. These were in response to events after they happened, not a commitment to schedule a different kind of program regularly, but we welcomed the opportunity anyway. A colleague broadcast a Korean War chronology after the cease-fire, and I won the other two.

On Thursday, March 5, 1953, the wire services rang their BULLETIN bells for the official announcement of the death of Joseph Stalin. Reports that he was ill, rumors that he was dead, had dominated the news for almost a week. Without the details that would come only much later, we had spent the week guessing and improvising. No later generation can quite appreciate how Stalin bestrode the world scene or the rumblings that were heard after his death.

He was an absolute ruler in dimensions unknown to European

tradition, more like an emperor of old China than any dictator we knew, but also one of our recent Allies, the one whose country paid most for World War II victory, and a proclaimed believer in benefiting mankind and righting injustice. Only later did his successors refer to him in opprobrious terms that only his most rabid enemies used about him when he was alive, reviling his words, degrading his memory, and even questioning his sanity.

During those nervous days, a man carrying a heavy, well-worn leather valise turned up unannounced at the cramped television news offices in the RCA Building. (We had been moved downtown from 106th Street because Bill McAndrew insisted we work where he could watch us.) The man was nondescript and skinny, with thinning dirty-blond hair and a light-colored, vaguely mauve, prominently striped, poorly fitting double-breasted suit. He claimed to be from Moscow, a film editor in one of the Soviet film studios; and he claimed to have defected. He unbuckled the two scuffed leather straps and opened the valise.

Inside was a jumble of film reels of all sizes that added up to a picture history of Russia, Stalin and Trotsky, the czar and the Revolution, World War I and World War II. He claimed he filched it. There was Grand Duke Alexander, the czar's uncle, skinny-dipping with the other generals who were supposed to be holding the Eastern front against Paul von Hindenburg and Erich Ludendorff. ("See, he grebs heem by the bolls.") There were scenes of World War II that we could get from our own library, but there were pictures in that valise none of us had ever seen before, pictures that added to what was known. Grigory Zinovyev and Lev Kamenev and Nikolai Bukharin, the early victims of the Stalin purges, pictures that official Soviet agencies, anxious as they were for dollars, would refuse to sell us. Trotsky organizing the Red Army, and other pictures we have seen dozens of times since but not before.

Some of the film was 35mm, some of it 16mm. Some of it was print, some of it was negative—not the original negative, but a negative made from a print. Some of it was clean and free of rips and blemishes, but most of it was not. Money was discussed and a deal was made in some other office, and on Friday morning I was assigned to put together a half-hour obituary of Stalin for broadcast Sunday afternoon. George Roney, the man with the valise, stood beside me as I worked, identifying whose picture that was and what he was doing. George was good at identification, but otherwise he mostly told jokes.

The program I put together, *Before and After Stalin*, tried to be historical. Roney's film provided about half the program, stretching back to Russia's disastrous defeat in World War I, the 1917 revolutions, his film of Lenin on the back platform of the train bringing him to the Finland Station, Stalin taking over, the purges that would leave Russia weakened when Hitler invaded, the personal exaltation of Stalin, all the usual stuff. . . . Then the news boys, especially Georgi Malenkov, Stalin's successor as the Party's general secretary (which to us sophisticates meant he would be the next dictator); Lavrenti Beria, head of the secret police, and Vyacheslav Molotov, the ultimate functionary, the Lepidus. It was all good stuff, pictures with the special scratches and jerkiness that signal they are history. If I had not seen them before that meant most of the audience had not seen them either.

The script marked a change in history and tried to speculate about what could be expected from those who were coming after. Reports out of Moscow identified Malenkov as having been Stalin's private secretary, and the script made some joke about history's most successful private secretary. Jack Gould, television critic of *The New York Times*, picked that line for special mention. He thought it was courageous. I found it a sorry use of words that the august *Times* could see courage in an American television network poking mild fun at a Soviet official. Gould was often hard to follow, but he was important—and he liked the program.

Jack Gould liked the program!

He had especially high praise for Henry Cassidy, the correspondent who read my script. But that is a condition of employment in my line of work. I was by then in my third year writing the *News Caravan* for Swayze, and I was used to it. What counted was that Gould, that the *Times*, had reviewed the program favorably. This was important to McAndrew because it was important to Pat Weaver, and to those in between, the people up the line. Gould's influence on how important people in television regarded their own work and that of each other has never been duplicated. A bad review by the drama critic of the *Times* can merely bankrupt a Broadway show by influencing the sale of tickets. Jack Gould influenced the bosses! He was not a very profound man, but he was honest and he tried. The ridiculous reach of his influence was not his fault. His judgments were old-maidish, his writing tortured, and his tastes unsophisticated, but his power was palpable.

Gould's approval meant that getting the next special program on the air would be easier. When workers in East Berlin rioted against the Communist government of East Germany, we asked again for a special time period. The anomaly that was West Berlin enabled Western journalists—and, above all, Western television—to see behind the border that the Communist governments tried to hold impervious against them. The arrangements among the Allies after the victory over Hitler had given each of them—American, Soviet, British, and French—a sector of Berlin to occupy, even though the city was more than a hundred miles east of the border between the zone of Germany occupied by the Russians and the zones occupied by the other three.

The Russian-occupied sector of Berlin became East Berlin, the capital of East Germany, and the other three sectors joined to form West Berlin, an entrepreneurial city affiliated with distant West Germany. As the two halves of the advanced world moved further and further apart, and faced each other with ever-increasing hostility, Berlin was where you could see it: the airlift, the East German brain drain, and, in time, the Wall. For West against East, it was a listening post, an irritant, a propaganda billboard. The terms of the Occupation dictated free movement throughout the city, for East and West Berliners and especially for military and civilian citizens of the four occupying powers. That included newsfilm cameramen. Nowhere else in the world did the Cold War and television mesh more closely. They needed each other, and they affected each other.

When East Berlin workers rebelled against production quotas, rationed food, inflation, and hardship, Western eyes saw their rebellion. It began when a handful demonstrated before the Ministry of Labor, which a camera with a reasonably long lens could see from the Western sector. There had been no warning, so the best that came out of that day were a few scenes. Over the next few days the unrest exploded into protest marches, still unheard of inside any Communist country, and the troops were called out. Western journalists tried to get close but were, illegally, kept or driven away. The troops opened fire, wounding and killing demonstrators. After it was over, the city of West Berlin held a memorial service for the dead of East Berlin. Konrad Adenauer, the chancellor, came from Bonn. The band played "Ich Hatt' Einen Kameraden." The bureau in Berlin supplied film to the *News Caravan* night after night. It was an amazing phenomenon, not only the revolt of the oppressed, but being able to see it.

By happy coincidence, Gary Stindt was in New York when it happened. He had to forgo his vacation to run his bureau by transatlantic telephone and helped us write scripts for *News Caravan*. Stindt and

I talked McAndrew into asking Weaver to give us time for a special report. The request was not welcomed, but neither was it dismissed out of hand. We eventually got the time, but not right away, when public interest was greatest. We would have to wait until after the Fourth of July, when audiences grew smaller, and to incorporate our special about the riots in East Berlin into a series Pat Weaver had always wanted to do. *Trouble Spots* it would be called, a look at various loci of international tension with explanation of the causes and history of whatever was the conflict.

Weaver's bent for the didactic, which I explained to myself as his wall against the audience, was nowhere better expressed than in this formulation for a series of which I produced the only "episode." The *Trouble Spots* idea seemed to me uniquely unsuited to the retelling of a phenomenal event. But we had progressed from 2:00 P.M. Sunday, when we had observed Stalin's death, to 8:00 P.M. Wednesday. It may have been the Wednesday after the Fourth of July, but we were actually going on the air in prime time!

After a short opening nod to the *Trouble Spots* idea, we told our story, from the little crowd that first day far away in front of East Germany's Ministry of Labor to the ineradicable images of men throwing stones at tanks in the Pottsdammerplatz. This was before Poznan, or Budapest, or Prague. That voiceless thousands inside a Communist dictatorship might rise up in protest, in physical defiance, was something we had never known, a possibility we hardly granted. And here it was, happening where we could see it.

The point of our program was: In our society, whatever its shortcomings, the fissures and rents were there for everyone to see, to criticize, to speak, or to act against.

The workers' riots in East Berlin were especially important, because events and conditions "behind the Curtain" could usually only be judged from smuggled hints, self-serving accounts, and often meretricious official versions. Showing the film of the workers' rebellion literally lifted the curtain. Berlin would serve the same function for international reporting that cloud chambers do for nuclear physicists, a place where the invisible can be tracked for the human eye.

It was, however, luck that brought Gary Stindt to New York while the riots were going on in East Berlin. He had come to interest McAndrew and NBC management in some film he had made on his own using that very long lens he had got in a pawnshop for two cartons of PX cigarettes when he had reentered his native Germany in 1945.

Seven years later, he had finally put the lens to use. He had spent the winter filming the last survivors of the Nazi leadership, who had been shut away from all human sight—except that of their guards—since the Nuremberg trials. It was an old-fashioned scoop.

The seven top Nazis who had not been sent to the gallows by the Allied War Crime Tribunal had been imprisoned in a massive red-brick prison in the once-independent village of Spandau in West Berlin. Stindt had rented the attic of a bakery across from Spandau prison so he could film through the window into the exercise yard. He fastened his 28-inch lens to a 16mm silent film camera and set it on a tripod looking out the attic window. Whenever he could spare a few hours, he would go to the bakery in Spandau, wait for activity in the exercise yard, and expose a few feet of film. If he was caught it would be a criminal offense. A few times that winter, boys pointed up at his attic window, and he had to move his camera back so it could not be seen from the street, but he was never challenged.

He kept on filming whenever he could, although he was too far away for his eye to see whom he was filming. After the film was developed and a print made, he compared the pictures of the shuffling figures in their dyed U.S. Army greatcoats and pillbox prisoners' hats with newsreels and still pictures of the seven Nazi leaders in their prime. This is how he puzzled out whose picture he had taken. Rudolph Hess, tall, stooped, skinny, was unmistakable as he hoed in the little patch of garden assigned to him. Konstantin von Neurath and Albert Speer were almost as easy to recognize. A couple of the others would occasionally come close enough to the wall of the yard so their features were distinguishable on the film. One of those was Karl Dönitz, the grand admiral whom Hitler, about to commit suicide in the bunker, had named Führer, an honor he had held for seven days. All that winter, an hour or two at a time, Gary made his films of the prisoners in the exercise yard, of the guards in the towers, of the ceremonial changing of the guard once a month, Soviet to American, American to British, British to French. It did not add up to a lot of film, but it was truly film no one else had, film of Hess, Speer, von Neurath, Dönitz, Erich Raeder, Walter Funk, Baldur von Schirach. In 1953, those were still names.

A half dozen of us were shown the film, and we were fascinated, none more than Bill McAndrew, who immediately scheduled a screening for some of the top echelon of NBC. McAndrew had the journalist's sense that here was something exciting because it was exclusive, because it was surreptitious, because the drama of the subject was all mixed up with the drama of getting the pictures. He invited Weaver and all the leaders of his programming staff; he invited his own superior and his superior's superior; he invited top people from Sales; he invited someone from each department. He also invited Brig. Gen. David Sarnoff, chairman of the board of the Radio Corporation of America, of which NBC was a subsidiary.

McAndrew asked me to come with him to the screening. Stindt was there and a couple of others. The hour arrived, and we were alone. No one had come to our screening. It was insulting, and it was depressing. Then, five minutes late, Sarnoff walked in. Bill introduced him to us, sat him down, locked the door to the screening room, and waved to the projectionist to roll the film. Sarnoff was as taken with it as we were. Meanwhile, word had spread through the halls that "the General" had come down from RCA and was in NBC, in a ninth-floor screening room, looking at some film of Billy McAndrew's. Vice presidents and executive vice presidents straightened their ties and hastened to the ninth floor. They pounded on the door. McAndrew ignored them. They rattled the doorknob, pounded on the door again, even shouted. Finally, Bill opened the door a crack and said, "We're already halfway through and I don't want to disturb the General. I'll set up another screening if you'd like."

There was nothing they could do. They went away.

Sarnoff, meanwhile, watched every foot of the film, and paid close attention to Stindt's descriptions and explanations. He liked it and congratulated Stindt. To McAndrew he said, "I think that ought to go on the television. Talk to Robert about it." Robert Sarnoff, his oldest son, was then vice president in charge of NBC's (entertainment) film division.

It illustrates the organization's sociology and politics that in the summer of 1953, when the founder of NBC, chairman of its corporate parent—by any measure the man who owned the store—said he wanted a program put on the air, it still took almost a year. News was so little regarded by the people who really ran the network that Sarnoff's approval was barely enough to get the program produced and shown at all. It finally went on the air, on a Sunday afternoon, when it would interfere with nothing important. That, too, is the history of broadcasting.

The wheels finally began rolling early in 1954, when McAndrew told me he had a date and a time period and asked me to make a program out of Stindt's film. For a dozen weeks or so after that, every lunch hour, I went from 30 Rockefeller Plaza to 105 East 106th Street where film and editing had remained when the rest of us had moved downtown. An editor and I screened the material. We also ordered from our library, and from others around town, newsreel footage of each of the seven, of the Nazi era, of Germany after defeat. The drama came when we showed those newsreels of Hess, young, in full uniform, eyebrows beetling, striding with his Führer, then marching with his troops, and finally cut to Stindt's pictures of the stooped figure in the dyed prisoner's overcoat, pillbox hat, under guard, a hoe in his hands. We did that with all seven, one at a time.

It was Ozymandias, but it was also Nazis. We mixed in pictures of Kristallnacht; we showed the liberation of some concentration camps. At the end, the script said we hoped that the Germans now so important to us in the new We/They world were not like the Germans we had just shown. We were not sure, but one had to hope. The commentator, who read the script, was Joseph C. Harsch, of the *Christian Science Monitor*, whom McAndrew liked to use from time to time partly because it helped fend off Weaver's constant wooing of "someone from the *Times*." Harsch told me that when he was next in Bonn, Adenauer scolded him like a schoolboy because of that script.

The Road to Spandau won me my first award, the Sigma Delta Chi Award for television writing, and it got me off the *News Caravan*. My new boss was Ted Mills, an entertainment producer from the famous "Chicago school" of television programs that flourished at NBC's Midwest studios at the dawn of television. Bored and unemployed, he had told his friend Pat Weaver he would like to do a fact series, to give NBC's nonfiction "new perspectives." McAndrew swallowed the insult but insisted the series be nominally within News, and that one of "his people" be number two in the production unit. My award made me acceptable to Mills as not simply one of those News dodos. The series would be called *Background*, the commentator would be Joseph C. Harsch. Thus, when *See It Now* was almost three years old, NBC News got itself a series—of sorts.

We did some good things: the British leaving East Africa; an analysis of the hostilities in the French colonies of Southeast Asia; the story of a nationalist Chinese student in the United States who had criticized Chiang Kai-shek, whereupon the Taiwanese embassy had tricked the State Department into sending him back to mainland China and certain imprisonment. But after a good evening time period or two during the summer, we were moved to Sunday afternoon; the promised weekly series appeared once a month. NBC did not believe in us. The death of *Background* was only a matter of time as inertia finally resulted in nonexistence. The publicity and promotion departments were not told to help; there was no effort to build an audience with continuity; there was no feeling of NBC's commitment to the series or to the idea of the series. And that was the way things would always happen at NBC. First the producer went, then Harsch found better things to do, and finally I became producer by default for the last two programs and we closed the books. Whatever it was, it was not Weaver's kind of news. There were no live pictures of the front pages of newspapers, no leaders of thought or government ducking the cameras or agreeing to say a few self-serving words. *Background* expired unmourned, by us as well as by Pat Weaver.

My closest dealings with Weaver were in 1955, on a program he had doubts about and I was sure should not be done. He ordered the program because it was all he or anyone could think of to replace a sudden hole in the schedule. I did it to get out of something I wanted to do even less. Unfortunately, it was just one of many good lessons I was to get in how television really works.

NBC's biggest nonfiction success up to then had been a series called *Victory at Sea*, the story of the U.S. Navy during World War II, no more than a compilation of newsreel footage but done with such style, skill, and breadth that it may well have been the outstanding hit of television's early years. The original score was by Richard Rodgers, whose record of it became a smash best-seller. The producer was Henry J. Salomon, known as "Pete," a young historian who had served in the navy during the war. Weaver's plan to put the project inside News foundered on Salomon's opposition and that of a tired old-timer named Frank McCall, McAndrew's predecessor at the head of TV news, who wanted nothing to do with it. It would only be trouble, McCall told me later.

After the success of *Victory at Sea*, Pete Salomon embarked on a history of the world. This allowed him to keep together some of the talented people he had assembled and find more drama and coherence in assembling old newsreels. The rise of Nazism, the rise of communism, the rise of the American cowboy—they sought new insights in the retelling of old stories. Once or twice a year a theme of epic dimensions, a lilting script declaimed in the elegant voice of a golden-throated actor named Alexander Scourby, would find its way to television while critics swooned. The series title was *Project XX*—for twentieth century—the separation between it and the News department being rigorously maintained by both sides. When the newsreel archives were exhausted, or too many other people learned to use them, postcards, still photos, and paintings were substituted in examining the lives of Abraham Lincoln, Jesus Christ, and others. The series continued for several years beyond Pete Salomon's death, always getting serious attention and high praise.

The very first of the series was scheduled for 8:00 to 9:00 P.M. Sunday, July 17, 1955. Even in summer, this was a desirable time. On Sundays at 8:00, CBS presented one of the stalwarts of early television, Ed Sullivan's variety program, and NBC put forth its rotation of some of the most successful comedians of the time, Dean Martin and Jerry Lewis, Jimmy Durante, even Fred Allen and Bob Hope. That hour was allotted to Pete Salomon to tell America about the rise of communism, the emergence of Stalin, the hatching of his international conspiracy, and the new dictatorship that had succeeded him. It was to be called "Nightmare in Red." A new dimension of entertainment and enlightenment was awaited.

An ABC announcement upset everything. Instead of the usual old movie, ABC announced that it would broadcast live coverage of the grand opening of Disneyland in Anaheim, California. The auspiciousness of the event was yet only partly appreciated, but that was enough to strike terror into Ed Sullivan. He charged home early from his vacation to bolster his run-of-the-mill off-season lineup that night with his physical presence, to seek out the best and biggest star available, who turned out to be Ethel Merman—close enough, especially for a summer night. Suddenly, "Nightmare in Red," sitting in its film can awaiting a cue to enlighten America, faced some of the biggest names in American show business: Sullivan, Merman, and, towering above them, Walt Disney, a presence as big as Stalin. The competition, moreover, was live.

Salomon wrote to Pat Weaver asking him to withdraw "Nightmare in Red" from its widely advertised time slot. The next day, he argued, all right-thinking people on the planet would focus their hopes on Geneva, where the leaders of the divided world would meet to resolve differences, ameliorate tensions, and restore confidence and tranquillity to mankind. President Eisenhower would be there, and Prime Minister Anthony Eden, and Edgar Faure, the premier of France. They would be meeting for the first time the new leaders of the Soviet

Union, the ones who had displaced the ones who had originally succeeded Stalin, Marshal Nikolai Bulganin, who had rebuilt the Red Army, and a fat little Communist Party functionary who usually traveled with him named Nikita Khrushchev.

Since "Nightmare in Red" concentrated on the evils visited by Soviet dictators both on their own people and on the world, it would be discordant for NBC to show it the night before the Big Four met. Would it not be more appropriate, Salomon went on, to do a program about the meeting in Geneva the next day, and how the world's hopes were wrapped up in its outcome? Salomon himself would be pleased to work up such a program if he were not so busy with his next attempt to make this a wiser, and therefore better, place.

During all this, I was involved in another Pat Weaver project, perhaps his favorite, an idea he had been promoting for several years to all who would listen and to all whose attention he could command. He wanted NBC to show, on live television, places and events all over the world, bringing them into one program to give a sense of simultaneous activity, the ultimate expression of television as a window (which is the way people talked back then). It would be called *Wide, Wide World*, a phrase taken directly from his Dartmouth College alma mater hymn. From time to time, Weaver would summon a meeting of a dozen or so of his closest executive associates and favorite producers for an unstructured discussion of how to get *Wide, Wide World* on the air. It was, as usual, all but impossible to get Weaver to put in words what he expected the program to contain, so ideas would be thrown in by the others while he would throw them back out. Finally, one of the producers present, said, "Pat, what you want us to show is what your social class does on a Sunday afternoon."

The logjam was broken when Pat put someone outside his social class in charge of the program. Barry Wood had been a singer on *Your Lucky Strike Hit Parade* in the heyday of network radio. During World War II, his had been one of the best-known voices in America because it was his voice heard singing "Any Bonds Today?," the U.S. Treasury song played every hour on every station. In television's early days, he had produced musical variety series at CBS with titles like *Places, Please* and *54th Street Revue*. He was a plodding, basic man who had made it the hard way, sustained by the attitudes and ostentatiously earthy vocabulary of people whose world is vaudeville.

Comedies, tragedies, and not a few operas have been built on the insertion of a humble son of the soil into the company of the effete and attenuated. Barry Wood was neither humble nor of the soil, but after all those others had talked and talked, it was he who took *Wide, Wide World* and put it on the air. A sample, or pilot, was booked for June 27, and he began by finding producers to do the segments that would add up to that first, experimental program. I could not pretend I was unavailable. *Background* had been decently interred, the *News Caravan* writer whom I had replaced when he was called back into the army reserves had returned from service, and I had nothing to show for my salary each week. Wood reasoned that a live segment from just inside the Canadian border and another from just inside the Mexican border would make the program seem international. Since I was from Canada, he sent me to prepare a quarter-hour segment from the Shakespeare Festival in Stratford, Ontario.

My problem was that all my experience was in news. My other problem was that I had no other job and could not turn this one down. I enlisted John Goetz, who had directed *Background* and also had extensive experience directing television entertainment. Together we went first to Toronto to visit the CBC—and the engineers and mobile unit managers who presumably would provide us with our picture, if we got around to having one. Then we went on to Stratford, a lovely little place, not at all overgrown yet, where we looked at swans on a river self-consciously called the Avon and the theater and the town. Goetz and I plotted where cameras should be and what would take place in front of them and might we be allowed into the theater—the answer was no—and such questions as what would be our beginning, middle, and end. All this time, I was wondering what was I doing there and how could I get out of it.

We drove back to the Toronto airport with two CBC technical managers who had come down to Stratford to walk through the sites and tell us if they would work. We were also joined by the executive producer Barry Wood had hired, Fred Rickey, a man of long experience in musical theater and variety, not unlike Wood himself in attitude and background, although physically quite different—thin, nervous, a chain-smoker. I was jammed in front with the driver and his partner; Goetz was in back with the executive producer and his secretary. As Lake Ontario slipped by in the dark, the CBC pair talked over their shoulders to the only one in the car worth talking to, the executive producer from New York.

They told him that one of the CBC national network's outstanding successes of the past season had been an hour given over to a French pantomimist named Marcel Marceau. The CBC had never had such a response—telephone calls, letters, reviews in the newspapers. The CBC program chiefs were planning to bring him back to do another program. NBC could do a lot worse than get him.

Rickey was duly impressed. He asked them to spell the name so his secretary could write it down.

The driver and his mate went on in their enthusiasm. They were sure NBC would have a bit hit if they devoted one of those big specials they were always doing to someone who would surely be an international star very soon.

From the backseat, silence. We were now east of Hamilton, moving moderately fast on an empty highway. I watched the lights and the lake. Fred Rickey spoke.

"This here Marcel," he said, "does he work in English or in French?"

When I got back to New York, McAndrew told me that I was relieved of the *Wide, Wide World* segment. Instead, I was to produce a program about the Big Four meeting soon to take place. *Wide, Wide World* went on without me. There was in fact a well-executed segment about the Shakespeare Festival at Stratford, Ontario, but it was on film, as was another from Tijuana starring the Mexican comedian Cantinflas. Why live television was replaced by film for the "international" segments of the program I was never told. I assume that someone had learned the hard way that putting a live camera in a given place at a given time did not guarantee there would be something to take a picture of.

The lesson was implicit when, that fall, *Wide, Wide World* went on to three seasons of distinction and excitement. It provided the most powerful example up to then—and since—of using television as the magic carpet some of the early visionaries, like Weaver and his nemesis, David Sarnoff, proclaimed it to be. To achieve it, however, all episodes were totally scripted, celebrities and actors brought to where the cameras were. This required interposing the intelligence, objective experience, and subjective taste of a skilled editor. It always does. The yearning for the found object is a faddish delusion, but no one ever dared tell Pat Weaver.

Meanwhile, proceeding with the utmost solemnity and humorlessness, my little band moved forward to let the American people understand the deep significances of the Big Four meeting in Geneva on the day before it took place. NBC's purpose in scheduling the program was to keep Pete Salomon's expensive film, "Nightmare in Red," from being chewed up in the ratings. My reason for agreeing to do it was that I did not want to work for Barry Wood. It is the subject of homilies that no achievement can be more exalted than the reason it was achieved, and our only instruction was to fill an hour.

At the center of this unusual effort I wanted David Brinkley. He seemed to me so obviously capable of more than his reports on the *News Caravan* and his radio chores. McAndrew thought it was a fine idea, and his superiors could think of no one else, so they acquiesced in their usual patronizing grumble. Brinkley himself took some coaxing, but I managed. He was, however, no help with content. I had to figure that out for myself.

What I finally did was set the scene the way I knew how, with film of past conflicts between Them and Us and the Cold War from its beginnings up to that important day; we re-created in careful detail the room in which the four leaders and their delegations would meet, and an NBC commentator walked from one chair to another saying A would be here, and B over there; we had experts share their expert knowledge. Joseph C. Harsch was induced to fly back from Geneva for the program rather than stay there and cover it; analysis can take place at any distance. Other NBC reporters narrated film biographies of the four principals (we assumed that Bulganin and not Nikita Khrushchev was the Russian principal, still a common mistake that month). Toward the end of the hour we would show filmed opinions from opinion makers, like William Randolph Hearst, Jr., H. V. Kaltenborn, Burma's prime minister, U Nu.

It was time to take the outline to Weaver. I was escorted by McAndrew and his superior, J. Davidson Taylor, whose approval was tentative, to get Weaver's reaction. We found Weaver sitting as he always did at his large desk, which was at a right angle to a conference table, the two of them forming an upside-down L. McAndrew and Taylor sat along the outside of the stem of the L while I sat in the angle. I joked feebly, "Who throws the switch?" The back of my head can be seen in a picture in *Life*, part of its profile of Pat Weaver. While the *Life* photographer popped up or squatted in funny places, Weaver heard me out, then said, "Well, okay. But that's not the way we're going to do it in twenty years." That was all he said. With that to guide me, I was sent on my way.

The solemnity with which the occasion was anticipated, the first summit meeting since the end of World War II, was not peculiar to

Weaver. Newspapers editorialized in the same holy tones. Only a few said openly that the country was tired of the Cold War, both at home and abroad, and hoped this meeting would end it, but that is what they all meant. Through shameless importuning, we got Bob Hope, the biggest name at NBC, to appear at the very beginning of the program to say that, like him, all four of the Big Four were fathers, and this was being done for the children.

Lacking content, we substituted activity. We used three live studios. Studio 8-H, the one built by David Sarnoff for Arturo Toscanini and the NBC Symphony, was our main studio, where Brinkley guided us through the evening and Harsch told us that, after Stalin, the Soviet Union had advanced from rule by dictator to rule by committee in which no individual would dominate. In our second full-sized, fully equipped television studio, a set designer had duplicated the Geneva conference room, and in the third an orchestra of two dozen musicians played our own commissioned music, composed to accompany the film segments. We ordered three rehearsals so they could hit all the film cues. The program may have been hollow, but we tried to put a shine on it.

Lest anyone was not sufficiently put off by the lugubrious air we assumed, NBC had taken out an ad in the Sunday papers, half a page across and the full page down, displaying the praying hands from the Albrecht Dürer drawing. The words printed with the hands in prayer began, "Tonight, while the world waits in hope on the eve of the Big Four conference, the National Broadcasting Company brings you . . ." Who, given this temptation, would turn to seeing Disneyland live or hearing Ethel Merman sing?

By midweek we had the answer. The entertainment trade paper *Variety* headlined its front-page story: "Summit's Zero Hour." The rating for *Meeting at the Summit*, as measured by Hooper, then a dominant service, was 0.7. Fewer than one percent of the television sets in the United States were tuned in to our message of comfort for a weary world! But we did set a record that has stood for years: We had the smallest audience ever reached by any network at 8:00 on a Sunday night.

We had nowhere to go but up. Soon after Labor Day, Bill McAndrew told me that I would be doing a weekly program—the "regular" series for which we both had wished—with Chet Huntley. Still looking if not for an "answer to Murrow" at least for a news broadcaster of sufficient presence to carry the NBC News guidon and get around

Weaver's lack of respect for Swayze, McAndrew had gone shopping in Los Angeles with the man he reported to, Davidson Taylor. They had been told about Chet Huntley and wanted to see for themselves.

Huntley had been working in NBC's Los Angeles bureau doing radio network news and television local news after terms at both the other networks and, as he used to say, "networks you never heard of." In those days, when broadcasters subscribed to a newsletter called *Red Channels* for guidance in maintaining their blacklists of performers who might be Communists, or sympathetic to communism, or had once been seen drinking tea with a Communist, he had attained a measure of extraparochial fame by suing some woman who had labeled him a Communist in public statements and in a campaign of letters to his employers and his sponsors. Not only did he sue, almost unheard of in the days when no virgin was more timid than a network lawyer, but the court awarded him some huge amount as damages. Unfortunately, the woman had no money in her own name, and he never collected a penny. The principle, however, was triumphant.

This had made him a hero to many in entertainment who envied his guts and to those show business liberals more noted for generous impulses than useful thoughts. McAndrew told me how he had been lunching in the Brown Derby the day the word was making its way around town that he had signed Huntley for the network news. Groucho Marx came over to his table to congratulate him and added, "Now, you treat him right or your name will be mud out here." McAndrew became furious all over again as he told me how someone he considered a baggy-pants comic dared lecture him about news.

The program with Huntley I was to produce would be a half hour every Sunday afternoon in the "intellectual ghetto" put aside by the networks for elevating discussion and noble ideas. These hours bridged the gap between Sunday dinner and expensive entertainment, while few watched and fewer paid attention. We didn't mind, because we still enjoyed what we were doing too much. We got to do programs the way we wanted to—and self-servingly insisted ought to be done. How we loved the "Sunday ghetto"! How we mourned when professional football wiped it out!

It was my opportunity to do a regular "magazine" program, allowing for longer and more skilled reports. McAndrew's interest was getting some network news on the weekend. NBC then had none. I was to keep five minutes open for news in every program, and be ready to throw away prepared reports when news broke. For years, the only network news on NBC on the weekends, other than bulletins, was our program, called *Outlook*, a name picked by Dave Taylor, who had also chosen *Background* as the title for my last undertaking. To me, both titles were sophomoric and patronized the audience.

Huntley came east that fall, a rangy Montanan in his forties, tall, good-looking, with a leonine head and a good baritone. He was easy to work with once he got over imitating Murrow, who had been his boss and whom he admired. I once told him to choose between being the second Edward R. Murrow or the first Chester R. Huntley.

For the sample program, the pilot, we did a long report on the problem of getting rid of nuclear waste—much too early, it turned out, no one knew what we were talking about—and a shorter one about tensions in Southern high schools preparing to desegregate. But what the executives to whom we showed the pilot liked most was Brinkley's spoken survival manual for anyone whose Washington job required attending three or four receptions an evening: You got a drink at the entrance, held it in your left hand as you shook hands with your right, and worked your way through the room without stopping until you poured it into the potted plant at the exit. The entertainment vice president found it especially funny and asked where we had been hiding that man. I told Brinkley how well he had been received. Typically, instead of being pleased he said, "I don't want to be thought of as some kind of clown."

The new program endured several false starts. Under pressure from RCA for a better showing on his books, Weaver had to cut some costs. *Outlook*, which had not yet seen the light of its first day, was an obvious target. The rule is that anything from News has the highest priority unless something else has a higher priority. The February starting time was abruptly canceled. When McAndrew called to tell me, a reporter from the *New York World-Telegram and Sun* was in our offices, there to give us publicity. The publicity he gave us was about the cancellation, which his editors played across eight columns on the TV page. NBC was so embarrassed we were reinstated. I was learning that television's top people are extremely sensitive to anything printed. As peddlers of a product that vanishes on sight, they are in awe of a medium that survives for an entire day.

There was even a press release heralding to the waiting world a new NBC News program called *Outlook*, to be reported by Chet Huntley, himself newly arrived from California, which would begin on April 1, 1956, at 2:30 in the afternoon. The press release neglected to identify

April 1 as Easter Sunday, a day no one watches television. It was a warm, sunny afternoon. An hour before the program, between rehearsal and broadcast, Huntley stood at a window facing 50th Street, marveling at the crowds lined up for the pageant in the Radio City Music Hall. "Why aren't those people at home watching television," he asked, "instead of outside on this glorious afternoon?" He had come all the way from California to talk to them, but they were lining up for "The Glory of Easter."

Outlook made its debut and settled into its routine. Vaguely sensing a political need for the debut program to look different, I had reporters report live about what people in the regions would find on the front pages of the next morning's newspapers on their porches. The image was blatantly out of Norman Rockwell, the idea wrapped in the deductive illogic that insists there must be other news out there somewhere. The novelty of live television still had its attractions for viewers, although not as great as the enchantment it held for us on the inside. We had one reporter in Philadelphia, covering the East Coast (not New York—that was too easy, and people would shrug). There was another in Chicago, a third in Kansas City, and a fourth in Los Angeles.

Each stood on a sidewalk, a cityscape behind him, the wind in his hair. Among them they talked about milk strikes and mayhem, water shortages and school budgets. Pat Weaver could not contain his enthusiasm. "I think you have a hit," he told McAndrew. "And you know I can smell a hit." Jack Gould looked at the same four men and called *Outlook* "the silliest news show of the season." They were both wrong. The only criticism I found useful came from my father. He reacted to the overlong but proudly and carefully constructed "teases" of our major stories with which we opened the program, presumably to entice a casual viewer to stay to the end. "Why did you tell those stories twice?" he asked me.

From that I learned that a well-crafted "tease" makes the story itself unnecessary, and that if the news in the boondocks were interesting we would have heard of it.

The stories we "told twice" included the updated report from the pilot program on the problems of disposing atomic waste—or, as we grandly dismissed it, nuclear garbage—and a study of the country's most important segregationist, Senator James Eastland of Mississippi. He was asked about repressive practices against Negroes in his state and his hometown. He indignantly rejected the imputation as incredible, because it would be illegal, a crime. He paused, then slowly and more quietly he said, "That is, if you could get the grand jury to indict."

He pronounced it "indaht" and we let it hang there. He smiled. His round face beamed and his wire-rimmed spectacles shone as the smile persisted. It was another of those small occasions that justify the existence of television. Eastland clearly knew what he was saying; he was playing games with us. In a newspaper report, the smile would not have been visible, and he knew that. But like so many in those days, even politicians, he had yet to learn about television. So he smiled as he said it. Inferring smugness or hypocrisy from that smile in a newspaper account would have been considered bad journalism. We could have cut the film at Eastland's last word, as though his words mattered but how he said them did not. Television news people who have no feel for television, in time the majority, would have done it that way. On television, we were able to follow his last word with a few milliseconds of smile, because pictures differ from words, and how they differ is not in degree but in kind.

Outlook lasted seven years. Later that first year, when Huntley and I were pressed into service to do the news every night, we insisted on keeping *Outlook*. Brinkley, who came with us to the nightly news, thought we were self-indulgent to stay with a weekly program purely as a hobby. Davidson Taylor offered to relieve us of it, not realizing that was the last thing we wanted. For us, there was a special feeling in being able to report with fewer time constraints, to dig into a story that was less sure to be on everybody else's television news program. I could keep two news writers we could otherwise not afford, but that was our only material benefit. Doing *Outlook* every week earned us no more money. We did not even get time off for the extra day (and occasionally two) we had to put in each week. We did it for the exercise, for the variety, for the fun; we did it because we wanted to, and because we would not trust anyone else with it.

We sought out stories and played with film. When the BBC sent us a wonderful film of Georgi Malenkov, Stalin's successor as general secretary of the Communist Party, visiting coal miners in Scotland and of his reciting to them Robert Burns's "A Man's a Man for a' That," we ran three verses—with English subtitles. (We did the same with Yevgeny Yevtushenko reading his dramatic "Babi Yar" to Oxford undergraduates while it was still brand new.) When Republic Aviation, on Long Island, New York, had a big layoff, three news writers roamed the area with three film crews for forty-eight hours, showing whatever they could find and interviewing everybody who would talk. We called it "Anatomy of a Layoff" and were accused of frightening people unnecessarily. In May, we filmed a lot of famous people speaking at a lot of college commencements and, without commentary or even identification, edited together an all-purpose, generic commencement speech. These later became common ways of doing things, but if they were done before we did them, we did not know about it. In our hearts we were adventurers.

Outlook traveled to the South for story after story on segregation. We showed the first films of the atom bomb test on Bikini Atoll as soon as the Defense Department made it available, running it much longer than any fifteen-minute network news program could. We dealt with a predicted shortage of American engineers, Algeria's drive to independence, the first wheat crop in Israel's Negev Desert, the San Andreas fault, the centenary of Clarence Darrow's birth (with Melvyn Douglas reading from Darrow's best-known summations to juries). We were a curious bunch, and we indulged our curiosity.

Over the years the name changed. When it seemed Huntley needed publicity—known in the trade as "recognition"—I changed *Outlook* to *Chet Huntley Reporting*. When that got tiresome, I reached into "Four Quartets" and brought out *Time Present*. Sometimes I put a colon after "Time" to make it look like a stage direction, sometimes not. At first, I had the announcer intone at the opening, over the printed title, "Time present and time past are both perhaps contained in time future, and time future in time past." This, with its wartime radio resonance, its hint of hidden meaning, and its redolence of sententiousness, seemed to me the perfect opening for an ambitious news series. But nobody noticed when I used it, and nobody noticed when I stopped. In 1963, when networks expanded nightly news programs to half an hour, NBC decreed that *Outlook*, or whatever it was being called at the time, should come to an end.

Sometime during *Outlook*'s seven years, it seemed to me that an age of innocence had ended. Like any human institution, television news, too, had begun in innocence. When I was writing the *Camel News Caravan* we assumed that almost everyone who watched us had read a newspaper that day, that our contribution, our adventure, would be pictures. The people at home, knowing what the news was, could see it happen. And it was the lure and excitement of picture that had enticed me to television; for words, I could have stayed with the newspaper. To be sure, television also had the bulletin function that was the heart of radio, the ability to dispense news immediately, without waiting to set it into type, print it, and get the finished newspaper to the street. But primarily, we were learning—by trial and error, for there was no one to teach us—what news looked like when it was published as pictures in motion, how to discipline those pictures the way editors discipline written words, and how pictures differ from spoken words as well as from written words.

I learned, or thought I learned, that exposition in detail is most understandable and easily accepted when written to be read. Seeing things happen, on the other hand, was knowing about them in a totally new dimension, one we were not used to or prepared for. Observed information was different information, different in kind. This difference, when recognized at all, is usually ascribed to the "power" of pictures, but it has nothing to do with power. Pictures reach different places of the brain, perhaps older, more primitive places—something we sensed rather than understood.

During the early years, we showed people, and places, and when we were lucky the events themselves, which had already been written about in that morning's newspaper—or perhaps yesterday's. The pictures rarely told me anything I did not already know, but being made flesh they told it to me in a way so different that it became different information. Did it matter that Eastland smiled at the notion of a Southern grand jury indicting white racists for a crime? Seeing that smile *made* it matter. Does it matter that a chief of state is tall or short or old or young or fair or homely? Seeing Charles DeGaulle surrounded by his cabinet or reading that he was six feet four aroused different responses to two forms of what was, after all, the same bit of fact. Did it matter that the teenager killed after volunteering information about a wanted criminal was tall, chubby, curly-haired, smart alecky like any city kid his age but to all appearance guileless and vulnerable? Perhaps it mattered less when we first showed him talking about Willie Sutton than when we used those pictures of him the second time, after he had been gunned down.

During this time of trying and learning, we knew there was an audience out there, but we tried not to think about it. When we had first learned the ratings of the *Camel News Caravan*, the director and I had determined to ignore them because it was frightening to imagine that many people. Our practical concern was our sponsor. We would pick the week's best newscast and order it copied to film, a kinescope recording, so the officials of the R. J. Reynolds Tobacco Co. might see what they were paying for, there being yet no television station in Winston-Salem, North Carolina. That alone was why kinescopes of the *News Caravan* were made. Kinescoping for the high public purpose of enhancing archives was then virtually unknown at NBC. Pictures of Swayze and the *News Caravan*, made then and since used repeatedly in all sorts of looking-back programs, television having become nostalgic about television, exist only because the sponsor wanted to see at least once a week what its money had bought and how its cigarettes were being sold.

Those arcadian days had to end. With more and more stations, and more and more programs, and more and more people watching, the stakes were mounting. The rewards of success were greater each day than they were the day before, the cost of failure higher. Television became the dominating medium in American advertising, and the advertising business grew as network television grew. Nourished by its symbiosis with network television, advertising became an economic power and a communications behemoth.

Television had become more than something to amuse technicians, a dumping ground for managers not bad enough to fire, a diversion from making money in radio. The Federal Communications Commission (FCC) had withdrawn its freeze on building new stations; sets maintained their healthy upward sales curve, and the incomparable ability of advertising messages on television to sell low-priced goods in staggering quantities (toothpaste, beer, headache pills, packaged food) was a lesson everybody learned. At the networks and at the advertising agencies, new hires and management trainees were exposed to inspirational pep talks proclaiming, "Television is not an advertising medium; it's a *sales* medium!"

News was still a very small part of this burgeoning institution called network advertising, but it was big enough to merit the attention of television's high managers and their concern lest it be judged only by the canons of journalism. The talk was still mostly of "image"— Weaver was bound and determined, for example, to replace Swayze because he did not reflect Pat's view of the "image" he wanted for NBC—but his, and all of management's, intensifying interest meant our happy isolation was drawing to a close.

5

The Huntley-Brinkley years at NBC began with the 1956 conventions. What would become a decade of unparalleled network news dominance began with accidents and compromises, managers accepting the suggestions of underlings because they could think of nothing better. When Chet Huntley and David Brinkley were finally approved at the very top as co-anchors of the convention coverage, the approval was so reluctant that public announcement, television's mandatory press release, was withheld for almost two months. When it succeeded, of course, everyone claimed credit.

This is my claim:

In late 1955, when Bill McAndrew asked me to produce the NBC News coverage of the 1956 political conventions, I convinced him I was not yet experienced enough. I offered instead to do the organizing and planning, and the fighting with Barry Wood, who would be the producer if I was not. Wood was Weaver's man, the "trouble-maker" (Weaver's own words) he sent down to shake up News.

Wood was all show business. He was also an aggressive vulgarian who thought people in news put on airs, and he worked out his resentments against them by regularly barging into McAndrew's morning staff meetings explaining at the top of his voice why he had to use

Bill's executive bathroom. Weaver thought that since Wood had made *Wide, Wide World* succeed when others failed, he might force NBC News closer to what he, Weaver, wanted but could not achieve. At one of McAndrew's convention planning meetings I raised the problem of having reporters on the convention floor who, in the absence of floor cameras, would have to be picked up by cameras in the balcony. The meeting was for all the departments involved, and my question for the technical department was: Could we devise a simple way for the floor reporters to tell us where they were so we could tell them what cameras to face? Wood suggested they wear bright beanies. He was quite serious, and became resentful and hostile when told correspondents of NBC News on the convention floor should not be seen wearing bright beanies. Later he suggested that as a promotional device all NBC reporters wear red blazers.

In 1952, NBC had plunged into convention coverage without adequate planning. As a result, while Walter Cronkite became a star, Bill Henry remained no more than a nice fellow. This time had to be different. First we agreed on a basic principle: to do news as news. My job was to plan and organize to get it done. This is not to say that appearance or pace, or any of the elements that make news more interesting would be discarded. Once I had set everything up, making it interesting was Barry Wood's concern; he was the producer.

My principal collaborator was Jack Sughrue; my principal source of information was John Chancellor. Sughrue's career as a navy fighter pilot had ended abruptly when President Truman ordered cuts in the Pentagon budget. When I met him, he was associate director of *Background*, a high-sounding, low-ranking job. Chancellor had been the most junior reporter for NBC's radio coverage of the 1952 conventions, which I had found the best place to learn what was going on, and I wanted to know how they did that.

Chancellor had cut his teeth in a Chicago city room before being fired in one of those self-indulgent exercises of City Editor as King that so color Chicago's newspapering legend. He had then taken the only job he could get, in television, and we first met when as shop steward of the news writers at NBC Chicago he came to New York to ask me what being a shop steward involved. (In the kingdom of the blind, the one-eyed man is a consultant.) I later got him his first network appearances as a reporter for a few of the *Background* half hours.

I took Sughrue to Chicago to survey the International Amphitheater. He was appalled that the nation's business would be conducted in such surroundings. The last event in the amphitheater had apparently been a farm animal show. On the lower level, where the committees would meet and delegations caucus, straw still covered the floor and enormous flies buzzed around us. The main floor, the arena itself, was cavernous and empty, and smelled organic and stale. He kept asking me, "Do they really do it here?" His sense of propriety was offended. I showed him where the dais would be, how the delegates' seats might be distributed, and what problems we would face in getting words and pictures into the cameras and out to the network. The biggest problem would be finding out what was going on among several thousand people pulling in different directions, and creating from that a coherent report which an interested citizen at home could follow.

A news process gathers, edits, and publishes. These steps are thought of as a sequence, but we were about to do them simultaneously. Radio aside, we were the first to try to bend the news process to live broadcasting: getting the news, reporting it, and distributing it all at the same time. (How does one edit a live report on television while the reporter is speaking?)

Sughrue taught me the carrier pilot's most important slogan: "Communication is control." We copied the navy's pattern of having communication arrive in one place, decisions made in another. Thus, we organized the control room into three levels: technical, decision, and the filter center. The filter center, an aircraft carrier term, talked to everybody; when it had something ready for air it notified the decision level, which would tell technical to put it on. Barry Wood was on the decision level with Bill McAndrew beside him. The director of the program sat with them because only they decided what would go on the air. I would sit in the filter center with Sughrue and Joe Meyers, NBC's director of news and McAndrew's principal assistant. In a few years all convention coverage was organized this way, and remains so to this day.

Chancellor's role was to explain to Sughrue and me how NBC radio news had been first to know what was happening on the convention floor in 1952, so we could do it on television in 1956. He said it had been Meyers's doing. The NBC radio reporters roaming the convention floor would report to Meyers with whatever news they picked up; he would move them around as he heard about stories beginning to develop or planned for events about to take place. His editorial acumen had given the story its drive. They had used an early version of the wireless microphone, which transmitted directly to the network without anchoring reporters inside a small radius, like dogs chained to their doghouses. By 1956, technology would give our floor reporters headsets by which they talked with their editors as well as broadcast. The short antenna sticking up from an earphone became the remembered hallmark of convention floor reporters.

Picking the hardware was simple; picking the anchor less so. Those with the authority to decide had no strong feelings, or even any sense of what the job entailed, so the discussion took months and was often surly. Bill Henry was the leading candidate. His work in 1952 was one of the few pleasant professional recollections of that difficult year. He was a good journalist, he was a good broadcaster, he was skilled and knowledgeable. I liked him, but I tried my hardest to convince McAndrew not to choose him. He was not only too old, I insisted, but, much more important, he was not of NBC News. His real employer was the *Los Angeles Times*, where he was still a featured columnist. Broadcasting was no more than his avocation, and conventions were too important for us to place an outsider in the lead role because only during convention coverage were we treated like grown-ups by colleagues and superiors inside the network. How well we did at these conventions would mark our position inside NBC and our standing with the public for the next four years. Look at Cronkite. Look at Swayze. McAndrew would not commit himself, but for the next sessions of his weekly meeting he kept the discussion away from who would be our anchor.

My candidate was Brinkley. Besides his obvious merits, wit, style, intelligence, and polished writing, I thought him more skillful in using television than any other reporter we had. He was uniquely comfortable with the medium, sensing the totality of impression and the place of his contribution to it. He was astute in knowing when to be quiet. Years later I told an interviewer, "Brinkley writes silence better than anyone else I know."

Meyers was pushing for Huntley. McAndrew was still for Bill Henry, and Taylor was even more strongly for Henry. But Meyers and I were the ones who had to do the work, and Taylor was manager enough to appreciate that the ones who do the work must somehow be mollified. At McAndrew's next meeting, Taylor tried to bring us around by suggesting pairing Henry with Ray Scherer, the White House correspondent. An older man and a younger man, he mused, would present an interesting contrast; Henry would explain the convention to Scherer. Shades of Cronkite's suggestion that he "explain" the convention to an "ordinary" man! But this dumb idea resolved the conflict between Meyers and me and gave us our solution.

When Taylor said "pairing" we had our answer. If it was to be two people, we knew which two it ought to be. Not Scherer and Henry but Huntley and Brinkley. We sold the idea to McAndrew in a matter of minutes. It took him longer to convince Taylor, but he managed. In time, the two of them even convinced Weaver. But he and the other people who ran NBC, whose decision this ultimately had to be, had so little faith in it that they held up the public announcement. We who had made the suggestion expected only that these two pleasant, youngish men, both experienced journalists and skilled broadcasters, would do a creditable job at the 1956 conventions. That the audience would see some special quality in them, that the combination would be greater than the sum of the halves, did not occur to anyone I know. Nor has anyone claimed he expected it to turn out that way. But that is how it happened.

The coverage was to center on as complete an information system as we could devise. Instead of merely carrying the party's proceedings, we would find out what was going on while it was still going on. Eliot Frankel, a colleague from my days at the *Newark Evening News*, who had come to NBC a few months after me and collaborated with me on *Outlook*, worked up the system that performed so nobly at the 1956 conventions and served well for years afterward.

First were the delegation reporters. They were the perfect news staff, all professional, all eager, all working for expenses and the sheer joy of it. We gathered them predominately from three sources: some were less eminent reporters and news writers from our own bureaus, who would otherwise not get to the conventions; some were part of a corps of affiliated-station news directors, willing to cover their home state delegations in return for fare, lodging, and some logistical help to get them on television back home; and some were friendly print journalists, like Les and Liz Carpenter covering Texas and the imposing Esther Van Wagoner Tufty reporting about Michigan. They were, as well, mostly hometown folks, and they managed to get housing in the same hotels as their delegations. Some of them actually got floor seats with their delegations during sessions.

To take their calls, stay in touch with them, and send them questions and assignments we put in an old-style news desk, under an old-style editor, with rewrite men to translate calls into short bulletins, and copy editors. To circulate the information, we rented old-fashioned, bulky, noisy teletypes, which we put at the news desk, in the anchor studio, the control room, our downtown newsroom, and so on through a list of less than a dozen. Thus we had our own wire service, which more than once was the fastest news source in Chicago.

The heart of the system, however, was the floor reporters. We had decided to have four for no better reason than it seemed symmetrical. From then on, and forever, it has been four. These would be put to buttonholing delegates, eavesdropping on party big shots, talking into their science fiction headsets, and then broadcasting some snippet of hot news. To broadcast, they had to face a camera. There would be at least one "creepie-peepie" on the floor, perhaps two, but these still produced crude, muddy pictures and got dark or wavy without warning. Sughrue found the solution to that problem in NBC's radio booth.

While the television anchors that year would still be in a studio in the network's work and office space, the radio anchor would watch the proceedings from a booth high above and behind the rostrum. Pauline Frederick, the first woman to anchor any network's convention coverage, was to sit with her producer, some technicians, and a lot of equipment at a twelve-foot glass window that looked out over the auditorium. Then along came Sughrue, who found two camera positions no one could take from him, because they were carved out of space already assigned to NBC. Narrowing her window to six feet would leave three feet on each side for a camera outside the booth. Everyone but Pauline and her producer was moved to the rear, unable to see what was going on, guided only by the producer's hand signals. The radio producer acquiesced because his boss, Joe Meyers, told him to. He was cramped and surly, but the radio booth cameras gave us the ability to cover the floor reporters.

However meager the mark made on history by the 1956 conventions, they were a time of excitement and opportunity for me and the little band I had gathered. The men who managed network news divisions had started and grown in radio and tended to be uncomfortable with all this talk of pictures and light levels. There was no need for us to know a lot, just more than they did. Mistakes were still inexpensive. Certainly Bill McAndrew, who relied too much on personal rapport when judging the professional competence of a colleague or employee, trusted me and my gang as he never could trust show business casuals like those around Barry Wood. They had been in television long enough, but they had no background in news and refused to accept that it was in any way different from drama or variety.

We set out for the conventions—the Democrats in Chicago, the Republicans in San Francisco—feeling we were blazing trails. Not that we believed we would be setting models for the industry, but that we would be pulling our own organization out of a slough of bad planning, sloppy organization, ineffective use of television, low public regard, and the constant frustrations that resulted. There was also the sense that this was for the long haul. Like all television programs, *Outlook* would eventually run its course. But conventions were an institution. They would always be news, and covering them right would be for the ages. We had no idea that in two decades conventions would become newsless and pointless, no longer a part of the process. It may have been predictable that the networks would keep covering them, because they did not know how to stop. Once conventions were being covered, their reporters would keep sifting frantically for grains of news. If there was no important news, unimportant news would inevitably have to do, gaining unwarranted attention by default. The growth of the primary system was not the only reason political conventions stopped generating news; the politicians wanted as little news as possible, because news diverted attention, they thought, from their using what to them was free television for political posturing and grandstanding. They looked on news as impinging on the audience they considered theirs; but, by drying up news, they destroyed that audience.

Although nothing at the 1956 conventions was of major consequence, we managed to eke out some news. Unsurprising or not, there was enough going on, especially at the Democrats' meeting, which was fortunately the earlier of the two, to hold the audience's attention. Also, seeing the conventions on television was still a novelty, fresh enough to hold the attention of many. Meyers had made up an appallingly short list of reporters he considered both available and qualified to be floor reporters, and he and I sifted through it many times. Three floor reporters were our own: Chancellor, Herbert Kaplow, and Merrill Mueller. These were not yet the "four horsemen" of subsequent fame, but each of them proved to be a savvy reporter with a nose for a story. For the fourth, we had to reach outside the organization, to Randall Jessee, news director of WDAF-TV, the station owned by the *Kansas City Star*, an old friend and collaborator, the one who had arranged for Thomas Hart Benton to make courtroom drawings at the trial of the Greenlease kidnappers.

With Ray Scherer, the White House correspondent, working the periphery of the hall, we had all the news there was to be had. Not all of it got on the air, because Barry Wood and the others on the middle deck did not know how to use the system, but the experience, the trial and error, the institutionalization of a logical, workable, simple news-collecting organization brought rewards in years to come.

Remembering the huddling and whispering of big-name politicians around the chairmen of the 1952 conventions, McAndrew had us hire a professional lip-reader for 1956. She sat with him and Wood in the center deck, but never read a lip; she did, however, marry one of the NBC technicians.

The big event on the first evening of the Democratic convention was to be the keynote speech by the young governor of Tennessee, Frank Clement, an orator whose style was modeled on that of his friend Billy Graham. Clement expected the speech to launch him into national prominence, which it did not. The convention managers had discussed dumping the keynote speech, replacing it with something new, a film, setting forth what the Democrats had done for America from the time of Roosevelt. Having it on television would make it the longest free commercial in history. Traditionalists opposed it, saying a convention is a convention, not some darned TV show. The result was a compromise: They would have both, first the film, then, after the film, the speech.

The film, called *The Pursuit of Happiness*, had been produced by Dore Schary, a famous director and producer. The script was by Norman Corwin, a giant of radio documentary before being lured to the movies. It was read by the young Massachusetts senator, John F. Kennedy, who, according to the party's press releases, had "partly rewritten" it. J. Leonard Reinsch, a broadcasting executive who every four years was in charge of the Democratic convention's operations, took a print of the film by hand to each network, delivering it gently to a higher officer. CBS refused to broadcast the film.

This set the stage for the first round of a fight that has lasted decades and may never end. In subsequent years, the fight over the film was usually between one or more of the networks and the Republicans, but it started with the Democrats in Chicago in 1956. With either party, however, the results were the same: Virtually no one in the hall could see the film clearly; virtually no one in the hall cared to see the film at all. The parties always claimed, however, that the film was an "integral" part of the convention.

After the film, which only ABC and NBC carried, chairman Paul Butler told the delegates: "One of our major networks has failed to keep its commitments to present this documentary film to the American people." (There had been no such commitments.) His statement was greeted with boos. When he then thanked ABC and NBC for "keeping their commitment," CBS was officially the culprit, and the booing grew to a roar. (Some of those booing were our own delegation reporters, egging on their friends from back home.)

Every four years, the pattern continued: CBS would skip the film. Cronkite would fill twenty or thirty minutes talking to the floor reporters who had been complaining all week that Cronkite would not talk to them. The floor reporters would be in the dark because the hall lights were down for the film. Nearby delegates said, "Shh! Shh!" But there is no "Shh! Shh!" in live television. At first, delegates agreed to interviews. Then convention managers ordered no interviews during films, so floor reporters and Cronkite talked to each other. Later on, live cameras were ordered off the floor during films. Reporters had to climb up to Cronkite's eyrie to talk. A politician too big to fear party bosses would come to be interviewed. From 1956 on, there has been film at every convention. Some have had two, even three films— simple-minded, uninteresting, but films. Like teachers, politicians think you can quiet the unruly with movies. But politicians make films as well as they write sonnets.

So CBS would stick to being principled; ABC almost always carried the film unless it was carrying nothing at all; NBC sometimes did, sometimes didn't; and newspapers pursued as news the squabble about television carrying "the film." In years when there was still business to do, deals to be cut, swaps to be made, and arms to be twisted, politicians found the darkened hall an ideal setting. Everyone else in the hall yawned and stretched and scratched. After 1976, with all political business decided before the opening gavel, it was everybody yawning and stretching and scratching.

When it came to the 1956 nomination, Adlai Stevenson got it on the first ballot. Before the balloting for President had even begun, floor reporters and delegation reporters had conceded to Stevenson and concentrated their attention on a choice for running mate. Two senators, John F. Kennedy and Estes Kefauver, led all the rest.

Minutes after Stevenson's nomination, the candidate told a dozen or so of the party's leaders, including Sam Rayburn, that he would not pick the candidate for vice president. That would be by an open vote of the convention. The leaders were horrified, but they could not talk him out of his decision.

There were two explanations for why he did it: he and his associates had promised too many politicians the second spot in return for their votes; or, he knew it would look good on television. The cameras picked up Stevenson making his way from the Stockyard Inn into the hall and to the podium. His heart was full and he was grateful. "I have decided," he told the delegates, "that the selection of the vice presidential nominee should be made through the free processes of the convention." He ended with a "God be with you" and went to bed. Sam Rayburn quickly gaveled adjournment to give leaders and manipulators extra time to huddle and politic and seek votes and trade votes.

The next afternoon came the roll call of the states, with Alabama yielding to Tennessee for the nomination of Senator Albert Gore. In all, thirteen names were placed in nomination and seconded, but it was Kennedy against Kefauver. Our floor reporters scurried all over the hall reporting stop-Kennedy movements, stop-Kefauver movements, compromises, favorite sons. On the first ballot, with 687 needed to nominate, Kefauver led with fewer than 500, Kennedy trailed with barely 300. Rayburn called for a second ballot, *the last second ballot for either nomination in either major party*. My problem, however, was not history but logistics. It was the kind of live television problem that dominates everything for minutes and hours, then seconds after it is over it is of no consequence, not even enough for tomorrow's newspaper.

Outside both Kefauver's and Kennedy's rooms in the Stockyard Inn were outlets for our one ultraportable camera, which was even smaller than the "creepie-peepie" but had to be connected by wire. Back then, television cameras, ultraportable or otherwise, did not take pictures as soon as they were switched on. The ultraportable took more than fifteen minutes to warm up. Should I place it outside Kennedy's room or Kefauver's? If I picked wrong, and it had to be moved, would I have the fifteen minutes for it to warm up at the new location for the shot of the winning candidate emerging? On the deck below me, Barry Wood got out of his chair, turned to face me, and leaned his arms across the shelf in front of me.

"Well, smartass?"

I picked Kefauver. Wood said, loudly, that I was wrong. The second roll call began.

There were very few changes, but mostly they favored Kennedy. At each, Barry Wood would ask me if I would move the camera and I would refuse. At 3:29, Delaware switched from the mayor of New York City, Robert Wagner, to Kennedy. Wood did not budge from his place, his arms across the shelf in front of me, his fat face a foot from mine, his eyes staring. At 3:44, New York State switched almost all its 98 votes from Wagner to Kennedy. Wood said time was running out. At 3:53, Texas switched from Gore to Kennedy, 56 votes, enough to put Kennedy ahead of Kefauver. Wood began pounding the shelf. The South was going for Kennedy, which made no sense to me, and I was moving from stubborn to nervous, but I kept the camera outside Kefauver's room. Officially, the second ballot ended with Kennedy at 618, Kefauver at 551½. Kennedy needed only 69 more votes. There was total confusion as delegation chairmen shouted for recognition.

Gore withdrew. Tennessee caucused. Oklahoma switched its 28 votes from Gore to Kefauver. Minnesota, then Missouri, then Michigan switched to Kefauver. Our tally by then had Kefauver once again ahead of Kennedy, 666 to 648. We switched to the ultraportable camera to show Kefauver entering his room in the Stockyard Inn. Barry Wood sat down. We switched back to the podium where Kennedy moved to make the Kefauver nomination unanimous. Again to the ultraportable camera as Kefauver left his room. In the center of a huge crowd, he moved toward the convention hall. His entourage burst out of the Stockyard Inn and disappeared behind a clump of trees near the hall's back entrance. We switched back inside where a resolution was being moved to thank the organist.

We left immediately for San Francisco to see the Republicans convene. We got there with Jack Gould's words ringing in our ears: Chet Huntley and David Brinkley had provided "the first real change in the network news situation in a long while." He had gone so far as to work up from press releases and one phone call a profile of Brinkley, the wry young man from Wilmington, North Carolina. As usual, other papers took their cue from the *Times*. (That, above all, is why Gould so frightened the pampered masters of the networks.) His use of "change in the network news situation" was Aesopian. We had challenged CBS and brought it off. Despite having only three days between tearing down at one convention and starting up at the other, we were full of high spirits and juvenile self-confidence.

That the proceedings in Chicago had been more interesting than we expected made us hope against hope for the same in San Francisco. Instead, it was an exercise in tedium. Nothing happened. There was a small fuss over a rumor that Eisenhower wanted to replace Vice President Richard M. Nixon. The hapless, well-meaning Harold Stassen was the principal actor in this sketch, but there were others. Needing a story, we made much of this one until it fizzled. That was all the news that week.

Otherwise, Randall Jessee got on camera with a Hawaiian delegate teaching him how to hula. The middle deck put it on the network; without real news it had to do. There was one historical highlight, or footnote. Eisenhower, who had not allowed live broadcast of his press conferences from the White House, became, in San Francisco, the first sitting President to allow the live broadcast of a press conference. He held it to say that Stassen would no longer oppose Nixon's nomination and would in fact be one of his seconders. Since no reporter had taken Stassen's campaign seriously, they seized the opportunity of this unique presidential press conference to try to elicit real news. They failed.

At 7:30 P.M. Pacific time, Thursday night, our convention coverage went off the air. Eisenhower and Nixon had been duly nominated and had accepted while the Atlantic seaboard was still awake. I had left for Los Angeles on Wednesday to work on Sunday's *Outlook*. Huntley joined me as soon as the convention adjourned. Suddenly, he and Brinkley were famous, recognized in public, treated with jolly regard by executives who months or weeks before had only reluctantly let their names be announced. Huntley was tired, but he enjoyed the people coming up to him with flattering words. He said we had to talk; I said we had to talk. He said Taylor's assistant had asked what he and Brinkley could do together to cash in on their success at the conventions. I said that could wait until 1960 because we had an important recording session the next morning for Sunday's *Outlook*, and perhaps, if we could swing it, an interview in the afternoon with Linus Pauling at Caltech for the following Sunday. He said he wanted some supper; I said I would pick him up at his hotel at 8:00 the next morning and returned to the editing room. I wondered long after whether we should not have done something triumphal.

In the September and October weeks that followed, the shape of NBC News was being changed in executive office meetings. Ben Park, Dave Taylor's assistant, suggested using the success of Huntley and Brinkley at the conventions by having them replace John Cameron Swayze. Proud as I was of pairing them for the conventions, I thought this was one of the dumber ideas I had ever heard. If news programs needed two anchors, they would already have had them. But it was a way to satisfy Weaver's poor opinion of Swayze—if truth be told, Bill McAndrew wasn't much enamored of him either—and the idea moved fast. McAndrew asked me if I would be interested in producing such a program. I said a producer rash enough to expose himself to the crossfire between two stars was asking for an early grave. Then I thought better of it.

(I would have been the "producer" because the term *executive producer* was not yet used in news. "Executive producer" is an inappropriate Hollywood locution, adopted because, to the uninformed, it implies enhancement. Since then, I have even heard "execproduce" spoken as one word and used as a verb. The accurate and descriptive word would be some variation of "editor," but that was precluded when anchorpersons preempted it; they wanted to be enhanced, too.)

On Friday, October 26, Swayze did the *News Caravan* for the last time. On Saturday we had a sort of rehearsal; on Sunday another. On Monday, October 29, we were on the air.

In memory, pairing Chet Huntley and David Brinkley would be seen as the one act that catapulted NBC to the top of whatever heap network news had become. Don Hewitt, who at one time or other produced both the CBS evening news and CBS's convention coverage, up against Huntley and Brinkley where they were most successful, would later say, "They came at us like an express train." They carved a hiatus in CBS News's half century of complacency and soothed NBC News's frustration at failing to convince its own superiors that, given support, it could do as well. Insiders credit adding Huntley to Brinkley with ending the fatuous practices of newsreels as well as stilling the affected resonances of wartime radio, providing news adults could watch without squirming. In fact, although what went before may have been bad, what succeeded was not always as good as later claimed. Nor was it born suddenly full-blown like Minerva, perfect and successful. It was a long time before we were home free.

On Monday, October 29, Israeli troops moved across the Suez

Peninsula to attack the Suez Canal, and Britain and France issued an ultimatum to both sides to cease hostilities or they would reoccupy the canal zone; Adlai Stevenson made a campaign speech in Boston blaming Eisenhower for earlier saying the Suez crisis had been defused; Soviet tanks crossed into Hungary from Romania on their way to Budapest to put out the Hungarian uprising, and the Hungarian Red Cross asked the world to help it care for up to fifty thousand wounded.

On Monday, October 29, Chet Huntley, David Brinkley, and a small group of reporters, news writers, and directors began a daily program unable, at least on that day, to cover much of the news on one of the heaviest news days in memory. For Suez, we had nothing from the scene, just Pauline Frederick at the United Nations. There was no reporter in Hungary, and the film, which had been reasonably steady since the uprising started almost two weeks before, did not arrive that day. Chancellor covered Stevenson in Philadelphia.

There were in those days two ways of switching the television picture from city to city. If it was available, you could rent a TV circuit from the city you wanted to include to the city where you had your control. The camera or cameras in the city you were adding would be as much in your control as the cameras in your studio. People in the two cities could be seen talking to each other. This was the effective and logical way to do these things, but it was very expensive. *Wide, Wide World* could do it this way, but we, with our puny budget, could not afford it. (The *News Caravan's* far-from-opulent budget was cut for us when we took over, presumably because we had not yet developed extravagant habits.)

The other way, which we could do with some stations but not all, was to tell AT&T when the switch would be made, and what word in the script would be the last word into the switch, and again out of the switch. At that time, hearing that word, an AT&T technician would unplug the network and replug it to go the other way. If it went well, the viewer at home would see a thick line roll up through the picture and that was all.

"Chet Huntley, NBC News, New York." *Switch*.

"And David Brinkley, NBC News, Washington." *Switch*.

When Huntley finished a segment, and Brinkley was next, Huntley had to say something that we could tell AT&T well in advance was the "switch cue" to Washington. When Brinkley was finishing a segment with Huntley up next, he in his turn would have to say something decided on and accepted in advance so we could advise AT&T of the switch cue back to New York. That is why Huntley would end his pieces by saying, "David," and Brinkley would end his pieces by saying, "Chet." When they became very popular, NBC Sales paid for an expensive survey to learn why people liked them. A big reason was the friendly way they talked to each other. But they never talked to each other. Those were switch cues for AT&T.

Huntley and Brinkley succeeded in a way no subsequent pairing, intentional or accidental, has been able to. There were reasons we puzzled over for years; some were obvious from the beginning. The horde of imitators seems to have missed the fact that Chet and David did different things; whatever one did, the other did not do. Brinkley covered Washington news. Huntley covered all other news. Unless one of them was on assignment or vacation, this rule was inflexible. Huntley usually led into switches out of town. It was thus rare that more than a third of any program was Brinkley's, and often enough on a slow day it took whips and chains to make him come up with two minutes. Yet most people thought they shared the time equally; Brinkley's presence was that strong.

As for being caught in the crossfire between two stars, as I had feared when I was first asked to be the producer, only once in my decade did anything remotely like that occur, and it was my fault. I had told Huntley in the morning that he would do a story, and then in the afternoon I told Brinkley he would do the same story. We did not catch the mistake until near broadcast time, which, among other things, left us short. They were both angry, for a few minutes, but it did not occur to either of them that it was anyone's job but mine to straighten things out.

That first night, October 29, 1956, sticks in my mind as the worst evening news program in the history of American network television. No kinescope recording was made, so I am at a loss for details, but I remember sitting at my desk when it ended, filled with abject despair. Huntley, Sughrue, and Eliot Frankel, the associate producer—that meant principal news editor in those days—asked me to join them for a drink, but my mood was too black. Then the network salesman who had entrapped Studebaker, one of the last of the small car manufacturers, into buying us one night a week telephoned cheerily from the private room at "21," the upscale restaurant, where he had been watching with people from the client and the agency.

Why didn't I come over? I said Huntley and I and some others were doing a postmortem. "Bring them," he said, unaware he was inviting a dozen of us to share his booze and expensive meat and to hear what a good show we had done from people who were drinking and talking while it was on. His jaw dropped as we paraded into that tiny top-floor room; extra tables were summoned. In the jollity, we were told over and over that Studebaker was in Mondays for the long haul. The same salesman had sold Tuesdays to Ronson lighters whose owner said he wanted to be to news what Gillette was to sports. By Christmas they had both left us. We did news better by then, but sold too few lighters and cars. Studebaker itself vanished, while Ronson was hit by disposable lighters and smokers quitting smoking. Even as a business, we did better than that. But it took time.

Earlier that terrible day, at about six o'clock, Sughrue had asked me, "How do you want the show to end?"

"What do you mean?"

"Well, the show has to end."

Yes, a show has to end. I rolled paper into my typewriter.

"Who has the last item?"

"Huntley."

I wrote: HUNTLEY (NY) Good night, David.

BRINKLEY (WX) Good night, Chet.

HUNTLEY (NY) And good night for NBC News.

Not long ago, the publishers of the *American Heritage Dictionary* published a volume of recent American quotations. There is one entry for Huntley and Brinkley, jointly, "Good night, David. . . . Good night, Chet. . . ." How do I complain?

Dear Mr. Heritage: They didn't write that; I did.

In fact, Huntley and Brinkley hated that closing. "We sound like a couple of sissies," they complained. I insisted a program must close somehow, that a close should be short, and that it must include both of them. I was willing to accept any closing they suggested if it met the requirements. Meanwhile, as our ratings approached inconsequentiality, others in the broad reaches of NBC News nominated themselves our successors. In New York, Merrill Mueller tried to convince Taylor he could do better. At NBC News Chicago, Alex Dreier, "Man on the Go," let drop that not only was he ready, he had been approached. The man who graced network television during the 1948 conventions analyzing the news while being shaved by Alfonse the barber trumpeted that the "good night" closing was bad form, unprofessional, "a couple of sissies."

. . .

The stage set is where a news program comes from, and the set from which we operated was different from any other in history. Swayze had sat at a desk in a make-believe library, Murrow in an actual control room. Sets have looked like living rooms, lawyers' offices (but not doctors'), newspaper city rooms, and appliance stores, to name a few. For election nights, Hjalmar Hermanson, a brilliant, taciturn Finn, put Huntley and Brinkley at an X-shaped desk because that is how ballots are marked. We never put a camera in the ceiling so you could see the X, but, sitting between its arms, they had room for the papers people kept pushing at them.

Our *Nightly News* set resulted from the histories of two men: Davidson Taylor and Barry Wood. Taylor had put NBC money into the design of a plastic globe conceived by Sam Berman, an artist in modeling clay who was known for creating "Mr. Esquire" when that magazine first began. He had designed an inflatable globe seven feet in diameter with raised physical features of the earth's surface, appropriately colored and accurate on a logarithmic scale. (I have no idea what that means; I quote from memory.) Taylor not only bought one, but gave additional thousands toward the cost of research. Under the broadcasting axiom that departmental budgets are scrutinized but program budgets are spent like water, he tried to get *Wide, Wide World* to pay for the globe. Wood used it once on his program, but he was not going to be suckered into paying the whole cost. So there it sat—until we came along. It became mine—whether I wanted it or not.

To McAndrew, sets were a show business matter, so he gave Barry Wood control over ours. Wood told his designer to design not just another news set but a set for a ballet about news. This flight of poetry haunted me until the next budget cut.

We had a medium-sized studio, large enough for a drama but not a musical. Across the width of this the designer, finding his news in classical times, put a semicircle of columns—that is, they looked like columns in wide shots (which we rarely took) but were actually curved like the blades of scimitars, with the narrow, or pommel, end at the bottom and the wide end at the top, holding up the capital. No matter what camera took what shot of Huntley, one of these things seemed to be growing out of his head. At the left end of the arcade of columns was a screen for maps and other graphics; at the right end, a TV monitor on which we could see Brinkley, although we could not show Huntley on Brinkley's monitor in Washington without paying an extra charge for the line, which we could not afford.

When reading the news or leading into Brinkley, or films, or reports from other cities, Huntley stood at the projection screen. During the out-of-town reports, or the films, or commercials, he had to run the full width of the studio to the monitor. When he was needed on the first camera again, it was a race back to the projection screen. Luckily, his high school sport had been track.

In the middle of the row of columns, at the very back of the studio, the designer left a gap for us to put our very own, exclusive, inflatable, plastic, seven-foot globe. The set was driving us to the poor house. We had little enough budget for covering news without this huge additional charge. Its initial cost was tiny compared to the upkeep. We only had the studio afternoons. Mornings, our set was hidden behind the morning program set, which was possible only once the globe was removed. Every night, two members of the Stagehands Union would deflate Mr. Berman's globe and hand it to three members of the Teamsters Union who would truck it to the NBC scene shop on 18th Street. Every morning, three members of the Teamsters Union would truck it from 18th Street to 30 Rockefeller Plaza and hand it to two members of the Stagehands Union who would inflate it and set it in place in our studio. It was an open wound in my budget.

Meanwhile, we managed. We got most of the news on. We got better at it. Acceptance would be too strong a word, but we were tolerated in the high reaches of the company, perhaps only until an acceptable replacement could be identified. Unlike most network programs, regular news programs may not be replaced with other kinds of programs, although those who do them may be replaced with other people. I was favored with lectures about the need for frugality and advice about how to do a news program. At one meeting, Dave Taylor expressed the opinion—his or Weaver's?—that we were unpopular because Huntley did not smile enough. He suggested I write "Smile" at intervals on his teleprompter copy. I didn't.

Early in 1957 we were saved; RCA ordered another budget cut. Had we continued as we were, there would be no money left for news at all. Drastic conditions make for drastic remedies. I told the meeting

Taylor had reflexively called that the only solution I could find to my budget problem was the "closet-to-closet concept." Taylor regarded me sagely and asked me to explain.

"The news is what Huntley says. The news is what Brinkley says. The news is not where it is said."

Taylor nodded.

"It would be the news even if they said it in a closet."

No one looked puzzled, or bemused, or outraged at this bare-faced scam. The proposition seemed self-evident, and all present accepted the corollaries: I did not need the big studio on the third floor of the RCA building, or Brinkley's big studio in Washington. (Brinkley, at least, had escaped Wood's nonsense about a "ballet" about the news; he sat alone among bare walls.) Brinkley, his drafting table with him, could fit in the tiny basement studio next to Washington master control. In New York, I had found a little room near the master control center on the fifth floor, the booth where announcers read station call letters, six feet wide and twenty-two feet deep. From there, Huntley could bring America the news. We would save enough in studio rental to maintain whole the system that gathered our news and film around the world. And we could finally—though I didn't dare mention it— get rid of our seven-foot globe.

The taciturn Finn put a false perspective flat on the back wall of the announce booth that made it look as though it stretched back half a mile. He made the top two-thirds of the back wall appear horizontal, the ceiling. The "ceiling" light fixtures were quadrilaterals of translucent plastic, lit from behind, shaped to force perspective. Below the dividing line, where the "ceiling" joined the "wall," he put clocks two inches in diameter to suggest the newsroom cliché of foot-wide clocks showing time in Singapore, Nairobi, and Rio de Janeiro—ours were not labeled. Barely visible behind Huntley was a door thirty inches high. Since everyone knows doors are seven feet high or more, the other false dimensions were forced into viewers' minds. Twenty-five years later, people still speak with awe of Hermanson's forced perspective set in the 5-HA announce booth. Once again, poverty had concentrated the mind.

During broadcasting, Huntley stood halfway back at a "leaner" that Hermanson had built to the height of his elbow, next to a latex screen for the projected graphics. With no room in the booth for the projector, it sat in the corridor with its operator, violating the fire laws. Maps and still pictures were projected onto the screen through the window installed long ago so out-of-towners on the famous NBC studio tour could watch an announcer announcing. Two cameras were side by side at the front end of the studio, one taking Huntley in close-up, one in a wide shot to include maps or other graphics as well as the supposed ceiling lights, international clocks, and the door that led to nowhere. The size of the room made the inevitable lights doubly oppressive, and Chet would end each evening soaking wet. At seven, when the first broadcast ended, I would walk from my office to the booth to discuss changes for the "repeat." Huntley would be in the corridor cooling off, greeting me with his imitation of Mel Allen: "And here comes old Case out of the dugout." For those eight months or so, NBC's news studio and newsroom were on the same floor, a simple, logical arrangement not available again for thirty-two years, and then achieved only by a vast rebuilding that cost millions.

CBS had moved its news program, with Douglas Edwards, from 7:30 P.M. to 6:45 or 7:15 P.M., the choice being each station's. This brought more money to the network, so NBC followed suit. We moved from 7:45 P.M., which we had inherited from Swayze, to 6:45 or 7:15 P.M., also at each station's choice. Some NBC affiliates in the South chose not to carry us at all, believing (but never saying) that the New York–based networks were in favor of racial integration. We were particularly suspect because of all those stories on *Outlook*. The grapevine quoted jokes about the Nigger Broadcasting Company.

Two of the five stations owned by Westinghouse were NBC affiliates, Boston and Cleveland, large cities. These chose not to carry *Huntley-Brinkley* for reasons not specified. So NBC arranged for ABC's affiliates to carry us in those cities. They reached smaller audiences, but they had good local news departments and gave us better regional stories than Westinghouse would have. (Later, when our ratings were high, Westinghouse claimed their rights of affiliation, displacing the ABC stations. I protested all over the building only to be greeted with amused tolerance.)

Getting out of the massive set in the studio on the third floor, the one Don Hewitt soon labeled "the Martian ballroom," had saved not only the budget but our spirits. We watched ourselves gaining control, doing what we were paid to do in the style we chose. No longer would Chet, David, and I need to continually reestablish, as we often would during those first months, that this was the news program we wanted to do. On the other hand, we fully expected to be replaced. It still puzzles me that we weren't. Ratings got a little better, but during the summer of 1957 there were whole days without any commercials. We went on the air *sustaining!*

Against that, the writing was getting better and tighter. My edict that the present tense referred only to the time of broadcast had rid us of the odor of newsreels that pervaded the *News Caravan*, where film scripts were written in the present tense, newsreel style, as in "As the cabinet watches, President Eisenhower greets the muscular dystrophy poster boy. A big day in the life of a brave, little fellow."

We did not judge all news equally solemn; some quite notable events were ridiculous, or uproarious, or ironic. This went against precedent in network news, but such attitudes were common in other media, and we were careful not to slop over into telling jokes, or exchanging banter. Above all, we made no assumptions about the intelligence of the audience except that it might be underestimated by most people in our business. This sounds noble, and it is meant to, but it is clearly easier to do a news program this way than to try to produce or write a program for an audience whose intelligence or interest level you consider substantially different from your own.

The organization, NBC News, was beginning to accommodate itself to our way of seeing pictures, to our proposition that television news was, above all, seeing things happen. Cameramen were enthusiastic, reporters and bureau chiefs less so. Our system was to have cameramen film news events, to edit their film into a narrative, then, as the last step, to write a script that included the description of the event and its news relevance. We did not use reporters on the scene, who would speak a script to which pictures would be matched—risking the danger of throwing away the best pictures because they had not been scripted for. So although we had some good reporters, we used them very little, far less than CBS did and perhaps less than we should have.

This way of doing things had drawbacks but also justifications. In our first weeks there had been two unnerving examples of reporters confusing themselves with the news itself.

The first was from Budapest. The Hungarian uprising of 1956 was another Cold War drama burned into American consciousness because it was on television. The last week of the *News Caravan* was the first week of the uprising, and we took it over, showing what we could, day after day, some from our own crews, some from a remarkable group of anonymous Hungarian newsreel cameramen who recorded what they could and sent it out to everyone they could reach so the world might know. Frank Bourgholtzer, one of our best reporters, was there, skilled, astute, and knowledgeable about Eastern Europe—but he had grown up in radio. One November day, after all the rumors, the fact: Russian tanks were finally where they could be seen, in Budapest's main square. Josef Oexle, one of our best cameramen, was there, but he did not film the tanks. The editor of a small newspaper had reached Budapest from the provinces and our reporter chose to interview him, bad English and all, around the corner from the square, take after take, while the light of the November afternoon faded and we could no longer film Russian tanks firing at the buildings where the last of the revolutionaries were holding out. The Hungarian newsreel cooperative saved us, but our cameraman missed the irreplaceable, unduplicable, once-and-nevermore picture. You can do a radio report from a hotel, phone your newspaper from the Foreign Office press room, but the cameraman must be there or there is no picture.

Those same weeks: Suez. Eisenhower told the British and French to turn tail, but the Israelis fought long enough to take a sizable number of Egyptian prisoners. We saw none of that until, in their own time, the Israelis allowed journalists into the prison camps. An NBC News reporter and a camera crew went to a camp in what has come to be known as the Gaza Strip. The next day we received one thousand feet of 16mm film, about half an hour's worth, a lot of raw footage for a spot news story. We gathered to look at it. In the center of the picture was our reporter, talking for the entire length of film, thirty minutes of nonstop gab. The camera started, stopped, turned here and there, but every frame had him in the center. Over his shoulder we could see Egyptians in uniform ambling idly, crawling into pup tents, drinking water from Lister bags, talking in groups, sitting. He was excited, overwhelmed, describing what he saw instead of letting us see it. What news he reported we had reported two days ago. The film was useless even as archive. We threw it all away.

Slowly things got better. As we saw it, we were showing a lot of newcomers to the medium how to do it right. In retrospect, there was more learning than teaching. What we thought of as "our style" was watching at a remove, allowing emotion to show only if it was not ours but a legitimately observed fact, and a readiness to see the absurd in human behavior. Above all, curiosity was reason enough. We each assumed, "If it interests me, it must interest at least one other person." We hired away from the London *Observer* their key Africa reporter, George Clay, and he showed Americans how colonies became republics. (When he was killed in the Congo several years later, even CBS felt obliged to report his death, saluting his role in teaching America about Africa.) When Tom Mboya, the black labor leader from Nairobi, made a speaking tour of the United States, I sent a reporter and crew to travel with him, showing a dapper, sophisticated, Kennedyesque politician spreading charm. As Huntley and Brinkley grew more popular, I could get away with such experiments, which gave us tone.

We showed lighter stories from Japan, like the pachinko craze, or how to eat fugu fish; beggars in Calcutta; the Polish black market in used American jeans; and long-lens pictures of Martin Borman's son and Heinrich Himmler's daughter. More than anyone else, we used reports from around the country by reporters around the country, in the affiliated stations. On a slow day in the news business—of which there are more than the other kind—we would call up four or five to survey national employment, or how this year's Christmas shopping compared to last year's. Cleveland would switch to Omaha, which would switch to Atlanta, which would switch to Los Angeles—all live television, each requiring an AT&T technician listening for a cue word and time so he could, by hand, change the place from where the network originated. Usually, it worked. Once it did not, and I kicked a large wastebasket across the newsroom. It was kept as a memento of the early days, the dent still showing.

Risks and all, these surveys and their Southern drawls and Midwestern vowels and Eastern lilts became part of our attitude of immediacy without hysteria. We soon had a repertory company of local reporters who understood us and liked what we did, and enjoyed the local fame from being on the big, powerful network. Over the years, several of them were hired as NBC News reporters, and at least two became "star" anchormen of local news on NBC-owned stations whose managers had seen them reporting for us. We did similar regional work on *Outlook*. On Sunday of each Labor Day weekend, *Outlook* would survey schools across the country as to what children and their parents would find Tuesday morning. The theme would be budget problems one year, desegregation another, curriculum changes a third, as we broke a national institution into its local bits.

For more than a year we developed a steadily better news program— more comprehensive, more interesting, better executed. But the number of NBC affiliated stations who chose not to carry the program changed little, so that the total stayed at fewer than half. Commercials were scattered and varied, and the ratings were not very good. Early in 1958, as one of his first acts as president of NBC, Robert Kintner approached Texaco gasoline through its advertising agency. He had this news program that would be perfect for them, if it worked. But he would not hide from them the fact that at the same moment he was speaking, clearances were lousy and ratings even worse. So he would sell it at a price they could not refuse, $100,000 a week for full sponsorship. If it didn't work after a few months, they would have lost little. By some alchemy, the chairman of Texaco, A. C. Long, seemed to like what we were doing.

He bought the program—the whole thing, five nights a week, all commercial spots. Within three years, Kintner had jacked the price up so high that Texaco had to split sponsorship with, of all people, Camel cigarettes, and after six months of that, they had to withdraw entirely because it was too expensive. In the meantime, news programming had acquired that unusual phenomenon, sponsorship, an advertisers's complete financing of a program—a system common in radio that had died early in network television. But costs were too great for all but a few companies, and even those learned that their advertising budgets could be more effectively spent by scattering it over a variety of programs on all networks. Such outright sponsorship was already dying when Texaco agreed to be sole advertiser in the *Huntley-Brinkley Report*, now the *Texaco Huntley-Brinkley Report*. In both cities, we moved out of the closets into proper studios so that representatives of the advertising agency, New York sharpsters all, could escort the oilmen on their trips from Texas to see what they were buying. In addition, the words *Texaco Huntley-Brinkley Report* actually had to appear on the studio set. I balked at this and there were discussions. A lot was riding on this seemingly minor matter, but no one wanted me to leave, which I sulkily indicated I was prepared to do. Finally I said that the new wording would have to be out of range of any cameras. Oh, said the man from the agency, that would be okay. That's not why they wanted it. So for more than three years, there was a sign, never seen on television, visible only to people from the advertising agency and the Texaco executives they so proudly brought around to show us off.

The sponsorship was delayed and kept a secret for months while the NBC department that deals with stations got them to get rid of "Esso Reporters" and similar oil company programs that might be adjacent. Texaco became our sponsor in June and was extraordinarily easy to get along with. During more than three years we received only one editorial demand, an incomprehensible official Texaco statement about flags of convenience—under which American tankers and freighters could be registered in places like Panama and Liberia to save money and skirt safety laws—which they insisted only Huntley or Brinkley read, exactly as written. Negotiations went on between NBC and Texaco, between us and our employers, while we were torn between taking a stand on principle and keeping Texaco happy with what was to us no more than a pointless and probably ineffective exercise. I took the coward's way out because we would never find another sponsor like them: I had Huntley read the statement.

The countervailing advantages were enormous, unique, and more than I could give up. The biggest was that whenever there was more news than I could squeeze into fifteen minutes, which meant barely twelve minutes of news, I would call our keeper at the agency and get his agreement to drop one or two, or even all, of the commercials, so long as someone said "Texaco" at the top and bottom of the program. It happened quite often, which was most unusual for commercial broadcasting and was not to be lightly dismissed. Besides, I had no passionate position on flags of convenience.

By the time Camel cigarettes became a half-sponsor, I was spoiled, and they were less friendly to the news and less amenable to losing commercials while paying for them. When news on one of their nights was more than I could fit in, I would ask someone to scout the news wires for any story about cancer. There was always one. It would be written into a ten-second item while I would tell the agency why it would look bad—for them!—if we ignored it. Grumbling, they would yank the commercial, a net gain for news of fifty seconds.

I never met A. C. Long, but nothing I heard about him told me why Texaco wanted to be associated with what we did. Whatever it was, the association did more than relieve our money problems or silence critics inside NBC and give us standing where we worked. Full sponsorship, especially by a product not sold in drugstores, was so attractive that almost all the NBC affiliates who had shunned us, whether for ideology or economics, now rushed to jump aboard. More stations meant, obviously, bigger audiences, and our ratings improved. It might be held by serious outside observers of the role of the media in American life that ratings should not matter, but in commercial broadcasting they mean survival, which is not without its own ethical connotations.

Texaco beamed when we looked good in Washington, which we did. September of the year before their sponsorship began was the first school year under *Brown* v. *Board of Education*, the Supreme Court's decision that separate education was not equal education, and that racially segregated schools were illegal. *Outlook* and the *Huntley-Brinkley Report* had reported story after story about the general situation and watched it refine down to the particular as the schools of the entire South prepared to reopen. Although not a meeting-prone group, we held planning meetings to prepare for the day after Labor Day, to choose who among the tiny group of reporters we trusted would be sent to where we expected the news to be. We chose McGee, Kaplow, and Chancellor. John was to go from Chicago to Nashville. On Labor Day afternoon, while we were at work on that night's program, Chancellor called from his office. He wanted to chat one last time about his assignment. He had dropped into the bureau to pick up some material before returning home to pack for the late plane to Nashville.

It was like all other telephone conversations I have had with reporters about to leave on assignment, until, as we were speaking, the copy boy put before my eyes an inch-wide strip of teletype paper, a bulletin that had just moved. In Little Rock, Arkansas, Governor Orval Faubus had asked for time on local television, and it was rumored he would call up the Arkansas National Guard.

I said to Chancellor, "Maybe you had better go."

"Do you mean it?"

I hesitated. We had planned for Nashville. There was no time for another meeting. Nervously, I changed his assignment.

Five minutes later, he called again. The only plane from Chicago to Little Rock that evening would leave so soon he had to go from the office to the airport without stopping at home for his suitcase. He got to Little Rock just as Faubus was on television. He checked into his hotel, made his contact at the *Arkansas Gazette*, and covered the story. He was the only national reporter (other than the education editor of *The New York Times*) present the next morning when the Arkansas National Guard drew up in front of Little Rock Central High School as nine black teenagers came to seek admission.

No one knew how long the story would last. Day after day, he accumulated a wardrobe; day after day, he covered the story, as every news organization in the country sent reporters and picture-takers and talkers. But he was first. Not only did he report every day; he flew to Oklahoma City to do so, and back when his report was done. AT&T had no originating equipment in Little Rock, and would make the requisite installation only on several days' notice and only if there was a firm order. For my budget, and to my stingy mind, a firm order for several days hence was more than I could afford. So at 3:00 P.M. Central time, the cameraman boarded a chartered plane to Oklahoma City, where WKY-TV was prepared to accept us and feed our report. At 4:00, Chancellor took a second chartered plane to Oklahoma City, arriving once the film had been developed and was ready to look at. When his report was over, he would get back on the plane, talk over the next day's likely locations with the cameraman, land, find some supper, catch up on what had happened while he was gone, and try to calm himself enough to be able to sleep.

This went on for a couple of weeks until I asked Huntley to read some lines. Perhaps, he told his audience with that resonant authority, they were wondering why John Chancellor, the NBC News reporter in Little Rock, was sending us his nightly reports from Oklahoma City. It was a sort of technical matter, he said; apparently AT&T could not send us his reports directly from Little Rock without going through a process that was too complicated to go into. Until this was solved, flying by chartered plane to Oklahoma City would be the only way Chancellor could bring us his reports.

It worked. The next day, Chancellor could report from KARK-TV, Little Rock; no more planes to Oklahoma City. The day after that, predictably, the NBC vice president in charge of getting along with AT&T brought his mournful countenance to my office and said I really should not do things like that, and would I not do it again, and please would I warn him if I was going to do it again.

Chancellor was on the air every night for the month that Little Rock was the biggest news in America. Orval Faubus, the kind of Southern governor who gets described in the Sunday papers of the North as a liberal, deployed his National Guard around Central High School because he had heard there would be violence, or so he said on television on Labor Day evening, September 2, minutes after Chancellor arrived from Chicago. The next day, the guardsmen barred twelve black teenagers from Central High School, where their enrollment had been mandated by a federal court. Twelve soon became nine, and in the weeks to come every journalist on the spot, every editor, copy editor, and rewrite man in New York, Chicago, Los Angeles, Atlanta, and across America, would know all nine by name.

Trouble, which was a surprise in Little Rock, had been expected in Greensboro, North Carolina, but none took place. It was also vainly anticipated in Charlotte, North Carolina, and in Louisville and Sturgis, Kentucky. There was in fact some real trouble in Nashville, where a bomb destroyed a school that had been ordered desegregated, and there was a bomb scare that did not materialize in Birmingham, Alabama. In both cities, the news establishment had been braced and expectant. All this was news that nervous September, all covered and reported, but the continuing story was Little Rock.

President Eisenhower would not accept the flouting of the law and the Constitution. We are still not quite sure what he thought of black children in white Southern schools, but his constitutional role was cruelly clear to him. All other avenues exhausted, he ordered the U.S. Army to take those children to school with bayonets fixed. That was Tuesday, September 24.

From the beginning, the story was too big for one reporter to handle, to cover for *Huntley-Brinkley* and *Today* and radio and the weekend programs, *Outlook* among them. But it was several days before McGee and Kaplow were moved over to Little Rock, along with more camera crews. By this time, every news organization of consequence had at least one reporter in Little Rock. That alumni association of news veterans of the civil rights struggle was formed in those days in Arkansas and still meets from time to time and will probably carry on, like Civil War veterans, until the last drummer boy has died.

In time, Chancellor left Little Rock, exhausted but with a wardrobe of new shirts. The following spring, a whole contingent of us went to the annual black-tie dinner given in a Washington hotel by the Radio and Television Correspondents Association. At these events, Washington reporters bring powerful politicians, generals and admirals, and high-ranking civil servants; New York producers bring advertisers, tough and successful men strangely prone to awe as they perambulate the corridors among famous political faces, who in turn had been brought to pay off a debt or set up a useful contact. Our guests were from our new sponsor, Texaco, and from its advertising agency. They were listening when, in one of the many standing-and-drinking rooms that surround such affairs, an important senator, Oklahoma Democrat A. S. "Mike" Monroney, was overheard saying, "When I think of Little Rock, I think of John Chancellor."

We had arrived.

6

While Americans moved placidly through Eisenhower's second term, television's propensity for turmoil persisted: Bob Kintner replaced Pat Weaver, there were quiz scandals, and news—that is, American television commercial network news—grew up. Our conceit was that the *Huntley-Brinkley Report* helped it grow up. In the week before Eisenhower's reelection, Chet Huntley and David Brinkley moved into NBC's daily network news lineup; they continued for almost fifteen years. For perhaps ten of them it was far and away the most watched television news program in the United States. It was also key to reviving the fortunes of the National Broadcasting Company.

My little repertory company had to face being the basic news for millions of people, with all the implied responsibility. Our excitement at the novelty of pictures as their own news medium was no longer justification enough. For better or for worse, to too many people, what we did was The News. We had to face that there was an audience of real people, individuals, even though advertisers and our own employers thought of them only in bulk, countable, salable numbers.

My colleagues and I exorcised the terrible vision of millions of pairs of eyes fixed on our work by imagining someone real to talk to: a woman not yet forty, one college degree, two children, a husband in

the professions, busy with PTA and either politics or do-goodery, wistful about being stuck in the home (these were the fifties), subscriber to a weekly newsmagazine, a letter writer whose sentences parsed. Thus, without market research or asking NBC Sales or management or NBC News, we decided for whom we should do the program. We felt that if we got them, the rest would follow. And they did.

Only later did I learn that it was an axiom that news and nonfiction appeal to older males, which was presumably the reason why we were sponsored by Texaco, a product males buy. We had also stumbled on a truth: Network news—that is, world and national news—interests mostly the middle class. But in the early days, viewers were all middle class. Only they and bar owners could afford sets. When the price of receivers became more affordable, and more people owned them, network news made no attempt to seek out new audiences. In the late sixties, when local television news suddenly expanded, it found a different audience, the one ignored by network news. Those who interpret Nielsen numbers have determined that viewers distinguish network news from local news even though both show up on the same glass surface with the dial set at the same channel; the audience for local news tends to be poorer and younger and includes more blue-collar workers.

For us, news was whatever we were interested in. The day was still to come when audience manipulation consultants gauged what interested the biggest possible number, and advised news directors how to cover those subjects and thus attract a larger audience, achieve a bigger rating, and charge more for commercials. For us, the old craft rules, handed down mostly by oral tradition, were still good enough. We were not without arrogance.

From the Age of Innocence we had moved to an Age of Bumptiousness, rooted in the middle fifties when the freeze on new stations was lifted and transmitting towers marched across the land. More stations were built, more receivers were bought, more Americans entered the world of television. The novelty of pictures in one's living room repeated itself over and over. As it was becoming old hat in Albany, it was new and exciting in Phoenix, and the networks had it almost all to themselves. Only the largest cities had more stations than the three network affiliates. (Because there were not enough stations to go around, the fourth network, DuMont, starved to death.) Such "independents" often suffered from not enough material to broadcast or money to produce their own.

By the 1956 conventions, "most" Americans owned television sets, and a surprising number watched, considering there was neither news nor spectacle nor relevance. Pollsters would determine in a few years that television had become the "principal" source of news for a majority of Americans, and they already showed it moving ahead, first overtaking newsmagazines, then radio, then at last looked to for their basic news by more people than looked to the newspapers themselves. Big names are rooted in that time: Murrow, Cronkite, Huntley, Brinkley. Documentaries flourished. And it was news to which the networks turned when the quiz scandals stained their reputations and imperiled their capacity to make a lot of money. News was noble; news was wonderful; news gave great image.

The scandals, which in that simpler time left millions feeling betrayed and aggrieved, grew out of an attempt by some program entrepreneurs to revise an old radio formula, quiz programs, by giving very big prizes. The most successful aped a highly rated prewar show built around a "Dr. I.Q." who would ask a series of questions, doubling prizes (2, 4, 8, 16, 32) until they reached $64. "And now for the sixty-four-dollar question" became part of the language. Revlon cosmetics brought it to CBS television as *The $64,000 Question*; the contestants were wholesome young people or engaging eccentrics who were placed in an "isolation booth" where they could hear only the questions. The game show host's asides, his revealing the answers to us at home, were unheard by the unfortunates inside their H. G. Wells-type phone booths, where viewers saw them sweat and grimace as they puzzled over their answers.

In the weeks it took for the successful contestants to reach the $64,000 "plateau," newspapers reported their least and silliest doings. CBS's ratings built to explosion points as the audience at home fantasized paying off the mortgage, affording a child's surgery or a better nose, or running off to Tahiti. NBC followed with its own big-money quiz, *Twenty-One*, in which scoring was based on blackjack, the casino card game. All these shows had the contestant choose whether to go on to the next level or collect his winnings and retire. The audience liked this part best—those in the studio cheering and shouting suggestions while those at home thrilled and sweated along with the contestants.

Then it came out that some contestants had been coached, that the ones favored were those most attractive to viewers—that is, best for the ratings. *Time* had hinted at this in the spring of 1957, but there was no pickup. In 1958, a contestant who felt shunted aside for a more telegenic one wrote CBS to complain but was brushed off. A year later, in 1959, the dam broke. A grand jury took testimony. A congressional committee held hearings.

Frank Hogan, Manhattan's district attorney, thundered that one hundred witnesses had lied. On CBS, it was testified, Patty Duke, the actress, had been fed questions by the producer's assistant, Shirley Bernstein (sister of Leonard, as all newspapers saw fit to note). Others were helped by fixing on their best areas as revealed in interviews, by repeating questions they had answered in audition quizzes, even by giving them time to study at home. Thus we had the shoemaker who knew opera, the navy officer who was a gourmet chef, the psychologist who knew prizefighting. All had been unfairly aided. All testified. All spoke to newspapers. All shattered faith and trust across the land—and in the houses of Congress.

The deepest disappointment, the worst loss of faith, was caused by Charles Van Doren, lecturer at Columbia University, scion of a distinguished family, skinny, boyish, nervous, endearing. He had become a hero climbing Fortune's ladder on *Twenty-One*, NBC's quiz show. His besweated brow as he squeezed his brain made millions of mothering hands reach out to the television set. And then it came out that he had known the answers all along, that he had only pretended to concentrate, to puzzle, even to sweat. *Time*'s cover story on Van Doren (February 11, 1957) was about the young Renaissance man who had set fire to the Nielsen ratings, about the boy and his family—the father, poet Mark; the mother, editor Dorothy; the uncle, biographer Carl. They learned from Clifton Fadiman and others about the little boy on the stairs in his pajamas listening to the talk of Sinclair Lewis, Franklin P. Adams, and Joseph Wood Krutch. *Time* hailed the American Century's reenthronement of the intellectual.

In November 1959, newly married, still such a figure of contemporary inconography that NBC had hired him at $50,000 a year as a "program consultant" to appear regularly on *Today* and utter capsules exhorting honest working people to pay heed to finer things, Van Doren came before Congressmen Oren Harris and confessed. Then it was the turn of Robert E. Kintner, president of NBC, who kept insisting that high-prize quiz programs were good entertainment and merely needed better rules, better enforced. Having started it all, CBS had canceled quiz shows before the hearings began and made the head of its network division walk the plank. Kintner, now alone, dug his hole deeper when, asked about enforcement at his network, he implied that it was the sponsor who should have done the enforcing.

Kintner had been president of NBC for less than two years. When he became president, not one NBC entertainment program was in Nielsen's top ten. He favored news from the beginning, both personally and to make news the engine to pull NBC back into contention, but it was not until after the quiz-show scandals that he started to pour all that money and all those people into NBC News in the way for which he would be remembered. It is not inconceivable that the congruent growth of news and the quiz-show scandals was coincidental. Everyone still around from those days—and not only those who were at NBC— insists and claims to document that the network news explosion of the late fifties and early sixties had been long planned.

Kintner was a schoolteacher's son from rural Pennsylvania who had been a major figure in Washington journalism during the New Deal. He came back from the war to the fledgling American Broadcasting Company. In time, he became president of ABC; then Edward J. Noble sold the network to Leonard Goldenson, and Goldenson fired Kintner. A month later, after the 1956 political conventions, David Sarnoff hired Kintner to be NBC executive vice president in charge of color coordination. Even though NBC's color programs were meant to help RCA sell color sets, Kintner had little interest in color television. The title was merely a parking spot. The General wanted him nearby for the inevitable day when he could no longer put up with Pat Weaver. As for Kintner, he said that after leaving ABC he had been wooed by both CBS and Hollywood, and had chosen Sarnoff's offer because of promises that had gone with it. He told a friend, "I don't take second-place jobs."

To us below, it was just another executive upheaval. In July 1958, Bob Kintner became my eighth NBC president. Sarnoff had reached the breaking point over Weaver's inability to make money while charting new paths in television, and he resented Weaver's heroic standing with the press.

After Weaver left NBC, he went to see William Paley at CBS, but Paley was having no free spirits today, thank you, so Weaver set out on his own. He never regained the influence he had enjoyed while at NBC, but his legacy is indelible. Morning television, for better or for worse, comes out of his insight that people would watch at those unlikely hours. There would have been morning television sooner or later, but he shaped it to the amiable nonfiction it now presents—all over the world. He did the same for the late evening, which became vaudeville's last stand, the last outpost of variety. His other contributions—the excitement of live television in *Wide, Wide World,* the glamour and surprise of upsetting announced schedules with "spectaculars" of great star value and lavish expense—soon lost their radiation and decayed into lead. But *Today* and *Tonight* set patterns now so universally accepted that few stop to think that they had to start somehow, and someone had to start them.

With Weaver gone, Kintner became executive vice president without modifiers. In the months before July 1958, when he became president and Bob Sarnoff became chairman, he steadily assumed control of the direction of the company; he worked it while Sarnoff saw to it that it worked. In February 1958, he was put in charge of all NBC television. *Variety,* the entertainment newspaper, which has an exaggerated reputation for clever headlines, expended its last memorable ones on these events as its banners rang the changes on PAT AND BOB and BOB AND PAT and BOB AND BOB. When Weaver left, the headline was PAT AND BOB BECOMES BOB & CO.—Kintner was never allowed to forget whose store he worked in as general manager. It irritated him; he felt hemmed in. He could be vocal about it with friends even though it was Bob Sarnoff who early in their relationship talked his puritanical father out of firing Kintner for being seen drunk.

His years at underprivileged ABC had taught Kintner how to program for maximum effect at minimum cost. He was good at cutting costs, and the way he saw television helped. He had little use for high-flown ideas of the future of television and its role in improving mankind. He canceled *Wide, Wide World* and almost all live drama. He saw that television entertainment was going to be mostly on film, and all this development of live TV machines and techniques, this coddling of technicians, could easily go. He set NBC's vaunted engineering development section, which recognized as its only rival RCA itself, on its long atrophy. Technical and financial executives brought from ABC ended practices like requisitioning favored technical directors, or even camera or sound or light technicians, which had been a tacit recognition of the creative contribution such people could make. A technician was a technician, to be ordered by how many you needed, not who.

Hollywood sold Kintner filmed series, some comedy and a great deal of what was known in the trade as action-adventure, meaning cops and cowboys, most of them from MCA, a very large talent rep-

resentation agency on its way to becoming as well a major movie and
TV producer. (The Department of Justice would soon force the two
functions to separate; the MCA bosses stayed with producing.) These
programs won NBC bigger audiences, which meant higher ratings,
translating directly to more income. This was fine with RCA, which
was always content for NBC to be number two, but wanted a better
number two than Weaver had achieved. To be number one entails
risk, and the factory managers and accountants who ran RCA did not
welcome risk in a business they would never understand. Their ideal
was an increasingly profitable number two, which is what Kintner gave
them.

It was Kintner who hired Van Doren as a consultant, imposing him
not only on *Today* but on me, for *Kaleidoscope*, a series that alternated
through the 1958–59 season with the notable *Omnibus*, which NBC
had won away from ABC. *Kaleidoscope* was supposed to be experimental, and planning meetings were full of aerated talk. Half the series
were to be produced by the entertainment department, half by the
news department. Bill McAndrew, who still had not learned to trust
other producers, wanted me to do the news programs in addition to
Huntley-Brinkley, which was going quite well by then, and the Sunday
program we did with Huntley because we liked to.

Since news was cheaper than entertainment, we got 40 percent of
the budget; and since entertainment took longer to do, we started first.
(With Davidson Taylor's help, we were always outvoted.) Huntley,
Sughrue, and Piers Anderton went to Berlin and in ten weeks we had
an hour-long study of East Germans who would board the elevated
trains, the S-Bahn, and because of the Occupation Statute ride un-
hindered to West Berlin. For East Germany it was a massive loss. We
showed doctors and engineers and teachers as they left the Communist
East for a different life. Our hour opened with the camera fixed on a
pedestrian tunnel whose walls were lined with tiles, which kicked back
spots of light. A man in an extra-long overcoat came into view carrying
a briefcase walking down that long tunnel, each step in his leather-
heeled cheap shoes echoing against the tiles. He climbed the stairs to
the platform, bought his ticket, and waited for the train to West Berlin
watched by two kinds of uniformed police. We called the program
The S-Bahn Stops at Freedom.

McAndrew called me in to tell me Kintner had decreed the series
would be "hosted" by Charles Van Doren. I had to edit some minutes
out of the now completed program to make room for him to introduce

Chet Huntley. It was insulting. "If anything, Huntley should be introducing him!" I said. McAndrew sighed, gave me that look, and said, "Just do it." So Van Doren "introduced" Huntley. Later that year, he "introduced" Bob McCormick's wrenching study of the movement to force American Indians off their reservations; Huntley's exploration of peaceful uses of atomic energy at Brookhaven Laboratories; our highly touted exposé of electronic eavesdropping that we called *The Big Ear*, and even the poetic, satiric travel essay by David Brinkley that was titled *Our Man in the Mediterranean*.

(During one of those prattling meetings we would have, a Tom Something from entertainment sputtered horror at "this . . . this . . . this . . . *newsman* doing a travelogue, for God's sake!" The day after it was on the air, he called burbling about what he chose to call "the 'Our Man' concept," and wanted to make plans for more.)

Those early years with Kintner emphasized news programs as never before, or since, on any network. There was money for reporters; there was money for documentaries; there was money for special programs. In his seven years as president, Kintner placed his stamp upon NBC as no one else in my four decades. And yet, like the rest of us, he just worked there. When that became unclear to him, it was time for him, too, to go. While he was there, however, the great weight of his presence was for more news, and news more prominently displayed. This resulted at least in part from his attachment to the trade he grew up in. Whatever the subsequent disclaimers, another motive, and not his alone, was to give the networks respectability at the time of not only the quiz-show scandals but specific complaints about disgusting programs and general ones about network cynicism and greed. Kintner's primary motive, however, was his need to fight CBS's enormous lead in entertainment, in audience, in income.

In a cover story, *Time* described Bob Kintner as five feet ten and a half inches tall. That must have been his press agent talking. The real Bob Kintner was dumpy, jowly, short-necked, thick-shouldered; his slitted pale blue eyes peering through heavy lenses; his well-tailored suit rumpled by 10:00 A.M.; white-shirted, bow-tied, patches of pale belly often visible between gaping shirt buttons; a vodka drinker, an alcoholic, a bully; brush-cut hair only slightly gray; a chain smoker with a low, grating voice; stubborn, impulsive, impatient, intolerant, deaf in one ear from a wartime injury, quick-witted, hard-driving, hard-working, and at least partly a genius. Subordinates, competitors, everybody in television, traded Kintner stories the way New York journalists of an earlier generation relished anecdotes about Charles Chapin, city editor of Pulitzer's *World*.

Although what he did for and with news gave him an enduring reputation, Kintner was a versatile executive. In his years at NBC, he suffered increasingly from cataracts, and it is not certain what he could see of the programs he ruled. But whatever its aesthetic merits, his entertainment programming revived NBC at a bad time, and his one-time juniors at NBC and ABC would years later recall him in awe as one of television's great salesmen. He was a skilled bureaucrat who knew how to change power patterns with the stroke of a pen. His first ukase was to have the head of NBC News report directly to him as president of NBC. No longer would Bill McAndrew, now a vice president, report to Davidson Taylor who reported to the executive vice president who was our channel to the top. No longer would it take four phone calls and two meetings to ask leave to interrupt a soap opera to give America the news that the sky had fallen. Taylor, not Kintner's type, was moved farther and farther aside, and finally out. News became a division, McAndrew a president. From complaining that our stuff never got airtime, we would soon be protesting we could not keep up.

Whatever Kintner's practical reasons for expanding NBC News, his obsession was to beat CBS, which he was intent on displacing as the television news exemplar. He lured away from CBS Irving Gitlin, an effective producer of strong documentaries who was chafing in Fred Friendly's shadow. Gitlin assembled some talented producers and inaugurated a series of attention-getting studies and exposés under the title, *NBC White Paper*. The press paid heed, which was part of the original purpose. Born under the Union Jack, I knew what a white paper was, and these weren't, but the term had a ring to it, so what the hell? In the years to come, I would use it myself.

Gitlin favored historical reviews, the U-2 affair, the death of Stalin, but he did come up with some disturbing studies of contemporary life. The earliest was on the civic bullying of welfare recipients in Newburgh, New York; a devastating look at how the needy are degraded. Gitlin's principal role, however, was holding the flank against CBS while Kintner developed his comprehensive campaign to make NBC News dominant, to condition the audience to turn to it whenever something big happened. In his single-mindedness and his dizzying intensity, we were never far from excess and sometimes he made us look silly. But the fact is he brought it off. For the very first time, NBC dominated broadcast news, and it lasted.

This is not to say that NBC had never before led with the amount or quality of news it presented, the money it spent, or the number of people it reached. But from the beginnings of Europe's slide toward World War II, CBS's coverage got more attention, especially from the press and from the kinds of people whose opinion in such things matters most. During the fortnight of the Munich crisis, for example, NBC had more and longer reports and special broadcasts from Europe, but CBS dominated the public consciousness, led by the clipped accents of the redoubtable H. V. Kaltenborn, simultaneously translating, reporting, and explaining. When I myself recall how as an undergraduate in Toronto I stayed glued to the radio for news of Munich, it is Kaltenborn's voice I hear. Kaltenborn was soon after enticed over to NBC, but by then, as the war raged in the skies over London, CBS had Murrow and his recruits—Shirer, Sevareid, Collingwood, LeSueur . . . the list goes on.

From then on, perhaps, CBS's reputation for news was earned for it by Edward R. Murrow. Certainly, when Weaver and other NBC executives bestirred themselves at all about news, it was Murrow they intended to "answer." But the perception was of longer standing than that and even antedates Murrow's radio dispatches from London. It may be that like so many puzzling phenomena of American corporations, it was rooted in the personalities of the founders. CBS's founder, William S. Paley, was born well-to-do, socially ambitious, a showman by instinct, who enjoyed news as well as the panache it gave him among people he wanted to impress. He enjoyed being seen about with Murrow, and actually named him to CBS's board of directors. One old CBS hand later recalled, "Paley thought of himself as a member of the old London gang."

David Sarnoff, who founded both RCA and NBC, was the classic immigrant boy, supporting a family while still a child, the self-taught engineer, the puritan who brought television to America but hired others to puzzle out what to put on it. Sarnoff was no less an ego than Paley. But while he believed broadcasting must provide news and never stinted in his support of it, he gratified his ego elsewhere. His greatest pride was the NBC Symphony, which he brought Arturo Toscanini, plucked from Italy just steps ahead of Mussolini's police, out of retirement to lead. It would not be the first instance of the idiosyncrasies of the founders of corporations affecting the actions of executives generations later. Whatever the reason, NBC was, and seemed willing to be, less important in news than CBS until Robert Kintner determined otherwise.

And yet, other than overburden us with attention and work, Kintner interfered little with what we did. He invited ideas but had few of his own; his concentration was on CBS, on beating CBS. This may have embarrassed us with colleagues, like having a parent with a foreign accent, but it worked. More important than the enjoyment he got out of a good fight was his unique awareness that being first was not an abstraction; it meant beating CBS.

When CBS News announced a new special program series, to be called *Eyewitness to History*, which would start life with eight special reports on President Eisenhower's trip to Europe, Kintner announced that NBC News would have *nine*. (Only then did he tell NBC News to do them.) Eisenhower's foray into personal, traveling diplomacy was the first of what was soon to become, for the presidency and for television, an institution, indeed a habit.

It had been a busy summer for me. Besides the news every night, *Outlook*, now renamed *Chet Huntley Reporting*, stayed on without the summer respite we would get in later years. In May, Bell & Howell, trying to be revolutionary, bought an hour special in prime time. McAndrew asked me to do it; it was so successful, Bell & Howell stayed in prime-time documentaries, but at ABC, where prices were lower. My group's big project that summer was two hours on emerging Africa—one in Rhodesia, about impatience; the other in Ghana, about a newly freed colony slipping off into indigenous dictatorship. Sughrue and Anderton went over to do them, and Huntley joined them in each country for a week.

Too Late for Reason, the one on southern Rhodesia, was scheduled for Labor Day weekend. We rushed to get it edited, scripted, recorded, and ready for broadcast so my family could get a promised week's vacation. We stayed at a motel on Long Island, at the very edge of the ocean beach. The weather was perfect, and we were together more than at any other time that year. We returned after dark one evening to find an urgent message to call Bill McAndrew at home. The two boys were in bed in our cabin, so I went outside, to the booth next to the light pole near the motel office. In the August night, moths and gnats and a menagerie of flying insects clustered and careened in that cone of light. I shut the door of the booth to keep them out; I opened it to get some air; I called McAndrew at home, gave him the number of the booth, and waited for him to call back. I was sweaty and itchy, and puzzled, and apprehensive.

Bill began by saying that "we" were short one of Kintner's announced special reports on Eisenhower's trip. His phrasing—that "we" were short—was clearly ominous, but I refused to accept that this was any business of mine. I had given over a couple of the Sunday programs to Eisenhower's journeyings and the rest of the nine were to be done by others. Why call me?

"Well, that Africa program, couldn't something be inserted to make it a report on the President's trip, or pretend to?"

"This is my vacation, Bill; I'm with my family."

"Oh, someone else in your group could trim a couple of minutes and you wouldn't have to come in."

"No, someone else could not; hour-long films are not made to be chopped from the bottom like wire service copy. Besides, Africa is not on Eisenhower's itinerary."

"Well, yes, but perhaps a minute to explain why he *isn't* going to Africa?"

It was like a nightmare. I stood in my shorts swatting bugs in an outdoor phone booth, arguing. I dug in. *Too Late for Reason* was broadcast as I had left it. McAndrew found Kintner his ninth report somewhere else, I do not recall where, but it was one more than CBS.

Not long afterward, Kintner got the head of Gulf Oil, Charles Whiteford, to go along with NBC for what we called "instant specials," which Gulf would agree to sponsor after only token prior discussion. Gulf Instant Specials, prime-time programs put together under forced draft to explain major news events that had broken upon the world a few hours before, were a useful and even exciting fixture for a decade, filling a major role in Kintner's campaign to push NBC News to some perceived "top"—dragging NBC behind it.

Naturally, the special would not displace an evening's most prof-itable program, but the one with the smallest audience, that night's stinker. Julian Goodman, who had come to New York to be Mc-Andrew's number two, would sit with an assistant at the ritual meeting when the new entertainment schedule was divulged to NBC executives, and they would try to pick the new season's leading targets to be bumped for Instant Specials. Over the years, Arthur Murray's dance program did well for us, as did something called *Klondike* and something else called *My Mother, the Car.*

The production unit set up to do Instant Specials was built around one of the best on-air reporters the medium has known, Frank McGee, and run by Chet Hagan, a solid producer. They were a hard-working group, always soliciting work, even when already doing something, because they were in fact free-lancers with no scheduled time to fill, never knowing when they would need to work around the clock or how long periods of total idleness would last. They got along perfectly with the people from Gulf and those from its advertising agency, not least because McGee's father had been an Oklahoma oil field worker, and when Gulf executives were in town and needing feting, McGee would dutifully attend and swap oil field yarns. Those close to him knew it was not something he did easily, but he was a good soldier. All this meant there was another producer McAndrew could trust and my load lightened, to which I had mixed reactions.

. . .

Roy Neal was our space expert, in addition to other duties. He had been a newscaster at NBC's Philadelphia affiliate when it was still owned by the Philco radio company and a frequent contributor to the *Camel News Caravan*. On slow days, you could count on him to get some scientist from Philadelphia's Fels Planetarium to explain something scientific, like a nuclear bomb's destructive range, with overlays on a New York City map with concentric circles centered roughly where I lived. In 1952, when the live network reached the West Coast, and the *News Caravan* needed its own editor, he was recruited as NBC News's first Los Angeles television bureau chief. He was a ham radio operator and a science buff, and a perfect candidate to report on space, although he did not know it yet.

American journalism first knew space exploration as grainy pictures of rockets blowing up on launching over the waters off Florida. The place was called Cape Canaveral, and the rocket was an Atlas. On vacation in Florida, I saw pictures in the *Miami Herald* of the second Atlas blowing up, which got almost no national notice. Certainly there was no film, no television coverage. Cape Canaveral was a military reservation, off-limits to newspeople. The newspaper pictures had been taken from the beach by photographers alerted by rumors and willing to wait days for something to happen. Back in New York, I called Neal, who called military friends, who leaked to him the frequencies being used, and, to the dismay of the accountants, I sent not only a reporter but a camera crew from California to Florida. They cruised the coastline eavesdropping and we had film of the next firing. And the one after that. We started reporting the story on *Huntley-Brinkley* and on *Outlook*, and Roy taught himself about space: the physics, the biology, the interservice rivalries.

On the last Sunday of 1958, we again begged an hour for a program we called *The Story of Atlas 10-B*. Until NBC followed CBS's profitable example of professional football Sunday afternoons, getting an hour on Sundays was still easy, usually needing only a phone call to McAndrew. Our hour was about the tenth rocket in the Atlas series. From a factory in southern California to its launching pad on the Atlantic coast of Florida, each Atlas rocket, still the most secret of projects, crossed the width of the United States. No closed vehicle was big enough, so it was chained on a flatbed truck and shrouded in what must have been the world's largest tarpaulin, its shape clearly outlined. The route was plotted to keep the Atlas from underpasses and overpasses too high or low to be negotiated, but there was no additional attempt to hide it from prying eyes, be they Russian, Chinese, or Roy Neal's. Finding out when the rocket was expected in Florida was easy, as was figuring out when it would have to leave California to get there. We placed three or four cameramen at obvious locations along the way to show it crossing the country.

The air force officers in charge at Cape Canaveral, and the civilians and officers from all three services trying to run a rocket program, were soon embarrassed by exposure of their attempts to hide failures from the public. Moreover, there had finally been some successes, and that may have helped. By that time, also, despite echoes of derision from CBS, we had rented a house as near to Cape Canaveral as we could get, and we were watching full time. The authorities finally bowed to the inevitable and invited Neal and his crew on the reservation for the launching of Atlas 10-B. Of course, everybody else was also invited, but we had the buildup, the journey, the sense of work in progress. In short, we had a story.

Soon there were Sputnik, and NASA, and John F. Kennedy promising to go to the moon. There was Mercury and Apollo and Shorty Powers and was solid fuel better than liquid fuel? Alan Shepard rode a capsule over the horizon; John Glenn became the first American in orbit; broadcasters talked about "hero-astronauts" and used words we would mock when spoken on Radio Moscow. Other than our regular news coverage, we handed space over to Hagan's group, to Frank McGee, who worked harder than anyone I ever knew learning his topic and became truly expert. Kintner, meanwhile, grabbed the space adventure as ideal for his plan. Gulf signed on without question. Most launchings meant hours and even days of delay, as McGee, in the rhythms of the King James Bible he had heard as a child in Oklahoma, explained and interviewed. Hagan presided over mobile units and assembled supporting casts, experts in weather, familiars with science, animaters who showed what was supposed to happen or was happening far from earthbound cameras. For the whole decade, the country got caught up in the adventure.

For space, Kintner demanded all-out coverage. Everything stopped at NBC, or almost everything. He himself would stay in his sixth-floor executive office day and night, along with Hagan in his fifth-floor control room and McGee in his little fifth-floor studio. Not only would Kintner stay in his office, sometimes for days, but he insisted other vice presidents and executive vice presidents and even division presidents stay with him. They had nothing to do, were not part of the coverage, but the boss wanted them there. One hapless executive, a man of considerable girth, who could not get from his office to the elevator without passing Kintner's door, which was always open during these interminable bouts of coverage, tried to creep past on hands and knees. It was his wedding anniversary, or child's birthday, or some such, and well into the evening. We had been on the air for hours, and he hoped Kintner was distracted by the pictures, or even napping. He was caught, a beached whale washed up in the corridor, red-faced and panting. Kintner acted solicitous, conscience-stricken, said it was okay to leave. Go ahead. But the poor man really had no alternative. He returned to his office for the night.

The amazing adventure of space—a dozen years from flaming rocket shards falling into the Atlantic to Neil Armstrong and Edwin Aldrin walking on the moon—was perfect for television because there were so many word-defying pictures. What words describing a rocket rising into the sky could possibly match seeing it yourself, even in two dimensions, in your living room? It captured national attention largely because the networks, with their broad reach and their endless hours, gave it national awareness. It had so many natural pauses for commercials. Above all, nobody was against space; it was *noncontroversial*.

Gerald Green, who had bullied me into television in 1950, liked to drift back to produce an occasional documentary in between novels and screenplays. He spent one afternoon in Chet Hagan's control room as all that sound and picture and energy swirled around him. He heard

McGee's careful phrases, polished as though written. He heard noises coming at him from all corners of the control room, radio from Ascension Island, telephone line from Mission Control, correspondents asking instructions, directors giving cues. He looked at all the pictures on all the monitors. Then he uttered the immortal words: "Space is for *goyim*."

But it was just another voice in Kintner's choir, and what Bob Kintner had wanted for his special needs as president of the company, McAndrew also sought as he tried to elevate the professional competence of NBC News. McAndrew had fought and schemed for years to build a professional department. Against him were arrayed the inertia of RCA, NBC's show business priorities, and the view of Pat Weaver's entourage that news was vaguely grubby. They favored enlightening the ignorant, explaining to the masses, seeking out the thoughts of the well-born or well-placed, and other high-end goods from the marketplace of ideas.

McAndrew aimed to recruit and develop and nurture reporters and editors who would put together news equal in value to news in other media, news done with the awareness of the special power that television, by its very nature, possessed. One of his most persistent campaigns was to have news presented by people with news credentials. No others would be tolerated; "presence," voice characteristics, even literary competence did not automatically earn one a place. Journalists only. This was a long, slow fight, especially with NBC's five owned television stations. In the early days, at all three companies, news on the owned stations was a responsibility of network news. NBC was the last to give up this system, although the marriage of the managements of the local stations and the news departments, like so many joined together too early, was being increasingly buffeted by their swiftly diverging interests. What a local station manager, responsible for his profit statement, wanted out of his anchormen was not what McAndrew looked for. That fight took several years to win.

Slowly a new NBC News took shape. The likes of Sander Vanocur and Frank McGee were hired. And, of course, Chet Huntley. Julian Goodman beefed up his Washington staff. Instead of Drew Middleton of *The New York Times*, whom Weaver had wanted, McAndrew hired Joseph C. Harsch of the *Christian Science Monitor*, who at least had some experience in radio and familiarity with broadcasting, and a voice that worked. He sent Harsch to London, for which Harsch, as reluctant as Br'er Rabbit thrown into the briar patch, extracted his price: the title Senior European Correspondent, no less. As a reward for Little Rock, John Chancellor became a foreign correspondent, first in Vienna, then in London to work for Harsch. Joe considered himself uniquely expert in European politics; he had studied a little in England as a young man and he was emphatically clubbable. After a while, Chancellor noted that fellow reporters were calling him "boy," going out of their way to drop it into conversation. It seems whenever someone offered a release to Harsch or suggested a story to him, he would say, "I'll send my boy around."

I was allowed to pick Chancellor's replacement in Chicago. The job was actually being the *Huntley-Brinkley* reporter from the Alleghenies to the Rockies and the Great Lakes to the Rio Grande, our only full-time staff outside New York and Washington. I interviewed and agonized, made at least one false start and had to explain to a disappointed reporter why I changed my mind, and finally settled on Vanocur, the Washington beginner who had been to the London School of Economics while working part-time for the *Manchester Guardian* and as a stringer for CBS radio. At first he would not be lured. He was Midwestern born and bred, and nothing ever happened in Chicago any more. Especially in politics, and he wanted to cover politics. I told him that in Chicago he would cover everything. He began to muse that his college roommate, Newton Minow, had become a lawyer in Adlai Stevenson's law firm. When he started talking like that, I knew I had him hooked. (Vanocur was lucky with roommates. His roommate at the London School of Economics had been Daniel Patrick Moynihan, who later worked for Governor W. Averell Harriman in Albany.) Sandy was well established in Chicago when Labor Day, 1958, rolled around and off he went to Little Rock, as Chancellor had the year before. There he was accepted into the fraternity of national reporters on the civil rights beat. He was adept at stories about the American pulse, and would go anywhere to do them. He set out to know everybody, and kept getting ever closer. He became the best political reporter I ever worked with.

So went McAndrew's war. I was one of his captains. Joe Meyers was another. Julian Goodman, in charge of Washington, was another, until Kintner ordered him to New York to be McAndrew's second in command and his own presumed heir, although none of us knew it at the time, perhaps not even he. To achieve his plan for NBC, Kintner took McAndrew and his news troops out of the shadows and put them in the van. He gave News money, airtime, and staff support, especially from press agents, writers of newspaper ads, and those who do "on-air promotion," those annoying ten- and twenty-second films extolling the merits of programs yet to be seen, the network's commercials for itself. As he had planned, when NBC News became famous, the entire network was launched on the road to recovery.

The argument is still unresolved between the academics and others who ascribe the expansion of news in those years to the need to repair the damage done by the quiz-show scandals and those, mostly exec-utives of the time, who claim that news was going to be expanded anyway. What the expansion of news stopped, whether by intent or not, was the undermining of network broadcasting itself. In a business subject to acts of Congress, what might otherwise have been only a damaged good name could have become a regulation limiting or even destroying the networks' ability to earn large amounts of money with relatively little work.

As for us helots in the fields, we did what we thought we were there to do, and we liked doing it. Civil rights was becoming more and more of a concern in the late fifties, which we covered often and variously, on the news each evening and in our little Sunday franchise. In February 1959, it was Atlanta's turn to face the crisis of school inte-gration. I sent the unshakable Bill Hill to put together a program of extra length. We tried not only to be balanced but to be sympathetic to people on both sides going through a difficult time. We called the program *The Second Agony of Atlanta*. Huntley and I worked out a conclusion in which he suggested that the National Association for the Advancement of Colored People (NAACP) itself might have be-come so inflammatory a symbol to some who might otherwise con-tribute constructively to solving the problem, it might help if it allowed other forces to carry the fight.

Boom! Bam! Smash! Phones ringing off hooks, switchboards lighting up like Christmas trees, and the other signs of vigorous public response. Roy Wilkins, head of the NAACP, and Henry Lee Moon, his chief public relations officer, called Huntley and McAndrew and me—and Kintner. McAndrew and I were in Kintner's office the next morning, my first time there. I learned then that he had no idea what I, or any producer, did. He ordered that the following Sunday's half hour be given over to Huntley mediating, live, a discussion between Wilkins and a Southern newspaper editor friendly to the White Citizens' Coun-cils. Wilkins said nothing surprising; the editor chewed over a lot of civilized-sounding statements about gradualism, the interests of children, and we all being people of goodwill. It was immediately for-gettable and soon forgotten.

What continued, however, was Kintner's ignorance of how things got done, what steps it took to translate his whims and instructions, the most challenging or the silliest, into something on television. With me in his office he wondered audibly why McAndrew had brought me. Producers, like me, were not among the elect that he cultivated. He had reporters and correspondents to his house, showed them off in public places, and ensured that their fame redounded. I would hear about such occasions, and it irritated me. Everybody likes to be invited when the boss has a party, and it was, to be honest, denigrating not to be included. There was, however, a positive side. If he had thought what I did was important, my attendance would have been required at the interminable meetings he held in his sixth-floor office, an-nouncing plans, cutting budgets, or just presiding over a dozen people staring at a television set. He may have been afraid of being lonely. The sessions ground on despite any other appointments or obligations that those in attendance might have. I could not have afforded to be at those meetings; my work involved getting specific television programs ready to be broadcast at a specific time, specific to the minute and second.

At his meetings Kintner spun his schemes. One was a year-end program to showcase our correspondents. News is scarce as a year ends. Legislatures are in recess; schools have shut; press agents are in the Caribbean. There are only disasters, natural and human, earthquakes and murders, train wrecks and mayhem. Worse than that, newspaper circulation is down so advertising goes down, and there are fewer pages for news, but still too many for the news there is. Out of this comes the institution in American journalism called "Ten Best." The ten best news stories are followed by the ten best movies, then the ten best athletes, which beget dozens of variations as each department fills its hole reporting not on yesterday and today but on the past twelve months, not philosophically but because there is nothing else to write about. True to form, broadcasting did it, too, without any understand-ing of how it began.

On New Year's Day, 1956, CBS News trundled out its biggest guns, with Murrow himself in the chair, and reviewed *Years of Crisis*, as civilization seemed rapidly going to hell and the West faced com-munism ineptly and poverty reigned and all that other stuff that was equally true in November. Murrow's group included at least one

Rhodes scholar, and the tone was spirited talk at the high table. The program won an Emmy for the year's "Best Coverage of a Newsworthy Event," the newsworthy event clearly being the discussion itself. CBS did it again the next year, and every year.

Then along came Kintner with his credo that anything they could do we could do better. As Christmas 1959 neared, the foreign bureaus of NBC News were emptied of reporters so they might be gathered in a New York studio to offer wisdom instead of news. The program ended with each telling us what would happen in the coming year. There were also parties around town, and, most important of all, a brilliant stroke, a luncheon in the main ballroom of the Waldorf-Astoria Hotel before the Foreign Policy Association to kick off its "big issue" for the year. Then off to half a dozen American cities to do the same in their biggest hotel ballrooms.

It was dramatically successful. Year after year, important people and powerful companies fought to buy tables and crowd the ballroom of the Waldorf or the New York Hilton. NBC's affiliated stations vied to have the itinerant troupe visit their cities, promising receptions at the very best country clubs, accommodations at the very best hotels, and social contact with the very best people. It was the kind of guided tour the mainland Chinese were at the time giving to Hungarian or Dutch television, who would then offer to sell us the film at exorbitant prices. My complaints to McAndrew that the foreign staff was for covering news not giving lectures got little attention. This was a big winner; ABC, and then CBS itself, started imitating us, pursuing big-name organizations to sponsor the Delphic wisdom of the network soothsayers. Every year since, in hotel dining rooms all over America, they still have these luncheons, tributes to Bob Kintner and how he did things.

7

Part of the Kintner legend was how he committed resources and energy to covering political conventions. True, by 1960, the crucial importance of live convention coverage to network news had ebbed a little. Television news was now not only accepted by the public but no longer the foster child inside the networks, its strengths not only in politics but in space coverage and in chasing Presidents around the earth. Millions watched the networks' evening newscasts seven days a week and their morning programs five. This was not enough for Kintner. What he wanted from NBC News was clear primacy in convention coverage, the perfect vehicle for his plan.

Conventions provided an arena where promotion could coax more people to watch than interest merited, and when three networks tried to do the same thing at the same time, it meant there had to be a winner and two losers. Such thinking was denounced by *Broadcasting*, the industry's trade paper and the particular voice of the station owners. Every four years the magazine called for a halt to what it saw as the networks' excessive live coverage. Station owners believed that convention coverage enriched only independent stations because it bored viewers, turning them away from the network affiliates with those endless hours of speeches and boilerplate resolutions thanking fire departments and caterers.

To Kintner, that was not the point, and history bears him out. To him, victory at conventions meant beating CBS. He would beat them in the news, in prestige, in ratings. Some independent's movie topping a night's numbers in one city would in no way dampen his belief that winning the conventions would bring NBC bigger audiences for its cop shows and its comedies. Bigger audiences do not simply mean bigger profits; they are how we keep score.

Kintner presided over NBC's political convention coverage only twice, in 1960 and 1964. It seemed like more, to us and to the world; he was that kind of figure. He persists in memory as the prime influence on convention coverage and how America saw its television. But although he gave this coverage priority over others in the company— their airtime, their budgets, their publicity—he had virtually no sense of what went into such coverage and he showed no interest in the months of planning that shaped it. On the other hand, he rarely demurred if we needed money, and he cozened and coddled and praised those of us who appeared on television. Not knowing what the others did, he ignored them.

When it came to the broadcast itself, Kintner would try to call the shots, but neither he nor (I finally understand) we appreciated how easy he was to ignore. The white phone would light, Bill McAndrew would pick it up, grunt into it a time or two, and hang up. "The boss wants . . ." he would say if it was early in the evening; later it became, "*He* wants . . ." Often it was easily done, would neither enhance nor distort, and I would do it. Or we were about to do it anyway. (The gravelly bark: "Let's see the floor reporters" . . . *click!*) Then it would become too much. McAndrew would turn to me and say, "He thinks this is going too long," and I would say, "Tell him to go fuck himself." McAndrew would pale, look away, and then, when the telephone rang again, he would say we were waiting for a commercial, or some other excuse, and that was it. Kintner would see something else he did not like, or have another idea, or merely try to show off for a visitor in his little cell of an office no more than ten yards from us, and the white phone would light up again.

"Signs," he would bark, "more signs . . . bigger signs . . ." In television they are called "supers" because lettering is superimposed over pictures; to Kintner they were "signs." He wanted identifications to be frequent and to stay up long. My rule was to identify someone on the screen only once, unless he talked for more than five minutes, and to keep identification on screen only five seconds. For Kintner, with his cataracts, this was not enough. At the 1960 Republican convention, he was once so insistent I gave up. On the podium was Dwight D. Eisenhower, still President, still hugely popular, the best-known living American face, but NBC News printed PRESIDENT EISENHOWER below his chin as he spoke to the convention. A friend from CBS called our control room to say, "You're kidding!"

Kintner was rarely in that control room, never when we were on the air. He was not at home in control rooms. He would sit in his cell chain-smoking, sipping vodka, watching three TV sets as NBC staff people from the law department or Washington would lure congressmen, commissioners, lobbyists, power peddlers, the practitioners and hangers-on who swarm at conventions, to come in their ones and twos to chat with him in his hideaway, or in the posh, well-stocked executive reception suite always a part of any network's convention work space. Licensed businesses have their imperatives.

We arrived in Los Angeles for the 1960 Democratic convention confident and feisty, a long way from 1956 but mostly the same people: Huntley, Brinkley, McAndrew, Sughrue, me. Again there were delegation reporters and floor reporters, Merrill Mueller and Herb Kaplow from 1956, along with Frank McGee and Martin Agronsky, a well-known journalist whom Kintner had enticed from ABC. Agronsky worked hard and had good contacts, but, like so many who had done well in radio, could not adapt to using pictures. For Agronsky, television was a place where people talked, he and others.

The day before the convention, he sought me out to boast about his treasured personal contacts, big shots and key players whom he had lined up to interview on the floor the next day.

"Martin," I said, "we're covering a breaking story. Those may not be the people we need. This isn't an interview show."

Upset and probably angry, he insisted I agree that the first name on his list, a governor, would inevitably be important as the convention began. I agreed, but told him to throw away the rest. He didn't approach me with the next day's list of names; either I talked him out of working that way or he did it more successfully, without telling me, with Eliot Frankel, my colleague of many years, who ran the floor reporters.

Agronsky hated machines. In 1960, technology could not yet give us more than two broadcasting frequencies for the floor reporters to use to talk to their editors, to talk to Eliot Frankel and his crew, as well as to broadcast over. We split the floor reporters into pairs, like the buddy system summer camps use for swimming safety. Each floor reporter had to be aware of what his buddy was doing, especially if his buddy was on the air. If he was, editorial chatter would go into the live coverage. It would be broadcast! Poor Martin had trouble adapting, and several times broke into someone else's broadcast. One time Eliot, goaded into losing his own discipline, shouted into millions of American homes, "Shut up, Agronsky!" (Martin later swore to me—"I swear to you, Reuv"—he was not on the floor at the time, but had drifted to the periphery for a morsel to eat. Faithfully wearing his headset, he had choked on his hot dog when Eliot's voice exploded in his ear.)

Sander Vanocur was not a floor reporter that year because he was the only reporter we had who knew the Kennedys well, and by convention time Senator John F. Kennedy was far and away the front-runner for the Democratic nomination. Sandy covered Kennedy because the previous fall he had called me to say there was nothing doing in Chicago and could he go to Wisconsin where the Massachusetts senator, whom he had not met, was going to test the waters for the primary the next spring. There he got to know the family, from the father and mother to the youngest brother, and it paid off in our coverage of the Wisconsin primary, Kennedy's first big step to the presidency.

New Hampshire had gone for Kennedy—and, less importantly, for Henry Cabot Lodge in the Republican vote—and we were doing well with our coverage, but Wisconsin became our story, and Vanocur did it. What else he did, of more interest to me, was put together a week's coverage for a Sunday half hour of *Chet Huntley Reporting*, a look at that growing institution, the primary, and, to a degree we could not know, a foretaste of the modern nominating process: energy wasted to the point of exhaustion, money to the point of nausea, the American political process showing again how well it caricatures itself.

Sandy and George Murray, a young film editor just promoted to director, wandered the entire length of the state with their camera crew, following now Kennedy and his tribe, now Hubert Humphrey and his band. There was a touching scene when Humphrey, at a factory gate with his teenage son in a freezing early morning, kept up the patter he was so good at but yet still could not suppress a father's concern: "How are you? . . . Good to see you. . . . We need your vote. . . . Stand in the doorway, Chip. . . . You need a President on your side. . . . The ordinary worker's side . . . Chip, get out of the wind. . . . I'm Senator Humphrey. . . . How are you? . . . Well, let's shake hands anyway. . . . Here, take this flyer. . . . Chip, let somebody else hand them out. . . . Put your gloves on, Chip. . . . My name is Humphrey. . . ." It was a telling image of American politics, but only we in the screening room could savor it. That same cold had slowed the camera and none of the sequence was usable.

The rest of the film was just fine. John F. Kennedy campaigning with his mother, two brothers, and three sisters; Robert as campaign manager and Edward, still in law school, handing out leaflets and doing chores. The women spoke and spoke, spoke together or each in her own little Wisconsin town, and when we got to screen the film it was wonderful how they were all saying the same thing. The voices were different and they looked different; they talked to different crowds in different places—auditoriums, suburban living rooms, Grange halls, rural parlors, classrooms—but what they said was exactly the same, wherever, to whomever. We intercut the film, not in the orderly way, ending each lady at the end of a thought, but one to the other in the middle of a sentence, once in the middle of a word. We used the Kennedy ladies several times this way, telling several stories from their well-rehearsed repertory, after which we showed a medium close-up of Hubert Humphrey, drained, alone in his campaign bus, saying, "I feel like a corner grocer fighting the A&P."

There was more to the half hour than that, of course. We had talk about Catholics and Protestants, of farms and cities; talk about Wisconsin's traditions, biographies of the two men, and all else that was usual. But we ended with the Kennedy ladies and the exhausted Humphrey. It was Vanocur's film, shaped by his command of the story and the people. And that is why he covered the Kennedys at the 1960 convention and was not a floor reporter.

We could afford more in 1960 than we had in 1956. Instead of the three-tiered control room, all three watching the same monitors, we could now afford two complete control rooms, at right angles: one for what was in the works, one for broadcast. McAndrew and I sat on a raised platform in the right angle, he with his phone to Kintner. Behind us, a glass wall sealed off a still higher deck, with upholstered chairs and a full refrigerator, where Julian Goodman was host to visiting big shots, mostly politicians but also some NBC and RCA executives too big to snub but in no way connected to what we were doing, who liked to watch the glamorous goings-on.

The most important device in that complex was the switch I pressed so I could speak into Huntley's or Brinkley's ear. What they heard was IFB, "interrupted feedback," the sound of the program as it was going out—"feedback"—which I could "interrupt" so I could speak to them. At first they used a simple earphone, then graduated to a molded device like a hearing aid, known as a Telex, after the company that makes it. By instructing them, I controlled the program. I told them where to send it next: to a floor reporter, a remote location, a news bulletin from New York, a commercial.

The program director, whose back was to me, was geared to hear what I said to Chet and David in the booth, and could ready his next pictures without my telling him directly. Every step we took had its preliminaries, choosing what to do next, the floor offering stories and we asking about rumors, chatter between control and remote units all over the city. Then the decision to do something or not to do something else, but nothing could happen until I pressed the key and told Chet or David where to send us next.

It was miraculous, the ultimate extension of Sughrue's dictum, "Communication is control." I ran the entire live coverage—six hundred NBC journalists and technicians, content, pace, flow—by no more than a word to Huntley or a word to Brinkley. (It helped that they trusted me.) In 1960, I had only one key and spoke to both of them at the same time, so Brinkley as he spoke would hear me tell Huntley to go to the floor, or a commercial, and Huntley would have to try to ignore my voice when I was talking to Brinkley. In later years, I could press "H" or "B" or "BOTH." Progress!

On the first day of the first convention, the first time we used the system, I asked for a lead to a commercial and they were taking forever to get to it while an NBC Sales vice president was reminding me for the third or fourth time how long it had been since we showed one, and I asked again without results and perhaps yet again, and I raised my voice into that little microphone, saying something unforgivable like, "Commercial, dammit!" They gave me my introduction to a commercial. After the session, quietly, casually, separately, both Chet and David sought me out to suggest that, busy though things were, I should try to remember that the little thing was inside their very heads and shouting into it was not helpful.

My little press-to-talk key to the anchors became an important part of television. It soon seemed as if every producer was controlling live programs this way, and, in time, it was also used in all programs where live and prepared elements are mixed, such as any regular news program. It became too common to merit notice, but so far as I can ascertain, I was the first to do it this way. Indeed, I knew, as the world knew, that Walter Cronkite insisted his cues be written on little cards by an assistant sitting at his feet, out of camera range, who passed on instructions from the control room, and that sometimes Walter heeded these written cues and sometimes he didn't. Cronkite's refusal to wear an IFB, in fact, was a contributing factor to the rise of Huntley and Brinkley.

The movie *Broadcast News* had, despite a silly story, the most authentic feel and structural interplay of television news that I have seen done by outsiders. In it, a bright, driven woman producer speaks into the IFB of the slow-witted, good-looking anchorman. The sequence is scripted to imply the man must be a boob because he needs instructions in his ear to know what to do next. This is unfair to many intelligent, experienced journalists—some of them even good-looking—who can without losing their places or contorting their faces hear from inside their heads that a picture they expected would not arrive or the order of items was being reversed or a foreign leader had been killed, things not known when they had sat down in front of the unbearable lights and hooked themselves by microphone to the world and by IFB to their only source of unexpected information.

The insatiable Kintner provided extra opportunities for Huntley and Brinkley, and all the others, to wear theirs. He had us doing special news programs almost daily beginning the week before the Democratic convention. Convention week was no different; every day but one we produced a major program in addition to covering the sessions. While Huntley and Brinkley sat (for the first time) in a booth above the hall, in a studio on the ground floor we interviewed panjandrums, gave summaries, and generally fed Kintner's insistence that we go on the air earlier than CBS and stay on later, and keep it going, keep it going, keep it going. Vanocur and Edwin Newman presided in the ground-floor studio when the convention was not in session, interviewing, anchoring, summarizing. If Vanocur was out after Kennedy, Newman sat alone, or Mueller or Richard Harkness or one of the others might be drafted to join him. Kintner had us broadcasting so often it felt as if everybody was on the air all the time.

The 1960 Democratic Convention opened in the Los Angeles Sports Arena on July 11. It was the first time a sitting President was barred by the Constitution from succeeding himself, and only the fifth time in the century that neither party would nominate an incumbent. The primaries had built up some anticipation, but the television camera's infatuation with Jack Kennedy had built up more.

As for Richard Nixon, the vice president, the almost certain Republican nominee, even in 1960 he was someone few Americans felt neutral about. In his party, he was the chosen leader of those self-made Sunbelt rich who were preparing to preempt the Midwestern isolationism of the Taft tradition and after that do battle with the Northeastern nobility, the ones who had nominated Eisenhower. To the Democrats, he meant the "Checkers" speech, the gutting of Helen Gahagan Douglas, and insinuations that their entire party was soft on Red Russian Soviet communism. The question Nixon faced was whether any limelight would be left for him, with the handsome young Democrat fighting his party's entrenched establishment with the prospective added spice of a nasty American fight about his Catholicism. But Nixon and the Republicans were not completely shut out of the public eye. Rockefeller decided to pick a fight with him, and that kept his face and his positions on television for a few extra exposures.

The Democratic primaries did not become a Kennedy bandwagon until after West Virginia, when he proved he could get the votes of fundamentalist Protestants, and forced Hubert Humphrey, his principal rival, out of the race. By the time they ended, in June, his opponents had little to claim except that he and party chairman Paul Butler were rigging the convention.

Then, the week before the Democratic Convention, we began that parade of special television coverage. On Saturday, July 2, Harry Truman was on all three networks supporting the charge of a rigged convention, insultingly suggesting that the young Kennedy let "someone with greater maturity" have the nomination. The next day: Rockefeller attacked Nixon's stands on the "burning issues"; Dr. W. A. Criswell of Dallas's huge First Baptist Church said in his sermon that Kennedy's election would mean the "death of religious liberty" in the United States; and Kennedy himself demanded the networks broadcast on live television the press conference he scheduled to reply to Truman.

CBS said it would cover Kennedy's press conference only as a news event, excerpting it in newscasts. Not Kintner. NBC went all out; the press conference would be covered live at 4:30 P.M. Monday, the

Fourth of July, a time and day when there was almost no audience to lose. But it was great for publicity, especially in newspapers, which may have been why CBS changed its mind and also carried the press conference live. By that time, NBC had captured the kudos. Jack Gould in the *Times* credited Kintner with "shaming" all of television into putting news before gain.

Lyndon Johnson announced his candidacy from his Senate office at 1:00 P.M. the next day, and Kintner carried it live. He added a special convention news program at 4:30, and again at the same time the next afternoon. By July 7, it had a series title, *Convention Preview*, and a better airtime, 7:30 P.M. While all this was going on, the Republicans managed to keep in the news. On July 8, President Eisenhower disputed Rockefeller's charge that America's defenses were lagging; Stevenson flirted with allowing his candidacy; and George Meany mobilized the AFL-CIO to oppose any place on the ticket for Johnson. Mutual of Omaha refused to share in sponsoring NBC's coverage unless Bob Considine, a Hearst columnist and sometime broadcaster, was included in our reporting team. Kintner refused. Mutual of Omaha went to ABC. By convention eve, Sunday night, we had broadcast dozens of hours. Newspapers speculated Rockefeller could not support Nixon because of what he had said about defense; Nixon sent the Republican platform committee chairman, Governor Charles Percy of Illinois, to reason with Rockefeller.

Whether the people watching at home responded to the accelerating tempo, or even noticed it, is one of those questions no one dares ask. A convention is a sealed world; the group covering a convention for any network a society unto itself. We were hardly even aware that there were other programs on our own network as we jumped in and out of the schedule with interruptions and bulletins. It was like living in a submarine. At every convention I had to restrain producers and directors from breaking into the network schedule with a tidbit of virtually meaningless news. Not only had we all become expert in the tiniest minutiae of political maneuvering, we thought everyone in the country should be. There were, even with these strictures, bulletins enough before the conventions began and when they were not in session. When the gavel sounded we were ready.

The day before the first convention began, Sughrue withdrew from the coverage organization. Newly married, he had been arguing with McAndrew about money, and lost. He stayed on the NBC News staff for several years doing occasional special programs, then left to do independent production. Thus, the night before the first gavel, I lost my co-designer and principal assistant, and I was not sure how it would work. Another director sat in for Sughrue; old friends and colleagues gathered round; what Sughrue would have done besides the actual directing fell to me.

Talk about hitting the ground running! By the time of that opening gavel, 8:15 that evening, Kennedy's nomination was a certainty, but the floor men and the other reporters kept the story boiling. Governor Pat Brown of California, the host state, declared for Kennedy early but could not get his Stevenson-loving delegates to follow, an excruciating embarrassment. When Stevenson arrived in the hall, the galleries erupted in the most spontaneous display of the week. Brown, frustrated and furious, demanded to know who had distributed the gallery tickets and to whom. There it was: All live! All on television! All before your very eyes!

On Tuesday, the convention's second day, Kintner ordered us on the air at 6:00 P.M. Eastern time. Our special program at noon had shown Johnson "inviting" Kennedy to debate him before a joint meeting of the Texas and Massachusetts delegations; at 2:05 we had a bulletin reporting that Kennedy had accepted; at 6:00—three o'clock in Los Angeles—the debate took place. It turned out to be a pretty mild affair. The knowledgeable politicians understood that Kennedy could no longer be stopped, and even Democrats stop fighting under those circumstances. On Wednesday, the convention nominated Kennedy on the first ballot. He beat Johnson by about two to one; no others came close. During the balloting, Vanocur asked me if I had a spare mobile unit. Somehow or other, I managed to "spare" one and sent it where Vanocur told me to. At 1:58 A.M., Eastern time, Governor LeRoy Collins of Florida, the convention chairman, announced that John Kennedy's nomination had been made unanimous. At 1:59, the band was playing "Anchors Aweigh" with everybody joining in whether or not they knew the words; Brinkley was saying that vice presidential possibilities had been summoned to Kennedy's "hideaway" somewhere in Los Angeles. At 2:00, we switched to the "hideaway" where Vanocur was standing in the street waiting for the candidate to come out. That was where he had told me to send the mobile unit, an address in downtown Los Angeles where the comedian Jack Haley had an apartment, which the Kennedy entourage had borrowed. Vanocur had learned where it was from the candidate's father. No one else had the picture. Hardly a landmark of American journalism, a reporter standing outside a building in the dark, but it drove CBS nuts. At 2:06 A.M., we showed Kennedy himself coming out into the street.

The only news Thursday was a bulletin that Kennedy had picked Johnson as his running mate. When we went on the air less than an hour later, we began with a taped summary of the day. The tape was edited in NBC's main California installation, in Burbank, where all the monitors we had in our control room were duplicated for recording everything on tape as needed. Television tape was still rather new. Few people knew how to use it, but one of them was Roy Neal, our expert on space, ham radio operator, and dabbler in electronics, who had taught himself the new skill. I had asked Neal to work as the producer sitting in Burbank editing tape.

In those early days, tape was far different from what ordinary citizens can now buy in drugstores. For the price of one of those early machines you could have bought the drugstore. Each was larger than a full-sized upright piano. The tape itself was two inches wide, the reel that held an hour of picture was more than a foot in diameter and very heavy. The picture-recording system was not yet something called "high-band" (a term I do not understand). So copying tape to tape noticeably degenerated the quality of the picture after a couple of generations; editing had to be physical, cutting it apart as though it were film, even though the eye could not see the picture. Modern editing methods, which apply the complex and creative processes of editing film to videotape by copying it in bits and stages from one tape to another to another, had to wait for devices not yet imagined. To edit the two-inch tape of those days required, first, painting along its edge with a liquid of suspended metal filings; the magnetism of the tape arranged these filings into striations marking each frame of picture; cuts were made only along these frame lines, the last known legal use of single-edged razor blades; two cuts of tape were spliced by a special metallic adhesive tape. Each splice took ten minutes.

At first, and for some time, we used tape to record and play back what we recorded. Only occasionally would we edit an important speech by excerpting one or two or at most three quotations and joining them. It was too difficult, too slow, to edit that wide tape as we had edited film, nor had we time to develop the steps, condition the reflexes, formalize the sociology, evolve the lore and the esprit to turn a mechanical function into a craft. But the day Kennedy put Johnson on his ticket, Neal and his editors assembled a drama. Knowing how it ended did not diminish the excitement.

The day's principal activity had been people moving up and down stairs between two floors of the Biltmore Hotel, between the seventh-floor suite where Johnson had his personal headquarters and the eighth-floor suite that was Kennedy's. One NBC reporter had stood at the top of the stairs, another at the bottom, neither aware of the other as he cornered politicians going in and out of doors. We captured the dance of politics on that stairway; grim, happy, talking, silent, Mid-westerners, Southerners, union bosses, city bosses, famous, obscure, but men only, political power on parade. From this raw material Neal fashioned that evening's opening, the process and interplay to a result already announced, Lyndon Johnson. He showed border state governors calling on Johnson; Kennedy going in person to the Johnson suite; Rayburn up and down; Bobby grim-faced. Governor David Lawrence of Pennsylvania, an organized labor state that had been crucial to Kennedy's nomination, joined Johnson and Kennedy in Johnson's suite. Before he entered, a shouted question:

"What's going on, Governor?"

"That's what I'm going in to find out."

Kennedy emerged and was vague. He said Johnson liked being Senate majority leader. Up to the eighth floor. Walter Reuther, president of the United Automobile Workers. Organized labor had openly declared its opposition to Johnson, but Reuther ducked questions. Fleetingly seen, Sam Rayburn, later identified as the one who talked Johnson into accepting. (He had told Mrs. Johnson that vice president was an easier job than Senate majority leader, and Lyndon had already had one heart attack.) Senator Henry "Scoop" Jackson of Washington, who had hoped to be the running mate, came out smiling, the good soldier denying rumors. Then the announcement, the two candidates posing for cameras arm in arm. Roy Neal had given us bits of picture and sound assembled into a story that kept its suspense.

Friday's last session, in the open air at the Los Angeles Coliseum, was an anticlimax and the audience was disappointing, but we had proved our point. In high spirits, we went on to Chicago and the Republican convention. Waiting for us at check-in were notes saying that our audiences had been greater than the other two networks' combined. Of 167 million Americans who watched at least part of the Democrats' week on any network, more than half watched us. Newspaper writers unanimously praised the Huntley-Brinkley style and approach, the floor reporters and our reporting system, what we did and the way we did it. "There came to an end something of an era," Jack Gould intoned in his pulpit at *The New York Times*. Kintner bought full-page ads.

CBS charged into Chicago determined to recover the primacy they had always accepted as divinely granted. They seemed to think the best way was more live television mobile units. They sent out a call for as many as could be corralled. But not all local stations owned mobile units, and those that did were usually reluctant to send them far distances. Mobile units were still things stations bragged of owning, and they wanted them available in case of a boastable major disaster. But in Chicago's streets that last week of July I recall seeing units from as far away as Oregon and Arizona. According to *Time* magazine, CBS that week "offered reporters bonuses for scoops."

On the Friday night before the convention, in an atmosphere of conspiratorial secrecy, Nixon flew to New York to see Rockefeller in his Fifth Avenue apartment. They met until 3:30 A.M. Saturday. Rockefeller presented Nixon with fourteen points and Nixon agreed to them. It became the lead in the newspapers on Sunday, the day before the Republican convention. The papers called it the Treaty of Fifth Avenue. Senator Barry Goldwater called it "Munich."

The Republicans had scheduled a Monday morning session so that any unseemly fights would not be fought on prime-time television. In fact, nothing happened, and our coverage was gladly interrupted to show the Nixons arriving at O'Hare Airport. Six NBC reporters were at the airport for the arrival, and ours was the smallest network contingent! Nixon's scheduled progress would take him from O'Hare by helicopter to Meigs Airport in downtown Chicago then by car to the Blackstone Hotel where he would stay. Charlie Jones, younger of the Jones twins, now a director in the Washington bureau, who had been drafted into Sughrue's job, insisted I give him enough mobile units to match what CBS was throwing against him. (Directors think like that.) I asked him if we had enough cameras so that when one lost Nixon the next would pick him up. Yes, we had. Then, I said, he had enough.

But this was war, mean and bitter and to the finish. Nixon may have been sure of the Republican nomination, but the struggle between NBC and CBS was still to be decided. The CBS publicity brigade got on their phones to everyone they knew. They coaxed Gould into making an exception in his parade of paeans for Huntley and Brinkley to say that CBS had better close-ups of Nixon. Kintner launched his counterattack. NBC press agents, in their turn, pointed out to the newspaper writers that ours was the only moving, wireless camera in the procession. Neither had anything to do with news—of the convention or anything else.

When Eisenhower arrived in Chicago on Tuesday, both networks repeated Monday's script—both the television coverage and the squabbling in the newspapers. With Kintner as our leader, we ate up more television time than anybody. At noon Eastern time, Newman appeared on the network with a bulletin: Eisenhower's plane was held up by fog. He was now expected in two hours. At 12:08, for five more minutes, another interruption, repeating that Eisenhower would be late and filling out the time with tape of a Rockefeller interview saying all was healed between him and Nixon, and he would second Nixon's nomination. At two, finally, Eisenhower. His progress was shown step by step through the streets of Chicago, which had proclaimed Tuesday, July 26, 1960, Thank You, Ike Day, and the mayor had asked the city to turn out and cheer. Hundreds of thousands lined the streets. It was like some medieval monarch's joyous entry.

At 3:30 we finished with Eisenhower. At 5:00, we were back with Rockefeller. He said Nixon would have New York's ninety-six votes. Wednesday morning, covered live, Eisenhower gave a breakfast for friends. He said his philosophy was the middle is always best. He thanked all who had worked with him in his presidency, many of whom were in the room. Impatiently, we cut to the Sheraton Towers, to the New York delegation. Nixon had come to thank them in person. Rockefeller met him at the door, wearing his patented grin and a "Nixon" button the size of a human head. They entered arm in arm. The delegates rose and applauded. Nixon and Rockefeller waved. Brinkley said, "If that isn't love, it'll have to do until the real thing comes along." For me, it was one of the week's two best moments.

The other came from the convention floor, during that night's session, after the convention was declared open for nominations.

"A - la - ba - ma!"

The roll call took an hour, from Alabama yielding to Oregon, so its governor, Mark Hatfield, could nominate Nixon in 288 words, through seconding speeches and demonstrations and pictures and interviews of the Nixon family, to the next state, Arizona. Governor Paul Fannin of Arizona nominated Senator Barry Goldwater. The aisles exploded in a spontaneous and very noisy demonstration. Frank McGee fought his way through the tumult to the Goldwater family box, one of the VIP boxes forming an arc around the floor but unusually high above it. McGee interviewed Mrs. Barry Goldwater, Peggy, and then their daughter, also Peggy. It was young Peggy's sixteenth birthday. Questions and answers were what they always are at such times, about how it feels, about family, lots of thank yous. The image locked in my mind is of McGee holding his microphone up the full length of his arm, young Peggy Goldwater bent almost double over the railing of the VIP box to talk into it, and Frank saying to Peggy, "Bless your heart, you're crying into my eyes."

Write me that in your newspaper.

Goldwater took the podium to withdraw in a famous speech, fore-shadowing 1964, and the post-1964 history of both the Republican party and the United States. "We've had our chance," he said, "we've fought our battle. Now let's put our shoulders to the wheel. . . . Let's grow up, conservatives. Let's, if we want to take this party back—and I think we can someday—let's get to work." The next day, Nixon announced his running mate, the ambassador to the United Nations and the former senator from Massachusetts, Henry Cabot Lodge.

Earlier in the day I had sent an assistant to downtown Chicago to buy a recording—instrumental, not vocal—of Romberg's "Stout-hearted Men" while my secretary compiled a list of credits to include everybody—producers, cameramen, gofers, directors, sound engineers and unit managers, secretaries and even vice presidents, everybody who had not been seen on the air during all those days and weeks. At 11:23 P.M. Central time, Friday, July 29, we rolled credits. They took three minutes, music swelling and fading, names rising through the picture in solemn array. I have never felt quite like that again.

> "Start me with ten who are stout-hearted men,
> And I'll soon give you ten thousand more . . ."

The next issue of *Broadcasting* wrote: "One of the biggest surprises of the Democratic and Republican conventions was NBC-TV's runaway sweep of audience and critical acclaim. To NBC News the biggest surprise was that everyone was surprised."

After Labor Day, my wife and I were on vacation in Europe. We spent time in Copenhagen with Chancellor and his family, whom he would not move to Moscow until the Soviet Foreign Ministry supplied him with a decent apartment. I was also in Moscow with Chancellor for a weekend. During a drive in the country, I asked him if, after missing the conventions, he would like to work election night. He would. I said I would see what could be done. He could help solve problems I expected to have. Besides, he and I went back a long way.

We met again in Studio 8-H, where I had been on the Tuesday after the first Monday of November every even-numbered year since 1950. Studio 8-H, where Toscanini used to conduct the NBC Symphony Orchestra, was once described by a magazine reporter as a huge cavity inside a midtown skyscraper. It was here that we set up for coverage of the 1960 election night, and nine election nights thereafter. The plan started with a deck extending over the floor, where Huntley and Brinkley sat, which that same reporter described as a huge pie plate. On it the laconic Hjalmar Hermanson had put the X-shaped desk. (A second reporter uncharitably described Hermanson's desk as two joined boomerangs.)

One floor below the Huntley and Brinkley deck was the working level, with editors and enumerators, messengers and pontificators, secretaries and vice presidents, the disciplined tumult of a network election night. Along the walls we put four bays of numbers. Here were posted, by state, the vote for President, senators, congressmen, and governors. Standing in front of the numbers, on platforms that were more like shelves, reporting the returns by region, were Vanocur for the Northeast, Chancellor the Midwest, McGee the South, and Mueller the West. There was the usual disagreement about what states are South or Southwest or West, and the usual arbitrary answers.

Kennedy was doing quite well when we went on the air, and he seemed on the way to an easy victory. Then, all night long, as the vote total swelled, his margin shrank. He never lost the lead, but the sure thing became a probable and then a possible. We stayed on in 8-H all that night and well into Wednesday. It was, finally, the closest presidential election of this century. From a location in the New York financial district, one of our reporters relayed the latest from an RCA computer that, like the returns themselves, had started the evening projecting a fat lead for Kennedy in both popular and electoral votes, then spent the rest of the night narrowing it.

I don't like election nights. I do not find them exciting, and I don't like producing them. Jimmy Breslin once called All the President's Men a movie about typing; election night is a TV show about adding. At best, the votes not yet counted have already been cast; the result is definite, except we still don't know it. We pretend all night that the result can change, but it can't. To escape monotony, producers rely too much on mobile unit pictures of a toothaching sameness: political headquarters where a band is playing, freeloaders freeloading, and the happy ones looking like the sad ones. The urge to use pointless gimmicks is irresistible. One of the best reporters I know talked the powers that be into letting him do election night from a neighborhood bar, patronizingly judged not only colorful but the locus of the American heartbeat. It was one more incarnation of Walter Cronkite's silly idea of the average man. Computers and survey techniques make it worse, not because they are unreliable but because they are *too* reliable. Soon they will never be wrong. I enjoy politics, and politics pays off on election night. I was in Times Square in the crisp November air of election night, 1940, with 100,000 other people watching Roosevelt gradually defeat Willkie in the electric letters circling the *Times* building, and it is a cherished memory. All those undergraduate years, and later in the army, and when I was a reporter, it was a luxury the next weekend to masticate at leisure the analyses in the Sunday paper, how farmers were the margin here, or why wall-eyed Ruthenians there confounded the experts. Now we told them on Tuesday night what once they had to wait days for, telling it better and more accurately, leaching out all suspense or romance or interest.

The evening wore on, and we were good. Everybody said we were good. We had everything, usually first. The way we showed it was easy to follow, and we were interesting, or as interesting as we could be. There was no time for style, little to be witty about, but Brinkley greeted Kennedy's lead in suburban Connecticut as refuting the tendency of Americans to vote Republican "as soon as they can afford a power mower." That was also the first night—of many—that he said our computer had had "its 2:00 A.M. feeding." Nor had we time to watch the other fellows. Later we learned CBS had gone all out, with every recognizable name except Ed Murrow's. (The press was told he had a cold. One account speculated that he was tired of having received, at both conventions, what it called the "you-be-Brinkley treatment." Perhaps, at long last, we no longer needed to look for "NBC's answer to Murrow.")

That it was a cliffhanger of an election night helped keep people interested—again, as many watching what we did as the other two combined—for much of that long, long night. We showed numbers and more numbers, then, after 3:00 in the morning, we showed Nixon saying that if trends continued Kennedy would be president, and he would wish him well, but things might change; then Kennedy's press chief, Pierre Salinger, saying the senator would not respond to what was not a concession. An hour later, Nixon's running mate, Lodge, repeating by rote, if trends continued. . . . Meanwhile on the boards around 8-H, the race grew closer instead of moving to a decision. At 4:30, when Kennedy needed one more electoral vote, Salinger was shown saying there would be no statement before 10:00 A.M. His lead in the total popular vote dropped below 800,000, then below 700,000.

Dawn.

Kintner, who had sent his troops into 8-H with a hubristic harangue about the race being not between Nixon and Kennedy but between CBS and NBC, now had something real to worry about. The six clients who had bought advertising in our election night program were entitled to so many commercials an hour until a President had been elected and our program was off the air. They paid the same whether the program ended at one o'clock or three or never, guaranteed a firm number of seconds every hour we were on the air. *Today* was due to start at seven o'clock, with its own commercials, its own sponsors, its own imperative to make a little money for the company. But if there was as yet no President, the election night program could not go off the air, repeating those other commercials yet once again for no additional income, while each unbroadcast *Today* commercial meant a specific loss of revenue. Word came down to declare a winner and get off the air. *Today* was waiting.

At 7:00, Dave Garroway joined Huntley and Brinkley on the deck, but it was still the election night program, not yet *Today*. Dave asked Chet what was going on. Chet told him. Then David told him. McGee and Chancellor, Mueller and Vanocur told him. Finally, at 7:20, the "concession desk" said Kennedy had won California, and Huntley said Kennedy having California was President-elect. Election night could go off the air and *Today*, with three quarters of its commercials intact, could take over. But Kennedy had not won California; Nixon had.

The race in Califiornia was very close. All that long night of counting Kennedy never had more than a small lead, but he led all night. At 7:20 A.M., when we declared the state for him, he still had a small lead, too small for a professional statistician to give him the state. I do not know who got them to do it—or how. Nixon got a majority of the absentee ballots, and that finally gave him the state. But we did not know that until eight days later. It left Kennedy with three hundred electoral college votes, enough to elect him, and a razor-thin margin in the popular vote. Our declaring California for Kennedy made no difference as far as the election went, but it did save most of the *Today* commercials.

While *Today* moved into the studio until 9:00, I sent Chet and David to bed; they had the news to do that night. The four bay reporters would take over their deck a half hour at a time in rotation, for bulletins or updates, resting in between. I and the others in the control room merely stayed on. Since in those days there was no network service to the Eastern time zone from 9:00 A.M. to 10:00 A.M., even we could relax, free until ten. I walked the halls, had coffee, went to the barbershop in the RCA building arcade. The barber's menu board advertised a facial massage. I had never had one, but now it seemed a good idea. Perhaps it would keep me awake.

Mueller came on at 10:00 with more returns; Chancellor at 10:30. From Hyannis Port, Ray Scherer reported Kennedy would say nothing until Nixon did. McGee at 11:00; Vanocur at 11:30. At 12:45, Herb Klein read Nixon's concession telegram. Kaplow was on the scene in California, Chancellor on the deck in 8-H, where he would stay. At 1:00 P.M., back to Chancellor. Now, surely, Kennedy would speak, and we could go home. Now, finally, he would come out of the house in Hyannis Port and go to the armory in Hyannis, as had been the plan for days. It was all anticlimax from here on, but we could not leave; the show was not over. Chancellor was talking, and nothing was happening in Cape Cod. Worse than that, the television monitor on the deck, the one that would show Chancellor what to talk about, broke down. He read wire copy and information from our own news wire. We showed tape of the Kennedys riding horses that morning. None would speak to the reporters.

When live pictures finally started coming through from Hyannis Port, Chancellor could not see them on his broken monitor, and besides, he had never been there. He had been in Moscow until the last weeks of the campaign, after which he caught up as well as he could. I could talk into the IFB in Chancellor's ear, but I, too, had never been to Hyannis Port, not as a journalist.

At that moment, by sheer luck, Vanocur showed up in the control room. He could not sleep with all this going on, and he knew Hyannisport well. I drafted him to stand beside me. He would tell me what we were seeing, and I would tell Chancellor in his ear what we were seeing—that is, what the audience was seeing but he couldn't because of his broken monitor. We started with scenic shots of the family compound, Jack's house, Bobby's house, the main house; then Scherer on the scene with Hyannis high school kids waiting, the President-elect in his white Lincoln, out of the car, shaking hands; photographers yelling for pictures, the victor, his wife, his father, his mother, his brothers, his sisters, children, whose children? Which were which? Kennedy read the telegram from Nixon and his answer; the telegram from President Eisenhower and his answer. At the end, he asked for everyone's help, a hint of tears in his eyes.

Eighteen hours after the election night program began, Chancellor signed off.

8

Memories of the Kennedy days are memories of television. From "what you can do for your country" to George Wallace barring the door to the University of Alabama to "Ich bin ein' Berliner," we remember less what happened than how it looked on television. Television news and television coverage were now welcome in American life, and the welcome had not yet been overstayed. It was all so perfect, the way the man and the time and the medium fit together, and the way it ended—in its way, also perfect.

Everyone in Kennedy's administration understood that success in politics had come to depend on success at being on television. Journalists, especially television journalists, had unprecedented access to the very top of government. The contrast with what had just ended was dramatic. Eisenhower's meetings with the press accorded reporters from broadcasting the same privileges given those from the print media: to sit and listen, to ask questions. First film was barred; then silent film allowed—of a President talking!— then the networks' big 16-mm Auricon sound-film cameras were allowed to line the back of the room as the President made his opening statements and reporters asked their tentative questions.

For all his popularity, his qualities of leadership, and his position in history, Eisenhower was not good on his feet. His syntax was clumsy, his verbs and predicates in frequent disagreement, his sentences often incomplete. His weekly meetings with the press were planned to end before noon, and Ray Scherer, the NBC White House correspondent, was famous for being able to rush to his telephone booth and ad lib a complete and rounded forty-five seconds live into the radio network's noontime news on the hour.

For television, however, we needed the man himself being seen talking. Bob Doyle, now the *Huntley-Brinkley* director in Washington, would attend so he might know what he and Brinkley could get out of the film that night. By four o'clock, film was out of the processor as Doyle and Brinkley puzzled over what to use, hoping that I had so much news in New York I would not need Eisenhower. They would agree on what was news and scour through the film for snippets that would add up to it, fleshing out a broken sentence or a hanging thought with a word or phrase from deep in the transcript or even some other answer. Then Doyle would call James Hagerty, Eisenhower's powerful press secretary, and tell him what they proposed. Hagerty said, "Okay." But grief awaited anyone who tried that stunt without clearing it. Brinkley dreaded coming to work on the days of the Eisenhower press conferences.

Brinkley and I were connected by an open telephone tie-line. We talked at least four times a day. On the day of an Eisenhower press conference, during, say, the third of these calls, I would ask—sometimes plead—what else he had, knowing there had been a presidential press conference and he had not mentioned it.

"Well, if you really need it, I can put together a few seconds of Uncle Fudd."

Then came Kennedy, "good television" all by himself, who liked press conferences. Quick-witted and a born performer, he was never in less than total command not only of the news but of the occasion. He enjoyed sparring with reporters, and they with him. When the subject was big and frightening, like the Cuban missile crisis, he had their goodwill on his side in a way none of his successors so far has matched. The cameras loved him, and it was not unrequited. Most of his press conferences were telecast live. So many reporters sought to attend that they were moved to a larger room, usually the State Department auditorium.

His whole family was made for television, and Kintner always wanted to put them on. Vanocur, now White House correspondent, was deluged by urgings to get "the first TV interview" with Mrs. Kennedy. Talk was already bubbling in the press room of a White House tour on live television. Vanocur, who preached one must never fawn on the Kennedys or they would know they owned you and need give you nothing, warned New York that if he got the interview NBC would not get the tour. Word came back to let New York handle that; you get the interview. He got it, and it made not a splash but a ripple, while all the White House connections at "New York's" command could not keep the tour away from CBS. We had had our turn.

The young, glamorous First Lady then led Charles Collingwood of CBS on a personal visit of the White House. Kintner was livid. He raised such a fuss the videotape was "pooled." This meant NBC, too, showed Mrs. Kennedy conducting a CBS News reporter, and the American people, on what became the classic White House tour. Either anger distorted Kintner's judgment or it was beyond him to realize how much worse this was than nothing at all.

In coming months, Vanocur had two more programs with Mrs. Kennedy, one on her European trip with her husband, when she had a striking meeting with Charles DeGaulle, France's war-hero president, the other when she went alone to India and Pakistan, both with "exclusive" interviews. But what history remembers is beautiful Jacqueline Kennedy taking CBS on that tour of the White House.

The Bay of Pigs invasion was Kennedy's first major foreign policy initiative. It was also his first disaster, the kind of disaster that echoes down through history, but both the polls and casual surveys by reporters showed his popularity up, not down. He told Vanocur privately that he himself did not understand it. The invasion of Cuba was reported when information was allowed, too late, of course. When, in time, film of the action was available, we used some on the *Huntley-Brinkley Report*, but more as a footnote to a past event than a news story. Most of it went into our Sunday program, by then firmly ensconced as *Chet Huntley Reporting*, which had the time.

As much as we liked spreading ourselves in "longer forms" and clever Sunday essays, our meal ticket was the nightly news program, now reaching unprecedented popularity. *Look* and *The New Yorker* came by to profile Chet and David. A reporter overheard someone telling me the ratings and quoted me calling them obscene. We still covered civil rights as a top story, weekdays and Sundays, now a little more respectably since JFK had telephoned Mrs. Martin Luther King, Jr., to offer help when her husband was jailed. This reporting still annoyed Southern opinion leaders, who made their annoyance known to the people who ran NBC's Southern stations. One said NBC's pretensions to objectivity and fairness were undermined by Huntley's eyebrows. When reporters called, Huntley disclaimed responsibility for his eyebrows, which for Huntley was a pretty good answer.

In our spare time we still did documentaries, more and more of them in a variety of forms and subjects, as Kintner urged NBC News on. After the 1960 election, Brinkley and I went to Hong Kong to do another *Our Man.* . . . We had a wonderful time and did what we thought was a colorful, provocative program. When it was ready for McAndrew to review, he brought Kintner. He may have mentioned our screening casually and Kintner insisted on coming because he had just been to Hong Kong, and had been given the tour correspondents give bosses. The screening was in a shabby room in 1600 Broadway, a building catering to free-lancers, casuals, and film business fly-by-nights, where we had rented extra editing space.

McAndrew and Kintner came from lunch, which promised trouble. Although what we showed was the complete, edited program, there were still gaps in the sound track, and the film print used for working purposes was badly exposed and, in the trial and error of the film-editing process, had been beat up, scratched, and gouged, with many blank slugs to be replaced later with pictures—in short, not fit for viewing by laity, especially laity who did not see well.

Kintner sat for the hour. He hated it, the film and the script. Brinkley's retelling of how the British stole the place from the Chinese, his acid account of the Opium Wars, the pictures of exploited mainland refugees working twelve-hour days for pennies, and Hakka women manhandling boulders on construction sites, all offended Kintner's unwavering regard for the rich and successful. Although we also showed the energy, the beauty, the variety of the place, he growled, "That's not the Hong Kong I saw." I was sure we would be canceled. I told McAndrew to promise Kintner any changes he wanted, but I would not make any. I think he did; I know I didn't.

Whatever his reservations about *Our Man in Hong Kong*—or he may have been led to believe that by telling us what changes he wanted he had made it acceptable—Kintner did not stint in support for it. We got publicity and press attention and many mentions on NBC television itself urging the audience to watch, which they did in substantial numbers. This was Kintner's way. He would keep after the appropriate network bureaucrats to enter as many News programs as possible for awards (of which the television business has a surfeit). At that time, Emmy winners were picked by vote of the Television Academy (today some, like those in news, are picked by panels), so he let NBC employees list their dues on expense accounts. When we did win awards, which we often did, at least in part on merit, he bought full-page advertisements proclaiming them in the major newspapers, and even in the expensive pages of magazines.

Any topic that seemed provocative was approved, and we usually suggested our own. That year's, on the Berlin crisis, entitled *Berlin: Where the West Begins*, was perhaps obvious; Spain was not. It was not even very prominent in the news. We aimed to show the Spanish middle class rousing the country from the slumber of centuries without disturbing its protofascist dictatorship. We were going to combine picture and history and impending change.

Huntley's relatively new wife, who had been the "weather girl" on NBC's Washington station—they had first met when Brinkley introduced them by TV monitor during rehearsal—had among her acquaintances an old-time Washington press agent and lobbyist whose big client was the Spanish government. Before long, I felt I had to convince Chet that in 1961 a journalist would look silly doing an hourlong news report on Spain without mentioning the Civil War or even Franco. Then Chet announced he needed no collaborators; he would write the script himself, in free verse no less. I could not meet the situation head on because he was obviously smarting from something somebody said or something somebody wrote, and he would not say what. (Perhaps, "Why is a writer listed on your programs?" Producers like me quake when anchormen arrive in the office repeating such questions.) It is not the kind of situation I am good at, so it was providential how well we came out.

The picture was evocative and dramatic. Huntley and I compromised on a script that made him feel good but included what I needed. The section I liked best intercut flamenco dancers with bullfighters to the excited twanging of a score we commissioned from a local guitarist. Network censors pressed us to cut out the actual kill. Since network censors have no say about news programs—which, at NBC at least, are the domain of network lawyers—they could only advise. I ignored the advice. For the first time on American televisoin, a bull was killed. (In fact, we filmed three and edited them as one.) The promised torrent of denunciation did not arrive. There were no letters at all, which was worse.

Perhaps my biggest, certainly my most difficult, achievement on *The Many Faces of Spain* was talking the director and the reporter out of quitting. The director was George Murray, who wanted it to be all about *penitentes* in their Easter processions, reflections on a brooding landscape, picture essays about penury and mysticism and the poetry of despair. The reporter, Piers Anderton, a versatile journalist and a writer who combined competence and flair in a way not often found, was famous among his friends for bursts of temper. A few years back, Piers had been the principal reporter on our two Africa programs and had written most of those two scripts. Seeing the convolutions I had to go through to get the hour on Spain done, he elected to become disgusted and resign. Somehow, I got both him and George to unquit. Anderton had been itching to go into the field, so I promised to put in a good word to Bill McAndrew. By summer, Piers Anderton was the NBC correspondent in West Berlin.

There has never again been such a time for documentaries in network television. *CBS Reports* kept on adding to its record, although its impact was diminished without Murrow; ABC News did one from time to time and tried sporadically to get a series going. At NBC, our group was in fact the least productive, what with our other work. Irving Gitlin continued the *NBC White Papers*, adding various danger zones of the globe to his historical accounts; Chet Hagan and Frank McGee often took topics from their assigned areas, space and Instant Specials, and worked them into more fully considered treatments. Not only did I like doing them but they got Huntley and Brinkley and me out of the building to where real people dealt with real problems, giving the world in which news occurs a tangibility it does not have in dispatches or film. Also, I wanted the audience to see Chet and David outside the studio, in three-dimensional places.

After *Our Man in Hong Kong*, Brinkley could hardly wait to do it again. He wanted to go to Vienna, the pudgy capital of a dead empire, a wonderful idea. The only complication was finding those news or news-appearing stories I demanded of them so as to "keep the franchise" on the nightly news program whenever they were off on other projects. But we could not expect to find news in Vienna, which was what made it so attractive a subject, a sleepy relic in a nervous world. One trip to a Communist border, perhaps Hungary, for the usual clichés was the most we could expect.

So many East Berliners were fleeing to West Berlin that it had become that summer's major news, on front pages day after day even in the American heartland. Going to Berlin on the way to Vienna is a nuisance, but covering any other available story as news would make us look foolish, so we went. It was a twelve-hour flight. We got there at noon on a Saturday, itchy and sleepy. We visited refugee camps, then went to the bureau to look at film Gary Stindt and Piers Anderton had prepared for us to pad out the stories we expected to do in the next three days, before going on to Vienna. When we could no longer keep our eyes open, we crossed the street to our hotel.

There at the desk was Charles Collingwood of CBS News, whom I had never met. Brinkley knew him well, of course, and introduced us. Collingwood invited us for a drink. Brinkley said we were too tired, having just flown overnight and spent the afternoon working. How about tomorrow?

"Gee, I'm sorry, David," said Collingwood. "Tomorrow I'm up at dawn. Don Hewitt has rented this videotape truck and we're going from West Berlin across East Germany to West Germany, making TV pictures as we go. Next time."

As I went to my room, my mood was black and my soul twisted by envy. What an idea! Driving live cameras across East Germany making pictures on videotape. Why hadn't I thought of that? If I had not been so tired, it would have kept me awake all night. As it was, I slept past 9:00 in the morning. I do not like breakfast in hotel rooms, and with no English newspapers available, I took a paperback to breakfast. At the second cup of coffee I thought the buzzing level in the room had increased. Conversation seemed too animated, too excited, for a normal Sunday morning. People were passing newspapers back and forth, and I peered over a shoulder. My German was not good enough even for headlines, but something was up. I went to the concierge desk and asked what was going on.

"Zey have closed ze border."

Who?

"Ze East."

Brinkley and I went where the news was. At the sector border, on the Wilhelmstrasse, shops with outdoor tables loaded with real and fake American blue jeans catered with great success to East Berlin's teenagers. Inside they sold rock records, posters, and the universal paraphernalia of youth. Shortly after noon, with the sun bright in a blue sky, Brinkley stood in the street talking about the sealing of the border between the two Berlins. Seen clearly behind him, East German conscripts planted square posts and strung barbed wire between them.

That was the Berlin Wall on its first day, Sunday, August 13, 1961. And there was Brinkley talking about it, and we filming him for Monday night, while Hewitt and Collingwood and their CBS tape truck were headed west across the Communist zone for West Germany! And since CBS and ABC had recently moved their German bureaus from West Berlin to Bonn, for forty-eight hours we were the only American television network journalists in Berlin.

Sunday afternoon turned suddenly gray, as it can on the north European plain. We heard that Russian tanks had been seen in an industrial workers' quarter called Wedding. We found the tanks deployed in a major boulevard where it crosses the Bernauerstrasse, the border street. Across the street, several hundred West Berliners shouted insults at the eight young lieutenants whose torsos protruded from the eight Soviet tanks. In chants, like English soccer crowds, they derided the Soviet Union and Walter Ulbricht, its East German proconsul. They stood together, a packed phalanx of middle-aged, beer-bellied humanity in straining gray Sunday suits. Brinkley and I watched from the sidewalk.

I said, "That could be the beginning of world war three."

Brinkley said, "It doesn't take much to draw a crowd in this town."

On Monday, Brinkley reported from the Brandenburg Gate. By Tuesday, the Wall had become everybody's news story, so we did one more piece and wrapped up. The night before we left, I sat in the bureau with Anderton and Stindt. We had been reporting about East German refugees at least since 1954, daily, on Sundays, in documentaries. We agreed no wall could stifle their impulse to leave. Most who might want to leave would be dissuaded, but surely not all. Somehow or other, there would be attempts to cross the wall, who knew how. Blessed with a daily program budget and a weekly program budget, I could tell Stindt and Anderton that whenever they could film someone trying to get out, or someone who had tried to get out, or who had got out, or how people got out, to do it without waiting for the go-ahead from New York. We would take care of the cost somehow, and I would flag them if they were overdoing it. Brinkley and I went on to Vienna.

Getting the story in Vienna was, if anything, too easy. It was so fat, so smug, so mired in imperial legacy, not only in the obvious funny ways but in its devotion to bureaucracy and to *Proporz*, which divided all government and all government jobs between red and black, the nominal Socialists and nominal Catholics. To help with arrangements, we hired a local journalist, Fritz Weiss, who turned out to be a man of sophistication and a sense of history. He quarreled with our nasty theses in his civilized way although, as a Jew, he owed little to Austrians. But Beethoven was important to him, and so was meeting kindred spirits in coffee houses, and Arthur Schnitzler, and the way many nationalities got along. Brinkley interviewed him on film, letting him refute a lot of what we said and implied.

I had brought with me two snippets of newsreel film, both of the day the Nazis had entered Vienna—one as they were greeted by the crowds and welcomed by the Cardinal at St. Stephen's Cathedral; the other showing them cheered by massed thousands as they rode past City Hall. We filmed the same locations from the same angles, in color this time, now deserted, green lawns and bright flowers sparkling in the lush August sun. In the film-editing room, we juxtaposed these pictures with the old black and white newsreel pictures, then and now, then and now. It lasted no more than a few seconds, but the Austrians never forgave us.

After *Our Man in Vienna* had been broadcast and pronounced a success, we heard that the Austrian Foreign Ministry had published a fancy pamphlet rejecting our description and took their revenge on the pleasant, civilized, middle-aged man who had been our contact and guide. I was told he had been denied work and could not earn a living. I called everyone I could think of, sent telegrams to editors I had never met, and tried to get the U.S. embassy involved. A year later a mutual acquaintance told me Weiss had put aside a bottle of good Tokay for whenever I came back to Vienna. Perhaps my efforts had worked, or, perhaps, nothing I did had helped, but, gentle soul, he wanted me to know that he did not hold me responsible.

My trip with Brinkley was my second to Vienna. I had first come almost two months before to prepare for the program, to see Vienna for myself and pick sites and pictures and even some stories worth telling. This is what is known in the trade as a "survey" trip and is often more fun than the working trip to follow, depending on what one is surveying, and where. I had arrived in Vienna a week after Kennedy left from his meeting there with Nikita Sergeivich Khrushchev. Chancellor, who as Moscow correspondent had been sent to Vienna to accompany Khrushchev and report on him, had stayed behind to introduce me to the city. Well after one midnight Chancellor was called to the telephone in the basement bar of the Bristol Hotel in Vienna. It was McAndrew calling to say Kintner wanted him to take over from Dave Garroway, to do *Today* as "host," or, as Pat Weaver used to say, "communicator."

When Kintner had decided to replace Garroway, he remembered Chancellor's ad-libbing for an hour on that Wednesday after the 1960 election night, describing scenes in Hyannis he could not see. He knew the ad-lib legends of radio—Gabriel Heatter talking all night as he waited for the signal that Bruno Hauptmann had died for the kidnap and murder of the Lindbergh baby, Milton Cross talking nonstop about a dozen other operas because the curtain at the Metropolitan Opera House was stuck and the performance could not begin. Was what Chancellor had done that Wednesday in the same league? Kintner thought so.

I urged Chancellor not to do it. It was not for him nor he for it. Nor was he himself enthused by the prospect, not that night. But as we talked he came to feel he had no choice. "They" were obviously in trouble or "they" would not have turned to him. If he did it and it did not work, well . . . But if he refused to do it, and whomever they then turned to failed, "they" would forever see him as the son of a bitch who had turned them down when they needed him. So he did it. It did not work. It would last fourteen months.

All this activity was merely part of the changes television news was going through both internally and in public acceptance. The biggest came from the building consensus that the fifteen-minute nightly news program was inadequate. Walter Cronkite got a lot of press attention when he had the words of one of his fifteen-minute evening news broadcasts set up against the front page of *The New York Times* and proved that it filled only two and a half columns. This could have been taken as criticism of the *Times*'s notorious penchant for over-writing and underediting, but it wasn't. Newspapers preferred to kiss off television news as merely a "headline service" and phoned around for comments. I said that although Walter's fifteen minutes used fewer words than the front page of the *Times*, they were still more words than Elizabeth Barrett Browning needed for the entire *Sonnets from the Portuguese*. No one used it.

There were more producers at NBC News now, although not as many as at CBS News. Chet Hagan had made it two, then Gitlin and his *White Paper* staff made it more than a half dozen, still not enough. Lou Hazam, who had long been associated with NBC News as a free-lancer, which he preferred, was dragooned into signing on and did distinguished and distinctive work, some historical, some pioneering in medical reporting for television, some sensing the American mood in a way that was arresting but more poetic than instructive or even insightful. Working with film can do that to you if you're not careful. There were some good ones who came and went, but demand exceeded supply, so we turned to filmmakers.

I am not the only one who reacts to the word *filmmakers* as Hermann Göring said he did to the word *culture*. Film as means and film as end are two different universes. The ability of moving pictures to carry information is very special, with the potential of involving the audience in a way the spoken word or the written word cannot. But the rules of information are good old rules, not to be trifled with. Too many "filmmakers" are like lawyers who start with the case to be made and seek out only such information as makes it. Any other information, crucial to the subject but damaging to the case, is left out. Partial information is partial, and is too often the arena of self-named film-makers. The film they are making is, they say, their way of "expressing themselves," or of "making a statement," which really means exerting a sort of power over those who watch, power they are not equipped to wield in any other way, not with their fists and not through debate. They smudge the line between what exists and what they have arranged. Their justification is, "Shakespeare did it."

Around this time, Frank Stanton, president of CBS, suggested a scheme of rotating prime-time news programs among the networks so that they shared equally in what was conceded to be a sacrifice. This, he said, would satisfy public responsibility. Or as more widely assumed, it could be impelled by a purpose greater than increased income, protecting the license to broadcast—that is, to make any money at all.

Documentaries often ran in prime time, displacing entertainment programs for a night, but series were different. CBS's documentaries were presented under the general title *CBS Reports* but were not a series until 1961. *CBS Reports* grew out of *See It Now*, the Murrow series that had blazed such trails from 1952 to 1955. For its last two seasons, *See It Now* was a half-hour series in prime time. In June 1955, as the second of those seasons was ending, *The $64,000 Question* was launched in the half hour immediately preceding it. It was a stunning hit, attracting such huge audiences that CBS knew they could make an almost equally large hit of any show that followed, if only it were not *See It Now*. From then on, *See It Now* was shown from time to time. In 1961, *CBS Reports* became a prime-time series, which was widely attributed to CBS's need for a shiny public face after the quiz-show scandals, primarily *The $64,000 Question*.

Whatever CBS's reasons, they were likely also NBC's when, in October 1961, it launched a weekly prime-time half-hour series called *David Brinkley's Journal*, and the next January, *Chet Huntley Reporting* was moved into prime time. To produce Brinkley's program, Julian Goodman recruited the brash and brilliant Ted Yates, who had practiced "tabloid" journalism on television long before the term was used, and brought to his skill with a camera a fearlessness bordering on folly, and Stuart Schulberg, gentle second son of a noted Hollywood family, who thought television ought to talk about the country's problems. They ventured all over the world for their pictures, sometimes attuned to Brinkley's uniqueness, sometimes not. There was a fair amount of footage about little wars around the world, including the one we were getting into in Southeast Asia, many people from the other side of the footlights, including wrestlers, and too many attempts to make fun of contemporary art. When my life became too busy for *Our Man* . . . programs, Yates produced three or four more.

I was busy with the news every night and with a Sunday program now moved to weeknight prime time, where it could be seen, and commented on, and suggested for, and otherwise interfered with. We managed some interesting things nonetheless. We tried whenever we could to let film and the sound of the occasion being filmed—natural sound, it is called—do as much story-telling without script as possible. This was not unique with us; everybody who enjoys film tries to do that, but each experiences his own adventures. In Texas, we found Billy James Hargis, a fundamentalist minister who ran something called the National Anti-Communist Leadership School. By making a lot of film of everything from registration to Hargis instructing and haranguing those attending to their lunchtime discussions we edited together a telling portrait with almost no accompanying narration other than Huntley's introductions to the two sections of the program, and his conclusion, which needed no heavy hand because the point had been made. Friends, even family, questioned this approach, saying I assumed too intelligent an audience. Perhaps, but there are worse faults.

Architect Eero Saarinen's last design, the TWA terminal at Idlewild Airport, a pair of huge brooding wings of shaped concrete sheltering passengers rushing to and from the gates, was completed after his death.

I sent a talented cameraman, alone, without a director or even a lighting man, to film whatever he saw. I found a composer willing to undertake an eight-minute score to accompany the edited picture, which we ran without any words. The result was not epic or immortal or perhaps even successful, but where else could something like that be tried? Perhaps less unorthodox but in the same mode, there was spring at the Berlin Wall, unemployment in Chicago's slowly dying meat-packing industry, "freedom riders" in Georgia, and the Detroit wedding of Jimmy Hoffa's daughter.

In 1963, the *Huntley-Brinkley Report* was almost six years old, the longest I had ever spent on one job. We were more successful than any standard news program yet—or since. The challenges and problems and failures of October 29, 1956, were long past. There was success, also, beyond ratings, and income, and even public recognition. NBC News itself was now established and eminent. There were other factors besides us, but without us it would not have happened, whereas without some of the others it might have. At least, that is how our little group, not noted for humility, saw it.

But it had become too easy. Anything I wanted to do I had done, and I had not discovered anything else that I wanted to do. Yet I had no other trade. I asked McAndrew and Goodman to relieve me, perhaps to let me do documentaries, since they were in such demand. I wanted to do them differently from the way I had been, spending more time thinking, doing more of my own work with fewer people to help me. I would carry on with the political coverage, if they wanted me to, including that year's election night, but the daily program had become too daily.

They let me leave daily news for other things. Already in the works was the program about people trying to escape from East Berlin, which I had discussed with Anderton and Stindt before leaving for Vienna. Nor was it too early to begin planning for the off-year election night. I wanted one more project because I was not used to doing only one thing at a time. Before I could find it, Goodman had one for me, the European Common Market. The Kennedy administration, especially those inside the White House itself—the President, the national security adviser, and such boosters as the under-secretary of state—was enchanted with the Common Market. To John Kennedy, a student of Europe, the dreams of Frenchmen Jean Monnet and Robert Schumann, chief architects of the slowly emerging economic and political union of Western Europe, were part of that grand design he liked to envision as the road to peace.

I have always wondered if that idea moved somehow from the White House to Goodman's office in the RCA Building. News executives like him, who served substantial tours in Washington, were more sensitive than the rest of us to what the movers from all three branches wanted, and paid greater mind to such desires than the rest of us could understand. He denies all this, going so far as to insist that the documentary on the Common Market was not his idea but mine. But I remember telling him it could not be done, because the heart of the Common Market was an idea, and you cannot take a picture of an idea. When he told me to do it anyway, I said it would be very expensive, perhaps the most expensive program I had ever done. He persisted, and I did it. A *Country Called Europe* cost about $165,000, a lot of money for a nonfiction hour in those days.

It certainly was not Kintner's idea. He hated even the thought. When McAndrew and Goodman, presenting documentary plans for his approval, mentioned that there was one in production on the Common Market, he objected and carped. It was sure to be dull; who cared anyway; it just wasted money and airtime. Then came Jack Gould himself, in *The New York Times* itself, commending John Chancellor's reporting and his script, a kind word for me and how I "deployed" my cameramen, calling the program "exciting, human and understandable," adding that even though we showed a lot that had been known, our way gave "arresting continuity and drama," all showing again the difficulty critics have in phrasing praise. But praise it was, from a source that mattered to many, to Bob Kintner most of all. If he had had second thoughts, admitting them would have been unlike him, but he was as always punctilious about the care and feeding of stars. From one floor above us, he sent a telegram (!) to be delivered by hand to Chancellor congratulating him—on "your good review."

One week before the broadcast of A *Country Called Europe* there had been *The Trouble with Water Is People*, a less happily named effort tracing the entire length of the Colorado River from the crystal freshets at the source to the man-made muck of the delta. That had filled whatever was left of my time since leaving the *Huntley-Brinkley Report* the previous summer. Both programs took months to do, and it was only coincidence, or some executive's ignorance, that they were scheduled consecutively. It made for hectic final days.

And then my liberty ended. One lovely, clear, late spring day in 1963, I parked my car in the usual garage about a block from the building. Robert Northshield, known to everyone as "Shad," an old friend and frequent co-conspirator, a talented producer, pulled up behind me. We walked the block together breathing spring, sometimes possible even in the city. Shad was one of those people with whom I would discuss ideas when they were not yet completely formed.

"What do you plan to do today?" he asked me.

"Sit in my office and wait for McAndrew to call."

"Why?"

"It was in today's *Times*."

"I haven't seen it yet."

"CBS is expanding Cronkite to a half hour."

"Oh."

I agreed to return to the daily program and see it to the half hour, but for two years and no more. The summer was spent expanding staff to meet new requirements, organizing around new ideas, and trying to establish, first for myself, in how many ways a half-hour news program should differ from a fifteen-minute news program. Our little trouble-making group would have to expand into a bureaucracy; our planning for future coverage would have to stretch its amplitude from weeks to months; jobs would have to be more narrowly defined. Most distressing of all, we would no longer be doing it ourselves. We suddenly had to rely on the entire corpus of NBC News, too many of them still schooled mostly in radio, others rigid in the way they thought, the way they approached news and how to report it, and successful enough doing things their way that it would be all but impossible to get them to do anything differently.

As I faced doubling the length of NBC's flagship daily news program, my most worrying prospect was how to get all those people I had never worked with to do things as I thought they ought to be done. They included famous and respected journalists, a decade or two my seniors, some of whom had rarely worked in television, some never. It was hardly my place to hold classes for them. My preferences were only my preferences, but, still, it was my show until it was someone else's, and I could not simply do nothing. I decided to put what I thought in writing. I did some solitary brooding; I consulted friends, mostly Chancellor; and I wrote a thirty-two page memo, always keeping in my mind's eye the face of a very senior NBC reporter, friend of Presidents and chief justices, who could not do a piece for television if his life depended on it. What I was trying to do was show him how.

The memo was mockingly called "The Bible" even by friends. It was later reprinted in journalism textbooks, circulated like a samizdat inside some foreign broadcasting organizations, quoted in speeches of NBC executives who missed the point, and accorded a strange life of its own. I quote some lines:

"The highest power of television journalism is not in the transmission of information but in the transmission of experience. Its other high power is that it is now accepted as authoritative, and this authority sustains it where it cannot rely on the impact of picture, and cannot shirk the mandate to inform comprehensively. . . . There are events which exist in the American mind and recollection primarily because they were reported on regular television news programs. We have found a dimension of information which is not contained in words alone. . . .

"Most people are dull. That is, they communicate ineptly . . . Those who communicate eptly, politicians, actors and the like, tend to be self-serving. It is natural and human and in many ways commendable that most of us recoil at being personally unpleasant to our fellow-men. . . . This is part of good manners. But an interviewer is not an individual human in conversation. . . . An interview which is not more than a conversation is less than an interview. You are wasting our time. . . . It is relevant here to recall an audience of up to 20 million Americans. A two-minute interview commands an aggregate attention of more than 600,000 man-hours. What effort we must make to justify this! . . .

"There is nothing more awkward than an interview in which the interviewer is more interesting than the subject. . . .

"A cameraman who cannot light is not a cameraman. A reporter who insists there is enough light is a fool. Film is not reality but illusion, at best an imitation of reality. Film is a strip of plastic overlaid with an arrangement of finely divided silver. The camera cannot always see what the eye can see. . . . Film is an arrangement of light and shadow. Lights disturb subjects more than cameras. Unlit, they are unseen. . . . Film takes time.

"The picture is not a fact but a symbol. . . . There are two important elements that are oftenest forgotten. The first is that hearing is a part of seeing. The second is that the setting is a part of the story. Natural sound is where you find it. . . . It is my experience with natural sound, whether shot wild or in synch., that the microphone should be farther back than the camera for wide shots, closer than the camera for close-ups. . . .

"Every news story should, without any sacrifice of probity or responsibility, display attributes of fiction, of drama. It should have structure and conflict, problem and denouement, rising action and falling action, a beginning, a middle and an end. These are not only the essentials of drama; they are the essentials of narrative. We are in the business of narrative because we are in the business of communication.

"Do not be misled by what the human eye sees. The eyes of the audience will see only the film. Do not rely too much on words explaining your pictures. Film something for the deaf. . . .

"There will be no tricks to gain or hold audiences we do not want. Controversy is to be neither sought nor avoided. . . . It is as true now as seven years ago [when *Huntley-Brinkley* began] that if we speak to our equals others will follow. There are methods of attracting the others for which we have neither the skill nor the stomach. What we can and are willing to do we do very, very well."

Eliot Frankel, who had taken over from me as producer the previous summer, went to London as the expanded program's editor and producer for Europe. Needing someone to do the same for the Far East, I found Jack Fern, a newcomer to NBC News who had accumulated good experience organizing coverage for CBS. Neither had let professional experience stifle native curiosity. They could still be interested, they could still be surprised. Although their presence helped the coverage of important—and obvious—events, it was their personalities that gave us some of our best stories. Eliot was sending us material on the Beatles long before they were recognizable names in the United States; we did a long report on them before their more famous appearance on the *Ed Sullivan Show*. At the other end, he covered the Prague spring of 1968 by going himself as producer to send us not only the blooming of political democracy but how theater was affected, and art, and the way people lived.

Fern was good at showing Japanese at home before most Americans were aware they ought to care, and at following the growing American involvement in Southeast Asia. I claim credit, however, in his biggest triumph. When the wires bulletined a major earthquake in Anchorage, Alaska, my years of slavish attention to the *Official Airlines Guide* paid off. As everyone was calling California to move camera crews to Alaska,

I wondered if a plane from Tokyo might get to Anchorage before a plane from Los Angeles. It could.

Fern and the Tokyo camera crews outdid themselves. We were a full day ahead of the competition with dramatic narrative pictures as we toured the ruins of half a city. No picture surpassed the one that Fern and one of the crews made while the reporter was off in another part of town. We saw a middle-aged man, disheveled, halting, searching through the rubble of what had been his store. There were slivers and fragments and shards, which he picked up and tossed aside, one by one. Unseen, off camera, Jack Fern asked:

"Mr. Golden, what do you plan to do now?"

The man stopped and turned toward the camera. "To tell the truth, Mr. Fern," he said, "an earthquake I didn't need."

Our life as a half-hour news program got off to a good start and held its lead for a fair length of time. I spent my summer producing as well as planning. With Frankel off to London, I had to double as producer of the fifteen-minute program until the day it became the half-hour. Meanwhile, I had to give the new program a new look, or I thought I did, and there were long discussions about what we would be doing and how we would be different, not only from the others but from what we had been.

Cronkite went to the half-hour format first, Labor Day, 1963. To signal the occasion, he interviewed President Kennedy. We went to our half-hour format a week later. To signal the occasion, Huntley and Brinkley interviewed President Kennedy. Both times, Kennedy wanted to talk about the goings-on in Southeast Asia and why our interests were affected. None of the three interviewers reminded him of the day between his election and his inauguration when he visited Gen. Douglas MacArthur in the Waldorf-Astoria Hotel and then told reporters waiting on the chilly sidewalk that the general had warned him against getting involved in war on the Asian mainland.

No one said why we expanded to a half hour a week later than CBS. That Cronkite's half hour began on Labor Day, one of three days of any year when audiences are smallest, did not affect the most important area of competition—for newspaper space. Thus challenged, Kintner had another public relations epiphany.

It began when a reporter whose beat was collecting television facts and facticles told an NBC press agent, inaccurately, that CBS News planned three one-hour programs on successive evenings about the year in civil rights. It had been a year of significant news indeed, schools desegregated, churches burned, a march on Washington, the heyday of the White Citizens' Councils, the emergence of Martin Luther King, Jr., as a major figure. The year had also seen Medgar Evers murdered and James Meredith entering the University of Mississippi. Yet to come were George Wallace in the schoolhouse doorway and the Sunday school bombings in Birmingham, Alabama. The press agent told McAndrew about the supposed CBS plan, and he told Kintner, who preempted the entertainment schedule for one whole evening, Labor Day evening, the evening Cronkite inaugurated his half-hour news.

Advertisers who had bought time for *Monday Night at the Movies* and that night's other canceled programs were allowed to withdraw their commercials without penalty, at the sales department's request. One advertiser did not withdraw. At NBC in those days, an old system was still in place whereby most "creative" participants in a program, not only those who were seen but writers, directors, and the like, were paid extra "commercial fees" if a program attracted any advertising. Most such fees were governed by contracts, personal or union, and for three-hour programs they were huge. Contracts did not say how many commercials a program need include. A commercial program was a commercial program, and the inclusion of one cut-rate spot from one advertiser obligated the network to the same fees as if the program had been sold out at premium. Someone calculated how much more those fees would cost than what one advertiser would pay for one spot in a movie during the repeat season. The sponsor was asked to withdraw. Then our press agents announced that not only was an evening's entire schedule being canceled for a program of national importance, but NBC would nobly not accept advertising for it.

Shad Northshield and Chet Hagan jointly produced a program that was never less than workmanlike and occasionally brilliant. In three hours, of course, their biggest job was organization, covering all that ground, effectively parceling it out among the best of the reporters and producers and others who could be strong-armed away from their regular jobs. It was unavoidable that they repeat much of what others had done, most notably an ABC program of two years before called *Walk in My Shoes*, astonishingly the first serious network effort to show American whites how American blacks lived. Shad made up buttons boasting, "I Watched All Three Hours," which only his staff wore honestly.

Kintner won his success. The press all but ignored Walter Cronkite's half-hour network nightly news for what it saw as a much more daring experiment in nonfiction television. There were no bad reviews. Some reviewers did, however, show fitful symptoms of fatigue. (Reviewers could still see programs only as they were broadcast. Tape cassettes to watch at home were yet to come.) Jack Gould of the *Times* positively burbled. What impressed them all was NBC destroying something of value, airtime, its only salable asset, for an apparently noble purpose. It is generally true that American commercial television gets brownie points mostly when it seems to be sacrificing something expensive.

Two months later, we went from the exhilaration that comes from putting one over—it was a good program, but still!—to the weekend of Kennedy's assassination, when we countered despair with as much work as we could do. The murder of John F. Kennedy was such an overarching personal event that we remember it more for what it did to us than for what happened to him. A President's violent death is shocking enough; this President's violent death changed our lives. I do not hold with the prattle about his being the victim of a violent society, his murder unmasking infection in our national soul. People who talk that way need conspiracy to explain every misfortune. Like children, they do not accept that bad things happen. Kennedy was killed by a diseased person, and, I believe, no others, and if any one of a hundred things had been different, it would not have happened, because that is how things are. But his death brought the end of optimism to my generation. He and I had never met, but we were in school at the same time and served in the same war.

What I remember of that weekend, from November 22, the Friday afternoon he was shot, until November 25, the Monday he was buried, shimmers in the memory like an impressionist landscape, all detail suppressed. We lived by adrenaline and reflex, fortunate in having too much to do to think. The bulletin moved from Dallas at 1:40 P.M. Eastern time, Friday, saying only that the President had been shot. At the time, the CBS network was active with a soap opera, while ABC and NBC were in what is called "station time," which means there were no network programs during that hour. Julian Goodman, reached by telephone in the luncheon club atop the RCA building, rushed to broadcast control, which controls television in New York. Shad Northshield, who, after his civil rights marathon, had become number three manager behind McAndrew and Goodman, still had documentaries to finish and was in a film-editing room. He went to the newsroom.

Bill McAndrew was not in the building, the last time he would spend his lunch hour outside the building except for vital necessity.

Everybody remembers where they were when they learned; I was at lunch. Like all tragedies, this one plays against a counterpoint of the ludicrous. The *Huntley-Brinkley* gang could no longer indulge itself in going forth in fours and fives as we used to when we were still at fifteen minutes, but this day we did, and it was a pleasant occasion, half business, half old jokes. Ellis Moore, an ABC vice president, waved as we came in. An hour later, he rushed over to our table to ask me if I knew the President had been shot. It could not be a joke, but it could not be real. He led me to the television set in the bar where someone was repeating the bulletin. At NBC, a reporter named Bill Ryan was in the little bulletin studio, soon joined by Frank McGee; Northshield was trying to keep the newsroom operating, while from all the offices on the floor, and other floors, people—executives, secretaries, clerks, journalists—had clustered around the central desk, getting in the way. CBS had just carried an unconfirmed report that Kennedy had died. Northshield saw me come in. "I can't go with an unconfirmed," he said. He was almost pleading. I agreed.

He waited until it was confirmed that President Kennedy had died. We were last with the news. After it was over, there was whispering that NBC had perhaps been a little slow off the mark, heh, heh, and in time some affiliate station managers asked out loud why we were so far behind. It was not my decision, but it sticks in my mind as the right one. Another thing Northshield said early that afternoon: "This is one goddam time we're not going to be edited by CBS!" He had someone clear out the newsroom; everyone back to his or her own desk and job. In broadcast control, a technician asked Julian Goodman when NBC would resume regular programming. Goodman asked him what he did. He saw to it that the right commercials played at the right times in the local station's programs.

"Son," said Julian, "get your coat and go home. We won't need you for a while."

Without anyone asking, at any of the networks, commercial broadcasting stopped. Toward the end of the weekend, there were rumors that some executive types from the business departments had asked testily how long all this would go on, but they had been denied. Mostly people just did what they thought they had to do. Control-room duty, which by midafternoon meant controlling the whole network, was rotated among three producers. The *Huntley-Brinkley* staff and I were assigned 6:00 P.M. to midnight, during which our program would have run. The first night we interrupted ourselves to use the *Huntley-Brinkley* opening and closing and report whatever other news there was that day, but the rest of the weekend was just one long special news program. Similarly, the *Today* group tried to do things their way, heavy on interviews and discussions, during the 6:00 A.M. to noon shift.

Television mobile units moved to the White House, the Capitol, and Andrews Air Force Base early in the afternoon; two were quickly readied in Dallas, one assigned to Robert MacNeil, then NBC's number two White House correspondent, who was our reporter on the Kennedy trip and therefore present when Kennedy was shot. There were units in New York and Hyannis Port, and then, for the world rulers coming to the funeral, a unit was sent to Dulles Airport. (MacNeil gave us the first direct accounts of what happened, his cameraman our first film. Then the engine of his mobile unit broke down. With no time for repairs, for the rest of that weekend it was dragged around Dallas by a tow truck, able to broadcast but not to move under its own power.)

Responding only to reflex leaves few memories, but I remember that first day wanting to use Kennedy's inaugural address. NBC News's always abysmal archives could not find it, probably had not kept it. We had run it unedited on *Chet Huntley Reporting*, so I sent to the New Jersey vaults where they store tapes of complete programs in case someone sues. We got it back in time to use before the evening ended. The first hours of the afternoon had been confusion, with snippets of news: about the shooting; about the man who shot Kennedy; about Governor John Connally of Texas, who had been wounded; about Mrs. Kennedy; about the new President being sworn in; what was happening, what would happen. And filler, filler, filler: how many Presidents had been shot, who they were, what is the oath of office, how had Kennedy spent that morning. Someone said Cronkite showed tears on the air; McGee and Huntley, who were at the bulletin desk with Ryan at the time, didn't—at least not on the air. Switch to the United Nations. Switch to Dallas. Switch to Washington. Irving R. Levine reported from Rome, radio only, over a slide, with something from the Vatican. Back in Dallas, Lee Harvey Oswald, who had allegedly killed Kennedy, had also shot a policeman. To Brinkley, in

Washington, with the latest funeral arrangements. It was approaching six o'clock, our time to take over the control room.

Air Force One landed in Washington, bringing the new President, the dead President's coffin, and the widow. There were statements of grief and sorrow, ranging from former President Eisenhower to senators to foreign statesmen to ordinary citizens. One wishes to be reminded of some special eloquence, but there was none. Yet the sorrow was real. We put together a sequence of Kennedy speaking—his inaugural address, his Cuban crisis speech, his civil rights speech. By then we had found them all. After that we switched to New Orleans for a year-old interview with Lee Harvey Oswald talking about his work for something called the Fair Play for Cuba Committee. Maybe he did it for Castro. We would learn at his trial, not before. The President's body got to the White House after nine in the evening.

When there was nothing else, statements from famous faces. Our own reporters talking. Edwin Newman said Americans tonight were a grossly diminished people. At 10:30, a report on Lyndon Johnson's first meeting as President with the secretary of defense and the acting secretary of state. Around 1:00 A.M., just before sign-off, MacNeil reporting from Dallas that Oswald had been formally charged with murder.

At the White House the next day, Mrs. Kennedy let cameras spend fifteen minutes in the room where the casket lay. We saw and heard the guard change. Tom Pettit was now our correspondent in Dallas. He reported from outside the jail where Oswald was being held. From Atlanta, an interview with Martin Luther King, Jr. Church services. Statements. Live pictures of Oswald being taken to the Dallas police Homicide Bureau. People in and out of the White House. Pettit kept the crime story alive, was told by Chief of Police Jesse Curry that the FBI knew Oswald was in Dallas but that they had not warned him. Film of Oswald's wife and baby visiting him in jail; he asked for a clean shirt. Police Chief Curry said the prisoner would be moved the next day.

Sunday morning I was home. I had slept. I did not want to watch. Just before noon I could no longer resist; I turned on the set, just for a minute to see what they were doing. Bill Ryan took over at noon from the *Today* crew. He talked about the upcoming funeral, switched to Pettit waiting in the jail corridor for Oswald to be moved. Back to Washington. Lines of people waiting in the cold. St. Matthew's Cathedral where Monday's funeral service would be held. Back to McGee in New York—for one minute and twenty seconds.

The legend in the halls of NBC is that at that moment Kintner called from home and told the control room to switch to Dallas. He gave no reason. On live television, we saw Oswald being led across the picture when, suddenly, from the lower right of the screen, the back of a man in a hat. He lunged forward. We could hear a shot. Pettit: "He's been shot! He's been shot! Lee Harvey Oswald has been shot! There is absolute pandemonium. . . ."

CBS's cameras were there but CBS had not switched live to Dallas. They did so in less than a minute, with Oswald already shot and the man who did it in the arms of policemen. ABC had chosen to place its cameras at the prison where Oswald was to be taken. The event, the NBC report, Pettit's shocked voice, have entered history as television's first live coverage of a murder, of someone being killed on camera. The moral changes rung on this unusual minute are numerous, all adducing that television itself must be evil to be able to do this evil thing. Afterward, Pettit told a *Newsweek* reporter that the words went from his eyes to his mouth without going through his brain. That was how most of us felt that weekend. We switched to Washington after seeing Oswald loaded into an ambulance headed for the hospital where Kennedy had died. The man who shot him was a nightclub owner named Jack Ruby.

In Washington, we saw the caisson arriving at the White House to take Kennedy's coffin to the Capitol, where it would lie in state. Muffled drums; riderless horse; the military, the clergy, the people. The family in cars. At the Capitol, Senator Mike Mansfield of Montana spoke the only eloquent words of the weekend: "There was a sound of laughter. In a moment it was no more. And she took the ring from her finger and placed it in his hand . . ." Others spoke, the Chief Justice, the Speaker of the House, but I remember only Mansfield's words from that weekend. Then to McGee with the news that Oswald had died.

A long procession of the famous and the ordinary passed the coffin in the Capitol Rotunda, moving slowly but never stopping. Some had been waiting twelve hours. At the airport, foreign dignitaries arriving for the funeral; developments in Dallas; in between, rather than more repetition or invention, we showed the people passing the coffin. Then more about Oswald, and by special courier from London, a tape of the special edition of the renowned British wit and satire program, *That Was the Week That Was.* This time its famous players favored us by being solemn and reverential. Many were impressed, but I found it tasteless and condescending, reaching an immortal nadir when Dame Sybil Thorndike belted out an instant poem apostrophizing Mrs. Kennedy, braying, "Oh, Jackie! Why, Jackie!" like a belabored donkey. McAndrew ordered pictures of the crowds filing past the coffin continued all night. For six hours, until morning, nothing was heard but feet shuffling, coughing, guards changing, some whispering, an announcer every hour, for five seconds.

When, on Monday, the control room first saw the heads of state filling the roadway from sidewalk to sidewalk, we gasped. Many of us had just read Barbara Tuchman's *Guns of August,* the story of how World War I started, which opens with the funeral of Britain's King Edward VII, with the massed crowned heads of Europe following the caisson on foot, the last time European monarchy would assemble en masse before the cataclysm that obliterated it. Now coming at us were President DeGaulle, tallest figure in the line, Emperor Haile Selassie of Ethiopia, King Baudouin of Belgium, West Germany's chancellor Ludwig Erhard, England's Prince Philip and Prime Minister Sir Alec Douglas-Home, Canada's prime minister Lester Pearson, Philippines president Diosdado Macapagal, Japan's prime minister Ikeda, Anastas Mikoyan from the Soviet Union, David Ben-Gurion, the queen of Greece, the Dutch crown princess . . .

There was an elite consensus that American television "matured" or "proved itself" or, worst of all, "earned its place" by what it did that weekend. From the crest of Olympus, James Reston, senior columnist of the *Times,* said television's coverage had united the country. Congress passed a resolution commending the networks and the industry for what had been done. Newton Minow, chairman of the FCC, who had coined the phrase "vast wasteland" to describe television programming, said of that weekend, "Broadcasting grew up. It was a turning point." The people I worked for were pleased to bask in unaccustomed approval, especially out of Washington. They did not resent the patronizing smell that clung to these pronouncements. I did.

NBC gave seventy-one hours to the Kennedy weekend, ABC sixty, CBS fifty-five. It was the kind of thing television enjoys bragging about, but this time the typical claims would have been unseemly. Kintner bought a full-page ad saluting all of American television for how it

had conducted itself. Other than being signed by the National Broadcasting Company, it bore no hint of the usual competitive boasting.

But the approval of the elite was not universal. In its issue reporting Kennedy's death, *Time* intoned: "Television wasted no time in making the most of its advantages" but "newspapers brought the message home as no transitory broadcast can ever do."

9

On Friday, September 14, 1962, twenty-six people, five of them children, three still infants in arms, went from a street in East Berlin to a street in West Berlin. The two streets were hardly more than a football field apart, but between them then stood the year-old Berlin Wall: barbed-wire tangles, some pyramids made of steel rails, and a wooden screen at the edge of East Berlin's "forbidden zone" to keep people on the two sides from waving to each other. To get from the apartment building in Schönholzerstrasse to the factory building in Bernauerstrasse, the people had crawled on their hands and knees through a tunnel that had taken a group of university students five months to dig.

Five or six weeks after they began, the students digging the tunnel ran out of money. All engineering students, they intended history's biggest escape route out of East Germany; their skillfully crafted drawings showed a more stable, more sophisticated, more lasting tunnel than the rabbit holes often used by fleeing East Germans, and they talked of rescuing hundreds. But their ambitious plan required money. To extend the tunnel away from the Wall in the East to dodge East German patrols required wood and steel and wiring, light bulbs and field telephones. In those days, escape organizations got their money to get started from a West German or West Berlin police authority. Theirs was soon gone and, embarrassed to go back for more, they came to us.

When the Wall went up, I had asked Piers Anderton and Gary Stindt to film what they could about the inevitable flight from East Germany. Tunnels had soon become the most common method, and they were being dug either by ad hoc groups of vaguely unsavory characters who charged large amounts to get people's friends or relatives out of "the East" or by students. Gary's weekend assistant, a former U.S. Army lieutenant who attended West Berlin's Free University during the week, had left word in all the student hangouts he knew in West Berlin that NBC would like to film in a tunnel. It worked. In May, he took Anderton to meet the students who had run out of money while building a tunnel.

Anderton met the project's organizers, two Italians and a German. One of the Italians, Domenico Sesta, known as Mimmo, short and blond, spoke good English. The other Italian, Luigi Spina, tall and dark, said only a few words. Anderton would always remember how the German one—Wolf Schroedter—sat in total silence, clicking the bolt on his automatic. They told Piers their tunnel was then sixty feet along, almost at the Wall, and they needed fifty thousand American dollars to complete it. The Italians were in it to rescue a friend, who had been at the Technical University with them until the Wall closed, and his mother, wife, and baby daughter. The German was a neighbor they had sought out because he was rumored to "know something about" tunnels. He wanted to bring out his sister and her child.

Piers was about to get married. He brought his bride-to-be to New York for the wedding and at a party we gave them took me aside. "I think we have our tunnel," he told me. He had been in it, crawling the sixty feet. It sounded promising, even exciting, but $50,000 was impossible. "They're crazy," I told him. I took it to Bill McAndrew. We agreed we would pay the students in return only for the right to film in the tunnel as it was dug. Anderton and Stindt would have them sign some sort of paper to that effect. We would all observe total secrecy; feeling ridiculous was not as bad as taking chances. Only those needing to know would be told. The money would be outside channels. We would limit it to $7,500. McAndrew would find a good time to tell Kintner.

On the day that started with his wedding breakfast, Anderton went from New York to Berlin with $7,500 in cash. By the end of the project, we had paid a total of $12,000, the rest in bits as the digging went along, needing more for this, more for that. It bought five tons of steel rail, twenty tons of wood, wire to light the tunnel, pumps when water main breaks flooded it, a compressor to get fresh air to the diggers and pipe to carry the air, pulleys and ropes to bring out the cart with the dirt, a motor so it need not be pulled by hand, and several months' worth of tea, coffee, and sandwiches. The steel rail guided the box with the dirt, which rolled on two wheels in back and a center one in front following the rail; the wood floored the 420-foot length of the tunnel, formed a ceiling for most of it, as well as supports every six feet—closer where the earth was crumbly—and four-by-four-inch crossbeams shaped by hand to fit snugly between the ceiling and the supports and hold it up.

Our film of the tunnel was a sensation even before broadcast. In both West Germany and the United States, newspapers ran stories for days; politics complicated the simple telling, and the three student organizers were accused, by Don Cook in the *Saturday Evening Post* and by some newspapers, of pocketing the money we gave them. In fact, Anderton and Stindt knew where every penny was spent, and as frustrations piled up, as the planned six weeks' digging grew to five months, they became the students' unwilling confidants, even father substitutes. Living close to such attractive, dedicated young people, they strained to follow Bill McAndrew's and my instructions to take no part in planning, express no opinions about action, and hold strictly to their roles as disinterested onlookers. When talk crossed the line marking the permissible, they changed the subject to politics or something young, like the future of mankind.

The project was never discussed on the phone. One had to assume being overheard; West Berlin telephone calls got to the West by microwave. Stindt called twice to tell me we had something to talk about, no more. I would not come to Berlin; resident American reporters in that inbred community, by then down to perhaps a dozen, would have asked questions if a New York big shot showed up. We held so tightly to the need-to-know rule, I didn't even know where in Berlin the digging was until the last day. But it was to be my documentary, so any problems were my problems. Off I flew, therefore, to talk in Paris where Piers and Gary and I dined grandly at Maxim's; the next time we met in London for dinner in the Savoy Grill. Each time I flew home the next morning. It felt foolish, but romantic.

Both times the problems we considered were water main breaks flooding the tunnel and stalling the digging. The first occurred when they were still inside West Berlin, the second after they had tunneled under the Wall and were well inside East Berlin. Our problem, the problem Stindt and Anderton wanted solved, was what if there was no completion, no story? My best answer was that we had not set out to do a program about a tunnel. For years we three had watched thousands "voting with their feet," draining East Germany of its intellectuals and its elite. With that experience, we had conceived a documentary about East Germans still trying to leave, even now that the Wall had gone up. This tunnel of theirs might end up as no more than one sequence of many, along with other tunnels, places where people jumped to their deaths, sewers with their resonance of Orson Welles in *The Third Man*, suppliers of forged passports, idealistic students and the cynical escape peddlers of the West Berlin demimonde. We would try to show what was happening behind the Wall while tour buses and souvenir stores swarmed along what had become one of Western Europe's major tourist attractions, the Berlin Wall. (See the Horror of the Century! Climb the wooden steps to the viewing platform, and wave at prisoners of Godless communism! Attractive souvenirs available.)

They went back to Berlin having heard more pep talk than advice. In the bureau storeroom, their hoard of film grew in time to twelve thousand feet, while in the tunnel itself the digging, and the filming, went stolidly forward. The tunnel was about three feet high and three feet wide. At its face, a digger on his back would thrust a spade between his legs into the earth before him, tossing the dirt behind him into a wooden cart, an apple crate with wheels. Behind him would be Peter Dehmel, the bureau's youngest cameraman, on his back, feet forward, his head upright, the camera against his eye; behind Peter, his brother Klaus, lying on his stomach so he could hold his battery-operated light next to Peter's camera. All three would be in front of the most-forward support being installed to hold up the tunnel as digging advanced. If the earth collapsed, it would collapse on them. Only the smallest, lightest, 16-mm camera would do in this pinched space. It held two and a half minutes of film. After exposing each roll, Peter would stop to reload, clumsily, because he had wrapped the camera in plastic to keep out water and mud.

In late August, McAndrew was visited by James Greenfield of the State Department information office, who had just been to CBS to warn them that a tunnel project they had been taking part in was a bad idea. CBS had agreed to withdraw. He hoped NBC wasn't involved in anything similar. Bill was noncommittal. Less than two weeks later, I got the final call from West Berlin: It was time to join them. I told Gerald Polikoff, who would edit the film, what we were involved in so that he became only the fifth person in the RCA Building to know, and we arrived in Berlin on September 13. On the way into town, Gary drove us past the site.

The Western entrance to the tunnel was in the cellar of an unprepossessing, bomb-damaged five-story factory building. Not all the floors upstairs were fit for use, but on one of them workers at plastic-extruding machines produced hundreds of thousands of swizzle-sticks. The students had dug the shaft 15 feet down from the cellar floor, and the tunnel 420 feet east from the shaft. All the rooms in the cellar were filled with dirt. Breakthrough was to be the next day, Friday, at dusk.

We spent Thursday screening the film Anderton and Stindt had assembled, our own and what they could buy, of dozens of escapes since the Wall had gone up, by jumping, by swimming, by sewer, and by tunnel—successes and failures. If our topic was to be all the East Germans trying to leave, and all the ways they tried, these would have been our film. Some of it was good film, but always the camera had arrived too late, only an open manhole to show, or a blank wall, a policeman, a hole in the ground, bystanders milling and gossiping. When, late in the evening, we finally got to Peter Dehmel's film from inside the tunnel, the actual digging, it was clear the other stuff was outshone. In the tunnel, we were there at every step, filming an event unfolding, seeing it happen.

There was still the breakthrough to be filmed, the escape itself, but I called Bill McAndrew in New York and said, "I may need ninety minutes, but I'll be able to tell you better Saturday."

When we had started filming the tunnel was a month along, so Gary made the organizers reenact what they did before we joined them, surveying the Wall, mapping crossing points, breaking into the concrete cellar floor. Reenactment is a touchy business in our trade so it was up to me whether to use this film. It seemed too useful to reject, but we identified it twice, once early, again ten minutes into the program, as Anderton said, "Here the reenactment ends. From this point all pictures were made as they happened."

The story as it unfolded, the story of the digging of the tunnel, was simple, claustrophobic, and frustrating. Up until their spring examinations, there were eight diggers; when the school year ended they grew to twenty, in three shifts, but security was the first concern. Anderton and Stindt and the Dehmels saw only one shift of the three. The others were just names in neat German script on the bulletin board above the hot plate. The pictures were of digging, of the two floods, of waiting, and of hauling dirt. When the box was full, about twenty-five pounds, the digger would lift the field telephone to call the hauler at the head of the shaft. They joked it was the only private telephone between East and West Berlin. The hauler would switch on the motor to pull the apple crate by its rope to the head of the tunnel, where it would be emptied into a wheelbarrow. The apple crate would return to the digging face while a third student moved the wheelbarrow to the room where they were dumping that day.

Digging tunnels means displacing dirt. For a tunnel being dug in secrecy, dirt must be dumped secretly. Digging a tunnel seems romantic, disposing of dirt mundane. Dirt outside the building would betray the digging, so it was stored inside. Before the tunnel was done, the cellar could hold no more. Dirt filled all the rooms, boards shoring it up like coal in bins to leave aisles for passage.

All Thursday evening and into Friday, we looked at pictures of the diggers of that one shift, pictures we would scatter through the narrative so that each became a person. There was film of a third Italian, the one who never said anything but was teased for wearing dark glasses in a tunnel. There was Hasso Herschel, an East German who had been jailed for an escape attempt, had reached the West on his second attempt, and now wanted to bring out his sister and her son. He had dark hair, piercing eyes, and a spade beard, and he dug harder than anyone except the two original Italians. One digger was known as Der Kleiner, or Shorty, because he was over six feet tall. A skilled electrical engineer, he installed the pumps and generators and other machines. Our film would include each of them as he dug, or hauled dirt, or sat around in futile idleness as the simple task they had set themselves was complicated by one external event after another, and the tunnel took over their lives.

When Gerry Polikoff and I came to edit the film, the puzzle was how to let the digging run long enough to let viewers feel the fatigue and the monotony, which were crucial as the gauge of the commitment of those young men who did nothing else that spring and summer. I felt we had to involve the audience in the ordeal, to make them experience it. But going too far would turn people away. There are no rules for solving this dilemma, only the feel of it. Watching unedited film those two days, I knew we had everything we needed to achieve this if only we did it right.

Each digger dug to bring someone out of East Germany. The two Italian organizers often visited the classmate who was their reason for digging. Gary taught Sesta, the short one, how to film. A bureau cameraman filmed him going through Checkpoint Charlie, and again when he came back. To this we could add Sesta's home movies, the film he had made of Peter Schmidt—the only name we were given— in a far suburb of East Berlin, his mother and his wife holding the baby, Peter playing the guitar. When the tunnel was almost done, Sesta did it again, returning with film not only of Peter's family but of the church where those who would come through the first night would rendezvous.

Other film captured the bleakness of the two floods, floorboards floating in puddles, water dripping from supports and crossbeams, diggers sitting or lying or reading or smoking in the ready room above the cellar; Spina and Sesta checking a map of the Berlin sewer system; the hand pump through which Sesta pumped eight thousand gallons the week Spina had his appendix removed. Peter Dehmel's professional eye made the most of muddy boots drying, hands brewing tea, Hasso Herschel studying for his driver's test. Then, glimpsed between the curtains of a window, West Berlin city workers repairing the main. By the second water main break, the one inside East Berlin, Der Kleiner had installed an electric pump, and for that reason or some other, when the flooding stopped the tunnel dried out. But they had lost three more weeks.

"The smell inside the earth itself is like no other smell," said Piers Anderton's script, "not like a forest or a field or a river or wet rock. It is a wet, old smell, a smell of undisturbed centuries, a smell of forever past and forever to come."

On June 21, Secretary of State Dean Rusk was taken on the visitors' tour of the Wall. In Bernauerstrasse he said, "The Wall must go!" At the tunnel site, almost immediately below him, Spina's appendectomy had delayed the digging. So had the security crisis when the students heard that another tunnel had been compromised. Those diggers, also students, came up into the arms of Vopos, the special East German border police. The news was a shock, a thunderclap; many in our group had friends in that one. They began to doubt each other. They kept one of their comrades under armed guard for days until finally deciding that he was not a threat. The rendezvous points were all changed. Who knew who had said what to the Vopos? Word of the changes had to be sent inside East Berlin. None of this happened when our camera was there. The Dehmels were told about it when they next came to film. On Friday, the day of the breakthrough, Peter and Klaus left in the early afternoon to film Sesta's fiancée, who held West German papers, crossing into East Berlin to serve as a courier. West Berliners were not accepted as West Germans by the Russians, and could not cross easily into East Berlin, but West Germans could. She boarded an elevated train, sat in an almost empty car looking out the window. At the last stop before the border, the Dehmels got off, leaving her on the train alone. The train crossed the canal that was part of the border dividing Berlin. It could be seen, and filmed, for more than a minute moving on the elevated tracks into East Berlin, then disappearing between two buildings. When the train was out of sight, they filmed the clock in the station. It was not yet two. She did not yet know, nor did they, that the other couriers would miss their rendezvous. It would be up to her alone to find all twenty-six people, the oldest of them seventy, the youngest six months, and direct them to number 7 Schönholzerstrasse.

The plan had the actual escapes beginning at about five, to take about two hours, and Peter and Klaus were to be back in the bureau by nine. It took longer than that, but things always do. We ordered food and waited. At 11:30, I had to get some air. I asked to be driven past the location. We did not stop, or even slow down. We could see well enough into the East even at that hour to be sure there was no special activity; nor was there any in the West, no police cars, searchlights, fire equipment, which would have been routine if the tunnel had been compromised. We returned to the bureau. Peter and Klaus got in at 2:00 A.M. They had left the film at the lab. Saturday at noon we saw the film of the escape.

Watching those black and white pictures unreeling on a stained white cardboard held me for an hour of tension and fruition like few I have ever experienced. A few minutes in, the camera was aimed down a hole dug fifteen feet into the earth to film the dirt walls and a crude ladder set against one wall of the shaft. Klaus Dehmel's battery light barely reached the ragged square of dirt at the bottom of the shaft. Almost four months of digging and filming and frustration and fear then came to a climax as, from screen left, a hand moved into the picture, paused, drew back, then a head, and then a whole person crawled out of the tunnel and stood up in the shaft. A woman. It was Evalina, Peter Schmidt's wife, the one Sesta had visited in East Berlin. She faced back into the tunnel as someone handed her the baby, whom she held against her as she slowly climbed the ladder.

Then one more, and two more, then the rest. First Sesta, who had left his post as a guard in the tunnel to help carry the baby. Then Peter Schmidt. Then Hasso Herschel's sister with her little girl. Crawling through the tunnel had worn six-inch holes in the women's stockings. After changing the babies' diapers, they stood half-crouched, two young women who had just met, sharing a basin of water to rinse mud from their scraped, naked knees. Others followed, young men, an older man, an old woman, her gray hair wild as the camera behind her showed her stopping on every second rung to get her breath. From Anderton's script: "These are ordinary people, not accustomed to risk. What must they be leaving to risk this?" It was not Anderton's line or mine, but Shad Northshield's. I had been showing him an early cut of the program to get an outsider's reaction because I was too close. Afterward, he did not remember saying it.

The Dehmels filmed only the twenty-six who came out Friday night. The diggers told Anderton and Stindt that three more had escaped on Saturday night. Students on guard along the tunnel that night were reporting that water was rising again. By Sunday night, when thirty more got through the tunnel was half-filled with water. The West Berlin fire brigade tried pumping it out but steady rain made that impossible. On Tuesday, the intelligence authorities, who had known about the tunnel all along, told the fire department to shut it down, and West Berlin announced publicly that a tunnel had been dug through which twenty-nine people had escaped from East Germany. City officials openly said they showed the tunnel to the press to warn others planning to use this escape route that it was no longer safe. As reported around the world, by radio or the wire services, the news was that twenty-nine East Germans had escaped through a tunnel to Bernauerstrasse. In the manner of the time, it was thereafter referred to as Tunnel 29. Only Piers Anderton said flatly, on NBC Radio, that fifty-nine had escaped.

Stindt fixed up a back room in his bureau and rented equipment so Gerry Polikoff and I could edit the program. We were dealing only with silent film so our needs were not great, and in little more than two weeks it came together, a beginning, a middle, and an end. The end was the party, which we gave. It would be too simple, too anticlimactic, to end with them coming through the tunnel. So during the week after the escape, we rounded up all who had not flown on to West Germany and laid on a heavy spread of food and whiskey.

The atmosphere was mostly sullen, but the mood was volatile, and there was only slightly more glowering than explosive laughter. It was fascinating to see. The tension was over, leaving only the uncertain future. The time for heroics was making way for the time for economics, and the adrenaline had drained. But there they were in fancy new clothes, the diggers sitting among them, Hasso Herschel and his sister, Spina and Sesta with Peter and his wife.

Late in the evening, Peter Schmidt agreed to play his guitar and sing. He had been refusing requests all evening, but by now, like everyone there, he was pretty drunk. He saluted his two Italian friends who had brought him and his family out of East Berlin. He acknowledged his debt in that mocking and partial way young people have; he sang to them in burlesque Italian, "Torna a Surriento," with mock-Neapolitan gestures.

> Vide 'o mare quant'e bello!
> Spira tantu sentimento,
> Comme tu a chi tiene mente.
> Ca scetato 'o sunna.

And that is how Polikoff and I ended the film. I was pressed into going with the sales department to Pittsburgh to help sell the program to Gulf Oil. It needed little from me. I told them what film we had, what I was doing with it, and they bought ninety minutes of prime time on Wednesday, October 31. I do not know what they paid. I know that Gulf, or somebody at Gulf, took the program as their own, identified with it, supported it through the bizarre history to follow, sometimes, I felt, more staunchly than NBC did.

By the time we came back from Pittsburgh, the world knew what we had done, or at least that we had done something. The timing of the announcement had not been of our choosing, and plunged us into a lot of meanness and politics for which we were unprepared. It had started when the West Berlin police had taken reporters to the site of the tunnel. NBC News's involvement became known through a peculiar circumstance. Until television news went to color, we were the only major organization to use DuPont film stock; the others used

Eastman Kodak. In the mob milling around the Bernauerstrasse cellar were news film cameramen, one of whom noticed on the floor a cardboard box with the DuPont trademark. "NBC was here!" he shouted. From that moment, we did our work on the program, editing, writing, music, all of it, in the glare of a spotlight. It slowed and distracted us.

At first NBC said nothing, then it announced that it had indeed filmed the digging of Tunnel 29. Then a full-dress press conference, McAndrew and Anderton and me up there on the stage fielding questions from a hundred reporters. Yes, we had paid, but not very much. How much? We would rather not say. And so on. Executives of other companies were sought out to be quoted saying they would never pay for news; CBS was especially voluble. They said they had been involved in a similar project but withdrew when the State Department asked them to. As we were to learn in the coming weeks, that was an incomplete account.

All this time, Anderton was in my office, at his own desk and typewriter, as we wrote the script together. The best film is sound film, not of people interviewed or showing off, but of the sounds that accompany every sight, noise in the distance, the horns and sirens of cities, the songs of birds not seen. But there could be no sound camera in the tunnel; sound cameras were too big for a narrow space not so deep as a well nor so wide as a church door.

Only once did they try to record the actual noises of the tunnel, made on a small audio tape recorder: the hum of the compressor pumping air to the work face, the motor pulling the cart with the dirt, shovels scraping, outside sounds heard inside—a streetcar, a tourist bus. The script asked, If the young men in the tunnel could hear what was happening on the surface, could the East German police in the street hear what was going on in the tunnel?

For the rest of the program we used music. I chose Eddie Safranski, once a well-known jazz bassist now a film composer who had done some work for *Outlook*. He wrote, orchestrated, and recorded a ninety-minute score in fourteen days; we had only seven weeks from the escape to the broadcast. The music implied tension when we needed tension, underlined monotony when we showed only digging. It had enough echo of Kurt Weill to say Berlin, but was not imitative. It was, necessarily, given how little time we had, simple, with few themes and few attitudes, but these benefited the film and accorded with it. Years later, I could hear in it a certain stridency, as I could in the script of which I had been one of the writers, but those were different days. On the positive side, not once did the script use the phrase *free world*, nor did the music play symbolic games with national anthems, theirs or ours. We put it all together, film and words and music, ordered prints for broadcast, and showed them to each other. It seemed to add up to a pretty good program.

Nor did the reporter become the story. Anderton could be seen talking only twice, after the opening and before the close. He opened with number 7 Schönholtzerstrasse seen from across the Wall in West Berlin. He closed during the party, with him outside the restaurant door saying that the tunnel had filled with water so not nearly as many escaped as the young men had hoped. "But there will be other young men, and other tunnels." Inside, Peter Schmidt was singing "Sorrento" to Sesta and Spina. End.

While Anderton and Stindt and I were in our own tunnels—in editing, in the recording studio, at our typewriters—important people tried to keep *The Tunnel* off the air. They almost succeeded. On October 16, the State Department said broadcasting the program would be "highly undesirable." An unnamed official told UPI that it would "complicate the Berlin situation." He did not say how. On October 18, Lincoln White, an official State Department spokesman, told the daily press briefing—that is, everyone—that such a broadcast would be "irresponsible, undesirable," and "contrary to the best interests of the United States." Strong stuff. We were puzzled and depressed; Kintner was nervous. Our diplomatic correspondent, Elie Abel, arranged for McAndrew and me to meet Secretary Rusk. We were received in his sumptuous seventh-floor office and told that it would have been embarrassing had the tunnel been invaded by East German troops to find "photographers" there from an American network. This is how memory reconstructs the conversation:

—But the tunnel was completed without incident.

—Yes, that was fortunate, but the possibility had existed, hadn't it?

—Was the Secretary saying that the program should not be broadcast?

—No, it would be improper for the Department to suggest such a thing. Any decision about broadcasting the program would be entirely up to NBC.

—But all these statements and newspaper reports added up to pressure to cancel the program.

—That was the farthest thing from [the Secretary's] mind. There was of course the matter of identifying those who escaped and endangering their families.

This was a new approach, that East German police needed American television to tell them who had left town. Escaping by tunnel, we pointed out, had already been widely reported in Germany, notably in an article in *Der Spiegel* about a scheme called "The Travel Bureau" *(Der Reiseburo)*, which got friends and relatives out under certain conditions. There was also a shady entrepreneur called "Fatty" or "The Fat Man" *(Der Dicke)*, whom newspapers in Germany and abroad had described as able to get people out for large fees. We had only recorded in pictures what was already known, and the State Department's actions seemed aimed at keeping the program off the air. (No, that was not the case, they kept saying. Showing the program was NBC's decision to make.)

Nevertheless, the next day, the Associated Press reported that the State Department still judged the project "risky, irresponsible and undesirable," but it "was not asking NBC to refrain from showing the film." Pressure? Perish the thought.

Earlier in the week, diggers not on the shift we had filmed complained publicly that the organizers had taken money for themselves. The West Berlin city council, the Senat, asked the Bonn government to ask NBC, directly and through the State Department, not to show the program. Kintner sent Lester Bernstein, a vice president for corporate relations, to Berlin to put out the fire. On October 20, the West Berlin Senat revised its view somewhat. Bernstein, who had been refused a meeting with Willy Brandt, the mayor of West Berlin, had talked to someone less well known but more important, Ernst Lemmer, Bonn's minister for all-German affairs. Lemmer was responsible for Bonn's relations with East Germans and the West German government's commitment to them. Bernstein told Lemmer what was in the film, and how it had been filmed. The Ministry of All-German Affairs then issued one of those third-person documents stating that "Minister Lemmer stressed that he had not given any comment on the disputed showing. However, he could only welcome it if the events in Berlin were reported to the world public as extensively and precisely as possible."

That should have done it, but it didn't. Sander Vanocur called to tell me that he had run into Attorney General Robert Kennedy, who had brought it up without any preamble. "That was a terrible thing you people did, buying that tunnel." CBS volunteered a sanctimonious statement claiming it would never do such a thing, again adding that in August a State Department deputy assistant secretary had visited Blair Clark, second in command of CBS News, to tell him American intelligence had learned that a tunnel-digging project in which CBS was known to be somehow involved had been compromised. CBS then pulled out of the project. That tunnel was indeed compromised and several people captured. The CBS statement made much of the fact that they had pulled out. It was that same day Jim Greenfield, the deputy assistant secretary, had visited Bill McAndrew to tell him what had happened with CBS, presumably as some sort of object lesson.

McAndrew had then told Kintner, who agreed, pugnaciously, to say nothing about what we were doing. No one was going to tell him, Kintner, how to cover news. Even after the West Berlin Senat had pulled back, after someone had somehow (we never knew who and how) quieted the student diggers, and after a Bonn cabinet member had given us as close to an open endorsement as governments can, the issue would not go away. Jack Gould preached a sermon in the *Times*, and Harriet Van Horne took swipes at us in the *World-Telegram & Sun*.

Caving in a little, Kintner ordered the faces of the refugees blacked out. We got that revised to exempt those who gave permission. Gary's staff rounded up signatures, but some refugees had left for who knew where in West Germany; their faces were covered with black rectangles like photographs of adulterers in exposé magazines. McAndrew told me that Kintner feared that RCA might lose its defense business. Courage was not holding at the top.

It was the time of the Cuban missile crisis, the closest the United States had been to war since V-J Day. McAndrew called me to his office to say that Kintner was postponing *The Tunnel*. No new date. Our ninety minutes on October 31 would be taken up by a program about the missile crisis. Shad Northshield would produce it.

"I'm sorry," he said.

I sat there for a long time. Then, to say something, I said that it was my time slot and the very least he could do was to let me produce the program. He was sure I would be busy, he said. No, the program was finished, ready to roll, and I saw no reason to change any of it— that is, if it was truly a postponement. He assured me it was. Shad and I would produce the program jointly. It worked out well enough. We called it *A Clear and Present Danger*.

That program over, I was thrown back to face where I stood. Kintner had postponed *The Tunnel* but would he ever reschedule it? I was deeply, perhaps unhealthily, involved in the program and convinced that postponed was a euphemism for canceled. McAndrew's assurances did not convince me. To me, beyond the program's merits as television reporting, it embodied values that were being denied for political reasons. I felt obliged to discuss it with my wife; it was not merely "something at work." I got her agreement before writing out my resignation. I wrote McAndrew I could not remain in an organization that could find no room for this program. He asked me to give him until the end of the year. I still had an off-year election night to produce and the Common Market program with John Chancellor to finish, so I held off that long.

McAndrew got *The Tunnel* rescheduled for Monday, December 10. Gulf, which had not only not wavered in its interest but had called me regularly during the turmoil to ask if there was anything they could do, would still be the sponsor. Although oil companies have at least as much to fear from the State Department as networks, Gulf had held firm. The broadcast was a triumph. The audience was enormous, not because of the program's merits since no one knew them until seeing it, but because the State Department had kept it in the news for weeks. It was the only time that season more people watched NBC than CBS's Monday lineup of star comedians: Lucille Ball, Danny Thomas, and Andy Griffith. All at once, vice presidents loved me.

And there have rarely been such reviews, except for Jack Gould's reservations—"little short of amazing" against "it would have been much more gripping condensed into a half hour"—and Harriet Van Horne's prim denunciation. She found proof of cheap theatricality among the credits, where it said "Makeup by Birgitta." As we were about to film Anderton outside the restaurant during the party, his new wife was bothered by how white his beard would look on television, so she darkened it with a makeup pencil. Later, putting together the credit list, still in the early euphoria, I used her first name as makeup credit. It was an inside joke, but harmless.

The other reviews wrote about "testament of freedom" and "epic courage" and "human adventure" and all the things we wanted to read. Spring brought awards tumbling at us. The day I got into a dinner jacket for the Emmy presentations, I considered it foregone that we would be the year's best documentary and we were. I said my prepared remarks, mostly nasty ones about the State Department. (It was no time to neglect the opportunity of a captive national audience.)

Piers Anderton won the Emmy for international reporting. (The *Hunt-ley-Brinkley Report* won its sixth Emmy, the first I was not called on to receive.) The evening's last award went to the "Program of the Year," which no news organization had ever won. I was surprised when *The Tunnel* was announced. Rehearsing in the shower what to say for the documentary award, I had not thought to prepare anything more. So I talked about the Dehmels and their heroism; I noted the support from Gulf; I mentioned the key role of Gary Stindt and Saf-ranski's great job. But, finally, it was those young men who had done it; we had merely shown what they did. I had nothing left to say. Bill McAndrew was at a table below the lectern, beaming, applauding. I looked at him as I said, "We've come a long way from night police." And sat down.

Program of the Year! The television academy discontinued that award a few years later, so *The Tunnel* will always be the only news program to win it. After the Emmys, there were the Overseas Press Club, which also recognized the Dehmels; Ohio State University; and more. Almost every foreign television service outside the Communist bloc showed the program; years later, foreign broadcasters I met knew me as the producer of *The Tunnel*. The USIA bought more than a hundred copies to show around the world as American propaganda, although that was a government action and meant no more, in its way, than the State Department's disapproval.

Perhaps no less. The program became one with the effort to keep it off television; the simple had become complex; the well-meaning had been besmirched. It bothered me for years that no explanation made sense. I finally used the Freedom of Information Act to get the State Department documents about the incident. An October 5 message to the U.S. mission in Berlin signed by Under-Secretary George Ball cited newspaper reports that NBC would show film of a tunnel on October 31. It added that Blair Clark had "justifiably" asked if his cooperation in canceling CBS's tunnel had "left CBS out in cold." It asked: "Was Anderton's enterprise carried out with US knowledge and approval? [This was apparently not inconceivable.] Was he asked to desist or was this an enterprise unknown to us?"

The next day, the reply, from BERLIN to SECRETARY OF STATE: "RE-PORTED ANDERTON ENTERPRISE NOT CARRIED OUT WITH OUR KNOWL-EDGE OR APPROVAL. SINCE WE HAD NO PRIOR KNOWLEDGE OF TUNNEL ESCAPE OF SEPT. 18 [sic] OR ANY ANDERTON CONNECTION WITH EAST BERLIN TUNNEL OPERATORS, WE WERE NOT IN POSITION TO REQUEST

ANDERTON TO DESIST FROM ANY FILM ACTIVITY . . . DEPARTMENT'S AT-
TENTION RECALLED TO OUR TEL 178 TO DEPT, 164 TO BONN, REPORTING
NBC ACTIVITY AND ALLEGED FILM FOOTAGE ANDERTON TOOK OF TUNNEL
IN AUGUST IN WHICH CBS PERSUADED TO CALL OFF SCHORR'S ARRANGE-
MENTS TO FILM ESCAPE . . ."

"Schorr" is Daniel Schorr, then CBS News correspondent in West
Germany.

After the tunnel it arranged to film had failed, CBS had promised
no more tunnels; NBC would not promise. In my State Department
Freedom of Information bundle was also a copy of a letter to Dean
Rusk from Kintner, of all people, setting out something I had not
known: The State Department had thought NBC was also involved in
the tunnel that had brought the warning to CBS. That was why James
Greenfield had come to see Bill McAndrew on August 21:

"It became clear from Mr. Greenfield's talk with Messrs. McAndrew
and Goodman," Kintner wrote to Rusk, "that his visit was prompted
by the erroneous belief that NBC had been participating as a patron
or purchaser of rights in an ill-fated tunnel venture involving the
Columbia Broadcasting System." Greenfield had told McAndrew that
the Department had learned through a double agent that this tunnel,
in West Berlin's Treptow district, had been compromised, and thought
NBC was involved because Anderton had been seen near the site when
the breakthrough into East Berlin failed. Kintner, or the lawyer who
wrote his letter, pointed out that the Department had since conceded
this assumption had been false after learning Anderton had heard about
that tunnel through other sources and was covering it as news.

Anderton told me what he knew of the rest of that part of the story.
Spina and Sesta had been involved in that tunnel, too, and from what
they told him and from what he saw the day that tunnel broke through,
he knew what had happened. Fewer than twenty students had dug a
short tunnel. They had planned to come up in a lumberyard storage
shack; they had come up into the watchman's shack instead. The
terrified watchmen had told them to go back West because he had to
call the police. The two diggers who had made the breakthrough
escaped, but the three dozen refugees waiting to escape were arrested
and all were sentenced to hard labor. Had the students blundered, or
had they been misled and entrapped? Anderton did not know.

In his letter to Rusk, Kintner was scathing about CBS and "its"
tunnel:

"The Treptow tunnel began in an open field, ran only thirty feet and ended in the house of a watchman at an East Berlin construction company yard. The organizer of this tunnel was an unsavory West Berlin character known as 'Der Dicke' ('Fatty') who has engaged in tunnel-building as a promotion. It had been bungled both in the digging and with respect to its security; while under construction it had become known independently to the State Department, the East Germans and NBC. . . . In comparing the responses of CBS and NBC to the representations of the State Department, it is relevant to note that CBS was being informed that the tunnel it was covering had been compromised and was already known to the East Germans. In these circumstances, it is hardly surprising that CBS agreed to withdraw its personnel. . . ." For Kintner, Berlin was merely another battlefield in the war with CBS.

The State Department's campaign to have NBC cancel the program had presumably been triggered by CBS's withdrawing from its tunnel and our failure to do likewise. While in Berlin putting out the fire, Lester Bernstein went to a cocktail party with the assistant bureau chief, Harry Thoess. (Gary Stindt was still in New York helping us with the script.) Daniel Schorr was also there. "I asked [Schorr] what happened to the tunnel that CBS had been trying to film," Thoess wrote me. "He denied any knowledge. I told him we had a roll of film shot by us that showed the CBS crew filming the escape attempt, which failed, and one could see very clearly on our film that the East Germans caught the people by force and took them away. Consequently CBS's claim that it had and would never touch such a project was false and what would CBS New York say if we would release our footage of their failure?"

Not CBS alone but all American reporters in West Germany were envious of the Dehmels' film, of NBC's achievement. From envy it may have been a short step to making mischief. On October 15, the U.S. mission in Berlin cabled the State Department that it had been informed by Don Cook of the *New York Herald Tribune* and George Bailey of *The Reporter* magazine that the two Italians and the West German who organized the tunnel—obviously Spina, Sesta, and Schroedter—had sold NBC the rights to film their tunnel "for personal gain" and without approval of the other diggers. In June 1989, I tracked down Don Cook in Philadelphia to ask him if he recalled saying this. He did, vaguely. Who had told him? Well, I knew how it was; Berlin was full of rumors. Did he really think that after buying supplies out of the money we gave them they had enough left for "personal gain"?

He had not realized. (Cook had written about that same tunnel, Tunnel 29, in the *Saturday Evening Post* and knew pretty well what was involved.) I also wrote to Bailey in Munich but got no answer.

I was no nearer to understanding why the State Department had done what it did than when I started. It was not reason enough that it was embarrassed because CBS had complied, and we had not, with a request that had in fact everything to do with CBS and nothing to do with us. But sorting that out was too much trouble for the State Department professionals. To them we were all one. Also, all government professionals, especially those in foreign affairs, wish only that the press would disappear so they can do their work. And here they were, caught in the middle. Nor could I doubt that the prim, lawyerly Dean Rusk was genuinely exercised by what might have happened, although it didn't. (With McAndrew and me in his office, Elie Abel, whom he trusted, had lost his temper, saying to him, "This is a program about human freedom. Does the Department consider that in the 'national interest'?")

Worst of all, the Department had been embarrassed because its mission had not known about the tunnel, or about the escape, until they learned about it from the newspapers. The United States had not known, but West German officials had known all along. (BERLIN TO SECRETARY OF STATE, September 19, 1962: "WE UNDERSTAND TUNNEL BUILT BY STUDENTS AND MONITORED BY LANDESAMT FüR VERFASSUNG-SCHUETZ.") The Landesamt für Verfassunghuetz is the West Berlin branch of what is usually translated as the Office of the Protection of the Constitution, a West German intelligence service closely connected to several of ours.

Yet all this was still not enough to justify in my mind the intensity and scope of the effort, our sense that it was being orchestrated. It was too big to stem only from the envy of journalists or umbrage in Foggy Bottom. Was there some other interest that was less obvious but just as real as competing reporters' or the Department of State's, and just as important? Over the years I have written myself a scenario that goes like this:

The official announcements, from West Berlin police and the West German government, said twenty-nine people had escaped through the Bernauerstrasse tunnel. That is why it was called Tunnel 29. But Piers Anderton, informed by the diggers themselves, said in his first radio news report and consistently thereafter that fifty-nine people had escaped, twenty-six on Friday night, three the next night, and the remaining thirty on Sunday, when the tunnel filled with water. Our script, as well as all other news coverage by NBC News, spoke of fifty-nine escaping, although we had film of only the first twenty-six. But no one could know that unless—or until—they saw the film.

The Department's unusual and intensive campaign ended as soon as the film was broadcast. Once seen, the film must have been judged to include nothing objectionable. But during all the public fuss no one had asked to see the film. Nor am I sure we should have honored such a request from a government agency; we tend not to. Until seeing the film, did someone fear what we might have filmed, whose faces we might show, perhaps the thirty who escaped Sunday night, which only we seemed to know about? Who were these thirty? None of the students knew them. They were not relatives or friends of those who had dug all that summer in exchange for the right to bring out a relative or friend.

How else explain Bob Kintner's strange involvement? He knew nothing of how film was made. And yet he told us to black out the faces of those who escaped. Was Kintner concerned we might show Peter Schmidt's wife and mother-in-law, Hasso Herschel's sister? Or did someone out of his lifetime of Washington contacts ask him to make sure, at least, that no faces were recognizable?

Years after the program was broadcast, having been in management and left, I attended one of the black-tie dinners so favored by Washington journalists. It was soon after Congress had investigated and publicly humiliated the CIA, which had then resolved to go forth to meet the people. Next to me sat a high officer of the CIA, who so identified himself. I steered our conversation to *The Tunnel*. He remembered the program but not the controversy, or the criticism from the government and in the press. I sketched in the story. Then I tried my theory: Could the thirty who came out Sunday have been CIA "assets," a dozen or so and their families? He said it was not the kind of thing he knew about, but he would check.

He did. Within days he telephoned me in New York to say that he had found no hint of what I had suggested. I cannot believe he would have confirmed it to me if they had indeed been CIA spies and their families coming "in from the cold," but for some reason I believed him when he told me they were not CIA. There are, of course, other intelligence operations in the United States government, some of them bigger and richer than the CIA, all of them less well known, which suits them just fine. All had interests in East Germany and East Berlin, so it could have been one of them.

No other answer is possible. The young students had spent a summer digging underground in return for the right to bring someone out, some close friend or relative. None of them knew the thirty who came out that last night. Long before the two Italians had come to us for help in digging the tunnel, they had received their initial capital from the intelligence section of the West Berlin or West German police, they were never specific which. It's not proof, but there is no other answer. It stands to reason such people would fear that we had the pictures of their agents or "assets" or whatever they were called. As soon as the program was broadcast—that is, as soon as they could see we had no such pictures—all objections ceased. Not a negative word was said. The United States government bought dozens of copies of the film to show around the world. This is not proof, but more than a quarter century later, it is all there is.

10

For NBC News, 1964 was the year nothing could go wrong. It was the good year between the year of the assassination and the one in which NBC, with its unique tradition of leadership turmoil, had itself the biggest, most wrenching shakeup of its history. In 1964, whatever went on in the world, everything we did about it seemed to work to our benefit. We rode high; we did well; we humbled the enemy. Bob Kintner's rasp mellowed to a mere purr.

The big, important story of 1964 was often a violent one: the relentless movement toward better civil rights. It brought cross burnings and marches, baseball bats and police dogs, picketers and courtroom dramas. With television now the chief source of Americans' news, it told in June of Michael Schwerner, Andrew Goodman, and James Chaney disappearing in rural Mississippi, and in August showed their bodies being found. There were place names like Princess Anne, Maryland, and St. Augustine, Florida, where the civil rights story centered for a day, a week, a month.

It was, also, a presidential election year, a political convention year with the tension and excitement—and status—for network news singularly noticeable that year. This would be our convention year—ours, not theirs. None of us doubted that the momentum established in 1960 would carry NBC News even higher; the *Huntley-Brinkley Report*, so successful it had forced CBS to replace Douglas Edwards with Walter Cronkite, kept on attracting a much larger audience; documentary producers—without me that year—were broadening the definition of current events to include art, higher education, and even popular culture, and in one wonderful instance used wit to report news, Ted Yates's chilling *Vietnam: It's a Mad War!* The commitment in Southeast Asia, still only a medium news story, was seen as something America was obliged to accept by the heady world role it had accepted after the Second Big War, one it could easily handle.

There was a lot of news that year and we covered most of it well, while a whole half hour each evening gave us what we, given our pasts, found to be ample elbow room to do it right. We were busy and we liked it, so that the political season came on us unawares. One winter morning, Shad Northshield and I, energized by what we saw as our superiors' complacency, decided to do something, so we chose the four floor reporters. Northshield, like me a producer by trade, co-opted for the moment into management, agreed with me that it was an urgent decision. We listed the five best-known names on our now well-known staff, crossed one off, and sent McGee, Newman, Chancellor, and Vanocur into immortality as NBC's "Four Horsemen." Since I had the news to do every day, Northshield made arrangements, beginning in February, when the networks were to meet the Republicans in San Francisco. It was there Don Hewitt stole NBC's secret plans.

What Hewitt did not know is that there were no secret plans. For CBS, the year was the obverse of ours and their frustrations were never greater. That February, Edward R. Murrow's onetime producer, Fred Friendly, had engineered a palace coup to replace Richard S. Salant, the corporate lawyer who was president of CBS News. As head of news, Friendly soon made himself known by a series of well-reported speeches on large problems he saw confronting American journalism, but the detail work was done by the people who had done it before. One of them was Hewitt; another Bill Leonard, who that year served as executive producer of political coverage and was among those at the San Francisco meeting.

At one dreary morning session in a public room in the St. Francis Hotel, broadcasters and politicians were working out details like placing pool cameras. Everyone was impatient to leave for lunch with the San Francisco host committee. NBC's chief unit manager for that convention, Allan ("Scotty") Connal, was there with Jim Kitchell, one of my directors. Hewitt was sitting behind them with Robert Wussler, later executive vice president of Cable News Network (CNN). Connal always kept his papers in a fat, black, three-ring binder. That morning it held lists of hotel rooms, staff rosters, a car rental contract, three bids for catering sandwiches and coffee to the NBC work space, and other arcane texts. It was labeled, "NBC Convention Plans '64."

The notebook was too bulky to hold, so Scotty placed it under his folding chair. When the meeting ended, he reached for it and found it gone. Hewitt and Wussler were also gone. Kitchell said that something similar had happened to him at one of the space shots, but he could never prove it was Hewitt. Connal is a hockey player, with a hockey player's muscles and a hockey player's temper. He asked if the doorman had seen two men, one with a black notebook. Yes, sir, they had just boarded a taxi. Knowing CBS was at the Fairmont Hotel, Connal hailed his own taxi and gave chase.

On the tenth floor of the Fairmont he hammered on Hewitt's door till it opened and demanded his book. Hewitt denied having it. Noise from inside the bathroom. "Whoever's in there, come out, you son of a bitch!," roared Connal. Wussler emerged, looking sheepish. Both again denied having Connal's book, but he had no doubt.

"I will count to five, and if I don't get the book," he said to Hewitt, "I will throw you out that window."

Scotty was angry, Scotty was formidable, and nothing they could say would divert him. He started to count. At three, Hewitt said, "The book's behind the door."

No hard feelings. Hewitt, Wussler, and Connal shared a cab to the Cow Palace for the City of San Francisco lunch. Connal, now less angry, told Northshield, senior NBC News officer present, what had happened. Northshield said it was outrageous—hilarious, but outrageous—but it was over, and no harm done. Nevertheless, word got around. Moments later, Connal was sought out by Joe Derby, the publicity executive in charge of getting publicity for NBC News, who wanted to hear the story from Connal himself. He then went back to Northshield and said, "I can get mileage out of this." Northshield wanted to forget the whole thing, and said no reporter would be interested. Derby told him he was obliged to "seize the moral high ground" for NBC.

By this time, everybody at the lunch knew what had happened and there was buzzing and laughter. Northshield, reluctant and embarrassed, approached Blair Clark, Friendly's second in command, a man known for rectitude and high-mindedness. "I think this is outrageous," Northshield told him while Derby, from behind Clark, gave him facial cues to say more, say more. Northshield could think of nothing more to say; what he had already said made him feel silly enough. He could not take the incident seriously, but Derby kept on gesturing behind Clark's back. Northshield worked himself up to, "I find it absolutely unconscionable."

Clark said, "Yes. I do, too."

Standing with them was Terrence O'Flaherty, the television writer for the *San Francisco Chronicle*. The *Chronicle*'s TV column the next day was all about Northshield's protesting an act he called "unconscionable," with which CBS News's Blair Clark agreed. So, for that matter, did O'Flaherty. Nor was that all. The *New York Herald Tribune* woke Connal that night to check details. The *Trib*'s story was page one; the wires told every paper in the country about it; London's *Daily Telegraph* used a front-page story "From Our Own Correspondent." And with little else to write about, O'Flaherty rang the changes on the theft of NBC's "secrets" all that week.

Although few newspapers, least of all the *Telegraph*, failed to use the incident as proof of how silly TV folks could be, they also included in their accounts NBC's ratings lead over CBS during the 1960 conventions and said Hewitt's theft showed the lengths to which CBS had been driven. There were rumors that Paley, or Frank Stanton, or somebody, wanted Hewitt fired.

How could there be "secrets"? Everyone knew NBC News's plans; we wanted them to. We would be set up as in 1960, Huntley and Brinkley in the booth, four reporters on the floor, others at outside locations. We would have again our anonymous brigade with the delegations, a news desk to rewrite their stories, a teletype system to get their news to those who would use it. In Kintner's, and indeed television's, hunger for attention from print, we held nothing to ourselves, and things we had no intention of doing were fed to newspapers to keep them sated and make them spell our initials right. But Scotty Connal had his fifteen minutes of fame; McAndrew, and sometimes Kintner himself, would call him mornings with what he was to say that day if newspapers called, which they did. Hewitt's theft was a windfall, keeping our convention coverage in the news until the larger political story took shape, which it soon did.

President Lyndon Johnson was, of course, assured the Democratic nomination. Senator Barry Goldwater of Arizona was almost as sure of the Republican nomination, but he might have been stopped if New York's governor Nelson Rockefeller won the California primary. After the *Huntley-Brinkley Report* on June 2, the day of the California primary, I drove to the RCA computer center in Cherry Hill, New Jersey. RCA was then the third-largest computer maker in the United States, which still meant in the world. I had no role in that evening's program but I wanted to see the vote analysis system in operation because I would be using it in the election night coverage on November 3. Shad Northshield, who enjoyed election nights more than I, was in charge of the voting analysis bureaucracy, while the program reporting the results of the primary would come from Los Angeles.

Raw returns would be collected precinct by precinct by brigades of volunteers organized by our election unit. The other networks did it the same way. Our voting analysis procedure, by now traditional with NBC, differed from theirs. It combined two distinct systems, one developed by a distinguished mathematician, the other by a distinguished social scientist. In those days, we projected a result before most votes were counted only when both systems agreed.

This is how they worked. Professor John Tukey, a Princeton mathematician, took the reported vote from precincts of established characteristics and projected the results to other precincts known to have the same characteristics, average income level, median education level, and so forth. By having established long ago the characteristics of all the precincts in the country, which he then stored in his computers, and done a lot of mathematical work, also stored in his computers, the votes from a few early precincts let him project final results in a lot of matching precincts. With the votes from relatively few additional precincts, he could project an election—for a state, for the country. His data came from the general vote-reporting apparatus. It reported all precincts; he picked out his.

The other system was developed by Richard Scammon, a political scientist and former director of the Census Bureau. NBC sent its own people to vote-counting headquarters in a whole bunch of precincts known to have voted for winners in previous elections. When enough of them were in, the ultimate results were projected. This second system needed very little special mathematics and would work using no more than adding machines, although computers would run it faster. Using both systems, we had beaten CBS to the call that year in Illinois and Oregon, but CBS had been first in New Hampshire, and Bob Kintner did not like it when CBS was first.

So there was Northshield in Cherry Hill with middle-level RCA executives hovering around him, and two long conference tables lined with people calculating, one chaired by Tukey, the other Scammon, each running his own system based on his own calculations using voting totals from separate sets of precincts.

Bill McAndrew, president of NBC News, was in the NBC studios in Burbank, where the California primary television program was being produced. Kintner, his boss, the president of NBC, in Los Angeles for a convention of the owners and managers of NBC's affiliated stations, for that evening only stayed in his elegant suite in the Beverly Hills Hotel, facing three television sets, at his elbow a telephone to McAndrew in the studio. When Kintner picked up that phone, McAndrew's would light up.

At 10:22 P.M. Eastern time, 7:22 Pacific, with polls closed in southern California but still open in the north, Kintner and McAndrew and Northshield, in Beverly Hills and Burbank and New Jersey, each watching three television sets, heard Walter Cronkite "call" the primary for Goldwater. Kintner picked up his telephone; McAndrew answered. Did you hear that? Yes, I heard that. Well, what the hell? I'll get back to you. McAndrew hung up one phone and picked up the one to Northshield. Did you hear that? Yes, I heard that. What do your fellows say? They're not sure. What do you mean, they're not sure? I mean one system gives Goldwater 53½ percent, but the other gives him only 50½, and I won't call an election with 50½ percent and half the polls still open. Well, he's been calling. I'm sorry, but you said to trust these guys and they say they don't have enough to make a call.

McAndrew telephoned Kintner. Kintner was not happy. So once again McAndrew telephoned Northshield, and this time the conversation grew heated. But all that night, rarely off the phone, Northshield held fast and, interestingly, was not countermanded. Not until well after midnight in the East, 9:50 P.M. in California, after even ABC, did the mathematician and the political scientist let him tell America that Goldwater had beaten Rockefeller. By the time he got to bed, he was sure he would be fired at dawn.

When Louis Harris, twenty-two minutes after polls closed in only half the state and were still open in the other half, had told Cronkite to say Goldwater would win with 53 percent of the vote he "called" it wrong. The actual vote was much closer all night long. After all the ballots were counted, Goldwater would lead by less than sixty thousand votes out of well over 2 million. But CBS had the winner, which is what matters in our business and to the people we work for, however silly Harris might look to his peers. In *The New York Times*, Jack Gould actually saluted NBC News for not yielding to competitive pressure, scolding CBS News for erroneous information. As comfort, it was meager, but it may have saved Northshield's job because he wasn't fired. Actually, Kintner rarely fired anybody, but that always came as a surprise.

The stop-Goldwater forces tried to rally around William Scranton, the governor of Pennsylvania, but they had too little time and a candidate whose only virtue was a willingness to be sacrificed. Eisenhower's support might have done it, but he refused to get involved. Dewey did not even bother coming to San Francisco.

Despite its hopelessness, the Scranton challenge would give us something to cover, a story to report. We would have that, and we would have civil rights, the issue that would dominate the proceedings and the news at both conventions. Civil rights and the Scranton candidacy—or rather the movement to stop Goldwater—came together many times during the week of the convention. During the week before the convention, they seemed to meld into one story as the platform committee met in the large, stately Colonial Room of the St. Francis Hotel, and George Murray, stealing a march on everyone, set up our coverage as a smaller version of the convention, with an anchor booth and floor reporters. Black leaders, shocked by the prospect of a Goldwater nomination, were flocking to the city; the Scranton forces were trying, clause by clause, bravely, with no success at all, to amend the platform closer to their position.

What we showed on television every day of that preconvention week was astonishing: the biggest guns of the defeated wing of the party— Rockefeller, Governor George Romney of Michigan, Stassen, Senator Hugh Scott of Pennsylvania, Lodge—pleading to temper the platform's language in measured sentences and careful argument, while the Goldwater majority remained silent, claiming little of the time due them in the debate, hardly answering at all. They knew they had the votes and saw no reason to waste their energies in rebuttal. When the question would be called, whatever it was, they would win, and they knew it.

All the conservative constituencies came to San Francisco to savor a victory they had been awaiting for years. This was no time to ponder how different they were from each other, what variations there were among them, the old Taft Midwesterners, the newly affluent Californians, Southern whites angry and frustrated by their comfortable society being thrown into disarray by outsiders and appointed judges, and those nostalgic for simpler times. Talk that was openly anti-Negro was rare; these were, after all, politicians. But outrage at the country's move toward civil rights seethed below the surface. Our reporters talked about something they called the "civil rights backlash." The convention included only fifteen black delegates and twenty-six alternates, mostly older men, lifelong party stalwarts, leftovers from the flowering of the Taft organization. Some began talking early about walking out of the convention if it nominated Goldwater. A few approached our floor reporters telling of clean-jawed young men dropping lighted cigarette butts into their pockets. One wept as he told his story.

The self-described conservatives in San Francisco were angry, opposed to everything around them, eager to hear talk about conspiracies and cabals. Having rarely experienced winning elections, wielding power, or shouldering responsibility, they favored simple, even physical answers. Four years before, Goldwater had urged them to, "Grow up, conservatives!" Some did, but most were irate and vengeful. They were hostile to the press—which they saw as an evil combine, monolithic, Eastern, and liberal—and especially television. Outside the Cow Palace, where Young Republicans sold souvenirs, the most popular was a button urging, STAMP OUT HUNTLEY-BRINKLEY! It sold out, and they had to send to New York for more.

This hostility achieved less frivolous expression on the second night of the convention. The speaker was the former President, Dwight D. Eisenhower, the only Republican President since Herbert Hoover. The Easterners had chosen him to lead the party; they had won him the nomination and organized his election and administration. What they believed was what he believed. But that Tuesday night none of that seemed to him as important as offering himself as the symbol of party unity. He actually reminded the delegates that the two world wars and the Korean War began during Democratic administrations. He did not accuse them of causing the wars, but the applause was deafening. Then he turned to the press.

The San Francisco Cow Palace is roomy and airy and its seats slope up easily to the ceiling. The anchor booths were not gondolas suspended over the floor, as in Chicago's International Amphitheater, but small studios at the back of the rows of seats. Eisenhower told the delegates to pay no heed to those "outside our family" who criticized the party and its leaders, especially "sensation-seeking columnists and commentators"—and the hall exploded in noise. The delegates on the floor, the audience in the seats, rose and turned toward the booths, above all the NBC booth.

Our floor reporters told me that, standing on the convention floor at that moment, they could barely see the NBC booth through the forest of raised and shaking fists. Huntley and Brinkley fully expected people to come through the glass at them. It was a moment of terror. When historians urge reappraisal of the Eisenhower presidency, to credit him for healing America's postwar exhaustion, for his gentling effect not only on politics but on the economy, I remember how he said "commentators and columnists"—"colyumists," he pronounced it—and how that let loose the beast in the mob, and what it felt like to be there.

After Ike's speech, the live cameras picked up a still photographer being ejected from the hall. Then there was a confrontation near the Puerto Rico delegation between a sergeant at arms and a television lighting technician. The evening was moving toward the most famous incident of conflict between that convention and the press: John Chancellor arrested and marched off the floor by two men in uniform. It started when I overheard Eliot Frankel, who edited the floor reporters, talking to Chancellor, who was telling him that he was at Alaska but a sergeant at arms wanted him to leave the area. The gavel could be heard in the background and the chairman asking that the aisles be cleared. Chancellor thought he would sit among the delegates in a vacant seat until the fuss died down and he could resume working. Eliot told him to check in when he was available again. Then, again, Chancellor to Frankel: "They will not let me sit down. They insist I leave."

I got into it. I told Eliot to have them make him leave. Eliot squeezed the button and spoke in Chancellor's ear: "They must make you leave."

How?

Eliot: "Make them carry you."

At that, I pressed my own button, saying, "Walk!" On the tape, which has been shown over and over ever since, Chancellor can be seen between two Daly City police officers, one holding each arm, slumping momentarily to make them carry him, then straightening up and walking out. Both Huntley and Brinkley—and others—thought it was funny. Not Chancellor. He found it humiliating, disconcerting, and unpleasant. He kept talking as he was led out, giving a running description of his own arrest, adding, "I formally say that this is a disgrace." He disappeared from camera view still talking, recovering enough of his sense of humor to sign off, "This is John Chancellor, somewhere in custody." (It made him famous, but with the passing years he wished more and more to be famous for something else.)

In minutes, he was back at the Alaska delegation, escorted by a higher officer among the sergeants at arms, with whom he shook hands. He resumed with, of course, "As I was saying . . ." But it was an ugly incident and an ugly experience, and playing it for laughs did not make it less ugly.

On Wednesday, Senator Goldwater won the nomination, with three-quarters of the delegate votes. On Thursday he accepted, saying, "I remind you that extremism in the defense of liberty is no vice . . . moderation in the pursuit of justice is no virtue." As he was speaking these words, the cameras showed Senator Kenneth Keating leading some of the New York delegates out of the hall. The black delegates stayed in their seats.

When the last session was over, earlier on Thursday night than we expected, I positioned the four floor reporters around the now empty hall so each could comment, sketch in details we had not had time for, reflect on what had happened in that hall that week. We were filling time, but they were good and very stylish. A few weeks later, at the Democratic convention in Atlantic City, it became something we did, with the four horsemen now together in the empty hall, talking to each other and to Huntley and Brinkley in the booth—several nights in Atlantic City 1964, *every night* in 1968! We chafed when Kintner insisted that we get on before CBS, and stay on after they closed, but this was something we ourselves wanted to do.

The Democratic party did not convene in Atlantic City until Monday, August 24, very late for a national convention and after an unusual gap of four full weeks between conventions. Meanwhile, the figures were published. Again, as four years before, NBC had attracted a larger audience than CBS and ABC combined. More important, only a fifth of the audience had watched something other than convention coverage. For us to capture more than half of those watching the convention was to give us fully 40 percent of the Americans watching any television those four evenings.

While we went about our business producing the program, company executives talked mostly about ratings. At the coal-face we learned such things later, although there were hints and winks throughout that we were doing okay. Only the major cities were then "rated" nightly by the Nielsen service. Those "numbers" were called from NBC in New York to very high ranking company officers who had come with us to San Francisco and whose journalistic role was to be awakened very early, California time, with the previous night's ratings, and call, hotel to hotel, to get the word to Kintner. (The "numbers" also provided small talk in the drinking with politicians.)

We were not the only ones involved with the Nielsen numbers; we were merely the only ones to enjoy them. At CBS, they caused no joy. On July 30, Fred Friendly, as president of CBS News, announced to a national intake of breath that Walter Cronkite would not be anchor for their coverage of the Democratic convention. That job would be done by two people, old-timer Robert Trout, who had been anchoring for CBS Radio, and Roger Mudd, a young Washington reporter who was a favorite of Friendly's. In extremis, CBS had stumbled on Davidson Taylor's rejected idea from 1956, an older man explaining to a younger man.

Friendly was careful to describe Cronkite's work during the Republican convention as "superb, but the story can be reported better by two men." (This is the first important example I remember of the fallacy that Huntley and Brinkley succeeded because there were two of them.) There were expressions of respect for Walter, loyalty to Walter, love for Walter, fealty to Walter. He would, after all, carry on the *CBS Evening News*, the "most important program" on CBS. The world was assured and reassured there was no thought of replacing him there with two other fellows. (Newspapers, however, speculated baldly that if the new team proved popular at the Democratic convention, replacing Cronkite on CBS's evening news was sure to be next.) Walter himself was called on to deny that he was thinking of resigning, first to newspaper reporters who phoned and then, when they grew too many, in a formal press conference on August 3.

"We took a clobbering in San Francisco," he told the reporters, "and it seems perfectly reasonable to me that management at CBS would like to try something else." He attributed NBC News's success to the "entertainment value" provided by Huntley and Brinkley and allowed this was not his strongest suit. He was being gracious only to a point; he wanted sweeter grapes. Don Hewitt, producer of the CBS convention coverage, was thrown off the back of the sled with Walter, and the two of them showed up in Atlantic City doing only the evening news, soldiering on bravely and accepting stoically the sympathy of friends and fools alike. Newspapers reported Cronkite's martyrdom in slavering detail, and it let late-night comedians talk of something people considered serious, which they relished, and did with appropriate solemnity. I have wondered if this triumphal moment for Huntley and Brinkley did not hide the seed of their decline as indignation and sympathy for Cronkite welled up in all honest folk. Certainly, his firing made him more famous than he had ever been.

As soon as it was announced that Trout and Mudd were replacing Cronkite, a story raced through New York television circles that is too good to risk by checking:

The scene is Cronkite's suite in a posh LaJolla hotel where he was staying when not at sea in his boat. It is after the Republican convention. The telephone rings and it is Eisenhower. Walter, one of the American reporters who spent much of World War II with Eisenhower, is a true familiar, and they are genuinely fond of each other. After the how-are-you's and How is Mamie? and How is Betsy? Eisenhower asks, "What is this I read in the newspapers?"

Walter replies, "Well, General, you know what kind of business this is, and what happened is just one of those things that happen." (All those old SHAEF reporters called Eisenhower "General" even after he was President, or so I have been told.)

"Well, I think it's just terrible."

"Well, thank you, General. It's good to know I'm in your thoughts."

"No, no. This is disgraceful. I really think something should be done about it. Perhaps I can do something."

"Thank you, General, but I wish you wouldn't."

"No, Walter. My mind is made up. I'm going to call Bill Paley." Nothing Cronkite says can dissuade him.

A few days later, the phone rings again, and again it's Eisenhower: "Walter, this is Ike Eisenhower."

"Oh, yes, General, good to hear from you."

"Walter, I called Bill Paley . . ."

"Gee, General, I wish you hadn't."

". . . and Bill said he didn't do it. According to him, it was some fellow in Chicago named Nielsen."

. . .

We expected the Democratic convention in Atlantic City to be without suspense. Lyndon Johnson's nomination for a full term was unopposed and foregone. When the nominee is known before the first gavel sounds, a convention becomes a balloon without air. This is usually ascribed to television, pejoratively, as if political conventions before television were assemblies of savants earnestly weighing national alternatives, veritable Socratic academies.

Against all expectation, however, this convention proved to be interesting as a spectacle, a television show. Partly, this was the conscious work of President Johnson; partly, it was the struggle for recognition by Southern black Democrats, refined down to one group, the Mississippi Free Democratic Party. Johnson's scenario and the black struggle for party recognition were often in conflict.

The Mississippi Free Democrats were a full delegation, not all black, led by Aaron Henry, a small-town druggist and president of the state's NAACP, who came to Atlantic City asking to replace the delegation put forward by the state's "regular" Democratic party. They argued that the regulars would not support the party's nominee, which would violate its new national rules, and that the regulars' delegation was chosen by whites only. The battle was never resolved, but while it was fought it held interest. The first battlefield was not Atlantic City, but Washington, where the platform and credentials committees met during the preceding week.

On Saturday, the climax of the week, the committee, and the national audience, were mesmerized by the testimony of Mrs. Fannie Lou Hamer, a sharecropper from Rulesville, Mississippi, a Free Democrat delegate, who told of being ordered by her "plantation owner" to withdraw her registration to vote, of being arrested for trying to get others to vote, of being forced to lie on a prison cot, and of two black prisoners ordered to beat her with blackjacks so she would regret her agitation. For the political semiprofessionals who form the bulk of convention delegations this was strong stuff, and their outrage was genuine. Mrs. Hamer probably cost the state's regular Democrats their seats, but that was still almost a week away.

The most attractive attribute of the Mississippi Free Democrats was their unadorned humanity, their dignity, their passion. What they were asking was simple and basic, and soon transcended the technical details of the argument in the minds of those watching. From the beginning of the convention, our reporters clustered around them, especially Frank McGee. They became the running story of Atlantic City, overshadowed for an hour or a day by something immediate, like the nomination or the Kennedy memorial, but threaded through the entire week and resonating in the memory.

There was a compromise on the seating that neither side accepted, so the regulars went home to Mississippi and the Free Democrats took up all the seats. Who had how many votes did not matter since no issue came to a vote. But as Vanocur said, having lost their bid in 1964, the Free Democrats won something bigger: Never again would a delegation be chosen by a segregated franchise.

All this agitated and displeased the President. McGee was interviewing Bayard Rustin, a senior leader of the civil rights movement, when Lyndon Johnson had a secretary place a call to Kintner for him. Kintner was not in his office; the telephone was answered by one of his entourage of executive outriders, who paled when he heard the president's voice, and turned even more ashen when he heard what the President said: "Tell Bob Kintner to get those [dark faces] off my television show or I'll make trouble." Or at least, that is how it was repeated in the corridors, which heard about it immediately. First, there was the buzzing among the not-very-busy executives, to whom "trouble" from that source could only mean losing a broadcasting license. As the worrying and whispering spread, it became merely gossip. But I was never told to trim coverage of the Mississippi Free Democrats. They remained our principal running story until it ended. (As recollection, Johnson's telephone call is most interesting to me for his use of "my television show," if that is indeed what he said.)

At about nine o'clock Wednesday evening, nomination day, while Governor John Connally was nominating his fellow Texan for the presidency, the picture cut to a small airport outside Atlantic City while convention sound continued. Out of the helicopter stepped the President of the United States. NBC News reporter Nancy Dickerson, a friend since Johnson's days in the Senate when she was a pretty young committee researcher, rushed to the foot of the ramp. "I'm happy to see you, Nancy," the President of the United States said on ABC, CBS, and NBC. "You've been doing wonderful. I've been watching you." Other reporters had now joined them, but he spoke only to her.

It was to Nancy Dickerson that he announced his running mate would be Hubert Humphrey. This was no longer news; he had hinted it to other reporters, leaked it, winked about it, played pattycake with it, come to Atlantic City to tell it to the delegates, but this was the first time he had said it publicly. This made it Nancy Dickerson's scoop and she mentioned it often in coming years; the biggest story of the 1964 convention and she broke it! He told her how he had picked Humphrey, how he had telephoned Mrs. Humphrey to tell her. After Humphrey was allowed to say a few words of his own, they got into the limousine to be driven to the convention.

Sander Vanocur had earlier come to the control room to ask if he could leave the floor for a few hours. I objected; he was needed. They all were. The session was full of lapses and monotonies that we had to fill, and who knew what our manic boss would want next. But Vanocur thought he knew where the President was going to be and he might be able to position himself there before the Secret Service sealed it off. As a result, while the speeches droned on, and the convention pretended to do its business, and we had to cover civil rights demonstrators on the boardwalk outside the hall, I somehow made do with three floor reporters.

When finally we reached the roll call of the states, for their unanimous votes, we spotted Vanocur in a VIP box talking to the Humphrey children. He took up position there and stayed for two hours, while on the podium and the convention floor the vote was completed, the President was escorted into the hall, the President spoke to the convention about his choice, Humphrey was nominated, and seconded, and seconded, and seconded, and the bands played, and the delegates ate hot dogs. Then Johnson made his way to the adjoining box, the one next to the one Secret Serviceman Rufus Youngblood had let Vanocur stay in because Youngblood had earlier lost his wallet and Vanocur found it for him.

Vanocur interviewed the President from 12:30 to 12:46 A.M. It was exclusive. It was without news, but it was the President live, and it was ours! The convention ground to a halt, and the other networks scratched to fill, while Johnson talked. ABC and CBS could show the President speaking to NBC News or they could look for their own news, of which there was none. In the CBS control room, Bill Leonard fumed. Where were his famous, expensive floor men? The Secret Service were keeping them away. He called for a headset and transmitter and dressed up as a floor reporter; he ran across the floor to the presidential box, risking the displeasure, to say the least, of the Secret Service. He got there at 12:42 A.M.

Vanocur saw him arrive. He let Johnson finish a sentence and said, "Mr. President, may I present my colleague, Bill Leonard of CBS. I'm sure you know him. He's a good man, Mr. President." Then

Sandy moved over to talk to Humphrey leaving Bill Leonard his few minutes with the President outside our picture. My lasting image of 1964 is of Vanocur presenting Bill Leonard to Lyndon Johnson. A "good man" indeed!

On the last day, Thursday, the nominations safely completed, at 8:57 P.M., Bobby Kennedy rose to introduce the film about his brother. Clearly there would be applause, but no one was prepared for what happened. The convention erupted in its only heartfelt demonstration of the week, and lost itself in affection and grief, nostalgia and aspiration. An uproar of cheers and shouts lasted for an unbelievable thirteen minutes—thirteen minutes without organizers or snake dancers or prepared posters or rehearsed music or assigned roles, thirteen minutes of cheering and clapping and waving such banners as were to hand, thirteen minutes of wishing things had been different.

No one who was there could ever after be skeptical of the "Kennedy phenomenon." He had become a symbol to those people now cheering in the hall. He had taken them outside themselves. Less than a year dead, he left them accepting something indefinably less, and because there was no point in crying, they cheered. Three or four times, when the noise seemed to subside, the passion to ebb, Bobby tried to begin, and that would start it again. His eyes were wet when at last they let him say his few words.

We managed to survive that prodigious week with only one embarrassment. The ground had been laid when, in the weeks before the convention, Nancy Dickerson, carefully getting Kintner's approval in advance, had filmed a "family album" session with the President's wife and daughters. The word came down to me that it was available, and then, never quite stated, that I would be expected to find room for it. It was less than twenty minutes long and there could "always" be a spot for "something like that." During the convention's first evening, with Bill McAndrew taking a short break, and George Murray sitting in his seat, the telephone rang—not the Kintner phone, the other one. George listened, and turned to me:

"When are we going to run the Johnson family album?"

I shrugged him off. I was on my own telephone call, with more important matters. I had two floor men covering the same story and we were having trouble coordinating them.

George stood up and shouted at me:

"When are we running the family album?"

"Who wants to know?"

"The President of the United States."

Oh.

"Tell him tomorrow night for sure." And Tuesday night, during the reading of the platform, we showed Lynda Bird when she was four, the three women getting off a train, the Christmas picture with Lynda Bird in Doctor Dentons, Lynda and Luci in look-alike dresses. (It was here that Bill Hill borrowed from Dorothy Parker and whispered, "Constant Viewer fwowed up.") There they were in Disneyland, there they were with the beagles. They talked to Dickerson and to each other about the role of the family in public life and the meaning of Christmas. Words cannot capture the banality. This was what President Johnson was referring to the next day when he said at the airport, "Nancy, I've been watching you."

We came out of Atlantic City still the leaders. Bob Trout and Roger Mudd had not improved CBS's ratings, which had been the one reason they were put there. There was actually one hour of coverage where the rating service showed us with 84 percent of the audience. Shortly after that, Northshield was in McAndrew's chair beside me when the Kintner phone rang.

"Hello."

"You guys are slowing down."

"For Pete's sake, what do you want? One hundred percent?"

"You're goddam right!" Slam.

CBS, frantic, asked for humor from Eric Sevareid and Harry Reasoner, "recognized as humorous essayists of long standing," as one newspaper coyly put it. (ABC hired television comedian George Gobel to make humorous asides.) The ratings were not helped. ABC's were about what they had been for their Republican coverage; CBS's slipped a notch, which we gained. It was fun to watch CBS keep attributing our edge entirely to Brinkley's humor. They could not bring themselves to accept that we did the basic work better than they, and only then went on to outshine them in the anchor booth. Brinkley, moreover, was not some fellow telling jokes. He was an experienced Washington journalist who was also gifted with wit and style. Huntley's solidity and Brinkley's wit put a stamp on our work. Also, they were both so self-assured that they shared airtime easily with other reporters. Thus, being funnier than Brinkley would not have helped ABC or CBS even if they could have been.

The capper was to be election night, and for this RCA, the "parent corporation" so revered by McAndrew and the other old-timers, had proposed the most, best, modernest, fastest computer system of all. The vote would be gathered by the News Election Service, a consortium of the three networks and the two major wire services under the aegis of an antitrust exemption, but what would happen to those numbers would be the province of the new magic. An RCA house organ had advised the company's salesmen, "If you have a customer who has any doubt about RCA's computer capability, systems capability, real-time capability, programming capability, or any other capability, this is the time to prove we're not just talking—we're doing. And we can prove our points right in their own living rooms—just get them to watch NBC." Third in the fledgling business of computers, RCA sought all the attention it could get. We were the vehicle.

McAndrew, Northshield, and I drove down to Cherry Hill to be shown what they were planning, including something they referred to only as a secret weapon. We saw the seven RCA computers and the hundreds of miles of wire so beloved of press release writers and the rest of this up-to-date system of reporting and projecting elections. John Tukey and Richard Scammon would again be presiding over their own systems as they had done for the primaries. The secret weapon was something called a Digital to Video Converter, shortened and glamorized to DIVCON. This would take all the stored material and all the night's material as it came in and translate it into a television frame without "posting" by human hands. Thus, John Chancellor, the analysis reporter, or Northshield, his editor that night, would simply press a key, and it would say:

INDIANA 63%
PRESIDENT
JOHNSON
TO CARRY BY
50,000 TO
130,000 VOTES

There were such frames for each state, for senator and governor, for summaries of the national vote. I fantasized that future election nights would require only one good reporter and a DIVCON; we could go back to Huntley's tiny fifth-floor studio from our poor, early days. Then someone else could do election night and I could go to the movies, or read a book.

Frank Jordan, in charge of the vote-getting part of the organization, had hired 9,000 temporary workers to feed the two systems and the machines. George Murray oversaw recruitment and distribution of almost 820 NBC people to work in Studio 8-H and around the country, including 22 correspondents besides those in the studio, 57 or 58 editors and news writers, Chet Hagan's 14 remote locations with their 60 live television cameras, and on, and on, and on. I could never have done it. First Sughrue had done this kind of thing for me and then Murray. I would tell them what I wanted to do and they had to enable me to do it, but I could not have accomplished my requirements myself.

While all this was going on, at the *New York Herald Tribune*, a newspaper going through the brilliance of its last days, Richard C. Wald, the managing editor, proposed to William S. Paley, his owner's brother-in-law, that the *Herald Trib* use CBS's computer material with due credit, which would be free publicity for CBS. Wald reasoned that much of the material so expensively gathered would not be used, or, given how broadcasting uses material, would vanish in the twinkling of an eye. Paley was intrigued enough to make the deal with *The New York Times*, which would pay him $25,000.

Wald was furious. It was his idea and Paley stole it. Knowing no one else in broadcasting, he called Julian Goodman with the same suggestion, in honesty adding the story of what Paley had done to him. Goodman asked him, "What are you prepared to pay?"

Wald replied, "Nothing, because you have no other papers to go to, so if you want the publicity you must come to us."

Julian laughed; it was done. Then other newspapers were invited, and there were soon places for about a dozen in a large room off 8-H. To the *Washington Post*, the *Chicago Tribune*, the *Boston Globe*, and the others NBC was prepared to provide telephone, typewriter, space to work, coffee, sandwiches, soft drinks, and all the material spewing out of RCA's seven computers. They would have returns; they would have the best projections for their editions as each went to press; they would have tables and charts so dear to editors of election editions. And NBC News would get publicity worth far more than the mere $25,000 Paley was getting from the *Times*.

Only one thing went wrong. The computers did not work.

A few minutes after eight that evening, in my place behind the high table separating the deck where McAndrew and I sat from the lower one where the directors and technicians sat, I saw Northshield's face rise up, drawn, pouchy, angry.

"The damned machines won't work."

"Who knows?"

"Well, I know. Chancellor knows. And, of course, the RCA guys."

"Don't tell anybody."

Luckily, weeks before, Northshield and Jordan had conspired to put together a rough backup system in case the computers failed. Jordan put extra people in four regional vote collection centers to get us results from key and tag precincts outside regular channels, by telephone if necessary. Northshield had those simple and sparse items fed into the DIVCON display device. The actual returns came in as they were supposed to, and were posted in the units around the huge studio as they were meant to be. I used Chancellor and the DIVCON as planned, often enough so it seemed to be something to boast about. CBS had only a small edge on us in projections even though their system worked perfectly. Huntley and Brinkley did not at any time that night know the computers were not operating. McAndrew did not know. In the *Times*, Jack Gould mentioned in passing that we were said to have had some computer trouble. He preferred CBS's coverage. But the television writer for the *Herald Tribune*, watching at home and not to be confused with its chief political writer in the room off 8-H with the others, said we clearly had the best presentation.

None of the big-name national political reporters knew the computers were not working. Dick Wald, back in the *Herald Trib*'s newsroom, knew because he had no numbers for the tables he had set in type and had to fill with slow stuff from the wires. (The *Times*, on the other hand, got all it needed from CBS, all $25,000 worth.) One service said we had slightly more audience than the other two combined, the other said we had slightly less.

Kintner held some kind of drumhead court-martial that had nothing to do with me. And RCA fired some people. When RCA finally withdrew from the computer business I wondered whether it had anything to do with the great debacle of 1964, but since that was seven years later it is highly unlikely. I thought that we had done a good job with the election night program, and losing the computers mattered little. All those smart people sitting right there did not sense it. The only reporter I know who spotted it was Edwin H. James, executive editor of *Broadcasting*, who wrote a brilliant article describing what went into a network's election night report.

"Considering the number of people who were intimately involved in the NBC show," he wrote, "it is remarkable that the best-kept secret of the election night of 1964 was and still is the utter collapse of the elaborate computerized system that NBC had counted on to issue automatic projections and analyses and to dazzle viewers with its virtuosity on DIVCON. Not a single 'take' of analytical material came out of the 3301. DIVCON was struck dumb."

Luckily, it was a landslide. (Johnson won.)

11

I had undertaken to bring the *Huntley-Brinkley Report* from fifteen minutes to a half hour, and stay two years. By January 1965, I could hardly wait for the two years to end. I could no longer pretend interest in the day's most important story, or what we should be covering tomorrow, or next month. I was not sure what I wanted to do, but I was more certain with each day of what I did not want to do. Daily news programs had become a grind. There was no challenge left. The restlessness I had felt when I left the first time was back. Beating CBS had become too easy and no longer made up for boring detail, the feeling one gets when the same news stories seem to repeat themselves day after day after day. I was newsed out.

There were other irritations. Kintner decreed early in 1965 that Huntley and Brinkley bump McGee out of anchoring space coverage, which was becoming an ever bigger story. It was a decision I disagreed with, and a nuisance to me, because it took them off somewhere during many nights of news. But it had begun to bother Kintner that over at CBS, Walter Cronkite was still their man on the space program. When Huntley and Brinkley's success on the news had forced CBS to replace Douglas Edwards on their competing program with Cronkite, he continued anchoring their space coverage. This brought him notice for doing both, the iron man, in the Molotov tradition.

Perhaps the survey people told Kintner that CBS got some advantage from all this; in any case, he was sure that if Cronkite could do it, we could do it. Huntley and Brinkley would not only do the news, they would anchor space coverage, leaving McGee as some kind of expert commentator, or so NBC told the press.

It was less than McGee deserved. Worse, it gave the job to two fine and talented broadcasters who had, at best, only casual interest in the topic, and it showed. It was around this time that CBS's space coverage began to get better notices and larger audiences. Gulf, which had opposed the change, complained without effect. Not even his stake in that relationship could make Kintner reconsider. It would violate his being to admit a mistake. He never learned there are Huntleys and Brinkleys who are exceptional at some things, and Cronkites who can be dependable at nearly everything. As different as they were, however, Huntley, Brinkley, and McGee shared a basic trait; their inner controls, their native taste, would have kept any one of the three of them from saying on the air, "Go, baby, go!" when a manned rocket was rising above the Cape, as Cronkite once did. But Americans seem to like their anchormen to say, "Go, baby, go!"

These were, however, details. Mostly, I had had enough. The business was getting more complicated, and I could no longer do things as I liked, while delegating beyond my small trusted coterie was against my nature. I met separately with Chet and David, told them I did not want to continue, and they wished me well. Then I asked for lunch with Bill McAndrew and Julian Goodman. I said I hoped they had other work, but if not I would understand. They insisted there would be something. I stayed at my job while we all considered the next step, mine and theirs. My personal services contract would expire at the end of June, the deadline.

One morning, while all this was working its slow way to resolution, I received a telephone call from a recruiter, a head-hunter. I had never met a head-hunter! Soon I was being romanced to be editor of the *Saturday Evening Post*, a magazine now on hard times, once part of the American fabric. It was a new experience, lunches in secret places, offers of large salaries, meeting the president of the Curtis Publishing Company one day, another day the well-known editor who would be "my" fiction editor if he accepted. But he didn't and I didn't. I do not believe in people who come in at the top, and I would not be one of them, so I begged off. But it was flattering.

Kintner, faithfully kept current by Bill McAndrew as Bill was by me, took the Curtis offer as an affront, which to me was an added condiment. He told McAndrew he would pull RCA's advertising out of all Curtis magazines, and he castigated McAndrew and Goodman for not renewing my contract earlier, sewing me up. Marvin Josephson and Ralph Mann, who represented me to NBC business departments, baldly used the fortuitous offer that I edit a magazine to get more money out of the company than we could have otherwise. It certainly was more money than I had anticipated when I had told McAndrew and Goodman that I wanted to leave daily news for a while. It was, furthermore, a contract for four years, without any of those little loopholes letting the company cancel at will, so common in television. I would produce unspecified programs, probably mostly documentaries.

The first was a documentary on eavesdropping, which worked pretty well. I was laid up through most of the production by a cracked vertebra, so this one even more than most was the work of others, while I tried to produce it from home. Ron Steinman, my associate producer, found a threadbare old private eye who told of being hired by J. Edgar Hoover to bug Eleanor Roosevelt's motel room during a trip to Detroit during World War II. That item appeared on many front pages, even *The New York Times*', the day after the program was broadcast. For Kintner and others, that was the real achievement.

That program was the occasion of my biggest fight with NBC's law department. Under our rules, news programs, including documentaries, were not cleared by the censors—the Standards and Practices department, as they were coyly called—but by the lawyers, basically for libel, invasion of privacy, and the other things one gets sued for. The fight I got into was over the victim, the one I insisted we have in every program decrying some social evil. It was not for us, I would insist, to get worked up about theoretical harm, the way lawyers do. To show evil we must show suffering. We found a minister who had been eavesdropped upon by some dissidents in his Baton Rouge congregation who wanted him ousted. They had succeeded because he was caught talking to a liberal, or some similar transgression. He had been fired and had brought suit in federal court—in Baton Rouge.

The law department newcomer assigned to this program said—and this was two days before the air date, with the program finished and ready to roll—that we could not use the ten-minute sequence about the victim, none of it. Why not? Because you will make it impossible to find an impartial jury. I insisted that was not my business, and he was killing my show, ruining the payoff. He was adamant; it would not go. That went on for a day and a night, when I had an inspiration. I called the Baton Rouge station to ask if they were planning to carry *The Big Ear*. Sorry, but no, they were not. I have spent a career producing programs affiliate stations are most likely to dump. It can irk. That time alone I was pleased that a station was dumping me. We could taint no veniremen in Baton Rouge. The question was moot. *The Big Ear* was broadcast uncut.

My next undertaking took me to the Netherlands for what I had hoped to be a study of a faith healer who had gained the ear of the queen and, so gossip had it and I hoped to prove, had brought into the palace influences strongly opposed to NATO. The reporter was Aline Saarinen, widow of the architect Eero Saarinen, an attractive woman of great presence and solid news background. I used to think she could have been the first woman anchor in American network news but for the illness that killed her soon after. The project withered when sources dried up. While we were working on what was left of this once exciting project, Kintner was fired.

On a misty, chilly November day, I returned from a meeting in Kiel to the Amsterdam Hilton's enormous lobby fireplace and a drink. I had barely sat down when I was called to the telephone. It was McAndrew in New York. Kintner, about to be both president and chairman of NBC as Bob Sarnoff moved to president of RCA, had instead been fired by Sarnoff. Julian Goodman would now be president of NBC, and Walter Scott, an executive I barely knew, would be chairman. He wanted me to replace Goodman as vice president in the News division. I said, "Bill, you know me well enough. It's not my kind of thing."

"You owe me one," he said.

He had never said that to me before.

I had no answer, except to tell him I would think about it and call him the next day. I spent the whole day thinking about it, whether I could in conscience turn McAndrew down. I decided I could not. I called him to say I would be back in a week. There had been no talk of money.

In New York, I pieced together some of what had happened—not all, because no one has ever been sure of all of it. There are many versions, but some facts were established. The first was that General

Sarnoff had moved to bring his son Robert to RCA while he was still alive. NBC seemed finally out of trouble, making large profits, and more stable than it had been since radio had made room for television. Kintner would not only inherit Bob Sarnoff's NBC titles, chairman and chief executive officer, but retain his own, NBC president. That had been announced and known for some time.

Then, in November, there was a meeting in Acapulco of the higher levels of NBC brass with the "board of delegates," the ongoing committee of the affiliated stations. Kintner had been on the wagon all summer, or so I was told by several who were close to him, but in Acapulco he fell off.

While Kintner was in Acapulco, Bob Sarnoff stayed in New York preparing for his new responsibilities at RCA. It was no secret to Sarnoff that Kintner drank, or how much. He had shielded Kintner from the General's anger and saved him up till then from being fired. But now, with Kintner's life's goal within his grasp, word was coming back to Bob Sarnoff from Mexico that he was drunk at meetings with affiliates, his behavior shocking. Whoever was reporting back to Bob Sarnoff pictured Kintner as getting worse each hour. Sarnoff sent word he wanted to see Kintner as soon as he came back to New York.

But Kintner did not return to NBC. From Acapulco he went directly to his Fifth Avenue apartment where he went to bed with the flu. At least, that message was given all callers, Bob Sarnoff included. Kintner himself would not come to the phone. It was more than a month before he returned. He met with Sarnoff, who said he could not turn NBC over to him, and they should devise some graceful exit. At that, Robert Edmonds Kintner walked out of his office, the executive floor, NBC, and the RCA building, to return only once, six years later, to attend the memorial service for Chet Huntley.

An era ends in broadcasting once a week, but this was not like those. Twenty-one years later, in the volume of reminiscences honoring NBC's sixtieth anniversary, recollections of executives, stars, affiliates and journalists, Kintner's name is the most often invoked, oftener than David Sarnoff's. I believe that he was one of those who cannot accept success but are destroyed by it.

Whatever he had objected to was being eliminated; whatever he had striven for was being realized. Bob Sarnoff would no longer be looking over his shoulder. The General would no longer be in wait for him, his face austere in silent reproof, when he went to RCA for money, for a program, for equipment, for buying something or building something. He had everything he wanted—and he couldn't stand it. Early the following year he became secretary to the Cabinet in the Johnson White House. Julian Goodman succeeded him as president of NBC and Walter Scott moved into the job of chairman of NBC. I would be a vice president. Tra-la.

Once I said yes, I was no longer wooed. McAndrew warned me not to expect the kind of money I got as a producer—under my treasured new contract, not yet six months old. I was engulfed by his instructions, by Julian Goodman's, and by the job that had to be done, instructions or no. McAndrew wanted me to plunge immediately into the pending strike in the New York City transportation system, buses as well as subways, because he was not sure the local news staff was on top of it. Shad Northshield, now executive producer of the *Huntley-Brinkley Report*, upbraided me because "my" news department was understaffed in Vietnam and insisted I do something.

My biggest problems were in network news, but the majority were in local news. News at NBC-owned stations was still part of the News division, a way of doing things that NBC was last among the networks to change, so the New York station's news department was my responsibility. I enlisted George Murray to move in and take over planning for the impending transit strike because that kind of live coverage was still a mystery to most local staffs. (They would soon be taking to it as an addict takes to a narcotic, sending cameras to random events of towering insignificance because they were within range of newly cheap Japanese-made live equipment.) The vice president for personnel came by to say what my new job's salary was "budgeted" at. It took Goodman's intervention to keep my cut in income to less than half. The charm of management was beginning to fade. At least we had agreed that I would do this for no more than four years, and then return to producing.

There were to be two news vice presidents working for McAndrew: one for news and news programs; one for special programs, long planned and instant, who would also be in charge of *Today*. There was a vice president for money and administration, and one for sports, which Kintner had thrust into the News division when he fired the previous chief sports executive for general disrespect. I was in charge of staff and those news programs known as "hard"; of news at stations in New York, Los Angeles, Washington, Chicago, and Cleveland; and of radio news, not only on the radio network but on the radio stations that NBC owned. I used to warn Goodman that I might go to jail some day because of something said by someone in Cleveland whom I had never met. CBS and ABC had long shed this system, which was a throwback to the networks' earliest days, but Julian liked it, and so, ominously, did the management consultants whom RCA would inflict on us at intervals, like locusts, who were more interested in a so-called farm team concept than in understanding how things got done.

Under a reorganization devised by consultants, NBC had five divisions, each headed by a president. (Entertainment companies tend to have more presidents than Latin America.) News became a division, so McAndrew became a president. Peculiarly, the money we spent belonged to other people, other divisions. They had sales departments, which sold our programs, so it was their money. We spent the Network division's money, the Radio division's money, and the Owned Television Stations division's money. For this reason, everything we did—I did—had to be negotiated. With the owned stations it meant arguing all the time, about every nickel. The network, in contrast, argued over the money we wanted only at budget planning sessions and budget review sessions. When we fought with the network, which was often, we fought for airtime. Time is the one indispensable commodity in broadcasting. You can get money, if you must, by robbing a bank, but without time on the air you do not exist. Time is finite. Someone must own it and allocate it. The time I needed belonged to the NBC Television Network.

Organizations like NBC are not collegial; they are federal, groups of constituencies in conflict. Tone and pattern are set by whomever they all report to. A network's news gets strength only from the head of the company. Not until I was in management did I grasp what Kintner had meant to NBC News: he gave us airtime. This took us to places we had never been, to national recognition; to a large, diverse staff; to new ways of doing news, some of which he himself disliked; but in his need for more and always more, he was, like all managers, finally at the mercy of the people who do things.

At first, documentaries or the programs we suddenly did when something important burst upon us, were specifically outside my responsibility, and it was these that were the source of friction between the News and the Network divisions. Every Wednesday, the president and top executives of the Network division would come to McAndrew's office for a weekly meeting originally mandated by Kintner. They would learn what documentaries were planned, what time would be needed for them, and other issues of mutual interest—almost always involving airtime. These meetings could proceed without me, which pleased me. McAndrew wanted me to attend, but I told him I was too busy for meetings. (He gave me his over-the-glasses look.) My urgent problems were network and local staff and local news.

Most staff problems involved people I knew and had opinions about. I kept many such judgments to myself because I had decided not to try to correct the mistakes others had made. It seemed unfair to make some incompetent pay because someone had given him an unsuitable job. I was always perhaps too aware that people fired had families and mortgages. (In my ten years in management, I fired fewer than a half dozen people. Is that good or bad?) Also that first year, I made the first of my three big mistakes as a manager: As American involvement in Vietnam increased, requiring more and more reporters, I sent only volunteers. Thus, our best-known people did not go. The other networks did not make this mistake.

Although some of our war reporting was brilliant, as a whole it suffered. My rule did not apply to bureau chiefs, mostly old colleagues whom I grandly assigned without right of appeal. Jack Fern, Jack Reynolds, Ron Steinman—if we did not always have the best reporters, we did have the best bureau chiefs, which may have kept down the damage from my first decision. My rule on reporters was sometimes bent but never broken; people might have their arms twisted to volunteer. When we found someone to send to Tel Aviv, we hired him on condition that he go by way of Saigon, for six months. New reporters who were not working out enhanced their career prospects by asking to go to Saigon for "seasoning." The manager who ran the news staff, the one in my inner group who disagreed most with this policy, once proved his point by getting a reporter to volunteer for Vietnam as the alternative to being fired, which he should have been.

Some of our best reporters—McGee, Vanocur, Jack Perkins—went to Vietnam because they thought they ought to, but they went not for a tour of duty, but for a specific project, which lasted as long as it lasted, and then they came back. McGee, who never flagged in his concern with the race problem in America, devised and completed one of the finest documentaries to come out of that strange war, *Same Mud, Same Blood*. He worked in the discomfort and danger of any front-line reporter, but after five or six weeks of this he left for home. Vanocur went to report on the politics of the prospect for peace. Perkins was sent by Shad Northshield, the executive producer of the *Huntley-Brinkley Report*, because he wanted better reporting than he was getting. Their work was strong and distinguished, but their presence depressed the spirits of the resident staff. I knew I would not myself welcome being assigned to Vietnam, so I would not assign anyone the job—only volunteers.

Most of my time was spent on what I secretly saw as my less important responsibility—news at the five owned stations. The president of the Owned-Station division had managed one of General Electric's television stations and imbibed their management attitudes. He even looked the classic manager, like a banker: fleshy face, strands of gray-blond hair efficiently arrayed across a tan pate, rimless glasses, always a vest. He was older than the rest of us, and serious about his work. He reduced everything to numbers, planned every step carefully, recruited and molded other managers, knew where every dollar went and where it came from. In our few personal conversations, he generously volunteered advice about tax shelters. When he retired, he bought a home on a golf course.

Usually I dealt with the vice presidents of his division, the ones who ran the stations. The one time I collided with the division president himself was when I granted Frank McGee's request to be relieved of the eleven o'clock local news in New York, where he was doing very well. Even though his long days and nights during space shots or his crash duties for Instant Specials had others replacing him on the 11:00 in New York, Frank was wearing out. Or so he told me when he came to my office as an old friend and colleague. Perhaps I was too ready to believe him. I told him to give me two weeks to find someone else. I did not think to clear this decision. After all, he worked for me, as did the whole New York news staff. I did not even inform anyone in station management. I did not yet know that the ten minutes of news over which McGee presided on the New York station was the most profitable local program of any kind on any station NBC owned. But I soon found out. Julian Goodman, the brand-new president of NBC, backed me. He could hardly do anything else, but I suspect he began to have doubts about how much I had to learn and how fast I would learn it.

I was always more comfortable dealing with news problems, even local news problems, than all the other problems I was saddled with. It was easy to be interested when the news director in Cleveland scolded me because we always sent Chicago staff to a story in Detroit, and showed me in his atlas who was closer. Back in New York I decreed that Cleveland should supply network presence in Detroit when local resources were insufficient. In Chicago, the vice president and general manager of NBC's station wanted news and more news, in the mornings, at night, all day Sunday from 8:00 A.M., when Sunday editions landed on doorsteps, until prime-time entertainment started in the evening. He wanted to drive the *Chicago Tribune* out of business. It made no sense to me, but he was entitled to boast; his local news programs did so well that his Monday to Friday 10:00 P.M. (Central time) newscasts were five of the ten top-rated local television programs in all categories. I told him if his boss okayed the money I would provide the rest. His boss, the division president, did not approve. By that time I had learned; I was just the supplier.

My first time in Los Angeles as a vice president—that is, as the boss—the local station news director, who was also the network news bureau chief—the pattern in all five cities—told me his early evening news was only a half hour long. Burgeoning, sprawling, diverse southern California generated too much news to squeeze into thirty minutes. I could not solve his problem. The station owned the time, and expanding beyond thirty minutes would upset schedules as well as go against precedent, and no one is more orthodox than managers of stations. They are notorious for doing nothing which has not already been done. I had, however, an idea that might help.

Los Angeles has the same sunny weather and the same temperature range for more than three hundred days each year. If he got rid of his weatherman, he would be depriving no one of useful information. All this business of scribbling on maps about highs over Hawaii and lows over Alaska just filled time since there was no change in the weather to talk about. In southern California, peculiarly, when weather changed it really changed and was important news, which would be reported as such. Meanwhile, he would be saving about two and a half minutes, 10 percent of his program time, to use for news. That is what he did. The ratings dropped immediately! Highs over Hawaii and lows over Alaska had a constituency I had not dreamed of. He had to restore weather to his newscast, scramble for a new weatherman, and trumpet to the world that weather on Channel 4, Los Angeles, would be bigger and better than anyone else's. It bore out what the president of the Owned-Station division had told me: "There is no such thing as too much weather."

Things went that way for my first year as a manager. I tried to apply twenty years of experience, of trial and error, to what needed doing, and learned I still had mistakes to make. I learned that things interesting to do are less interesting to supervise. I learned that the essence of management is spending other people's money, to other people's purposes, but almost nobody thinks of it that way. I learned that having a friend in a high place is better than being that friend. I learned to fear the people who worked for me more than the people I worked for because the people I worked for could only fire me; the people who worked for me shaped what I did. I earned the respect of some colleagues but the cooperation of few, because management is not something to be savored or enjoyed for itself but a means, a means to more—more money, more status, more management—while sharing achievement can delay advancement. What I did not have to learn was how to make decisions; producers make yes-no decisions all day long, like binary gates. I did learn to be surprised at how few people are willing to make decisions, to realize that the wrong decision is usually better than no decision at all.

The New York transit strike was barely over when the spotlight hit network news itself, as it sometimes does, exposing its inner mechanics on front pages across the country. It began when the antiwar leader in Congress, Senator J. William Fulbright of Arkansas, chairman of the Senate Foreign Relations Committee, had Secretary of State Dean Rusk before his committee and savaged him. It was "good television," and long film excerpts made that evening's news programs. The next day we all sent live cameras, hoping for more, but got only a parade of expert opinions. The drama was over before the live cameras arrived.

In the days of dull hearings to come, Fred Friendly, not yet two years into his CBS News presidency, wanted to carry everything all the time. His boss, John Schneider, CBS's equivalent of our Network division president, refused. At the time, CBS had by far the most successful daytime schedule of the three networks, its audiences almost twice as large as NBC's, with ABC even further behind. Schneider felt the hearings drove away viewers, also ruining the rest of the day. He was willing in return to give up an hour of prime time each night for review and summary, which always seemed to me "better television" as well as more "responsible," but CBS would resume its schedule.

Friendly quit as president of CBS News and left CBS forever. Textbooks say he looked up to see George Kennan, diplomat and scholar, speaking on NBC, while CBS, his home, his heart, was showing an episode of *I Love Lucy*. In any case *The New York Times* printed his many-thousand-word letter of resignation whole, as it earlier had the text of the Treaty of Versailles, and thus ended the shortest tenure of any president of any network news division. There were those who speculated whether Kennan had more to do with Friendly's resignation than that little border incident had with Hitler's invasion of Poland.

Dick Salant came back to be president of CBS News. Friendly went on to the Public Television Laboratory, an experimental approach to what would soon be called a newsmagazine program, funded by the Ford Foundation, with whom Fred had established a relationship that would last a long time, and produced for the newly reorganized public television. He recruited some talented people, including a couple of ours, notably Tom Pettit, an old colleague, and Pat Trese, one of my original, pre–*Huntley-Brinkley* gang. (They came back with tales of what it was like working in a control room with Friendly screaming, countermanding, and second-guessing. It was one of many occasions when I was to learn that CBS's control rooms were noisy and contentious whereas in ours people usually whispered. A former CBS News executive once blithely said she could tell things were going well when people in the control room screamed and fought. I told her that we always beat the hell out of them without raising our voices.)

In a young institution, anything a few years old is a tradition. Thus it was the tradition at NBC News that it be run by two people in lockstep, the division president and executive vice president; knowing each other's thoughts, supporting each other's actions; the president dealing with NBC and the world, the executive vice president with the division itself. It was a system with drawbacks but it made for consistency. As a tradition, it dated from the time Kintner had bullied Julian Goodman into leaving his comfortable job as head of the large and important Washington bureau to come to New York and be Bill McAndrew's alter ego. It was a system Julian and Bill liked. With Julian now president of NBC, Bill had no executive vice president. After about a year I became he.

Under the arrangement, the money vice president would continue to report to McAndrew as would the one for sports, so only one vice president reported to me. I was told to find another, my own replacement. I got a raise, even RCA stock options, solemnly described to me as an earnest of the company's regard and a great way to get rich. Luckily, I never exercised the few options I was given; the market price of the stock when I could buy it was always lower than the option price, which would have lost me money. Corridor gossip had it that under the same conditions a high officer of NBC had exercised his options with borrowed money, putting him so deeply in debt he had to defer his retirement several years to come out even.

Reporting to McAndrew, I was in charge of everything we called news, including documentaries, instant specials, and even *Today*. This meant I could no longer ignore McAndrew's Wednesday meetings with the Network division. One such Wednesday I presented the case for a unique documentary. Lucy Jarvis, who always gained access more successfully than she produced programs, had filmed the disgraced Nikita Khrushchev, newly the "nonperson" in the Soviet cosmogony. Her contact was Victor Louis, Moscow stringer for a London newspaper and widely considered an agent for the NKVD or the KGB or whatever was that year's label for the Sons of the Okhrana. The proof usually cited for his secret police connections was that he drove a Mercedes around Moscow. Exploiting former contacts, and demanding huge amounts of money for himself and for Aleksei Adzhubei, Khrushchev's son-in-law, Louis had offered to let Lucy make silent film of the deposed dictator, now aged and bent, to show the daily routine in his dacha, to make sound film and audio tape of him, in Russian, of course, even to interview him. For whatever it was we were paying, we would have one crack. Louis was peddling the book rights separately. I had approved the project and now the film and tape were in house being edited; Edwin Newman was working on the script; the rough cut looked promising. The time had come to brace the Network division for broadcast time.

When McAndrew's agenda reached new programs, I pitched for a time suitable for a bona-fide exclusive on a subject of drama and importance. The president of NBC Television went into his customary huddle with his lieutenants, then replied. I surely understood, he said smoothly, such subjects attracted a predominantly male audience. The ideal time, if I agreed, would be following the forthcoming major league All-Star Game. The game would be over by 10:00 P.M., or a few minutes later, with a large audience having been assembled by NBC, predominantly male like all sports audiences, so that the fewest might switch away, as many regrettably did from documentaries. It seemed reasonable and I agreed. I could see McAndrew smiling less than a whole smile, the intelligent parent letting the child learn through mistakes. After the meeting I told him there was nothing wrong with the scheme. Although the Network would gain something to put on after the All-Star Game, it was to our benefit also. McAndrew said merely, "I never trust that gang."

The 1967 All-Star Game was the longest All-Star Game in history, fifteen innings long. *Khrushchev in Exile*, an exciting and important program, well written and put together, could not go on the air until the clock passed eleven on its way to midnight. As the night went on, McAndrew was no longer supercilious. When crisis struck, this was his division and his show. Sports was also his. He called the control truck in Anaheim, California, with specific instructions: Once each inning, he ordered, the game announcers were to mention this important program, to be seen after the All-Star Game—whenever it ended. McAndrew was the boss and they did as they were told. I can still hear the voice of one of America's best-known baseball announcers repeating, "A reminder for all you Khrushchev fans . . ."

Earlier that year, AFTRA, the American Federation of Television and Radio Artists, the performers' and talkers' union, conducted its first strike against the networks. The greatest impact was felt on news programs, both the network programs and those on the stations they owned in New York, Chicago, and Los Angeles, where AFTRA also went on strike. There were enough "management personnel" to ensure that all news functions, down to weather and sports, were uninterrupted. And there were no threats to good order, as there may be when an accountant flies your plane during a pilots' strike, but there was some loss of revenue, and the newspapers enjoyed writing about children showing up at the picket line for autographs.

The strike lasted thirteen days, from March 29 to April 11. Soap operas and most entertainment programs were replaced by tapes of past episodes, so public attention fixed on news programs and what was happening on them. At NBC, the director of religious programs became the New York local weatherman, his bluntness and nervousness leading him into awkward colloquialisms that gave his work a strange and unique charm. At ABC's New York station, a black secretary did so well substituting for a big-name anchorperson she was hired as a permanent member of their news staff when the strike ended. At CBS, an administrator named Arnold Zenker sat in Walter Cronkite's chair. He was the most famous strike substitute, getting a big job after the strike anchoring local news programs outside New York, but his glamour evanesced and he found another career.

Huntley chose to work. This became big news. For Chet it was a position of principle, quixotic but real. He had long objected to having to join AFTRA before he might work at a network. He was not anti-union, but to him a union made up "overwhelmingly" of show folk could not speak for newspeople. He had been saying this for thirty years, and now he would not observe AFTRA's strike. Walter Cronkite stayed out, as did Peter Jennings at ABC. Brinkley stayed home; he did not picket, but he did not appear on television either. McGee and some others agreed with Huntley and met their assignments, but they were mostly radio and their quarrel was not as blatant as Huntley's. His had been a last-minute decision; others were in place to do the program, and we had not asked him to work. With almost no warning, he did it himself, for himself.

After the strike, all was as before. Relations between Huntley and Brinkley were unchanged. They continued as cordial colleagues; they had never, in fact, been friends. Nor was there any change in their public acceptance, in the ratings—at least not right away. In time, of course, things changed. Their popularity did diminish, and the AFTRA strike may contain a hint. It was, after all, no small thing. In the years of network television, no other news program has attained the same dominance. There are always the bromides: it is a cyclical business; no one stays on top forever. Nor was the erosion sudden. People moved gradually away so that in a few years the balance tipped the other way.

In her book, *The Evening Stars*, Barbara Matusow speculates that the war in Vietnam made the world too serious for their detached approach. It is an intelligent argument, but I do not accept it. Their dominance held well into the Vietnam War. Then there was Cronkite's public disgrace when his removal from anchoring the conventions had attracted sympathy to him, making him famous. Still not enough. There had to be something else.

Long after the AFTRA strike, too late to ask for a survey or an opinion poll to check it, I came to believe that Huntley working those two weeks of the strike and Brinkley not working eroded their audience. It was not merely that one was working alone, without the other, since that happened often in the course of any year, during vacations or special assignments. But this was not a routine absence; everyone who read a newspaper knew that Huntley was working during the strike and could easily see that Brinkley was not. No one said so and it may not have been true, but it appeared that Brinkley disagreed with Huntley, that there was a rift.

It always annoyed me to back off from my position that we did well because we did the news well, to accept the findings of the "research" departments with their polling statistics and ratings analyses. They would say to me, both when I was the producer and after I had become an executive, that the *Huntley-Brinkley Report* was popular because Chet and David talked to each other. But they did not talk to each other, except to say, "Good night," because it was short. Well, they insisted, people *believed* they talked to each other, and that made them popular. What we were so proud of, how we got and edited the news, our style, figured less, they told me, than the impression we gave of two friends chatting, so middle-class matrons in their living rooms could say to themselves, "That's nice."

If that's so, if some perception of friendship or at least cordiality between Huntley and Brinkley swelled audiences, then it is conceivable the public was put off by what it saw during the strike. If people had been attracted to these two men because they seemed to be friends, it made them uncomfortable when that was disturbed, like children when their parents argue. It is not that people chose sides, but that what had attracted them had been withdrawn. I do not know that this is what happened; I do know that in television that is all it takes.

12

More books have been written about 1968 than any other year of recent memory—about what happened in the United States that year, about what happened abroad, about single events and the dizzying parade of events, even books about the year itself. At each of those events, television news was somehow there, with film cameras or live cameras, for minutes or weeks. What happened and how it was covered are tangled in the recollection. During that year, between the murder of Bobby Kennedy and the Soviet invasion of Prague, I became president of NBC News.

The rush of news had started in January when the Communist authorities of North Korea seized the U.S. Navy communications ship *Pueblo*, accusing it of entering their territorial waters to spy. The American Right demanded armed rescue and bloody revenge. Governor Ronald Reagan of California and Senator Everett Dirksen of Illinois wanted action before it was too late. Like notes of a muted trombone, Dirksen's somber syllables echoed in the Senate chamber: "The clammy spirit of fear and timidity seems to be upon us." President Johnson called up several thousand reservists.

North Korea published a confession elicited from the ship's captain, Cdr. Lloyd M. Bucher. He was made to speak on short-wave radio;

film was distributed of him and his crew, Bucher bowing stiffly in formal subjection before North Korean officers in uniform. Using those pictures in news programs brought letters of protest, the first of many times that year that we would be upbraided for showing what we showed by people who did not challenge its accuracy.

It would take all year before diplomacy brought the *Pueblo* crew home. By then they were just one of the year's crowd of events. Two weeks after they were captured came the Tet offensive, and attention returned to Vietnam. Vietnam's three-day lunar New Year celebration began that year on January 30. Previous Tets had been observed with some sort of cease-fire, but 1968's would enter history for the most effective campaign yet mounted by North Vietnam and the Vietcong. Its success was enhanced by the television journalism that reported it, as reporters and cameras ranged the country for something specific to show Americans back home.

The Cold War as Television, which for me had reached a kind of apotheosis with the heroics of *The Tunnel*, had evolved into nightly scenes of the fighting in Vietnam, reporters trying to pluck individual narratives from a conflict fought in the air, on water, but most of all on land, hundreds of square miles of it, an entire country. Viewers cozy in their living rooms—an academics' image about to be born— could only sense what their troops were learning: what it is like to be hated, a new experience for Americans.

Tet, 1968, was the topper. After seeing seven years of war in that exotic landscape, Americans now watched enemy soldiers penetrate the U.S. embassy compound in Saigon, bursting out of mysterious tropical forests into familiar-seeming streets, the very downtowns of South Vietnam's cities. The theater commander, Gen. William West-moreland, said his headquarters had anticipated the offensive all along, but *The New York Times* later found and published memoranda, signed by him, proving the opposite. Yet he continued trying to counter the impression of unpreparedness that was the dominant implication of the television pictures.

From the government to the hustings to the think tanks, it had been whispered, then stated, then trumpeted that the enemy had suffered a major defeat but television's coverage had switched the defeat to our side. At a background briefing, Secretary of State Rusk, a mild-mannered man, shouted at reporters, "There gets to be a point when the question is, Whose side are you on?" Things were going bad because whether or not Americans at home thought what they had seen was a debacle, they found reason to wonder why American troops were there to begin with. If the explanations they got were true, what they saw could not have happened.

The enemy was soon driven from the embassy compound, but not before it was filmed for posterity. For three tortured weeks, the Communists held Hue, an old city with historic and symbolic meaning for the Vietnamese. The troops who retook Hue found mass graves with more than a thousand bodies—the city's military, political, and business leadership—along with some French priests and other foreigners. Newspapers and networks reported the discoveries immediately, in detail, but afterward, whenever we told of an atrocity by American or South Vietnamese troops, we got a flood of audience mail asking why we had not included the North's atrocities in Hue last January.

Tet provided one of the two indelible images of that war. (The other was a naked little girl running screaming down the road, her clothes burnt off by napalm.) On February 1, the third day of Tet, South Vietnam's police chief, Brig. Gen. Nguyen Ngoc Loan, in cold blood and at point-blank range, shot a Vietcong lieutenant brought before him as a prisoner. The Associated Press picture of the event, the general holding his pistol at arm's length, the officer's face grimacing, his eyes closed, already dead but not yet fallen, is an icon of the history of the time. While Eddie Adams, the AP photographer, took his picture, Vo Suu, an NBC News cameraman, was filming beside him.

Vo Suu was giving Adams a lift downtown in his jeep when they saw Loan on his corner. Suu parked to wait for something to happen. Adams grew impatient, but it was our jeep. MPs brought over the prisoner. Disdaining the cameras, General Loan shot the VC. Another American network cameraman present—like Vo Suu a South Vietnamese working for Americans—knowing Loan's reputation for violence, shot no film, so only the AP had a still picture; only NBC News had film. The AP picture was on every front page in the world the next morning. Even by satellite, our film could not get to New York before evening. Adams won all that year's photojournalism awards. That NBC had the only film is rarely mentioned, but viewers wrote to complain of being "subjected"—the word used—to such pictures during dinner.

At that, the film had someone judging at every stage how much gore is too much. In Tokyo, where it went first, it was easily edited: Two military policemen pushing the officer, Loan raising a pistol, the shot, the VC falling, his body on the sidewalk, blood oozing from the head. The only problem was how long to show the blood flowing. Too short would be prissy, too long would look exploitive. The reporter pared the first edit to shorten the blood, then shorter still, then sent the film by satellite to New York. Shad Northshield, the executive producer, watched it coming in and thought the blood flowed too long. He asked that it be trimmed. It was, to his satisfaction.

In my office, I saw the film on a closed circuit. It seemed to me blood oozed too long. I asked Northshield to trim the shot further. Thus, every time it was seen, it was trimmed, but many still wrote to say it was too bloody. At each stage, from the reporter screening unedited film in Tokyo to Northshield and me in New York to the viewer watching in his home, the shock was at the first sight. Of us all, however, only the viewer saw it only once.

Then, too, as the nation was splitting over the Vietnam War, the public could not accept television's coverage, in general, as neutral. No matter how hard we tried, many in the audience, patriotic and frustrated Americans, saw in the pictures we used or in the fact that we used them proof that we were supporting the enemy. Television reporting was used to validate all positions, from our providing comfort to the enemy to our whipping up war hysteria. This made us valuable to the politicians. In every administration, of whichever party, there is always someone high in government who is especially skilled in deflecting criticism of what they are doing to criticism of those reporting it. Although television's coverage of the war in Vietnam was a sitting duck, the accusation was also directed at the reporting of every contentious issue in that contentious time.

Thus, those frustrated at how slowly the nation addressed issues of race and civil rights were sure things would improve if reporting were more "constructive" and "responsible." President Johnson's commission to look into 1967's "long, hot summer" reported, on February 29, 1968: "The media . . . have not communicated to the majority of their audience—which is white—a sense of the degradation, misery and hopelessness of life in the ghetto."

"If only the media . . ." It was 1968, I think, when news professionals began to show signs of a new paranoia, convinced by polls that the public did not love them anymore. They missed the point; the public rarely likes news or its mongers. It is the years when they are popular that are the exception. But in 1968, news managers took to justifying themselves in print, wearing out the tired image of the messenger killed for his news, a shard from an American past when classical allusion was part of daily language, even in newspapers. The Commission on Violence, under Governor Otto Kerner of Illinois and New York's mayor John Lindsay, concluded that a different kind of journalism would lessen the damage and lectured journalists on how to help the country and the problems it faced.

Bill McAndrew and I met the commission at a weekend retreat in a monkish conference center maintained by IBM in New York's leafy Westchester County. In formal and informal discussion, and, because I was so exercised, in letters afterward, I harangued the commissioners that it was not journalism's role to tailor reporting to achieve a desired good end. No one was very convinced, the one least swayed being Roger Wilkins, nephew of Roy Wilkins, who had for many years been head of the NAACP. It had been Roy Wilkins who appeared with Huntley on that Sunday back in 1959 to refute Chet's implication that the NAACP had become an irritation to white Southerners, making school desegregation even more difficult. I remembered how, chatting before the program, Roy Wilkins had told me that if the NAACP were not leading the fight, it would be taken over by "extremists like Martin Luther King." Nine years later, Roger Wilkins, a keen-minded man who later wrote editorials for America's two most important newspapers, turned down my position that the country would suffer if newspeople set out to change society, even for the better.

Not quite at the same time but close enough, some Saigon news bureau chiefs dined with the U.S. ambassador to Vietnam, Ellsworth Bunker—stately and gracious, an envoy for all occasions. These were the men who ran the bureaus of the more important American news organizations—the networks, the major wire servies, the bigger newspapers. Among the diners was Bunker's newly assigned deputy, Robert Komer, whose responsibility was the "pacification" program, the one that would win the "hearts and minds" of the peasantry. He had gained a measure of fame by using a computer model to give every Vietnamese hamlet a higher or lower grade for safety. He interrupted the amiable chatter by rising to his feet to address the gathering. As recalled later by one of those present, he said: "I think the gentlemen present should know that they are not helping. They are not doing their bit to get this war won. I do not impugn their patriotism, but they should reflect on what they are doing."

All through March that year, war and politics fought for news space and airtime. Politics won. We reported when the draft was increased, and there were rumors that General Westmoreland had asked President

Johnson for 206,000 more troops. Our cameras filmed the rumors becoming charges hurled at Secretary Rusk as he delivered his yearly report to the Foreign Relations Committee and its hostile chairman, Senator Fulbright. It looked like last year's news.

The new news was politics. Richard Nixon went on television that week to announce his candidacy for the Republican presidential nomination, pledging to end the war in Vietnam, the first step to becoming the only President elected twice pledging an end to the same war. Our crews reported from the New Hampshire Democratic primary as Senator Eugene McCarthy of Minnesota, the antiwar candidate, all but upset Lyndon Johnson's high-powered write-in campaign for the popular vote, and won twenty delegates to Johnson's four. President John F. Kennedy's brother Robert, now the junior senator from New York, announced he, too, would run for President, promising to "deescalate" the war.

On March 31, a Sunday, President Johnson preempted the best entertainment hour of the week, 9:00 to 10:00 P.M. to announce to the 70 million viewers on all three networks that he was ordering a halt to the bombing of North Vietnam north of the demilitarized zone. At the end of his address, not included in the advance text handed out to reporters, was this sentence: "I shall not seek, and I will not accept, the nomination of my party as your President."

Johnson finished at 9:40, leaving twenty minutes of airtime before the next regularly scheduled program. News staffs were caught unprepared, dumbfounded, hyperventilating. On CBS, Roger Mudd wished he could sleep on the news and be asked about it tomorrow. Edwin Newman, on NBC, did better, but he, too, could offer no more than speculation. During those twenty minutes, while the commentators floundered, Johnson accepted an invitation, sitting in his drawer as it does for every President every year, to speak the next day to the opening session of the National Association of Broadcasters' annual convention. It was barely enough notice. Schedules were juggled; the mayor of Chicago, Johnson's old ally Richard Daley, had to change plans to get there; Lowell Thomas, the venerable radio news broadcaster who was to get the NAB's "lifetime achievement" award as that session's highlight, instead introduced the President—ad libbing until he arrived. To a packed hall, Lowell Thomas welcomed Johnson, a rich radio and television station owner, "back to the broadcasting business." The President told his friendly hearers he had taken the first real step to peace—it seemed real enough to send the stock market soaring—then lectured the assembled station owners on their public obligations when presenting news.

He spoke to them as a colleague, flattering them about the "awesome power" they had, lulling them with assurances that they used that power well, entrapping them as he defined the obligations that "must accompany" such power. "History," he told those owners and operators of high-earning broadcasting properties, "is going to be asking some very hard questions." In news, "the face of hatred and bigotry comes through much more clearly, no matter what its color, and the face of tolerance I seem to find is rarely newsworthy." If there was doubt that the Vietnam War coverage enraged him, it was dispelled by, "Historians can only guess at the effect that television would have had during earlier conflicts on the future of this nation." He reminded them they were in a licensed business without using the word: "Men and women of the airwaves fully as much as men and women of public service have a public trust."

I was in Chicago because, later in the week, I was to take part in a panel confabulating on television news coverage of the "inner city" riots that were becoming a fixture of the American summer. The term *inner city* had already become the code word for black people, especially young and disorderly ones, and how their rioting was shown on television was making Americans far away fearful and querulous. (Sander Vanocur, back from that year's trip to meet politicians and sniff winds, told me of a Montana town with almost no blacks where the leading candidate for mayor was ahead because he was for "law and order"—that is, against the black rioters on television.) The questions I was expected to answer in that panel were: "Had television overplayed the militants?" and "Does the presence of television cameras change the nature of a story being covered?"

The questions as worded implied preferred answers, but I accepted neither. We had analyzed stacks of NBC News scripts and found we had dealt far more with "civil rights moderates" than with "civil rights militants." I proposed, "This year's militant is next year's moderate." I said that among the written criticisms that we had not shown the more moderate civil rights leaders, the name of Martin Luther King kept appearing. But a few years ago, a civil rights moderate had described Dr. King to me in conversation as an irresponsible militant. (I did not use Roy Wilkins's name.) Now, Dr. King was again being called a militant for his stand on Vietnam and his work right there in

Chicago. Those were words without meaning. The next day, Martin Luther King was murdered.

I was on an airplane when it happened. As so often in management, my job that day required me to waste time at a head table for a hotel lunch. I left as soon as I politely could, to fly back to New York, nagged by a general sense that no one was minding the store. When I called the office, Bill McAndrew had gone home; Julian Goodman was out. I tried Shad Northshield, who would be in the turmoil of the *Huntley-Brinkley Report* and have no time for small talk, to ask what was "going on." He was tied up with that evening's special, he said. What special? On Martin Luther King. Why a special? He told me: King had been shot as he stood on the balcony of a Memphis motel. The President would talk at nine o'clock, and we were following at 9:30 with a special. Shad and Chet Huntley.

We would in the days to come do more than twenty hours of special programs and live coverage of and about Martin Luther King, Jr. Mostly, we showed events: the march in Memphis, the funeral in Atlanta. King had come to Memphis to help city sanitation workers, most but not all Negro, fight for better pay. The mayor had refused him permission to lead a march to City Hall. After King's death, he allowed a procession along the same route to honor his memory. When the march reached City Hall, King's widow, Coretta Scott King, suddenly a public figure, pleaded for a more peaceful society.

The funeral service in his native Atlanta, at his church, the Ebenezer Baptist Church, drew some of the major names of the time, both Senators Kennedy, Robert of New York and Edward of Massachusetts; Governors Nelson Rockefeller of New York and George Romney of Michigan; Hubert Humphrey and Richard Nixon, the present and past vice presidents. Many were glimpsed in passing as they stood against the walls of the crowded church, having given up their assigned seats to famous and ordinary women who had come to do honor. The most dramatic presence was John F. Kennedy's widow. The crowd engulfed and frightened her, and cameras caught her all but losing her composure. After the service, the ornate mahogany coffin, on a worn farm wagon, was drawn by a pair of mules to Morehouse College, King's alma mater, for a service, then to South View Cemetery. All three networks began their coverage at 10:00 in the morning and ended at 5:30 in the afternoon. Two days later they covered live President Johnson's signing of the broadest civil rights bill in American history.

There was parallel news—important, dramatic, disturbing, and within reach of cameras—but of that news none was covered live. King's death had set loose riots in America's cities. The week between his murder and funeral saw burning and looting that were a frustrated howl of defiance. Covering the riots American journalism was faced with its trickiest role, *Tout comprendre c'est tout pardonner*, trying so hard to explain as to end up excusing the inexcusable. When reports from around the country were collated, 125 cities had known serious riots. National and state governments had deployed 55,000 armed men, 21,000 from the army, the rest national guardsmen. Forty-six people had died—among them eleven in Chicago, ten in Washington, six each in Baltimore and Kansas City.

Our news crews were at almost every riot. It was not cameras that angered the crowds; it was the lights. Turning them on could expose film crews to real danger. Cameramen used more sensitive film so they could film without lights. At times, a mob's leaders might insist only Negro cameramen film, and somehow enough were found. The networks did not send live television to riots, although they were fully reported on news programs. This was not some "policy" developed in a meeting, at least not at NBC, but something that felt right, and we did it without prior discussion. Nor did anyone suggest we cover riots live.

This news overlapped still other news, of a different tenor and in a different place. March 1968 saw the birth of the "Prague Spring," the most rigid of Communist states relaxing civic life, the economic system, and, most notably to us foreigners, controls on cultural expression, bringing back what we had known as the Czech tradition. The landmarks of Cold War history are the landmarks of Cold War television: Poznan, East Berlin, Budapest, and now Prague. Correspondents swarmed to that city in search of the newly open meetings and discussions they had been told about, breathing the new air of that stunning, brooding Gothic city, while from it the world happily received paintings and motion pictures and poems and novels. Eliot Frankel went from London to produce as many stories as he could fit in before heading home to take part in convention coverage. Czechoslovakia and the "Prague Spring" were welcome news when we could make room for it.

Also that spring, the administration of Columbia University, after several years of student protest, summoned New York City police to the campus to disrupt demonstrations and the occupation of dormitories and offices. The leader of the Columbia students was Mark Rudd, a new name in the news. Some Negro students occupied the economics building at Cornell; a wire service picture of one of them holding a rifle struck terror into the hearts of Ivy League alumni everywhere, and it lives on as one of those symbols of a moment. There were student riots in West German cities, West Berlin students outside the printing plants of conservative publisher Axel Springer chanting, "Ho! Ho! Ho Chi Minh!" It was one world after all. West Germany's students were led by Rudi Dutschke, another new name in the news. The French student leader, Daniel Cohn-Bendit, became still another momentary American TV news star with the nightly reports of shouting and clubbing and tear gas in Paris, the city of light.

On April Fools' Day, I finally had someone to pass work to. When Julian Goodman had bumped me up to executive vice president, he urged me to add to NBC News management someone from "the outside" to counter our reputation for incestuous insularity. Among the few I talked to was Richard Wald, the last managing editor of the *New York Herald Tribune*, who on its demise had moved to the *World-Journal-Tribune*, an exotic slurry of three moribund New York newspapers, which lasted the twinkling of an eye. I wooed Dick more than a year until, after six months with the *Washington Post*, he overcame his snobbish distaste to enter the world of network news. In revenge, I gave him local news at the five stations, making him deal with the Owned Stations division, as mean an introduction to the business as I could devise.

In politics, the fight for the Democratic nomination was growing fierce. It was even conceivable the Democrats would name someone who opposed Lyndon Johnson on the Vietnam War. Two major candidates, Senators Eugene McCarthy and Robert Kennedy, were peace candidates. McCarthy had the purer antiwar record; Kennedy drew the wilder crowds, especially on campuses. In the emotions of the time, the men themselves were transmuted into symbols of passion. The third candidate, carrying Johnson's banner in the fervid contest, was his vice president, Hubert Humphrey, the Minnesota liberal who twenty years before had shamed the Democratic party into moving forward on civil rights. The showdown would come in the California primary.

The Republicans had several candidates, Governor Ronald Reagan of California among them, but the nomination of Richard Nixon, the former vice president, seemed certain. Herb Kaplow called to say Nixon wanted a meeting with Bill McAndrew. Kaplow had stayed in touch with Nixon after his defeat by John Kennedy in 1960 and was the only network reporter to go when Nixon toured the world for his law client, Pepsi-Cola. A few weeks later, Nixon was host at lunch in the Racquet and Tennis Club in New York City's East Sixties. He brought two aides; McAndrew brought Kaplow and me. The sterile WASPish environment was almost as strange to McAndrew as to me, and I wondered, in fact, who in the candidate's entourage had got Nixon in. Protestant he might be, but born poor, which in those surroundings would make him anomalous.

We made lunch talk. McAndrew, a political gossip addict, tried to draw Nixon out on his candidacy, the Democrats, the war. Nixon wanted to talk about George Wallace. He looked on every vote for Wallace as one he would have lost. Alabama's governor was by then the principal focus of Southern white indignation at the progress of civil rights in the legislatures and courts, and he was sure to run for President as an independent when, inevitably, he was refused the Democratic nomination. George Wallace was why Richard Nixon was having us to lunch. We were not there to chitchat, trade political stories, or be amused by each other's company.

Nixon had taken time from his campaign to come to New York to ask a couple of news executives he did not know (and there may have been other such lunches) this one question: Would we include Wallace in candidate debates? We said we would have to wait for Congress to set rules when it amended the Communications Act, but if Wallace became a national candidate, it would not be up to us to keep him out. Nixon did not like the answer, and that ended lunch. (Both party leaderships then decided that including George Wallace in debates was worse than not having any, so Congress did not amend the act. There were no presidential debates in 1968.)

Despite Reagan and some others, in practical terms Nixon had the Republican field to himself, while the Democrats had to go through the full primary drama, grueling for them, news for us. We moved people, spent money, soothed financial vice presidents. New Hampshire was pretty much as usual both in effort and in cost. Then Huntley, McGee, and Vanocur were sent to Wisconsin, the primary after Johnson announced he would not run. It built from there. By the end of the primaries, we had sent west not only the special program unit, Chet Hagan, McGee, and the rest, but the entire *Huntley-Brinkley*

Report. They started in Oregon, from there they moved to California, where, even more dramatically than usual, the narrative would reach its climax and conclusion. On Memorial Day weekend, while they were in California, Bill McAndrew died.

Bill died from a silly household accident. A fall had broken a rib that had punctured a lung, and by the time it was diagnosed it was too late. He had called me at home the night he fell to talk about the problems we were facing those days, the people who had to be shifted, the bases that had to be covered. He said he was sorry to add to my problems, but he would not be coming to the office the next morning. The doctor thought he ought to stay home a day or two. The next morning he was taken to the hospital. The funeral was on a Monday. Huntley, Northshield, Vanocur, and Don Meaney flew to New York for the funeral and then back to California for the Tuesday primary. (Meaney was the News vice president in charge of special programs, like primaries, *Today*, and documentaries.) Until Goodman made other arrangements, I was in charge. It was not what I had anticipated in the Amsterdam Hilton lobby that cold, rainy evening almost three years earlier when McAndrew had telephoned to tell me he wanted me in management.

Bill McAndrew was shy in public and spoke poorly. Executives at the other networks did not know what to make of him. NBC News's rise, they would say, was clearly due to someone else. Even inside his own division there were those who dismissed him as an "Irish pol" overfond of fires, resenting that he was so important in their success. He could also be unforgiving, and the road was lined with the bones of those who had underestimated him. He saw himself not as doing news on television but making it possible. He was the shield. We disagreed often, but he liked me personally, which meant he trusted me professionally. (He only trusted professionally those he liked personally.) We had been through a lot together.

During one of my short periods at home that weekend, the telephone rang and it was Bob Kintner. He wanted to know about Bill McAndrew but did not want to call anyone else. Perhaps he chose me because he hardly knew me, or perhaps because I had had nothing to do with his leaving. While we were speaking he began to sob, loud and uncontrollably. He regained his composure gradually while I told him what little there was to tell, what had happened, how Mrs. McAndrew was, where the funeral would be. He thanked me and wished me luck. He was sure I would do well. "You were always very budget-conscious," he said. I believe he meant it as a compliment. It was the only time we ever talked on the telephone.

Primary day in California, June 4, the day after McAndrew's funeral, found us in place and ready to go. Huntley and Brinkley were there for the news, McGee to anchor a special program with the results, and our best reporters were deployed around the state and with the candidates. Again, we were careful with projections, which kept us on the air long after CBS had declared Kennedy the winner and shut down. But there was no longer a Kintner to complain. As we prepared to end our coverage that long day, I was still in my office with an open telephone to Don Meaney in Los Angeles. Things had gone well enough. I did not mind that we had not been first to "project" Kennedy winning. We had just shown him at his headquarters claiming victory and were back in the studio with McGee wrapping up.

I said the usual about thanking everybody for me, and told Meaney what hotel I would be in for the few hours left of the night—it was after 3:00 A.M. in New York—when he said, "There's something going on. I'll call you back." We stayed on the air, in total confusion, which gradually cleared. First, there had been a shooting in the Ambassador Hotel soon after Kennedy had made his victory speech. Then we were told a man had been shot in the hip. Then, it was Bobby Kennedy who had been shot, and not in the hip, in the head.

The turmoil at a time like this cannot be imagined by laity, who know only their human, private puzzlement. We in news have that, too, but it is submerged by our obsessive need to be doing something, anything, fulfilling our roles, acting out how we see ourselves. By-standers are corralled and bullied into telling what they saw. People still in shock are thrust before cameras. Rational thought is a luxury as reporters and production associates race to get anyone at all before a camera, while directors move cameras to where they can get a picture worth showing and producers scream that we need new material. Eyewitnesses and reporters said:

• Rafer Johnson, the track star, grabbed the assailant.
• A busboy put a rosary into Kennedy's hand as he lay on the floor of the hotel kitchen.
• His brother-in-law, Stephen Smith, was also shot.
• Stephen Smith was not shot.
• The man who shot Kennedy was not seized by Rafer Johnson but by Roosevelt Grier, the football player.

We are out of live interview subjects; we need more. Fill time with anything. Show the tape again, confusion, girls screaming, one sits and cries. There are two suspects in custody. There is one suspect in custody. There was a girl. She had nothing to do with it. Vanocur interviews bystanders: "the ratatat of bullets . . . I thought it was fire-crackers, then I saw blood . . ."

There was no tape of the shooting itself, only film. Because film is film, it would not be seen for hours. Nor was it our film. It belonged to the local NBC station; the reporter, Piers Anderton. His film was shown several times that endless night. Piers had traveled a long road from Berlin to California. After Berlin he was sent first to India because he had somehow displeased Kintner; he quit in anger, got a job with ABC in New York, then moved to his native California to work for KNBC-TV in Los Angeles. Now his was our only film of the shooting of Bobby Kennedy. There is always one more irony.

Huntley and Brinkley, who had left the studio before the shooting, returned as soon as they heard. So did Northshield, who had heard on his radio that Kennedy was being taken to a hospital other than the one first reported. As Northshield entered the NBC parking lot, a mobile unit was about to leave. He diverted it to the right hospital. That fluke gave us the best camera position outside Good Samaritan Hospital all that Wednesday and into Thursday morning. There Frank Mankiewicz, the campaign secretary, standing on the hood of a car, would read bulletins and announcements of progress, life signs, sur-gery. From the studio, from all over the city, there were reports and interviews, more eyewitnesses, more doctors. The night's talisman: The longer there is no news, the better the news is.

That is how it went into the morning, through the afternoon. A mass in St. Patrick's Cathedral in New York. More doctors describing what was happening, reaction from the President, from the vice pres-ident, from congressmen and senators, from Europe. Press conference of Los Angeles's police chief. The shooter, booked as John Doe, had been arraigned. In the afternoon, regular programs, interrupted twice an hour with bulletins. As afternoon ended, the assailant was identified: Sirhan Bishara Sirhan. The ineffable Mayor Sam Yorty of Los Angeles made the unauthorized announcement. A special program at 10:00 P.M. Eastern time, the President speaking at 10:06.

In the early hours of Thursday, just before 5:00 A.M. in New York, 2:00 in Los Angeles, inside the hospital, in its press room, Frank Mankiewicz, his eyes reddened, his face a furrowed landscape of grief, stood at the podium, waited for the television lights to be turned on. He said, "I have a short announcement to make which I shall read at this time." His eyes shifted to the card in his hand. "Senator Robert Francis Kennedy died at one forty-four A.M. today, June 6, 1968. With him were his wife, Ethel; his sisters, Mrs. Patricia Lawford and Mrs. Stephen Smith; his brother-in-law, Stephen Smith; and his sister-in-law, Mrs. John F. Kennedy. He was forty-two years old." Slowly, Mankiewicz turned and left the podium. The television picture followed him out of the room, then cut to the street outside the hospital where crowds waited in the dark.

Twenty hours later, we went off the air, 1:00 A.M. Eastern Daylight Time, Friday, June 7. As a matter of course, all commercials had been canceled. Those newspapers who called to ask were told this cost the network about $1.25 million, its affiliated stations that much again. During those twenty hours, in addition to interviews, recapitulations, autopsy reports, Mayor Yorty's press conference blaming Sirhan's act on Communist influence, jeopardizing the integrity of the trial, there was the event only live television can encompass:

The coffin was taken to Air Force One to be flown east, the two Kennedy widows and the surviving Kennedy brother in the first car. We saw the widow and children watching the casket raised into the plane. Mrs. Kennedy invited Mrs. Martin Luther King to fly with them, and also Charles Evers, brother of Medgar Evers, the black Mississippi mayor killed that year. The plane reached New York at 9:00 that evening. We could not show the motorcade in the dark and were limited to pictures at the airport and in the streets outside St. Patrick's Cathedral, but these, too, had the special texture of live television. In both cities, along the routes, black and white faces, some weeping, people throwing flowers.

Vanocur was also on the plane. He went directly to the RCA Building to join Edwin Newman and John Chancellor on the air. Our picture switched between reporters in a studio and crowds outside St. Patrick's. After reporting on the flight, Vanocur shifted to how the Kennedys thought Mayor Yorty was using the event for his own publicity. Chancellor said Vanocur had not slept in two nights. He said it on network television but it was a message to me. I went to the cramped bulletin studio to get him out of there. (The director switched to St. Patrick's as I went inside. Executives do not walk into studios while they are feeding out live pictures.) Sandy, all wound up, wanted to keep talking. I insisted he go to bed. As we walked down the long, empty hall, a camera shooting through the door of St. Patrick's caught just a glimpse of Ted Kennedy standing at his brother's coffin.

Off the air at 1:00 A.M. On again at 5:30 A.M. with crowds outside St. Patrick's. They had stood all night. Crowds kept collecting outside St. Patrick's all that Friday, an incredible outpouring. At 11:30 Friday night, Johnny Carson gathered some of Robert Kennedy's friends, Vanocur among them, for ninety minutes of remembering. All that night, crowds moved slowly past the coffin in St. Patrick's, as they had moved past John's coffin in the Capitol Rotunda four and a half years earlier. By 8:00 Saturday morning, when the cathedral was closed for the funeral mass, more than 150,000 had moved past the casket.

After the mass, with the cathedral packed with the famous and powerful, television moved back outside where yet another motorcade brought the casket to Pennsylvania Station to go by train to Washington, and again by motocade to Arlington National Cemetery. At every step, people in their hundreds, some no doubt only curious, but most because they felt a need to be there. At 11:04 P.M. Saturday, after Robert Kennedy's body was buried not far from his brother's, NBC resumed scheduled programs and NBC News caught up with what was happening in the rest of the world. Some events—assassinations and beginnings and ends of wars—drive out other news. When they end, we pick up by conditioned reflex, going through motions.

We picked up where we had left off with politics. Both conventions were scheduled for August, which is late. We again covered the Paris peace talks, almost every meeting ending with the report that they were deadlocked. In Czechoslovakia there was Soviet pressure to reverse what had happened in the spring and those who cared braced for trouble; in Vietnam the total of American dead reached 25,000. There was film of marines pulling out of Khesanh after six months of pummeling. We showed Resurrection City, which would have been Martin Luther King's next project, shacks and tents in the prettiest part of the monumental Washington, bringing poverty and deprivation to the attention of the nation's leaders. That was June.

We expected the Republican convention in Miami Beach to be the first dull one of the television age. If so, our system, built around digging out news, would do less well because there would be less news to dig out. We still outrated the others even though Cronkite, since 1964, had become genuinely famous and ABC, on some days but not all, gave highlights rather than carry the proceedings. We did well, being more skilled because of more experience. But there was too much solution for not much problem, as though the Yankees were at Des Moines. We all sensed it, but we did what we had always done because we thought that it was why we were there. Having studied us hungrily since 1956, politicians had learned how to maneuver us. For example, parliamentary gambits deliberately dragged out the proceedings in a move to bore the audience and send it elsewhere while a stop-Nixon coalition was attempted. (It failed.)

I had moved from acting president to president when Julian Goodman published a gracious organizational notice calling me Bill McAndrew's choice. While McAndrew was alive I had let him talk me into the executive producer's chair for another pair of conventions, in the right angle between air control and preset control. George Murray would again run the machine itself, the organizer, translating between news and machines. Murray would have to make every decision I used to make until the moment I moved into the executive producer's chair. It was where he had aspired to sit, but, glowering, he did everything he had to better than anyone else would have.

With the story barely alive, even arrivals were news. Forgotten was 1960, when CBS had the mobile units and we had the news. Our reporters might still be best, but, as the legacy of Kintner's pampering, we, too, now had more mobile units than we needed. When Governor Rockefeller arrived on Saturday, we showed his plane landing; we showed him getting out of his plane and into his motorcade; we showed the motorcade along the route from the airport; we showed him arriving at the Americana Hotel.

The arrival in the hotel was a virtuosity. Murray had set up no less than three camera positions, one outside to catch Rockefeller getting out of his limousine and walking up the steps, one in the lobby for him and his entourage to move to the elevators, and one to show them as they disappeared into the waiting elevators to ascend to their penthouse headquarters. None of this added to public enlightenment except we now knew that Nelson Rockefeller had reached Miami Beach and was presumably at that very moment washing his hands and face after his trying journey on his personal jet.

Not much else from those weeks became cozy recollection. Our relations with politicians were getting tense. The week before the Republican convention, during a final meeting on news arrangements, Donald Ross, vice chairman of the Republican National Committee, objected to the networks' escalating requests for access to the floor. "The Republican party leased this building from the city," he sputtered, "and we decide where you can have cameras and phones. Broadcasters didn't lease this building and they have no right to decide." Competing to show off, we may all have asked too much, but he picked a stupid way to say so. Print reporters present noted George Murray's expectable statement about the public's right to know, and Ross's chilling reply: "You have no right to be in this building." Each network was finally allowed two portable cameras on the floor to work with its four reporters. Along with the cameras in the anchor booth and other high positions, these would be enough, but we objected formally anyway. It was all foretaste.

In Chicago, where the Democrats would meet once the Republicans had ended in Miami Beach, and where there was no danger of a dull convention, union telephone installers had been on strike since May. It was they who would install our cables and connections. Without them there could be no live television coverage. In June, John Criswell, in charge of the Democrats' convention arrangements, speculated whether the convention might move to another city rather than do without television. Also, the "counterculture" had targeted the Democratic convention in Chicago for a massive demonstration against the Vietnam War, and the city was having an attack of nerves.

For our part, almost all of us in television were sure that the telephone installers' strike had been engineered by Richard Daley, mayor of Chicago and the one and only boss of its political machine. We had no evidence, but Daley was a virtuoso manipulator and the city's craft unions were in his fief. When Criswell spoke out publicly about moving the convention, Daley called union and company into his office and locked the doors.

They emerged agreeing to restore live coverage: The strike would go on, but three hundred of the striking installers would, unpaid, prepare the hall for the convention and for television. (Their union, the International Brotherhood of Electrical Workers, also oversaw telephones, crucial since Kennedy's nomination in 1960, to enable candidates' headquarters and staffs to control their tactics and allies. The Eugene McCarthy organization later complained that the Hubert Humphrey organization got better telephone service. It is not unlikely.)

Illinois Bell would pay the money these men would have earned, straight time and overtime—and double time and triple time—into an IBEW strike fund for all striking members to share.

There would thus be live pictures, but only from the hall. The formula "could not be" extended to remote sites, like hotels. Party chairman John Bailey hailed the deal. "We're used to Mayor Daley performing such miracles," he said. John Criswell spoke no more of moving the convention from Chicago. It did not matter to them that only proceedings in the hall would be shown, since that is all they wanted shown, the free TV that conventions had come to mean to politicians. Daley, with Hippies and Yippies and all the other unshorn and unwashed poised to descend on him, had, he thought, denied them the coverage that was all *they* really wanted. Their sole interest in the convention was all those cameras in one place. Daley was now sure he had kept them off television.

While all this was playing out in Chicago, we in Miami Beach could not ignore it. George Murray's advance team called daily with reports of work being held up, requests for instructions, and general gloom-sharing. Newspapers asked about our plans should there be no television in Chicago. I worked up a stock reply that if there was no live television, we would use film; if film was forbidden, we would try Polaroid; and if that was denied, we would hire sketch artists. Somehow we would honor our commitment to cover the convention. It sounded nice, but I had no idea what we would do.

The Republican convention opened on schedule and proceeded according to plan. The only roll-call votes were for choosing the nominees for President and vice president, the only credentials battle over one Iowa delegate. As always when a nomination is a foregone conclusion, the buzz all week was about the running mate. Most guessed a liberal. Nixon chose Governor Spiro T. Agnew of Maryland, an obscure politician known as a sort of moderate but a hard-liner on "law and order" who had said of the Kerner commission's report, "If we want to pinpoint the cause of riots, it would be this permissive climate and the misguided compassion of public opinion."

Rev. Ralph Abernathy's Poor People's Campaign was present in small numbers outside the convention hall to almost no attention. Convention week saw two protest rallies in Negro sections of Miami, both of which turned violent, one in Liberty City where several were injured, and the other, on the night of the acceptance speeches, in Central City, where three died. On that last night, after the acceptance speeches, while Huntley and Brinkley and the Four Horsemen were summing up, we showed the film we had from Central City. Newspapers and audience mail, some of it angry, commented that the pictures seemed to point up the evening's theme of the Republicans' break with Negro voters, but that had not been our intent. We had merely used the pictures when we got them.

We left Miami for Chicago. I had two jobs: producing the coverage, and running the division, because McAndrew's death had left no time for making changes. It meant hitting the ground running the week between the conventions, the busiest "week before" I can remember. It meant trying to keep up with history while enmeshed in housekeeping trivia, reporting conflict while deflecting charges that we were abetting conflict.

On Tuesday of that week, August 20, Soviet tanks rolled into Prague, and the Illinois National Guard was ordered to Chicago. Both actions were justified as preventing subversion of authority and promoting order. Tass, the Soviet news agency, said the action was for "the purpose of peace."

The invasion had been foreshadowed by intensifying official criticism, in the Soviet Union and throughout the Eastern bloc, of the Czech experiment in giving "a human face" to socialism, an experiment that had, wisely or not, uplifted many Americans, both for what it promised and as a scrap of good news at a time of bad. Thousands of soldiers of five Warsaw Pact powers—all except Czechoslovakia— had been wheeling and deploying along the Polish and Hungarian borders on "routine" maneuvers and exercises. It was clearly only a matter of time, but when the invasion was finally loosed, its brutality shocked the whole world. The Warsaw Pact troops suppressed all the new free forms, and the Czech leaders who had written an inspiring new chapter in postwar history were summoned to Moscow for talks whose outcome was predetermined. Perhaps the high hopes were foolish.

By that Tuesday, young people had begun to gather in Chicago for the Democratic convention—the perfect stage for their challenge to the war in Vietnam. There were two groups of organized activists: the somber radicals of the National Mobilization Committee to End the War in Vietnam, led by Tom Hayden and Rennie Davis, the Mobes as they would be called; and the Youth International Party, the Yippies, followers of Abbie Hoffman, whose weapon was ridicule and who proposed to nominate a pig for President.

The largest group were the sympathizers or merely bystanders, students looking for summer excitement, all of them against the American presence in Vietnam, of course, but content to let others do something about it. Most were unkempt and startlingly dressed, the majority from comfortable and conventional families, and almost all glibly talked violence. The city refused them permission to sleep in parks or parade through the streets to the convention hall.

Also on that Tuesday, on the advice of Mayor Daley, Governor Samuel H. Shapiro of Illinois had called up 5,649 members of the Illinois National Guard for duty at the Democratic National Convention. Then reporters learned that 6,000 U.S. Army troops had just completed riot-control training at Fort Hood, Texas. And advance parties, drivers, cooks, and clerks were already setting up at military installations near Chicago. The day's last announcement was that all 12,000 Chicago police had been put on twelve-hour shifts. Secret Service and FBI added perhaps another thousand. The number of students totaled more than ten thousand, yet there was more than one Chicago cop for every long-haired kid, and better than twice as many when one included the Illinois National Guard and U.S. Army. A chain-link fence a mile long, topped with barbed wire, encircled the convention hall. It persists in the memory as the symbol of those two weeks: the 1968 Democratic National Convention met behind barbed wire.

Our coverage each night began by showing barbed wire framing the International Amphitheater; it became the theme, the trademark. Editorial? Of course. But journalists from all media had been injured by police, and in many instances they had been sought out:

"I'm from *Newsweek*."

"Fuck *Newsweek*!" And his glasses were smashed.

It had begun on Sunday night, the night before the convention. Police broke up a demonstration in Lincoln Park with tear gas. They roughed up two film crews—one ours, one CBS's. On Monday, John Evans, an NBC reporter, had to be taken to a hospital. Whatever animus Daley and his police felt for antiwar demonstrators seemed more specific and personal, more exquisite, more gratifying when exercised against the press. The demonstrators were just unspeakable kids, but the press gave them status, legitimized them, took them seriously. This is not to imply journalists were hurt worse than demonstrators. But beating up on kids was just good, clean fun, while we were seen as the bastards who were making a big deal out of it. By

Tuesday, the AP noticed there had been enough journalists attacked to do a special story on the total. That day the total reached 21.

Live television coverage of the convention was possible from only two locations, the International Amphitheater, down by the stockyards, and each network's permanent Chicago headquarters and studios. Ours were in the Merchandise Mart, a squat commercial building taking up a whole block just outside the Loop, along the Chicago River. The telephone installers' strike prevented microwave transmissions from anywhere else. We used microwave to send the live signal to the Mart, and from there to the network. (In all the United States, only in Chicago were these microwave installations within the union jurisdiction of IBEW telephone installers.) Then television mobile units were banned from the front of the Michigan Avenue hotels. So they parked a block away, behind the hotels.

We were convinced this was Daley's doing, or some flunky helping the boss keep antiwar demonstrators off television. But Daley or his flunky had outsmarted himself. The demonstrators, knowing where the mayor and the Chicago police had situated the mobile units—there and nowhere else—came to them. The pictures might not be live, but there would be pictures. Mobile units came with generators and could record pictures on tape. Couriers could take the tape by motorcycle to the Amphitheater or the Mart to be fed into the network. When the turmoil reached its climax, that is exactly how the pictures came to be shown across the country and became part of the permanent recollection.

We never knew if it was Daley or President Johnson for whom television was the enemy, but we had been singled out. The installers' strike and the restrictions on mobile units were proof enough, but another came Monday morning, the day the convention was to start. All the previous week, our requests for floor credentials, to give access to our reporters and their cameras, had been brushed aside. Now we were summoned, the presidents of the network news divisions, to a 9:00 A.M. meeting in a room in the Stockyard Inn, next door to the International Amphitheater. We were on time, but no one came from the convention management, not at 9:00, not at 9:30, not at 10:00. Dick Salant, president of CBS News, was outraged at the affront and sought to storm out. Bill Leonard, one of his vice presidents, and I kept him in his seat. This was too important for dignity. We needed those floor passes. The officials arrived at 10:30.

In came J. Leonard Reinsch, who every four years since 1936 had taken a leave of absence from his executive post at NBC's Atlanta affiliate to run the Democrats' convention. With him was John Criswell, who seemed to us our special nemesis. They had met all night with Speaker of the House Carl Albert, the permanent chairman of the convention, and others high up in the party. They dropped hints, but nothing specific, that there had been "input" from the White House. Criswell said, "The electronic media infringe on the rights of the delegates." His solution was to give each network floor passes for one floor camera, and only one, plus two reporters for television and two for radio. This would add up to seven passes each. (We had each asked for fifteen, for television alone. Radio was separate.) The outcry was immediate, loud, and anguished. Criswell left the meeting so there was only Reinsch to complain to.

What faced us was the gutting of our system. During convention sessions, only two of the Four Horsemen could be on the floor at a time, and there would be only one camera and crew to cover them. They could, of course, be found by cameras pointed down from the anchor booth and elsewhere, but this was clearly censorship by restricting access, the most effective kind. Then, in what he made seem an afterthought as the meeting ended, Reinsch gave us each six messenger passes. Salant found it insulting, but Bill Leonard and I grabbed them. Messengers go anywhere. Chancellor, for one, roamed the convention floor that week because his card said "Messenger."

The convention opened to the usual speeches and the traditional conflicts. In his welcoming speech as host, Mayor Daley asked, "Did you see those rioters at the other convention? No! They came here to wreck *this* convention." To loud applause, he promised law and order as long as he was mayor of Chicago. There were the usual struggles over seating, rules, civil rights, and who was a Democrat. But the Vietnam War lay over every speech, dominated every debate, and influenced every point of view and the outcome of every issue.

Over the next two days, Tuesday and Wednesday, August 27 and 28, more than at any time before or since, a national convention exploded into a national drama. It would not have happened if television were not there, but all we did was be there. It began Tuesday with the platform debate, the committee majority backing President Johnson on Vietnam and a minority report demanding an end to the bombing. The day had opened with Anita Bryant singing "Happy Birthday" to the President. Long before deciding not to run again, Johnson himself had arranged that the convention meet the week of his sixtieth birthday, and, to accommodate Dick Daley, his ardent supporter, it would meet in Chicago.

There was even the fantasy of his first settling the problem of Vietnam at a summit meeting with Soviet premier Alexei Kosygin. Now the peacemaker, he would descend on the city in triumph, to be drafted by acclamation for another term. Kosygin had reportedly hinted he might be available. That dream died when Soviet tanks rolled into Prague the week before, but rumors the President was coming to Chicago persisted and so, we learned later, did his plans to come.

On Tuesday, his birthday, reporters spotted Secret Service men downtown. We kept cameras "hot" at O'Hare Airport where his plane would land and the downtown heliport where he would come by helicopter. That was how he had come to Atlantic City. We got word from Daley's office that the banned mobile units could broadcast live from the airport if they were covering the President's arrival. The telephone installers would defer to the "presidential" occasion.

The following week, *The New York Times*, using White House sources, confirmed that the President had canceled his plans to come to Chicago that Tuesday only at the very last minute when his people on the scene told him he would not be "warmly received." Even after the chimera of a settlement with Kosygin, Johnson had wanted to lecture his party on the Vietnam plank in its platform, oppose any unconditional halt to the bombing; he had conceded enough. Now they must come to him. He had seen the need to give up the presidency, but he could not tolerate his party rejecting his policy. So it was reluctantly that he agreed to stay in Washington, but his lieutenants must hold to his positions. This hardening made everything worse, outside in the streets and inside in the hall.

It was after midnight in Chicago, already Wednesday morning, when Speaker Carl Albert called platform committee chairman Hale Boggs to the podium with his eighteen-thousand-word report. The leadership was ready to go to 3:30 A.M., but the tired, angry delegates balked. This helped the minority whose call to halt bombing in Vietnam had got only a third of the committee's votes. Its sponsors believed it would do better on the floor, but their big concern was television.

Debate might bring new life to the antiwar movement, but not in the wee hours of the morning. They wanted prime time.

Wisconsin moved to adjourn until 4:00 P.M. Wednesday.

Albert: "The Wisconsin delegate is out of order. Adjournment is not a recognizable motion."

Delegates started chanting, "Let's go home! Let's go home!" There was shouting and rhythmic clapping. Our floor reporters said there was a movement to walk out of the hall. Albert, one of the least effective Speakers of our time, lost control as the noise grew. Daley took the Illinois microphone to ask recognition. Boos from the galleries and the convention floor. He threatened to have the galleries cleared. "These people are here as guests, and if there is anymore of this, we'll clear them out."

"Let's go home! Let's go home!" More booing, louder now, and sustained.

Television cameras showed Albert conferring at the lectern with Boggs and party chairman John Bailey.

Albert: "Will the convention please come to order!"

From the floor a long, loud, derisive "Nooooooo . . ."

The cameras caught Daley in his seat, making the traditional throat-cutting gesture with the flat of his hand.

Albert: "I recognize the mayor."

More booing. Delegates and galleries, standing by now, waving arms and papers, some shaking fists.

Daley: (Scarcely heard in the din.) "I move to adjourn until twelve noon tomorrow."

The ayes had it. The delegates straggled out in a disorderly rush. The floor reporters went after the leaders of the antiwar delegates, who hailed postponing the debate until the next day as a triumph. Noon was not prime time, but it was better than two in the morning. The delegates headed for their hotels to try for some sleep, to be politicked by both sides in the coming debate. We stayed on the air. There was tape to be shown of police breaking up demonstrations in Grant Park. There were the Four Horsemen to hear from. This was now the second night that we had not shown any of the police activity during the session but only after it was over.

What we saw was the demonstrators in Grant Park chanting, "Hey! Hey! LBJ! How many kids did you kill today?" On the other side of Michigan Avenue were bystanders, some from Chicago, some from all over the country. Police were in a double line. Our reporter described the scene as he would have if it were being broadcast live, which became part of our pattern for tapes. That tape ran two minutes, ending before the confrontation. From the booth, Brinkley added that in the time since those pictures had been recorded, police had clashed with demonstrators.

Wednesday, at noon, the convention met to decide its platform. Boggs's reading was interrupted by booing, and Daley again threatened to clear the balconies. A Wisconsin delegate told Vanocur, "We are seeing the demise of the convention system."

Resentment against Daley simmered all day. The most persistent complaint was that delegates could not move easily about the floor, being constantly channeled, challenged to prove identity, even searched. Women told of having handbags pawed through. Never had armed police presumed to intrude on a major party's convention. Their animus was directed as much at reporters as at protesters. Dan Rather had been punched in the stomach the day before; that day Mike Wallace was roughed up. (In our control room, unworthy thoughts were uttered that if they were pounding floor reporters, why not ours so we might enjoy the publicity. I speculated grandly that ours were better known than CBS's, which gave them a kind of immunity.)

When the debate came, supporters of the President's plank alternating with those demanding an end to the bombing, we stuck with it, most of our excursions to the floor coming as speakers left or took the rostrum, a tedious process. There was chanting of, "We Want Peace!" and "Stop the War!" and much waving of signs, but it was a more orderly debate than expected, at least until Congressman Wayne Hays of Ohio, backing the "majority" plank, praised the Chicago police for "the patience of Job" and referred to the opposing plank to end the bombing as the "Hippie" plank. He derided the demonstrators' clothes, their hair, their bathing habits. Many delegates cheered Hays's attack on their own children, voicing the frustrations of a decade. Texas cheered; California booed. Although no delegate had been unaware of what was going on outside, now it had come inside.

When the roll-call vote was taken, the "majority" plank supporting the Johnson policies won by only three to two. More than a thousand delegates had voted against their President, and many voted for him rather than publicly repudiate him regardless of how they felt personally. The party split was now open. We then showed a tape from Grant Park, described by reporter Jack Perkins as though we were broadcasting live: demonstrators throwing stones and bottles at police; police firing tear gas; demonstrators shouting, "Sieg Heil!"; a young man bleeding; police arresting someone who had tried to tear down a flag.

Back to the convention, where the chair announced the vote on the Vietnam plank—and the platform—and adjourned the session, but neither could be heard. New York's delegates, in black armbands, were singing "We Shall Overcome" while on stage, at Mayor Daley's cue, the official band played brassy, happy music. "Four Leaf Clover" and "If You Knew Susie" and even the Democratic party fight song, "Happy Days Are Here Again!" Against them, "We Shall Overcome," California joining New York, and then delegates all over the floor, swaying and singing. Then the "Battle Hymn of the Republic." The floor rang with "Glory, Glory, Hallelujah!" But for the audience at home, it was drowned out by the official band; the singing was not included in the pooled sound supplied to the broadcasters. We sent our floor reporters to California and New York. They got the singing, thin and tinny, through their wireless microphones. Up to the booth to repeat the final vote on the party platform, 1,567 to 1,041, as we went off the air—for an hour. Then back for the night of nominating.

Breaking Chet and David for supper would be a problem. There was still the *Huntley-Brinkley Report* to do. It would include a report from Douglas Kiker about two thousand Yippies chased from Lincoln Park to Grant Park by police firing tear gas, and the National Guard arriving. The protesters would march on the hall tonight, he said. Then we had Elie Abel in New York with that day's film from Prague: Soviet tanks and troop carriers in the streets, people crying. While the newscast was on the air, I was in my corner planning that night's coverage before it was upon us.

Working in a control room is, as I said, like living in a submarine, an environment unto itself, sealed off and seemingly secure. It was doubly so at conventions because we lived there for a week at a time. Except for sleep and breakfast and walking on the lakeshore, my days passed there. News came to me there—from Prague, from the world, from the delegation hotels, from Michigan Avenue. I did not know what was happening; I knew what was on tape. Outside, twenty thousand troops and police diverted traffic, told people where to go and where not to go, used force to stifle expression, prepared for insurrection. The air throbbed from the rotors of helicopters watching Americans from above, but I knew only what I was told about it, or what I saw on a glass rectangle, three-fifths as high as wide. A few yards from my chair, in the hall, delegates, reporters, our copy boys, submitted to sophisticated electronic screening and to physical searching as they went from here to there, and once more when they stepped beyond, but I knew little of that. Security was casual in the area where I worked, scrutiny lax at the early hour I arrived. Nor did I myself smell tear gas. I knew about tear gas because I saw tape of colleagues and friends where tear gas was fired, listened to them describe how it smelled, heard them coughing.

Our convention coverage began at six that Wednesday evening. We signed off at one the following morning. In between, candidates for the presidential nomination were put forward in the traditional, comfortable way: nominated, seconded, and greeted with music as delegates circulated through the aisles. But little was traditional or comfortable that night. The confrontations in the streets reached their climax. In the hall, tensions between the two sides—"hawks" and "doves," there was no other issue—erupted in speeches, demonstrations, arrests, protests, threats to take the convention elsewhere, frustration, tears.

At the center, Mayor Daley manipulated from his seat what happened in the hall, sending squads of city employees into the balconies—the famous "sewer workers"—to cheer him when others booed him, managing security through his police. He became the focus of the anger of the "doves" and the approval of the "hawks" both inside the convention and all over the country. Hubert Humphrey said, "We ought to quit pretending that Mayor Daley did something that was wrong." In the networks' offices, we experienced an unusual volume of hostile telephone calls and telegrams.

I always felt obliged to run nominating speeches in full, no matter how long, but during seconding speeches we sent the floor reporters out to cover the news all over the convention. It would be hard to follow that rule tonight. Reports of trouble on Michigan Avenue were reaching the hall from all kinds of sources, not only ours. Delegates huddled at radios and used such phones as the establishment had granted them to keep up. If proceedings inside had no effect on events outside, what was happening outside was shaping and altering the convention inside. In the hour before the opening gavel, while we tried to squeeze in the news we had to cover before the roll call of the states, our mobile units in their dictated fixed positions were taping clashes between police and demonstrators.

I was huddled in my corner, listening with one ear to Eliot Frankel telling me what the next report on the floor would be, keeping the director and staff in air control to my right informed, whispering cues for Huntley and Brinkley, drawing their attention to delegation reports on the teletype, telling this or that floor reporter please to wind it up and whom to throw it to.

Inside control was to my left. Farther back on my left were Shad Northshield and outside control. From the time we got to Chicago, those monitors had been dark, devoid of live pictures from mobile units. Now the monitors were flickering; someone was rolling tape. George Murray was saying, "Shad wants you," but I was busy. So Northshield stood on a chair, thrust his upper body through the window between us and bellowed:

"Look at me, you son of a bitch!" I looked.

There, on two monitors, I could see running and clubbing and bleeding, confusion and violence. Tape had arrived from outside the downtown hotels, and I had to decide whether to show it—not knowing quite when it was recorded—or stay with the convention. Two weeks earlier, during the Republican convention, we had used little of the violence in the Negro sections of Miami, showing it only after the sessions had adjourned. It had seemed to me that although they were news, they were not news of the convention. By conditioning, or instinct, or perhaps prejudice, without time for debate, I decided that what was happening at Michigan and Balboa was truly part of the news of the Democratic convention, and I would have to fit it in.

Daley forces were bringing outsiders into the hall to demonstrate for Humphrey when he was put in nomination. The rules of that convention forbade outsiders in demonstrations, only those accredited to be in the hall. McCarthy's and McGovern's managers ran to the floor reporters to be outraged. We were not yet at the roll call of the states. For the first time during a session, not waiting until it ended, I ordered up Northshield's tape.

We heard Aline Saarinen reporting from Michigan and Balboa. We saw demonstrators marching south past the Hilton Hotel on their way to the convention. Police charged with tear gas. Aline told us how tear gas was unpleasant and burned the nose and eyes. We could hear her choke, cough, blow her nose. Tear gas filled the Conrad Hilton Hotel lobby. The demonstrators marched through the tear gas without breaking step. "This is my first experience with tear gas, and I don't like it," she said. I got some information to the booth, telling them it had been recorded almost an hour before, about seven o'clock. Brinkley could also say Aline had been treated for the tear gas and was all right. Later in the evening, with communication disorganized and events in the hall accelerating, I could sometimes give Huntley and Brinkley only a sentence or two for them to set the scene.

We started to carry the first nomination. Governor Dan K. Moore of North Carolina. Brinkley interrupted to say police were using night-sticks on demonstrators and loading them, bleeding, into patrol vans.

Then, during seconding, tape from Douglas Kiker, a half hour after Aline's, perhaps recorded by the same cameras; we had no way of knowing. Marchers, police in phalanx, clubbing. Inside the hall, a New York delegate, outraged at the ringers brought in by the Daley machine, refused to show his pass when challenged. An usher called a cop; there were more cops; he was dragged out. It was a pointless gesture, perhaps, but the atmosphere was getting uglier. Echoes of events outside, fragmentary reports, and the amplifying effect of one telling another added to the pitch.

Chancellor: "There is an awful mess in the aisle between South Dakota and New York. Guards with linked hands are driving people before them. This is a perfect indication of the mood on the floor. Six Chicago policemen with billy clubs are dragging people out of the New York delegation."

The Governor of Iowa nominated Senator Eugene McCarthy. When his speech ended we showed new tapes from Michigan Avenue, Aline Saarinen with demonstrators being clubbed outside the Conrad Hilton; Gabe Pressman of NBC's New York station with disorder and arrests on Balboa. There were cameras on Michigan Avenue; there were cameras on Balboa. There were no cameras in the Hilton lobby or near the hotel restaurant called The Haymarket.

Bystanders and some demonstrators fled police and tear gas to seek refuge in the restaurant; police pushed some through a plate glass window; other police ran into the restaurant randomly clubbing those inside. We saw none of that; we read about it in the next morning's newspapers. What occurred away from the cameras was worse than what we showed, and thus was not shown on television, not seen by the American people. Most of the horrors testified to later at the commission of inquiry were in fact not seen on television, police shouting, "Kill 'em! Kill 'em!," or clubbing kneeling young women and well-dressed, middle-aged bystanders. But what we did show sickened those who watched, and they hated us for showing it to them.

While Carl Stokes, the black mayor of Cleveland, was seconding Humphrey, we showed tape an hour old on which we heard for the first time, "The whole world is watching!," the demonstrator's slogan soon indeed heard around the world. The march to the hall was broken up. We could see the last demonstrators chased back into Grant Park by guardsmen with bayonets. Then another tape, Aline again, guardsmen marching down Michigan Avenue, the bayonets no longer on their rifles. These two tapes should have been played in reverse order, but we had no way of knowing. (We saved tape of Stokes's speech for after the session. It was half past midnight in Chicago by then, but it was a gesture.)

Soon after ten o'clock, Senator Abraham Ribicoff of Connecticut nominated Senator George McGovern. Looking directly at Daley seated fifteen feet below him in his delegation, Ribicoff said, "With George McGovern as President of the United States, we wouldn't have Gestapo tactics in the streets of Chicago." The crowd roared. The picture cut to Daley jumping to his feet, his palm against his mouth and nose to amplify his voice as he shouted obscenities. He was not heard on television, but no one needed a lip reader.

A cordon of plainclothesmen took up positions around the Illinois delegation. Strange men wearing "Humphrey" buttons or badges of the Textile Workers' Union took to shadowing our floor reporters. Dissident delegates found their floor microphones turned off. Humphrey was nominated on the first ballot with 1,317 voters, which became 1,760 after states were permitted to change their votes. He had needed 1,312. It was midnight in Chicago.

We stayed on for another hour. We showed the downtown tapes again. Playwright Arthur Miller, a Connecticut delegate, talked to Newman about hate for the young and bitterness of the aging. Again, we heard "The whole world is watching," and saw medical students treating the injured. Also that Wednesday, Illinois Bell and the IBEW agreed to end the telephone installers' strike.

The next day, Senator Edmund Muskie of Maine was nominated for vice president. Defenses were being marshaled for what had happened, especially that television had not shown the "provocation" the police were subjected to, the spitting and name calling. The popular instinct was to hate what was seen and us for showing it. A national poll supported Daley and the Chicago police three to one. It was not until the year's end, when an official report introduced the term *police riot* into the language, that this feeling began to ebb. But it never went completely away. It did not help to explain, as Brinkley did that last night in response to all the phone calls, that we showed what we could, that our locations were circumscribed and what we showed was unedited. Congressmen, among them Senators John O. Pastore of Rhode Island and Warren Magnusson of Washington, left Chicago promising to investigate why we had not shown the "provocation" but only the violence. It had been a bad year for us so far, and it was not going to get any better.

The last images of the convention itself were of yearning and dis-
enchantment, sadness and anger. Daley had packed the gallery with
city workers, personally seeing them past the guards, and they were
shown waving signs saying "We Love Mayor Daley" and a long banner
that said "We Support Mayor Daley and the Chicago Police." Aline
Saarinen interviewed the Humphreys, first Muriel Humphrey, then
the candidate. We were trying to be normal.

With no issues left to be decided, it was to be an evening of gestures
and formalities, culminating in the acceptance speeches. First, after
a filmed introduction from Senator Edward Kennedy, who had decided
not to be present in person for any part of the convention, there was
the convention's film in tribute to the martyred Robert Kennedy. The
narration was by Richard Burton, over scenes of Bobby Kennedy's life
and career, with repeated references to poor people and to peace. The
film changed nothing and added nothing in any objective way, but to
the people in the hall, after what they had already lived through that
week, that year, it became a moment of self-revelation and emotional
catharsis. When the film ended, and the lights went up, everyone in
the hall stood and began singing "The Battle Hymn of the Republic."
They joined hands and swayed, this time everybody in the hall, and
"Glory, Glory, Hallelujah!" echoed back from the walls and roof. This
time the official broadcast sound let us hear it. The cameras ranged
the rows for faces, many of them crying, some of them famous.

Not all were equally moved. Texas and Illinois sat while the rest
sang. The cameras kept returning to large men in short-sleeved shirts,
their meaty arms folded, glowering through the entire quarter hour
the singing lasted. The claque in the balcony had tried to drown it
out with shouts of, "We love Daley! We love Daley!" Picture and
sound combined to form the mordant expression of an ugly time, an
image of class division that even in private moments we dared not
admit, the tearful well-to-do of New York and California against the
working poor of the balconies. It made no sense, this shouting match
between those who worked for Daley and those who yearned for Kennedy. They had not been enemies. To Bobby Kennedy, Daley had
been the crucial ally. But they had become symbols, and, as symbols,
they were enemies.

One could not be unaffected witnessing such scenes, but they were
undeniably news, what we were in Chicago to report. What stunned
me personally, and many others that final day, had taken place before
the session started. Richard Daley was invited to Walter Cronkite's

anchor booth to be interviewed, admittedly in response to the protests CBS had received. "We've had hundreds of telegrams," Cronkite said, "a lot of telephone calls supporting your position and how things have gone here in Chicago." So had everyone in television. This was not objective, but abject. It got worse. The mayor first told Cronkite he was a welcome guest in the Daley home every evening. Then he read a short statement: "Terrorists came here equipped with caustics, with helmets, and with their own brigade of medics . . . Fifty-one policemen have been injured. Sixty percent of those arrested did not live in Illinois and seventy percent did not live in Chicago . . . In the heat of emotion and riot, some policemen may have overreacted. . . ."

Cronkite interjected, "That's the problem with having your face out there as the head man. You get all the blame."

Daley: "I've never seen on television a picture of a wounded policeman laying on the street, seen them badly hurt. Is this the kind of coverage of the news we should get? . . ."

Cronkite: "We know that these people met and marched at some park. . . . They had a high strategy meeting for this disruption you're talking about. There's no question about their plan to disrupt this convention."

Daley: "That disruption they practiced, Walter, and I never saw it in some newspapers. They practiced guerrilla warfare."

And later:

Daley: "Don't condemn the majority of our police department. The majority—I know you—"

Cronkite: "I have—personally, I have—"

Daley: "I'm saying that the police department—"

Cronkite: "—the greatest sympathy for them, standing there taking those taunts—"

Daley: "Yes. And the language. You can't show it on this thing."

Cronkite: "No."

Daley: "The language that was used last night until four o'clock, you couldn't repeat it."

Cronkite: "It must be very difficult for any police officer or any other individual to stand there and listen to that and look at that and the filth and the dirt and the spoken—"

Daley: "Would you like to be called a pig? Would you like to be called with a four-letter word?"

Cronkite: "No—"

Daley: "Well, that's what happens."

And further along:

Daley: "The television is just like a fire department. As soon as you bring a television camera out in the neighborhood, in certain neighborhoods—"

Cronkite: "We recognize the problem. We've been working on it."

Daley: "And you have a responsibility, your industry, the same as anyone else."

Cronkite: "We certainly do, a very large responsibility in this regard, and we recognize that . . . I don't envy the mayor of any big city in the United States today."

It was not a tough interview.

Daley left the booth and CBS's convention coverage paused for a commercial. In later years, Cronkite would tell friends his invitation to Daley and that night's interview had been his worst professional mistake. Clearly, he had not come to fight. At best, it was a victory for the fatuousness of deadpan journalism. I looked on it as consorting with the enemy. CBS gave Daley a platform all his own, to attack with no one defending, to make unchallenged, unrebutted excuses for four days of what, when they happened in other countries, we called human rights violations.

Hanging over us was the certain prospect of a season of unprecedented trouble with Congress, not for all of broadcasting, but for the networks alone. Congress would embrace Daley's basic defense, and that of his supporters, that it was our fault, that we were the villains; we were arrogant; we must have made it up.

To us, the wonder was that, in a city under siege, we had managed to cover the convention as well as we had. But that was the cause of our trouble. As *Broadcasting* magazine put it, "If Chicago was a garrison city last week—most would agree that it was—it was a garrison city in a fishbowl." Network television did that. We had not led protests or clubbed demonstrators; we had not goaded police or fired tear gas. Our sin was being there—with cameras.

Congressional Democrats feared that what was seen on television might cost them the presidential election and damage them individually in their districts. Indeed, it may have. Nor was hostility to the networks confined to Democrats. Republican whip Leslie Arends proposed that the House investigate "the role of the networks in our national affairs and just how these federally licensed activities ought to be allowed to get into the business of influencing the public." That was stating it plain, right down to the magic words *federally licensed*.

Calling for a "full-scale" investigation, Senator Russell Long of Louisiana opined: "The city of Chicago was convicted by the television media without its side ever being heard." There was a day-long attack in the House. Michigan's powerful Democratic congressman John Dingell called the coverage "biased" and "irresponsible."

Pastore's Senate Communications Subcommittee stretched its scheduled hearings into violence in television programs to include the news coverage in Chicago. Sniffing the wind, the FCC asked each of the three networks to consider the mail it, the commission, had received charging they had shown bias, and to aid the commission in formulating a response.

Congress's hostility to the networks lasted until it was deflated by a report from the commission on American violence named by President Johnson after Robert Kennedy's murder. In the uproar following the Chicago convention, the commission chairman, Dr. Milton S. Eisenhower, President Dwight D. Eisenhower's brother, had asked a panel headed by Daniel Walker, a lawyer for Montgomery-Ward, to find out what had happened there. On December 1, it published Walker's report, tellingly entitled, "Rights in Conflict." What the report said had happened was largely what the networks had reported at the time, dismissing as insubstantial the claims that police had been unbearably provoked. The worst incidents were blamed on what the report labeled a "police riot." Television, it said, may have made things worse, and there had been too little analysis of the protest groups, but that was said in a low key. In contrast, it called the police violence "unrestrained and indiscriminate." Congress turned to other concerns.

The aborted congressional inquiries and the FCC asking us to sweep our files for them had meanwhile cost the networks hundreds of thousands of dollars worth of lawyers' and clerks' time to find and organize and copy documents, and of film and tape editors making copies of what had not been broadcast. Many of us spent hours answering questions and trying to recall, and all of us read and reread transcripts of all thirty-five hours of our Chicago coverage.

The transcripts showed that of the thirty-five hours, exactly sixty-five minutes was devoted to the demonstrations, including twelve minutes of tapes shown a second time. Of the sixty-five minutes, thirty were in prime time. This was important because Daley was demanding an hour of prime time from each of the networks to answer "charges" against him and his city. Our transcript showed no one reporting for NBC News making charges against Daley or Chicago or statements critical of the Chicago police, and I am sure the others were roughly the same. His allegation that we had not shown provocation, the complaint most widely echoed in Congress and by the public, was simply not true. For example, the tearing down of the American flag, the provocation he most often cited as ignored by us, was shown not once but three times, and several of our reporters, at different times, had talked about how the demonstrators had set out to goad the police.

There was no point in public denials. Not only would it be playing Daley's game; it would have convinced few. He claimed he had received forty thousand letters of approval, and I am sure he did. The obverse was the mail we received that disapproved of what NBC News did, or what we were perceived as doing, in heavy proportion and great volume. Daley wanted his hour of prime time and the networks refused to give it. CBS refused outright. ABC and we offered to put him on an interview program, in our case *Meet the Press*, which we would expand to an hour for the occasion. I felt, as I had when I saw him interviewed by Cronkite, that it was not our job to provide him a platform. Our job was journalism, and there cannot be journalism without journalists. It might be news if he answered reporters' questions, but I could not accept "giving" him an hour to "answer" what we had shown and said. From the Senate floor, John Pastore of Rhode Island urged us to reconsider, but I felt it would be wrong, and Julian Goodman, president of NBC, supported me.

There matters stood until someone came forth to give Daley the time he wanted. The offer came with much fanfare from Metromedia, a company owning stations in New York, San Francisco, Los Angeles, Kansas City, and Washington. By Sunday, September 15, more than 130 stations, including, of course, the *Chicago Tribune*'s WGN-TV, had joined to carry Daley's "answer." Most film in it had been supplied, at Daley's request, by the networks. The "original" pictures were of Chicago police officials and civilians talking about provocation, and of policemen awkwardly holding Molotov cocktails, loose bricks, and a baseball bat with "Kill the Pigs" painted on it.

It was a letdown. The *Times* said it "showed no more provocation than network television had shown while the convention was going on. But it eliminated most footage of clubbing by police." The only pictures of Daley himself were from the interview in Cronkite's anchor booth, on the last night of the convention.

With the broadcast of the film, the Daley incident evanesced. The fuss had been about carrying it and that had become moot. The unshakable case he had promised was shaky. Those who believed in him mumbled and grumbled but, without the ammunition he had promised, lost stomach for the fight. They still knew we were wrong, and evil as well, but they could not prove it. (One woman, whose complaint I had answered with lawyer-imposed reasonableness and a small array of facts, wrote back: "You networks always have an answer!") As the thunder died away, it seemed to some of us, with little to go on except taut nerves and tired muscles, that Chicago 1968 was where network news had lost its innocence. After years of telling poll-takers they trusted television above all other media of news, the American audience, history's most middle-class majority, was writing to us and telling newspapers and whoever would listen that the era of trust was over. We, who had once been so loved!

If not everybody responsible for network news felt this way, apparently we all felt something. There had never been such a time for news executives to agree to appear, to volunteer to appear, before groups and in panels, lecturing, pleading, wrapping ourselves in the First Amendment, American tradition, English common law, and anything else available. We warned and expostulated and cajoled that what happened to the free flow of news would happen not to us but to them, our hearers, the citizenry, free government. We did not know what good practice this would be for the years of Richard M. Nixon and Spiro T. Agnew, who would be elected that November.

Before we reached that day, there was the campaign to cover, New York City's worst and most famous teachers' strike, the Vietnam War, the Paris peace talks, the passionate movement at home to end the bombing. There was the logistical nightmare to face of the first Apollo mission since January 1967 when three astronauts had been burned to death on the launch pad.

And so, on the last Thursday in October, the organism finally rebelled. I had returned early from a business lunch feeling internal distress. Despite recourse to antacids and analgesics in my private bathroom (the only perquisite of office worth having), the mirror showed someone pale and sweaty. After ten minutes of this, I asked a secretary to find a doctor. NBC's had left at noon, but she found Rockefeller Center's. He came with his stethoscope and his laconic gloom and solemnly advised me it might be a heart attack. My doctor was informed and arrangements were made.

By now I was feeling less uncomfortable but I had been strapped onto a stretcher, wheeled into an elevator and out to the ambulance, through the usual midtown New York lunch-hour crowd. Someone asked who that was. I could hear the answer: "Some NBC biggie." Dick Wald rode with me in the ambulance. By the time they wheeled me into Intensive Care I no longer felt ill. Wald told jokes, and we were so noisy a nurse ordered him out. They kept me for days of testing, since no test could find anything wrong. It wasn't my heart; perhaps my gallbladder, but if so it was only temporary. Nonmedical to a fault, I concluded that something inside resented being exploited by this nonsense and had refused to go on.

What matters is that I was still in the hospital on election day. It was the first even-numbered year since 1950 that I had not been in Studio 8-H. I got a second telephone but there was no time, given hospital bureaucracies, to bring in more television sets, so I had to watch all three networks on one set, switching among them by a slow "bedside" device. I do not recall actually doing anything besides being a nuisance to Shad Northshield, who was producing, but I did keep them on the air another half hour when they wanted to close. All night, I dozed and woke and said a few words into the open phone.

It was an exciting night for returns. Coming out of Chicago by far the underdog, Humphrey had almost closed the gap. His staff would later claim that, given one more week, he could have won. (One of them, in an airport encounter years later, claimed if NBC had not shown the Chicago rioting, he would have won. He was still angry. Not at the police, not at the demonstrators, not at Daley, but at me. By then it was two Presidents later, and he was in another business.)

Coverage of the 1968 election was much like that of 1960. Again, the program finally signed off at 7:30 A.M., still without an official winner. *Today* came on and went off and still no sure result. Again, as in 1960, we had been saying all night we would wait for California but ended up waiting for Illinois. This time Illinois voted Republican; Daley could not hold it. It was after 10:30 Eastern time, Wednesday morning, that we at last projected the Nixon victory. He and Humphrey were barely half a percentage point apart in the popular vote, and Wallace had taken 13½ percent—and five states. Wallace claimed credit for the Republican victory, but by Nixon's own reckoning, without Wallace it would still have been a Nixon victory. In the hospital, I hung up the phone and finished sleeping. I was to have more tests that afternoon.

The Wednesday after I returned from the hospital, on November 13, the usual Wednesday meeting between the News and the Network gathered in my office. With me were two vice presidents for news, another for money, and a fourth for sports. By then, Sports was part of News only as a formality. Bill McAndrew and Julian Goodman had enjoyed the association, but everyone knew that my interest was at best meager. I liked going to games but was bored by palaver about rights and licensing fees.

And yet the presence of Sports at the News meeting with the Network was essential; many Wednesdays we had nothing else to talk about. It was at one of these meetings that the Network's engineering vice president had told the Sports vice president, Carl Lindemann, that not only was slow-motion replay not yet available, but it was, in the judgment of his scientific experts, impossible in theory. (The next Saturday, in its college football coverage, ABC used slow-motion replay, inaugurating a new age in television sports.)

At this November 13 meeting, the Network's delegation was headed by the division president, Don Durgin, and his deputy, Robert Stone, the only man I knew on *Fortune* magazine's list of America's Ten Worst Bosses. (Once, when I had told just such a meeting that the White House wanted network television for the President's speech the next evening, Stone asked me, "Does the White House know we have two premieres tomorrow?") There were also some vice presidents, including, of course, the engineering vice president, but that day Bob Stone held the floor.

Stone described NBC's coup in getting a single sponsor, Timex, at a large price—newspapers said $850,000—for an expensive and important children's special program the coming Sunday. It was the classic *Heidi*, starring a new, beautiful ten-year-old, with a supporting cast that included Michael Redgrave, Jean Simmons, Maximilian Schell, and Walter Slezak, whom even we News types could recognize. If it did not begin on the dot of seven, if it was delayed or "joined in progress," the tykes would switch to ABC's *Land of the Giant*, which NBC had promised Timex would not happen. "So," he said, shaking his finger under Carl's nose, "that football game better end by seven." It all seemed strange to me, but it was Carl's business, not mine.

My wife had asked friends to dinner Sunday now that I was back from the hospital certified no worse off than before. My younger son, then fourteen, distracted by all the grown-up noise, had escaped to the television set upstairs to watch the New York Jets play the Oakland Raiders. As we were sitting down to dinner, he came charging down the stairs, shouting, "What are you people doing?"

I asked him what was he talking about. He told me NBC had cut away from the Raiders-Jets game with less than a minute to play. It dismayed him that I was not surprised. I asked what the score was. The Jets were leading 32–29. He went back upstairs to learn what happened from the radio. What happened was this: After a grueling and exciting game, full of the kind of gory battling that always lubricated meetings of these two teams, the Jets pulled ahead with barely a minute left. When Oakland got the ball, its first play was a twenty-two-yard pass putting them in scoring position. With fifty seconds now left to play, NBC cut away for *Heidi.*

Unseen east of the Mississippi, the Oakland Raiders scored two touchdowns in the last fifty seconds of play and won the game 43 to 32. NBC became a national scandal and *Heidi* a national joke. As I would learn the next day, every NBC station in two time zones was swamped with telephone calls, and our New York switchboard was inundated by an estimated ten thousand calls at once, burning out its fuses and some wiring. (When NBC did not answer, hundreds called *The New York Times* and the New York Police Department.) Those switching to radio learned who won the game; those watching *Heidi* had to wait eighty minutes, when a ribbon of lettering moved across the bottom of the picture saying Oakland had scored twice and won. (The ribbon of lettering, or "flashcaster," was repeated later, disturbing the scene in which Heidi's paralyzed cousin tries to walk for the first time.)

The late Sunday evening news programs on CBS and ABC held us up to ridicule; Monday's newspapers were scathing; the mail was outraged. NBC made lame statements about protecting children's programs, and even lamer explanations about this one calling that one who tried to call the other one but could not get through. We started off looking silly and ended up looking venal. Finally, NBC proclaimed that henceforward, when showing a live sports event, we would keep on showing it until we knew who won, and by what score, and that we would delay—or "slide"—the openings of all the following programs long enough forward to make this possible. This was now an absolute, unshakable rule, to be broken only in cases of assassination, war, or catastrophe. We might not show a sports event from the beginning; but we would show it to the end. Inside NBC, this is known as the "Heidi rule."

On December 24, we covered the return of eighty-two crew members of the *Pueblo* and the body of the eighty-third. There were family reunions and talk of the holiday season, with an undercurrent of unease as the Navy named an admiral to investigate and the captain of the *Pueblo* wept on reaching American soil. But that night, Christmas Eve, Col. Frank Borman, Capt. James A. Lovell, Jr., and Maj. William A. Anders became the first humans to orbit the moon. As their Christmas greeting from space, they read in turn from the opening verses of Genesis.

Anders opened with, "In the beginning, God created heaven and earth. And the earth was without form and voice; and darkness was upon the face of the deep," and Borman closed with, "And God called the dry land Earth, and the gathering together of the water He called the seas! And God saw that it was good."

They went around the moon ten times and NBC alone stayed on the air all night. On December 27, they splashed down, and talk turned to men actually landing on the moon in the New Year, in 1969. "In this decade," John Kennedy had said.

On December 27, waiting for Apollo VIII to splash down in the Pacific, Chet Huntley filled time reading letters NBC had got about the latest adventure in space, about the orbit of the moon on Christmas Eve, about seeing it on television, about Borman and his colleagues reading from the story of Creation, as human eyes saw for the first time the "dark side" of the moon. But there was more than awe and wonder; some letters pointed out that Borman was in a government vehicle when he read from the Bible, which violated the separation of church and state. Huntley welcomed Borman to television, where no matter what you say someone will write to object.

13

When we left Chicago, with all its detritus of the 1968 Democratic convention, I turned my attention full time to running NBC News. Being division president involved the same work I had done as McAndrew's number two, but the texture of my days was different. Old colleagues on their way into my office would ask my secretary about my mood, and newspapers judged me quotable, often more than I liked. People who ran news organizations had become persons of interest, with the managers of broadcast news organizations the most interesting of all.

The Vietnam War did that, and it never went away. The public's attention fixed not only on our prejudices and conspiracies but on our minutiae, the programs we broadcast, the people who did them, even the other news we covered. From the smallest detail to the least connected event, we were seen by viewers, by politicians, by ourselves in the light of our coverage of the war and how our coverage was perceived. During my time as division president we did many different things, some of which seized momentary attention, but we were known to everyone, and forever, by how we covered the war.

My immediate problem was getting it covered. As the rules dictate, I tried to keep my personal attitudes out of such decisions, but that is an unattainable ideal. My personal attitude toward Vietnam, as it had been toward Korea, was shaped by serving in uniform during World War II. Like most of my generation, like the presidents themselves, I never doubted that that was where I should be. But from the start, this was a strange one. Some young men were drafted while others were not. The rightness of the cause was neither self-evident to the country nor proclaimed by its leaders. This was not Normandy, or Okinawa, or even Pusan. John Kennedy tried to pretend it was not a war; Lyndon Johnson tried to pretend it would not cost much; Richard Nixon tried to pretend he was withdrawing.

It was, to begin with, my nightmare that a president would ask for a declaration of war, especially Johnson, because there was a time Congress might have given him one. A declared war would have meant censorship at the source, our color film held in Saigon to be run through some murky soup in an Army Signal Corps lab rather than being sent to Los Angeles or San Francisco or Tokyo for developing. What scared me was not what they might cut—American censors have never been that bad—but the physical damage they might do the film.

War was never declared; Congress was willing to pay for it only if it did not have to declare it. We filmed, and we shipped our film freely, scolded by admirals and generals and colonels and captains, but never threatened. Each time I visited Saigon I would marvel again to see on the bureau bulletin board the schedule of military shuttle flights to Da Nang, to Hue, to the Delta, to the major points of the country, flights available to journalists. At the bitterest of the fighting, at the worst of hostility between the brass and the press, reporters and camera crews were taken to the action by the military, to the nastiest action, to the stupidest command mistakes. And if the next flight was booked up, there would be another in about an hour, like a streetcar.

I visited Vietnam not because I had doubts about the coverage or wisdom to give those charged with it, nor to "learn for myself" how things were really going. I went to Vietnam so the staff could complain to "New York." They were physically the farthest of all our people from where their work was used. They could barely communicate with us, at best on scratchy radio circuits ordered in advance, always overloaded with the needs of radio reporting, or by a teletype system that took so long to move a message that one bureau chief would punch and insert the tape, then go to dinner while it was being sent. A rare telephone call might get through, and, even rarer, you could hear it. And once a year they talked to me in person.

The bureau chief would give me an office, and one by one they came in, if they cared to, and said something, which I would note— to be acted upon, or transmitted, or even ignored as the fulmination of someone under stress, facing danger when working and boredom when idle. Just listening was function enough. That was the war in the field. The war at home was something different.

At home, the war not only brought on the demonstrations at the Democratic convention in Chicago and ended the American public's simple trust in the news it got on television, it led to open hostility between the White House and American journalism. The best-remembered event in the annals of that hostility was Vice President Spiro Agnew's speech to a regional Republican conference in Des Moines, Iowa, on November 13, 1969, where he said a "little group of men," conspiring to dictate what America saw, exercised a "concentration of power" that Americans would not tolerate.

"The credibility gap," he said, "is not in the offices of the government in Washington but in the studios of the networks in New York."

Agnew's Des Moines speech ranks as a marker in American history. It launched the Nixon administration's effort to put blame for opposition to the war on the way it was reported, to direct the public's displeasure to the coverage as the easier target, and, after Chicago, we were easier indeed. Although the press has always been fair game, it now became the enemy, with television news singled out as the foe within. Agnew's speech is the best remembered of the steps in the Nixon White House campaign against the networks.

Long after he pleaded no contest to corruption, resigned as Vice President, and vanished into well-upholstered obscurity, Agnew's name still evokes the Des Moines speech, which had not even been on the conference's agenda. Someone had called from Washington to ask that room be made, and dutiful Republicans shoehorned the Vice President in before their first session, a time set aside for late arrivals to get hotel keys and have a drink with friends they had not seen since last time. The White House needed a platform for Agnew right away; Des Moines was what they found.

That morning our Washington bureau chief had read me excerpts from the advance text. Whatever else it was, it would clearly be news, and we must carry it live. Such things took days to arrange. We would need to bring in enough equipment to cover a football game or the opening of Congress, and that was only part of it. AT&T would have to juggle circuits so that, instead of flowing across the country from

New York or Los Angeles or Washington, picture and sound would flow from Des Moines both east and west. As I feared, we were too late for all that. It turned out, however, that an Iowa educational station had TV equipment in the hall to record the conference on tape—not Agnew's speech but the meeting itself. The phone company strained to get that picture to the connecting point. The other two networks had joined us, and we never knew who was first and who last in deciding and arranging, but all three carried Spiro Agnew's message using an educational station's black and white pictures.

After he spoke, we strained to explain the severity of his attack, the harshness of tone, the clear intention to "take on" the networks. Neither Nixon nor Agnew was known for confrontation. Nixon, indeed, was becoming adept at indirection. His style was to appeal to station owners over the heads of their liberal networks; to invite chiefs of the networks and other media companies to the Oval Office for chats, dispensing presidential golf balls and ashtrays, cuff links and matchbooks; even, it was said, to use Internal Revenue agents or the FBI to spread discomfort, to keep the "enemies" list. Confrontation may have suited Patrick Buchanan, the White House staff writer credited with the Des Moines speech, but, if so, what had set him, or them, off on such a rampage?

The only adequate answer is frustration, and the big frustration of the time, America's and Nixon's, was the Vietnam War. Nixon had been elected the previous November because enough voters had thought him the more likely to attain peace there. The following March, however, he admitted to reporters he saw "no prospects for a reduction of American forces in the foreseeable future." In April, American battle deaths in Vietnam passed those in Korea. As antiwar protest spread and grew respectable, Nixon had to respond. He would shift the burden of fighting to South Vietnam—what would be called "Vietnamization"—and vowed to cut American troops to 200,000 by the end of 1970. but as our ground strength shrank, bombing of North Vietnam increased, producing charges of civilian targets and dead children, swelling the protest even more.

Against this background, Nixon presented himself on November 3, 1969, for what we were advised would be his definitive policy statement on Vietnam. All three networks showed him speaking earnestly into the camera: "North Vietnam cannot defeat or humiliate the United States. Only Americans can do that." He gave the vocabulary of the Right a new phrase when he asked for support from "the great silent majority" of his fellow Americans. The announced new policy itself, however, was no more than had been foreshadowed, withdrawing ground troops and handing the conduct of the war to the Vietnamese.

Ten days later, in Des Moines, Agnew said: "Monday night a week ago, President Nixon delivered the most important address of his administration, one of the most important of our decade. . . . For thirty-two minutes, he reasoned with a nation that has suffered almost a third of a million casualties in the longest war in its history. When the President completed his address . . . his words and policies were subjected to instant analysis and querulous criticism." Thus another homeric epithet entered the armory of the news-bashers, "instant analysis." Nobody had called it that before.

America responded to Agnew as it had to Daley. There were letters and wires to the networks, to the news divisions, to me and my counterparts by name—some orchestrated, some merely inspired—asking who elected us, and by what right we faced their President with our knee-jerk (a favorite term) liberalism. The storm reached such fury that the lords of CBS found it prudent to ban "instant analysis." Comment on major statements, presidential and other, would be deferred for one whole day, by which time no one would care any longer, which they soon found out—but not before they had been denounced in major newspapers for "knuckling under"—and big names in their own news staffs publicly deplored their managers.

Agnew had said in his speech that the President spoke for "thirty-two minutes," and that is the hidden key of one of the great fusses of history. Broadcasting has always divided its hours into neat fractions. After events like speeches or sports a network or station will "fill" to the next half hour before starting another program. When radio dominated the story of Europe sliding down its path to war, with audiences huddling at radio sets whenever there was news, "fill" became opportunity for prestige and even fame. House journalists volunteered themselves in place of organ music. Networks took to having them answer, What does it all mean? In time, this was accepted as part of the jealously held mandate of uptown journalism. But it started as "fill," and that was always its basic function.

Thus, if President Nixon had been able to have his say in twenty-eight minutes rather than thirty-two, the analyzers might not have had time to get up to speed. A minute or two of summarized highlights and we would be returned to "our regularly scheduled program." But he left them too much time. In the President's mind, this was an important occasion, his most serious address about America's most vexing problem, his first substantial opportunity since elected to stake out stature. Nixon, a self-dramatizer of the Walter Mitty sort, built to a noble climax, perorating with benisons. The effect was then ruined by yammerers and pickers of nits. His balloon deflated, he sent his point men to lash the networks with his furies.

All of which has been much gone over. But one circumstance that had been ignored emerges on reexamination. Of the networks, ABC took the most seriously the job of filling nearly thirty minutes of empty air. In contrast to CBS's and NBC's three talking heads each, ABC News sent eight, one of them an outside "expert." He was W. Averell Harriman, millionaire, public servant, ambassador to Moscow, pillar of the Marshall Plan, governor of New York, cabinet member. Of all who commented on Nixon's speech that night, Harriman had been the least critical. It would be "presumptuous," he said, to "give a complete analysis of a very carefully thought out speech," adding, "No one wishes him well any more than I do."

Nevertheless, Agnew savaged him at the very top of his speech: "To guarantee in advance that the President's plea for national unity would be challenged, one network trotted out Averell Harriman. . . ." He said that as America's chief negotiator at the Paris peace talks, Harriman had appeased the North Vietnamese; he made the usual populist joke about the shape of the bargaining table; he accused Harriman of a "compulsion to justify his failure to anyone who will listen." Attacking Harriman instead of such inviting targets as the three anchormen made no sense—even from Agnew's own point of view. This was not rebuttal; this was not even having a go at the networks. This was spitting anger.

Since Harriman had said almost nothing, it must have been the mere sight of him that set Agnew off. Harriman was a Roosevelt Democrat, a New Dealer, whose very voice and accent bespoke privilege. People who claw their way up from impoverished respectability, like Nixon, and Agnew—and Buchanan?—hate people like Harriman. They have, to be sure, their own rich friends, but these are the self-made rich, Bebe Rebozos and Robert Abplanalps, not Harrimans or Rockefellers.

The Agnew speech shook every broadcasting professional, but not all in the same way. Proprietors of the affiliated stations publicly declared support for the network news divisions, but they told reporters from behind their hands that there was a lot in what Agnew said. A

Los Angeles–based network vice president, not otherwise identified, told *Broadcasting* magazine: "Don't quote me because my opinion, of course, is drastically different from that of my home office in New York. But I'll tell you this—Agnew's blast was a long time coming. Why, these news guys, even in my own place, get away with murder."

FCC chairman Dean Burch asked for transcripts of the summary and analysis with which the networks had followed the President's speech to the nation on November 3. It may well have been, as he later insisted, a perfectly innocent request, prompted only by his un- derstandable wish to find out what was causing all the fuss. The net- works, equally understandably, reacted as though the hangman was asking to borrow a rope. Remarkably, Burch's request had been made to the networks on November 5, two days after Nixon's speech, and more than a week before Agnew spoke out in Des Moines.

The White House preoccupation with television, always high, now became total. Eager young men were assigned to watch all three net- work evening news programs, their morning programs, their special programs, recording and evaluating and writing reports that circulated throughout the national executive, from the Oval Office to the sub- basements. The process reached a high point more than a year later when one of these "scorecards" was "obtained" by Jerry terHorst of the *Detroit News* at the same time it was "provided" to right-wing syndicated columnist Victor Lasky. TerHorst wrote about the White House compulsion to monitor network newscasts; Lasky took the ma- terial as his and did his usual media-conspiracy column, belaboring the networks for negative reports on the fighting in Laos. Both columns, terHorst's and Lasky's, stemmed from President Nixon's public irri- tation, at a news conference, with how the networks were depicting his Laos adventure and his cherished plan to have the South Viet- namese Army fight and win on the ground, with only logistics and air "support" from the United States.

The circulated document itself, eight single-spaced typewritten pages, is of value—and was then—only to illustrate the Nixon circle's mesmerized attention to television news, its fascinated hostility, its obsession with detail. It said that "the evidence is damning—partic- ularly on the part of our old friends at NBC." (I admit to reading this with a certain pride, the same pride Brinkley felt at being the first journalist denounced by name by Spiro Agnew.) ABC and CBS got their share, but ours was the lion's:

"February 10 [1971] NBC told us that the 3 million people of Laos have now become unwilling pawns . . ."

"On the 12th, NBC emphasized 'the most withering enemy anti-aircraft fire . . .' "

"On the 15th, NBC neglected to report ARVN claim that parts of [the Ho Chi Minh] Trail were cut . . ."

On the eighteenth, NBC "had a film report on U.S. wounded . . ."

On the nineteenth, "NBC report from a U.S. base near DMZ saw it in perilous position . . ."

"On the 20th, NBC said: 'The invasion of Laos has run into serious trouble . . .' "

"Continuing downward on the 21st, NBC said: ' . . . Things are not going well for the South Vietnamese . . .' Chancellor said: 'In the Northern part of Laos the war is also going badly.' "

And so on to March 1, when the White House summary felt obliged to note: "NBC gets a clean bill this evening."

The point is not the invasion of Laos, or whether the South Vietnamese could win without American ground troops, or even whether, as the report says, NBC was "irresponsible." The paper is of consequence because it was read and believed by the President of the United States, one of a series of monitoring reports and "scorecards" of network coverage made at his, and his advisers', direction. Reflecting and reinforcing their attitudes, these anonymous memoranda influenced what they said, and what they hoped to do. These in-house evaluations were what Nixon and Agnew and Chuck Colson and most of the rest of the administration relied on to know how they were "playing" in the media, especially on television. Locked into a war they inherited, determined not to be seen as surrendering while being seen as ending it, needing above all the public's good opinion, which they thought only a docile journalism could give them, they became more and more a band besieged, trusting only each other. It is hardly surprising that as reelection time loomed, someone was sent to break into the Watergate office of the Democratic party's national chairman to see if he knew something nasty that he might *leak to reporters*.

The campaign against the networks built up steam. Wyoming's Clifford P. Hansen, a White House point man in the Senate, took from the television news archives that Vanderbilt University had recently begun compiling "the complete television presentations dealing with the recent Laos incursion from CBS and NBC evening telecasts from February 25 through March 5, 1971." The quotation is from the covering letter Hansen sent to newspaper and magazine editors with the copy of his speech. To close the circle, he also included a copy of Victor Lasky's column. On the Senate floor, and in his letter to the editors, he also said:

"American and allied soldiers are today fighting two wars. One is in Southeast Asia where American and South Vietnamese fighting men are serving their nations with the highest distinction. The other war is here in the United States where the television networks are oftentimes unfairly reporting the highly important Laotian operation. . . ." He accused the networks, by "design or negligence," of presenting only negative reports, charged them with "subtle brainwashing" and "selected interviews" and used charged words like "the network hierarchy."

"When history records the winning of the peace in Indochina," he concluded, "it must also record the great obstacles which were overcome to achieve peace. Those obstacles were not only in Vietnam; they were also in the news offices of Manhattan."

Senator Robert Dole of Kansas, then also Republican national chairman, accused "the president of NBC News and the other media masters of distorting television reports of the Laotian incursion that give a false impression of defeat to the American people." Was this history repeating itself, as when German generals from World War I proclaimed they had not been defeated in battle but by a "stab in the back" at home? That had led to Hitler. Now, the back-stabber was network television news. Perhaps because so little of it stuck, it is hard to remember how intense this campaign was, how extreme the accusations. I, and others like me, sometimes answered in forums, with speeches and the like, but not on the air. On the air, we went about our business. But a great deal of our business had to do with the war in Vietnam, and all of us were affected by it.

George Murray, an infantry lieutenant in Korea, went to Vietnam many times, invading my office every time he came back with requests, pleas, and demands on behalf of the Saigon staff. For about a year, he produced a weekly program called *Vietnam Weekly Review* for which I wheedled some money and a shifting time slot on weekend afternoons so we could explain what was going on without the constraints of length and immediacy that governed the *Huntley-Brinkley Report*. (There, executive producer Shad Northshield, a World War II infantry lieutenant, tried notably to explain with good maps and background stories.) The Network's money-handlers wiped out the

Vietnam Weekly Review as soon as they could, although it cost little and filled a need. They said few people were watching, and I said they had given me a time when few could watch, but it was their money so they won. A year later I revived it, with Murray again the producer, under the title *Vietnam: The War This Week*, but they saw through my subterfuge and knocked it off in a month.

It was a victim, as I have said, of the peculiar accounting system I lived by. I had, in fact, no budget of my own. Under NBC's unique system, NBC News did the programs but the money came from the other divisions: television news programs from the budget of the Television Network division; local television news paid for by the owned-stations division; and radio news, both network and local, controlled by us but billed to the Radio division. Each year, I would ask for the money I needed for the programs I expected to do for each of the divisions. After much argument, that became my budget for the coming year. But it was a fiction. The money was in the coffers of others. The *Vietnam Weekly Review* had not been allowed for when the year's budget was written, even though I stole from other projects to pay for it. Not enough. It was the Network's money and I must not spend it. It died.

It did not matter if these programs satisfied important professional and general criteria for what news divisions were expected to do. Or that they were well done. Or, for that matter, that they helped recruit the "volunteers" for Vietnam assignments by giving them another place to be seen on television, always an important consideration, hard though it may be to explain to a roundtable conference on the role of the media.

There were at least twenty-five "volunteers" who reported for NBC News from Vietnam over more than a dozen years, usually for six months at a time, rarely for more than a year. Some went for advancement; some, knowing they were not very good, went to save their jobs; some were hired by NBC News only because they volunteered to go to Vietnam; some wanted to be war correspondents; and, indeed, some went because it was the biggest story of the time. Not all were bad. Some worked wonderfully well, both there and when they came home. Two or three, hired in haste barely out of school, were brave under fire, feisty at the army's daily briefings, which history knows as the "Five O'Clock Follies," and both responsible and interesting when telling what was going on. Two decades after the fall of Saigon, they were still important reporters in an NBC News where the reporting corps had shrunk to favor presentation over content and where new proprietors were in a panicked search for ever larger audiences at whatever cost.

On the other hand, I could hardly condone the two who brought their wives and found them Hong Kong apartments. One took an extra week before reporting to Saigon because his new bride, born to wealth, needed time to unpack the china, while the other, married to a younger woman of dramatic physical attractions, would use even short breaks to fly back and partake of them. My Saigon bureau chief wanted their heads. So did my harried colleagues in New York who were charged with getting a world of news covered. But I did not fire them. I managed, I am not sure why, to find them other work—at which they were quite successful.

Some reporters on the staff who were not very good, proved first rate (or close to it) in Vietnam, and then came back to be, again, not very good. Having Vietnam on their records understandably enhanced their job security, but almost all in time drifted away on their own. One came back to see me with "demands" when his second tour in Vietnam ended. He was a moody man, not very likeable, good-looking to the point of prettiness, introverted, a loner, not at all the cliché war correspondent. But his work showed a special feel for men who fight, and the pieces he did ranked high among the battle reporting still remembered by old-timers. He left Vietnam believing that he had attained television stardom, and when I would not be convinced he went to ABC. Whatever it was he was seeking he did not find, and not long after he took his own life.

There were only a few Americans among our camera crews. Most were Vietnamese, and the rest were "third country" nationals from our other bureaus, notably Israel and Germany and, of course, Japan. Good news film awes me. Making it takes guts and savvy and training and art, and three out of four will not do. You cannot get your picture from an eyewitness's memory, crib it from a colleague's carbon copy, or phone it in from a hotel room. Cameramen must be close enough to get it on film. This ours did better, I am persuaded, than any of the others. They sent us unsurpassed drama, day after day, season after season, engagement after engagement; on land, in the air, and in the mud and marsh of the delta.

The Vietnamese were the best of them, and they uniquely were never rotated home. Outstanding among them, and their teacher, was a sturdy, handsome, mustached North Vietnamese named Vo Huynh who, with his family and younger brother, had come to Saigon when the country was split in 1954. Later, when Saigon had become for our reporters not a visit but a bureau, he joined as one of our earliest cameramen. Vo Suu, his brother, soon followed. (It was Vo Suu who filmed Brig. Gen. Loan shooting the Vietcong lieutenant standing before him on the sidewalk during that famous Tet.)

As the staff grew, Vo Huynh clearly became the leader, not only to the Vietnamese film crews but to all of them. With the years, bureau chiefs took to sending him out with a new reporter on his (or her—we had the first of those, too) field assignment. He would report whether he thought the rookie could handle combat. He himself was fearless, to judge from his films, but he was as wise in battle as an old marine. There were times he would back away from action, or go to another sector, without explaining why. He distrusted foolhardiness like a bloodied grunt, and complained to the bureau chief if he saw it in a reporter. When conditions daunted the highly regarded stateside cameraman who came with Frank McGee to film *Same Mud, Same Blood*, Vo Huynh went into the breach and saved that program. All of our film staff, as well as the Vietnamese cameramen working for American (and other) television organizations, looked to him for leadership, for tone. One recalled, "He was the Godfather."

(The brothers and their families were among our Vietnamese staff who got out in 1975 during the evacuation. They were fitted into the domestic camera staff as well as union rules allowed. Vo Suu drifted off to work for an uncle in Maryland; Vo Huynh remained on the NBC News staff, but for several years this man, who made the best combat films of my experience, had to accept the pay and union grade of assistant cameraman.)

The Eden Building, which housed our Saigon bureau, was a dark, cool, stone warren of a half dozen floors; wide and narrow stairways; two creaky, open-work elevators; rows of closed doors to offices and workshops and apartments, corridors crossing corridors, usually empty but sometimes one saw children playing on the floor and at others one passed Frenchmen or Americans or Vietnamese, their heels clacking or their sandals shuffling along the stone floors. One entrance to the Eden Building opened a block behind TuDo Street, the one with the bars and the girls and the motorcycles, Americans in uniform crowding sidewalks at all hours and Military Police jeeps cruising day and night. The other was on a quieter street a block behind that. At each entrance was a brass plate bearing a message in French and Vietnamese. The

French read: "L'usage de l'ascenseur est interdit aux coolies, aux boys et aux boyesses, sauf si celles-ci accompagnent des enfants des loca- taires," which I translated as, "Native servants may not use the elevators except for maids escorting the children of tenants." Not only "coolies" but that blinding "boys et boyesses" summed up for me the whole history of colonialism, including how England taught the rest of Europe. I had not known that French colonials used the English word, "boys," for native labor.

Although Vietnam dominated, other events marked those years, like the voyage of Apollo XI, when men first walked on the moon. The exalting symbolism of the act obscured the monotony of the details. Another leap into the unknown by three white American males, knights of the golden mean. In our homes, watching television, we could hear the roar and feel the vibration of the great rocket shaking the earth as it left Florida. Then hours and days of Frank McGee waving little models; animated films provided by a hardly disinterested NASA taking us through jettisoning fuel tanks, orbit insertion, and the rest of the now-familiar litany; Brinkley and Huntley at their x-shaped election night desk, so good to pile papers on, repeating bulletins, switching to other reporters—in Houston, in Washington, around the world— in colloquy with someone from an assembled corps of weathermen, scientists, astronauts from once and future space voyages, the merely famous—all explaining, evaluating, filling with a parade of words the hours we waited until it happened.

The capsule would land on the moon on Sunday evening, July 20, 1969. The plan called for Neil Armstrong and Edwin Aldrin to remain inside for six hours to nap, to restore their energies for this ultimate adventure, the first human step into the firmament. The world would not begrudge them the extra time. But what about television? By monstrous coincidence—one tended not to credit NASA with this kind of imagination or wit—the astronauts' vehicle would be on the moon's surface with them inside napping during just those hours when more Americans watch television than at any other in the week. ("In prime time viewing hours, 7 P.M. to 11 P.M., Mr. Armstrong, Mr. Aldrin and Michael Collins [piloting the 'mother ship' rocket orbiting the moon] will be asleep," wrote *The New York Times* archly. "Tele- vision will have nothing to report.")

With two Americans actually on the moon, we dared not stop, even with nothing to add. Returning to scheduled comedies or dramas or musical variety was unthinkable. Each news division agreed to fill four prime-time hours to divert a tensely waiting world. ABC interwove Steve Allen musing about the moon and romance at a piano in and out of some science fiction writers, a Nobel laureate physicist giving a chalk talk, clips from science fiction movies, and anchormen talking to students. CBS enlisted Orson Welles, Arthur Clarke (who had written one of the movies ABC showed), an astronaut remembering, the director of Britain's Jodrell Bank Observatory expounding, and brief film biographies of fifteen men described as "little known but important to the space program."

George Murray, in charge of covering the moon voyage for us, took charge of the four hours of Sunday prime time as well. Murray, who never had a small idea, opted for music and poetry. He arranged for the NBC Orchestra, no longer Toscanini's but still a mighty throng; the Mormon Tabernacle Choir; and Beverly Sills, at the height of her career as a leading diva. To these he added, among others, John Chancellor, Aline Saarinen, Danny Kaye, and four well-known actors to read inspiring verse. All were pleased to be part of the night's adventure and asked only their union's minimum pay.

They were in Studio 8-H, rehearsed and ready, when word came that Armstrong and Aldrin, no less impatient than we on earth, would emerge early. Rather than send his stars home, Murray taped the four-hour extravaganza he had so grandly arranged. Then that decent man, Neil Armstrong, aspiring to poetry but achieving only history, said, "One small step for a man, one giant leap for mankind."

After the unforgettable lunar walks with men in their H. G. Wells space suits jumping around in low gravity, kicking moon dust and planting the flag, they left the moon, rejoined Michael Collins in the rocket, and returned to earth. All those days, as we interrupted scheduled programming with reports of the return journey, sometimes with pictures, usually without, Murray would haunt my office demanding to be allowed to use portions of the tape of his four-hour concert. All those wonderful people, all that wonderful entertainment, a wonderful NBC exclusive, all going to waste!

We did use some of it, as respite from McGee and the NASA animations, from Huntley and Brinkley with the latest from the wire services. Beverly Sills sang "My Sweetheart Is the Man in the Moon," and a lesser singer sang other songs of lunar significance, like "Harvest Moon" and "How High the Moon." We showed Van Heflin, James Earl Jones, and Julie Harris in a dramatic reading of Thomas Wolfe's insufferable poem "This Is Man." But it was not enough for Murray.

"You can't do that to people like that," he sulked. We returned to Beverly Sills, bursting with American pride, in an aria from "The Ballad for Baby Doe," and for one song from the Mormon Tabernacle Choir. The rest of George Murray's debut as impresario is lost to history. It was time for splashdown in the Pacific.

There is surely no one who has not at some time seen those pictures of Armstrong and Aldrin walking on the moon. In what we call the Western world, including Japan, all life stopped that night to watch television. In Milan, in Budapest, in Edinburgh, strangers shook the hands of American tourists, wished them well—thanked them! Visitors' books at U.S. embassies overflowed with messages of congratulation. The world saw walking on the moon as an occasion of hope, less because of the science than of the refusal to accept limits. There were those in the United States who said that such money might be better put to righting society's imbalances; those in Moscow and elsewhere who said America was seeking military hegemony in the vastness of space; and a significant number who said it was a fiction, a performance in some television studio. No one listened. An event of science had been transformed by the presence of television—not what anyone did but its mere existence—into an experience of sobering universality.

There were four moon journeys still to come, and we carried them all, but those pictures hardly mattered, not even with strange, jeeplike vehicles bumping along the surface of another celestial body, landing sites with hills instead of plains, or finally seeing the moon in color. Nothing matched the first time.

. . .

My favorite venture as an executive was starting a new program series. One series I launched was that weekly report on the war in Vietnam that lasted barely a year. Another, in 1970, was about man's abuse of the environment, which I called *In Which We Live* and managed to coax Edwin Newman to present and Shad Northshield to produce. The inaugural hour dealt with the destructiveness of DDT, and presented a fascinating segment, beautiful to watch, about Pacific islands where wildlife was coming back from its depredations.

Later programs dealt with radon (not bad for 1970!); how nuclear plants in the Northwest might affect salmon hatching by warming the Columbia River; the Alaska oil pipeline, then under construction; recycling sewage; overpopulation—all concerns that would in little more than a decade be chic and "green" and discussed at parties, but we were too early and collected mostly indifference. After two months, there was the usual meeting. The Network official who best understood budgets had his say. The commode flushed. Once again, I was dazzled by the virtuosity of the explanations of this tall, curly, bespectacled, brilliant Harvard man, who could add columns of figures at one glance. I always thought of him as the adder.

Somewhere, however, a sensitivity was evolving. There was an attempt to keep secret the cancellation of *In Which We Live*. NBC issued no press release, made no public statement, and the dozen or so people involved were asked to be quiet about it. Perhaps they were, but not all of their friends were. (Whenever journalists become executives, even Julian Goodman, they try to obscure information that might embarrass them and tend to sputter when the reporting reflects badly on them. "How do reporters get these stories?" they ask, or worse, "What makes *that* so interesting?") Within a week, a *Times* reporter was on the phone and I had to confirm killing a noble-sounding program that cost $25,000 a week to do, a pittance even then. He also called Shad Northshield, who told him, "I guess they noticed that all the ecological problems have been solved so there's no need for the show." "Why does Shad have to talk like that?" Goodman asked me. "What would you have him say?" I responded.

The series on the Vietnam fighting and the one on the environment took up only junk time on Saturday and Sunday afternoons. They were consigned to oblivion because of their truly quite insignificant cost, not because of the revenue they might displace. One series I was involved in during those years was in prime entertainment time, which meant it did displace real (or potential) income. I learned a great deal about how television really worked from that experience, or so it seemed to me at the time, but I may have been learning only how NBC worked—with a special nod to RCA. It was lesson enough.

It had started while Bill McAndrew was still alive. The two of us were at the 1968 winter meeting of NBC executives with the "board of delegates" of the affiliated stations. Delegates are a cross section, from large and small stations and the regions of the country, who are expected to maintain constant contact with the managements of other stations and to represent their consensus as well as their dissidences to NBC executives. There were two such formal meetings a year, one before the full spring convention of the affiliates, in whatever city that meeting was held, and the other early in the New Year, at one of those deluxe resorts where most American business is now done.

This meeting was near Palm Springs, in a desert resort set in a plain of irrigated greenery suffused with crystal air and ringed by shredded-wheat mountains. I was still new to these affairs, and divided my time between trying to remember names and observing the roles of golf and health club facilities, where massage and colonic irrigation are offered in the American economy. We from News had few problems to discuss, and those we had were of little interest to the delegates. We outlined our plans for covering the conventions in Miami Beach and Chicago that summer—as we did last time, we said airily—and our documentaries. Whatever problems NBC itself shared with its affiliates, or whatever divided them, I was not yet paying attention to things like that. McAndrew filled me in on the gossip when we met for a drink before each night's convivial dinner—such meetings usually last three days—and otherwise, being neither golfer nor tenniser, I kept busy.

One morning, Julian Goodman asked McAndrew and me to a private meeting in his cottage. He wanted us to consider carefully a suggestion from the Television Network. The Network had raised with the delegates the prospect of adding *Monday Night at the Movies* to *Saturday Night at the Movies* and *Tuesday Night at the Movies*. It had been a hard sell, but the board agreed. Now the Network proposed to share its windfall with News, to whom it was offering the prospect of taking over one of those additional two-hour movie periods once a month to produce what the vice president for programs described as a "blockbuster." Sensitive to the needs of News, Goodman had told the Network that with *Tuesday Night at the Movies* known to a sizable audience while the yet-unborn *Monday Night at the Movies* had still to find one, they must allot us a Tuesday night, not a Monday night.

Granting his good intentions, I found it hard to accept the videothink that assumes the audience for last week's horror movie would be kept transfixed by the perils of nuclear waste, or even a saucy travelogue of a Persian Gulf sheikdom, while it awaited the coming week's torrid romance. This was an example of the scholasticism that suffuses the discussions of those attempting to determine what Nielsen ratings mean. How many angels can dance on the head of a pin is sober inquiry compared to how many millions will stay tuned.

One source of problems was, of course, RCA, to whom NBC was a cash cow. NBC always made money, always enjoyed a large "cash flow," which RCA always seemed to need. When things went well it might need just enough to make dividends a little fatter; when things went poorly, enough to cover up the bad news. Sometimes RCA demanded, and got, enough money to damage NBC. An example: Most successful programs become so after years of gestation, of planning, of trial and error, of investment. One year, to satisfy RCA's demands, NBC had to cut its program development fund to zero. The result was felt years later.

RCA's depredations were one cause for NBC loading its entertainment schedule with a third night of movies that had been shown in theaters. Another was an "inventory" of movies of low quality, contracted for years earlier in order to get better movies that were part of the same unbreakable "package." There were not, however, enough of those leftover clinkers to increase by half the movies NBC Television would offer next season, so NBC News was graciously invited to fill every fourth night of the new commitment, to dumbfound the world with twelve two-hour "blockbusters."

This dozen "blockbusters" would not, however, be simply added to the other programs we expected to do. The Kintner legacy, still in effect, was that every year NBC News would present thirty-five or so hour-long programs, most of them entitled to be called documentaries. This new scheme would count against those hours, taking up twenty-four of the thirty-five traditionally imposed—by fiat of the president of NBC—on the entertainment schedule. (A network is a federation of constituencies in continuous conflict. Whoever is at the top decides conflicts. NBC News flourished when it was upheld by the head of NBC, languished when it was not.) To the Network's added advantage, twelve two-hour programs would "ruin" half as many nights as twenty-four one-hour programs.

Finally, I set my own trap and walked into it. If we were to do a two-hour program one Tuesday a month, I asked that it be the first Tuesday of the month, which was agreed. We would call the program *First Tuesday*, which I found an attractive title, quirky, easy to remember, advertising the day of broadcast. And so it was, but I had forgotten that every other year, on the first Tuesday of November, NBC News displaced the evening's entertainment schedule with election returns. Now we would be taking over our own time. We would displace ourselves.

As for the program itself, I never doubted that we would do it, that we would swallow losing twenty-four hour-long documentaries and get on with this, whatever this was. Nor was the prospect unattractive. Whatever accident brought it about, it was a new idea, at the least a new program shape. We did not, however, accept the Network's vision of our mandate, something cooked up in a meeting.

My reconstruction of what led to the Network's unusual invitation to NBC News, based on the answers I got when I asked old friends how it happened, goes like this:

Programming executives held a series of meetings to decide what to do about the shortage of new programs resulting from killing program development (and, unadmitted, too little imagination and skill). A third night of movies was arrived at only reluctantly because in the trade it would be seen as a public declaration of bankruptcy, and besides, it was very expensive. Lacking a better solution, they went ahead, only to learn too late that the planning had been even worse than they had known; NBC did not own enough movies for a third night.

Then someone said, "Why not have News fill the gap?"

The discussion veered away, found no easier solution, drifted back. Perhaps some kind of news program really could make up for the shortfall. What kind? Then low-level desperation became slowly transmuted into low-level enthusiasm. What a great showcase for News! Especially if they really did it smart. They have never had two hours. What an opportunity! Other networks don't give their news divisions two hours. They could do their scoops, exclusive interviews like the President, DeGaulle, Cary Grant. Jimmy Hoffa would tell them about the money he stole! A blockbuster every month! If those guys in News play their cards right, this could be the biggest thing in television. Can't you just see the press release?

It need hardly be said that was not what we did. We accepted the two hours, and started from there. The program I proposed to McAndrew and Goodman was the one I longed to do myself. It would be a "magazine" program, a term just gaining currency. While I was explaining *First Tuesday* to McAndrew and Goodman, Don Hewitt was getting the support of Bill Leonard and other CBS News executives for *60 Minutes*, and from them on up the line all the way to William Paley. With CBS, however, it was not a matter of solving a scheduling problem. A CBS News producer had an idea for a new kind of program and they were refining it and testing it and deciding how to make room for it on the schedule—to make room for it by denying room to something else, to an entertainment program. I had made similar proposals several times over the years, as had other NBC News producers, but NBC did not consider a news "magazine" until the Network's entertainment schedule needed rescuing.

Like programs I produced myself, *First Tuesday* aimed to have a star but not be a star vehicle. He would do reporting of his own; provide a presence in the studio; connect to the audience, telling them what they were about to see, and why it seemed worth showing, and add his own touches. The first would be Sander Vanocur. The executive producer would be Eliot Frankel. The producers of the individual reports would include some of those who were frozen out of documentary work by the network's crafty excision of twenty-four of those hours, the younger ones, the feistier ones, the ones who were always complaining we never did anything different. The two-hour length would allow for frequent forays into topics that would otherwise take an hour but could be well edited to, say, forty-three minutes. It would allow for many shorter pieces, eight minutes or ten, too long and too different in tone to fit into an evening news program or even *Today*. Pieces had to stand up as journalism, and be well filmed and well written. That left a lot of latitude. I made my pitch. Bill McAndrew tended to let me have my head in such things. Julian Goodman suppressed his reservations. We were on our way.

As early as spring it had been rumored, then confirmed, that CBS, too, planned a magazine; then that it would be called *60 Minutes*; finally, that it would begin with the season itself, in September, and, worst of all, also on Tuesdays. Meanwhile, *First Tuesday* had to leap another hurdle. Someone checked the arithmetic, or inventoried the film vaults, discovering there were more movies than orginally thought. They would have to be "burned off" or, for some reason, the investment in them would be lost. That delayed *First Tuesday* until January 1969. Vanocur and Frankel and Tom Pettit, who would be the senior reporter, and the rest felt double-crossed. So did I, but McAndrew was no longer around for me to complain to.

From the beginning, *60 Minutes* was star journalism, the reporter as hero, his personality more important than any picture, his questions more interesting than the answers. The first two were Mike Wallace and Harry Reasoner. My preference was always for picture reporting with a heavy emphasis on style and writing. The general range of subjects on *First Tuesday* were not unlike those on *60 Minutes*. The differences lay in presentation, in form. At first, our way was more successful than theirs, but history has shown that Hewitt was right and I was wrong.

The first edition of *First Tuesday* was broadcast on January 7, 1969, with an insightful report on how Castro was trying to raise a new, revolutionary generation of Cubans and a poignant essay on what ever happened to Rita Hayworth, who had been out of sight for years—we were apparently the first to ask. The first show did well. Twenty years later, as network magazine programs continued to elbow each other on and off the air, an executive at another network asked which of all of them had attracted the largest audience for its first edition. The surprising answer was *First Tuesday*, which had started well and stayed up there for as long as it was left alone.

Such statements, it must be understood, are relative. The audience for *First Tuesday* was higher than the audience for *60 Minutes*, which was broadcast for an hour on alternate Tuesdays, with hour-long documentaries on the Tuesdays between. To us, when it came to ratings, beating *60 Minutes* was all we cared about. In NBC's entertainment and money departments, as well as at the top of the NBC pyramid, the grown-ups saw things otherwise. With both CBS and NBC expending their Tuesday evenings on long-form news, which everybody knew had limited appeal, ABC installed at 10:00 P.M. Tuesdays a serial drama about a doctor. *Marcus Welby, M.D.* was the first ABC program to break into the "Top Ten" since 1967, the highest-rated network series of the year and one of television's historic hits. It helped make NBC third in the ratings for the first time ever, leading in time to NBC's period of internal turmoil, executive shakeups, demoralized staff, and endemic disorder—all of which the press and public found amusing but rather foolish.

Denied the gift of prophecy, we kept doing what we were doing as well as we could do it. The second edition of *First Tuesday* was an achievement worth long remembering. Half of it was given over to Tom Pettit's outstanding, ultimately multi-award-winning examination of chemical and bacteriological warfare, a topic new to almost everyone in the country but a major occupation of America's military. Tom had been working on the story for a full year. He divided his film into parts: a chemical weapons depot, the Pentagon, an unknown U.S. Army research facility in Canada where work on new gases had started before World War II, and so forth.

Frankel and Vanocur organized the report so that as Sandy was on camera bridging between film segments, compressing, explaining, supplying what film could not, to be seen beside him was a large fuzzy rabbit placidly chewing lettuce. The film had shown such rabbits during the poison gas tests in the very first segment, but we did not say this one was one of them. Among those watching was the wife of a congressman named McCarthy who called him in to look at what was going on. McCarthy, from Buffalo, New York, first name Richard but known as Max, was as fascinated and horrified—and enlightened —as his wife. He introduced a bill, which became law, abjuring chemical and bacteriological warfare by the United States. (Having thus dramatically made history, Max McCarthy ran for the Senate and lost, and then returned to his trade as a newspaper writer.)

History has found some escape clauses in the law banning chemical and bacteriological warfare, and the United States is still in the poison gas business, but for drama, skilled reporting, and public benefit, Pettit's contribution stands with the best of them. There was, however, a price. Because the first Tuesday of most months is followed by the first Wednesday, the day the boards of RCA and NBC meet, I found myself in an unwelcome spotlight. I had just been named one of the NBC board's "inside" directors, replacing Bill McAndrew. One of the "outside" directors on NBC's board, also on RCA's board, was Adm. Lewis Strauss, a friend of David Sarnoff, an avid establishmentarian, a banker who had been Eisenhower's Atomic Energy Commission chairman then his only cabinet nomination rejected by the Senate. Strauss had seen Pettit's report the night before and added zest to my first board meeting by grilling me. Once he had me on the ropes he grumpily accepted my assurance that every statement was based on research, and the board went on to other business. But the day after every *First Tuesday* there was a board meeting, to which I always went wondering what awaited me.

Other moments in the short life of *First Tuesday* persist in memory. There was the visit to white-ruled Rhodesia by of the Rev. Billy James Hargis and his Anti-Communist Christian Leadership Crusade. There was a remarkable film showing poppy extract shipped from the "Golden Triangle" in the north of Burma by leftover Chinese Nationalist generals down the rugged mountains into Thailand, and then to Hong Kong and Bangkok to be processed into heroin for the United States. The guts this one took! It had been urged on me by Otto Pfeffer, a short, round, bespectacled film editor, whose trip and budget I was finally coaxed into authorizing by Eliot Frankel. Otto, who had never directed a film, made the frightening trip himself, hiring a local cameraman and returning with his astounding report. Somebody wrote a script and it went on. The program was that flexible.

Not all of it was film. Once they thought to interview a Russian émigré who had served long years in the gulag system, which Solzhenitsyn had just brought brutally to American attention, but the émigré's English was impossible. So Eliot sat him down with a writer and a stage designer to whom he described gulags he had been in, what they looked like, where the guard towers were, how many barbed wire fences and how high, what color the barracks and the guards' quarters were. The designer built a ten-foot-square detailed model. The writers wrote a script for live cameras to follow. As Vanocur described it you could all but see the *zeks* huddled in the cold, marching out before dawn to chop trees or dig holes in the tundra.

Another time, a friend of Dick Wald's suggested *First Tuesday* buy from the Capitol architect the plans for the new FBI headquarters then being built. The plans cost five dollars. Again, the designer built a precise model. He played up J. Edgar Hoover's sybaritic bathroom with its gold-plated faucets. Before the program, I got official protests, each from a higher FBI level than the last, questioning NBC's objectivity, questioning my patriotism, hinting at organized public outcry. But Hoover himself never wrote, and no specific threat was ever made. It was fun. After it was broadcast, the FBI asked to borrow the model to install in their old building to show tourists on their very popular tour how their new headquarters would look. We agreed, trumpeting our generosity in a press release.

A whole year passed, and another was well along, and *First Tuesday* was becoming known. We suffered one election night, the diminution of documentary hours, and recurring budget cuts, balancing against that our success with stories that needed covering but fit nowhere else. Style and tone were maintained, even remarked upon. When Vanocur went on to other things Garrick Utley took over, while the program kept improving. Ratings held up pretty well.

Nevertheless, *First Tuesday* had not been born as our idea but as the solution to somebody else's problem, and now the problem had gone away. The bad movies had been used up and NBC had come to the end of *Tuesday Night at the Movies*. Other programs would fill those two hours on Tuesdays, programs that needed regularity to develop faithful followings, regularity that could hardly be interrupted every month for a newsmagazine. The sentencing panel suggested moving *First Tuesday* to Friday. The talk was gentle, even deferential, and I was never actually told I could take it or leave it. I didn't like Fridays. I didn't like "First Friday." Too gloomy. (Someone suggested keeping the title *First Tuesday*. Like the *Saturday Evening Post*, which went on sale Wednesdays.)

I huddled with the staff. No one had a title. I doodled, settled on "Chronolog," which I did not like, nor did they. But no one had a better title. *Chronolog* ran one season. Then, for some reason, we were returned to Tuesdays, for only one hour once a month, but *First Tuesday* again. Once a month we got as much time as *60 Minutes* now got once a week. The gang tried; topics were well chosen and well done, but it was over. The regularity the Network said its series needed was denied to ours. *First Tuesday* slowly, quietly died, an NBC magazine strangled in its crib, not the last; *60 Minutes* became the most profitable network series ever. The adder himself might have paid heed had he known.

By this time, NBC News's public face had changed; Chet Huntley left. Early in 1970, he had casually told me he would not stay after his contract ended in August. He had some businesses, a resort in his native Montana for which large corporations were providing financing, a broadcasting company he owned with partners, which, because of new FCC rules, he could not expand while a network employee. He wanted to write, and especially to quit while ahead, rare in his occupation. Anchors die at their desks, like McGee and Frank Reynolds, or leave when pushed, like Swayze and Edwards, Cronkite and Chancellor, even Brinkley. Some liked to mock Huntley, but he alone quit when he was ahead. Interestingly, no one high in NBC tried to dissuade him from leaving, not that it would have worked. Nor, since he was not joining a competing network, did NBC have any legal claim.

Privately, I have since often wondered if one of his reasons was an awareness of being an outsider among such as Bill McAndrew and Julian Goodman, who believed only working in Washington made an important journalist. Huntley, the generous romantic, was not always taken seriously by them, and he must have sensed this. He was a large-souled man, comfortable in his values and rarely angry, good-humored rather than humorous, but not invulnerable. He had to have heard at least a little of what I sometimes heard. Why not indeed quit when he was ahead? He was in no one's debt.

On the last night, Huntley said, "Good night, David," and Brinkley said, "Good-bye, Chet." There was a small dinner at Lutèce where Julian gave Chet a palomino horse.

That left the problem of what to do after Huntley. My solution grew in part out of a sort of windfall. It seemed that some months earlier a high officer of Esso, as it was still called, wanted to show a niece what a control room looked like and asked to go into the control room of the CBS evening news program, which Esso sponsored *in full* Saturdays and Sundays. (By then almost no one still sponsored anything in full.) At CBS News, where the least inconsequentiality was a matter of high principle and committee review, they brushed him off in a way he found rude.

For years, I, and Bill McAndrew before me, had envied CBS News their regular half-hour news programs on both weekend nights. We took time in the Sunday descendant of Chet Huntley's *Outlook*, now done by Frank McGee, for some minutes of late news, but on Saturdays had no regular network news. It wasn't the money, we were assured, but simply that not enough stations would carry such programs to enable NBC to charge enough to pay for them. So it *was* the money.

I told the sales vice president I might let a sponsor's niece into our control room if it meant sponsorship on Saturdays and Sundays and if she kept her mouth shut and did not tell us how to do the news. He agreed. Esso moved from CBS to NBC, and we had our seven days of news. Thus it was the money, after all. Nor did the sponsor or his niece ever come to see the control room.

When Huntley left, I changed the name of the program from the *Huntley-Brinkley Report* to NBC *Nightly News* because that is what we had become, *nightly*, every night, seven nights a week. When it came to who would anchor, I made what I still consider—and colleagues agree—my worst mistake as a manager, even more damaging than using only volunteers to report on Vietnam:

I assigned David Brinkley and John Chancellor and Frank McGee, three anchormen for seven nights, two each night in a rotation maintained by the executive producer, whom I instructed to treat all three equally so that no one was saddled with too many weekends. In retrospect, it was obviously stupid. But if I was stupid, how was it allowed by those who had to approve, the president of NBC and its sales department, if no one else? The answer is simple. The three men I had named were by far our best-known journalists, so the Nielsen analyzers agreed sagely it might staunch the ratings hemorrhage expected from Huntley's leaving, while everyone else expressed or pretended enthusiasm. This presumably objective assessment obviated the involvement of subjective judgment.

Inside the News division, the three were referred to as the "troika" while the audience was furnished a mystery, because no viewer could know which two of the three he might see any night. And audiences don't like mysteries. To a viewer, a news anchor is a reference, an assurance, a familiar. We had lost the simple and elegant logic of Huntley and Brinkley, each with his clear mandate, so that when you saw Huntley you knew before he spoke it was about somewhere in the world, and when you saw Brinkley you knew before he spoke it would be about Washington. Now we had the troika.

It didn't work. I knew when I first saw it that it didn't work. But that is not the same as doing something about it. Surprisingly, the ratings held up well. The drop-off was less than the experts had expected. The silly way I had set up the program did not do any damage, which saved me from facing the most excruciating decision of all: If there was to be only one anchor, as good sense dictated, who would it be? One of the three, certainly, but which? All were real journalists and skilled writers. They were also friends with whom I had shared crisis and triumph, and my decision would be the ultimate professional accolade for one, a blow or at least an insult to the others, and I am a coward.

My private beliefs were: Brinkley might be the most talented journalist in television, but his talents did not include anchoring a half-hour regular news program alone; McGee could best attract an audience, but though a skilled reporter with a powerful television presence, he lacked some of the knowledge and experience he needed and I had seen him looking foolish orating on subjects he knew too little about; Chancellor was best fitted to anchor alone by intellect and the universality of his curiosity and was unencumbered by Brinkley's feel for the ridiculous or low boredom threshold, but he did not have the aspect of a star performer and would be a gamble. So I fretted over my poltroonery and hoped for a miracle.

One man's miracle is another man's cataclysm. At about this time Hugh Downs let it be known that he, too, wanted to leave. He would stop being host of *Today* when his contract was up. The top executives of NBC and of its sales department, who had accepted Huntley's exit with such equanimity, added up what Downs's might cost in lost revenue and pronounced it a black day for journalism. Downs was popular; Downs did commercials; Downs was loved by affiliates. Given the enormous profitability of *Today*, the terror following his announcement is understandable. Efforts to change his mind were made "at the highest level," but he was firm.

Hugh Downs, a decent, friendly man with long experience in broadcasting, had few pretensions to journalism as a trade. He ably practiced a skill unique to show business: He was a "host." He had been an announcer for NBC in Chicago—as had Garroway—and became in time the announcer for *Tonight*, NBC's late-evening variety. In the manner of such programs, members of the "cast" often engaged in banter, Downs among them, along with the band leader and one of his musicians. Downs was interested in science, and in scientific things, and knew a lot of little-known facts. He often had answers to obscure questions and was considered an intellectual, first by Jack Paar, then by America. For a time, he also "hosted" a mind-twister of a daytime game show called *Concentration*, which helped that reputation.

When Bob Kintner's bold stroke of sending John Chancellor in to replace Dave Garroway as "host" of *Today* failed so badly, the Television Network rushed Hugh Downs in as replacement, and he stayed nine years. He gave *Today* tone and calm and class, and helped it to success and high earnings. True, the program still had a virtual monopoly on weekday mornings, but people could always choose not to watch, and, as with Chancellor, we had learned that when too many chose not to watch, earnings were meager and life difficult.

I was determined the new "host" would be from News. Nine years before, despite Kintner's moving *Today* under News, it was the Television Network that picked the "host" because the program meant so much to NBC's profits, an area where News was not considered competent. No one fought them then; I was prepared to now. As soon as I learned Downs was leaving, I moved to make McGee host of *Today*. He seemed to me perfect by aspect and experience. His controlled, interesting baritone, his measured speech and lyrical way with a phrase, his lifetime in news, his capacity for long hours, and his pleasant face, attractive without being too handsome, added up to my idea of the perfect host or anchor or chairman of *Today*. Obviously, I was aware that this would also solve my other problem, to my mind and perhaps to mine alone the more important problem, *NBC Nightly News* and the troika, but first I decided on McGee for *Today*. Honest.

Next, lunch. McGee said he knew something was up because we did not do this often. My fault, I replied, but I was very busy. He said he was only teasing. After we waltzed a little, I brought it up: Would he care for Hugh Down's job? He thought not. He knew only news, and it was his experience that once you left it you were never allowed back. I said whether *Today* was news, and to what degree, might depend

on him. We chewed that over for a course. I said talking about money
would be for his representative and someone on my staff, but it might
well be more than he expected. I did not mention I knew he had
bought a large farm near Washington, D.C., for a high price and a
large mortgage, where he hoped to retire in ten years or so, perhaps
to write. I did keep coming back, gently, to how much money he
might make. That may have been what worked. His last words were
he would not do commercials.

Then Julian Goodman agreed, provided the Network did not object.
When I told them the next Wednesday, they objected. They thought
McGee was a terrible idea. He was associated with politics and other
controversies. He was not a star. He had never done it. Would he do
commercials? (I knew the answer, but I said I would ask.) I was reminded how NBC's profits were helped when the *Today* host did
commercials. I preempted more discussion by saying the new host had
to be from NBC News; I might accept someone besides McGee, but
only someone from News. They didn't want anybody from News but
equally they didn't want the responsibility for *Today* back in their
department. It had become too much of a news program, not only in
content but in the minds of the audience, of the press, even the
advertisers—none of which they would admit in public. James Reston
had actually written in his Olympian column in the *Times* that *Today*
"set the agenda" for America.

I had too much on my side. It was McGee.

It worked very well. McGee was at least as good as I had anticipated
and had predicted—to Goodman, to the Network, to my own associates. His presence—his "projection"—was remarkable and he was
as always a craftsman. You could not tell by watching how his innards
churned whenever he was on the air, or waiting to get on the air, for
all those minutes and hours. I knew, because I had seen it during all
his days and nights of space coverage, and everything else he had done,
the good soldier, like Huntley the outsider, but smarter than Huntley,
also more prone to nurse a grudge.

Then there was a problem with Barbara Walters. She had come to
Today as a staff writer after a few years in publicity, advanced to field
reporter, then to that silly institution the *Today* "girl," and finally to
famous interviewer with second billing after—quite a bit after—Hugh
Downs. She now aspired to equal billing. McGee would have none
of it. To him she represented the nonnews things that he distrusted
about *Today*, that had made him reluctant to take the job, that he felt

he had to keep far away from now that he was in the job. I also suspect he was not at ease with professionally equal women. They grew openly hostile, and there were noisy scenes off camera. But by the time their antagonism became newspaper gossip, Dick Wald was president of NBC News and I was out of it.

After I had left management, McGee and I would sometimes meet to talk, as friends. Once, in an elevator, he said he wanted to see me about something important. I said it must be that day or the next, because I was leaving for Beirut on a program survey. He did not call before I left so I never knew what was troubling him. In Beirut I got a cable saying he had died. He was on the edge of fulfilling an enormous promise. Almost until the day he died, suppressing illness and pain, Frank McGee was at work, the best "host" in *Today*'s long history.

My participation in both *Nightly News* and *Today* was mostly picking stars, reviewing spending, and, when I thought things were going so badly that I must act, replacing the executive producer. I was less inhibited when it came to documentaries, and often met with their producers to talk content and plans. At one such meeting with Fred Freed, informally Gitlin's heir as cosmic issues specialist, I wrote on a piece of paper: "Who killed Lake Erie?" and handed it to him. He produced a highly honored program by that title which was exciting, a little frightening, and even useful.

Shad Northshield tackled equally large subjects, but his films sought your soul, either the issues or what he did with them. *Suffer the Little Children* was about how the fighting in the streets of Belfast warped those growing up there; *The Sins of the Fathers* dealt with mixed-race children of American servicemen who had left them behind in Vietnam, a subject later to become "good copy" for sociologists, supermarket tabloid writers, and reporters from local stations; and *Guilty by Reason of Race* retold the story of the World War II internment of Japanese in Manzanar and other camps, almost twenty years before Congress found out.

Lucy Jarvis did her usual big deals, specializing in being permitted to film where no one had before, like the Louvre and Scotland Yard. She organized a birthday homage to Picasso that wound up with a live transatlantic auction. Aline Saarinen, as producer, marked an anniversary of New York's Metropolitan Museum of Art—she got Mayor John V. Lindsay to be her narrator—and later conducted us through the Prado. It was traditional that any year's NBC News documentary schedule include one or two about art, because we liked to and because we thought we ought to. No one from Network or Sales suggested we leave such stuff to public television or complained it was hard to sell. There were always advertisers, and there were always audiences, not big, but big enough.

There were other producers, some born free-lancers who worked for us a while then left; some from inside NBC News who would do one or two hours then return, to *First Tuesday* perhaps, or daily news work. Some were better than others. One of the best, and strangest, was Martin Carr, who had done good work for CBS News, had a falling out, came to us, did work of real distinction, and left. His first, called *Migrant*, celebrated the tenth anniversary of *Harvest of Shame*, Edward R. Murrow's renowned documentary on migrant farm labor. Carr proposed opening with a clip of Murrow opening his program ten years before. I think he was surprised when I okayed it.

Migrant offers a rich case history of the interplay sometimes occurring among networks, advertisers, and news divisions. Among its sequences was a short one showing how migrant workers harvesting Minute Maid's orange groves were housed. Minute Maid had recently been bought by Coca-Cola, which got wind of the program. We had, as usual, fed it on the network during idle (local) time so affiliates could see it. One of them broke all the rules, including decency, by allowing someone from Coca-Cola into the viewing room. Coca-Cola, thus informed, complained we had blind-sided them, that they had plans to make things better but too little time to put them into effect.

Then a lawyer for the Florida Fruit & Vegetable Association demanded television time to reply. (Why don't you show the *good* things?) Otherwise he would seek redress in the courts, or so he wrote to the FCC, to Julian Goodman, and to me. He also wrote to every NBC affiliated station threatening to challenge the broadcasting license of any station carrying the program. Carr had endured worse in the field. He and his crews had been harassed, threatened at gunpoint, and, more than once, run off. An interview of an old, poor black woman in her shanty on the Minute Maid property had been interrupted— on camera—by a company representative who ordered it stopped— on camera. The problem would not be these complaints, the growers', or Coca-Cola's. It was bigger than that.

A trade paper had the president of Coca-Cola, J. Paul Austin, "screaming" at Julian Goodman by telephone that NBC "was doing a bitch job on Coke." Goodman denied there was such a call. It seemed to me possible Coca-Cola might genuinely intend to improve the housing, so I made Carr put in a clumsy, last-minute script change to say so. But there would be no change of what was shown or how it was edited. That was July 1970. In December it came out that Coca-Cola, which in the last quarter of 1970 had spent more than $2 million in NBC programs, would not advertise on NBC at all in the first quarter of 1971.

"At the same time," said *Variety*, "Coke has upped its scatter buys on ABC for the first quarter by about 50 percent according to the network. CBS says it has no Coke business for the first quarter, yet the network in its Saturday night news aired a long and 'soft' feature on the new wondrous life of Coca-Cola's migrant workers." Three weeks later, *Variety* reported that CBS had got about a million dollars in extra business from Coca-Cola, which it would not admit. McCann-Erickson, Coca-Cola's advertising agency, told reporters that *Migrant* had nothing to do with the change in commercial placement; NBC's "demographics" were the cause.

At no time did Julian Goodman suggest that I make any change in *Migrant* or comment when I told him of the change I had decided on, neither agreeing that it should be made nor suggesting that it was not enough, or too much, or anything other than "interesting." If the law department or the Washington lobbying office thought changes might be wise, and I have no cause to think they did, he did not tell me. Nor did he tell me that the president of Coca-Cola had called him; I learned about it from newspapers. On the other hand, Julian brooked no public criticism of Coca-Cola, who would, one hoped, return one day as a valued advertiser.

Almost all of NBC's affiliated stations showed *Migrant*, among them all seven in Florida, although one prefaced it with a spoken disclaimer. Three NBC stations had baseball commitments and could not have carried it even had there been no controversy; Dallas–Fort Worth did not carry the original broadcast but reconsidered and played it at a later time. Baltimore and Syracuse refused to carry it for editorial reasons. (There are employers of migrant workers in Maryland and upstate New York no less than in Florida.) Carr's next hour, a study of juveniles in detention called *This Child Is Rated "X,"* also offended a sponsor: a Spokane lawn-mower dealer protested to Goodman that the program maligned American law enforcement. He yanked $1,300 of advertising from NBC's affiliate, but soon decided that selling lawn mowers outweighed principle and restored the advertising.

It is interesting how many of the underlying issues were the same whether dealt with in the sedate rhythms of documentary production or the frenetic ones of presenting news daily. Those were years when outrage led to violence that would reach summertime crescendo both in antiwar protest and in the dissatisfaction seething in the poor black enclaves of America's cities. Augusta, Georgia, Jackson, Mississippi, and Hot Springs, Arkansas, were added to that roster of violent cities begun in the sixties. "Long, hot summer" was accepted as a recurring phase of Nature, like the seasons or sunset.

Our film crews and reporters, especially those covering local news in the five cities where NBC owned stations, learned to cover news in hard hats and bullet-proof vests. None of our people were killed or badly hurt, but we were simultaneously hated and exploited by the rioters, and disliked and harassed by the policemen struggling to control crowds. When what we covered moved from local to network news, Americans snug and distant took fright, and "law and order" grew to be an even stronger political theme than in the days of Newark and Watts, while campaign dialogue was besmirched with a number of code words for black.

At the same time, antiwar protest grew ever stronger, the confrontation between the two sides uglier. No attempt to bring the two protests together had succeeded, not even Martin Luther King's. They were merely simultaneous, which strained the resources of news organizations and increased geometrically the ordinary American's sense of threat and revulsion. There is no way to measure how much of the antiwar protest was anger at what the demonstrators saw as a new American colonialism holding cheap the lives of distant races, and how much of it was well-to-do young people fearing the draft. On May 1, 1970, President Nixon, speaking informally to Pentagon employees, said, "You see these bums, you know, blowing up the campuses. Listen, the boys that are on the college campuses today are the luckiest people in the world, going to the greatest universities, and here they are burning up books. . . . Then out there [in Vietnam] we have kids just doing their duty." He was voicing a widespread feeling, both disapproval and puzzlement. On May 8, we covered construction workers attacking antiwar demonstrators in New York's financial district, shouting, "Love it or leave it!" and "All the way, U.S.A.!" American flags were painted on fire engines, like tanks going into battle against an enemy.

Circumstances dictated that my 1970 trip to Saigon be in May, later than I liked because I dislike tropical heat. Because NBC Sports reported to me, even though only formally, Julian Goodman asked me to be in Tokyo in the middle of May when NBC would celebrate its purchase of the television rights to the 1972 Winter Olympics in Sapporo. As an occasion it was much like the signing of the Treaty of Vienna, but with raw fish instead of Sacher tortes. Rather than suffer the jet lag of two Far East trips, or delay Southeast Asia until I was finished in Japan, when it would be even hotter, I worked out a trip ending with the Olympic signing. I went from Hong Kong to Saigon, then to a place I would not otherwise get to, my reward to myself for making each trip (this year it was Taipei), and finally to Tokyo, where Goodman, accompanied by his wife and mine, was due for the formalities. This schedule would keep me from that year's meeting of the NBC affiliates, unusual for a division president but not unprecedented.

My few days in Taipei were in a very fancy hotel, a servant for each room plus others who polished corridor floors by skating over them on little cloth sacks containing beans that exuded a wax. On my last morning, the English-language newspaper at my door headlined that four students had been killed by U.S. National Guardsmen during an antiwar protest at Kent State University in Ohio. Years before, I had not known where Pearl Harbor was. There, in Taipei, I was not sure I had ever heard of Kent State University. I was as depressed as I have ever been. The Taipei newspaper's account was skimpy; I was alone in some void unconnected to home or work, and I could not get better information or find anyone to talk to about this horror; and whatever it was I did not know, I did know that four kids had been killed by other kids, in uniform.

In the Tokyo bureau I could read the wires, call New York, find out what was happening, what we had done about it, how well or poor our coverage. As always when I showed up in Tokyo, there were ceremonial visits to be made to Japanese networks, the one run by the government and the one that was our collaborator among the commercial organizations, and then some others. One drank a lot of tea. In two days, it was time to meet Goodman's plane from San Francisco. Less than an hour after his arrival, we were due at the U.S. ambassador's residence for a reception. As he got off the plane, Goodman's first words to me were, "That is the last time you will miss an affiliates' meeting," and off we went to the reception. It was hours before I found out what he meant.

Each network meets its affiliates once a year, two hundred so in the case of CBS and NBC, a few fewer for ABC, at least back then. The meetings are almost always in May or June, so the network can tell its affiliated stations what its plans are for programs in the coming season. Presenting the new schedule is, therefore, the centerpiece of any of these meetings. Affiliates are important. If your network has no affiliate in Dubuque, your program will not be seen in Dubuque, and if you are cursed with too many Dubuques, not enough people will see your program to justify the price you are asking from advertisers. In the early days, affiliates were obliged to carry the networks' programs, but the Department of Justice put an end to that, so networks tried to buy their loyalty with cake and circuses. One constant at conventions of networks and affiliates was network officers pleading with stations to carry this or that program that was having trouble getting a profitable audience because they were not helping. They would defect for a week of Billy Graham or the baseball season or any of a dozen reasons, all costly to the network.

These events were usually sopping with good fellowship. At a time when most television stations were affiliated with networks—almost all "independents" were in the very big cities—a network schedule was a key concern to a station's managers. The amount of money a station received was only a trifling portion of what advertisers paid the network to advertise in the program; the station made much of its money selling advertising in the adjacent "station breaks" or the local advertising gaps in the network programs. Network programs that were locally popular enabled stations to charge premiums for this advertising.

That is what these meetings were about, with three-legged races on the Sunday before and special luncheons for wives. Although most interest centered in the entertainment programs and the most energy and ingenuity spent on announcing them, there was also talk about sports—affiliates love sports!—and about news. At the 1970 meeting, I would learn, the talk about news exploded. And I was not there! I had missed the affiliates' revolt against NBC News.

Nor were we alone. CBS had met its affiliates the week before NBC's convention. Alerted by distant rumblings that they were in trouble, CBS executives arranged that their last session be in Studio 33 of Television City, their big Los Angeles studio complex. Walter Cronkite flew in from New York to do his news program for the first time before a live audience. More than five hundred people—owners and managers of CBS's affiliated stations and their wives and children and cousins—watched Cronkite perform. Included in that night's program was a correspondent in South Vietnam interviewing troops about to leave for Cambodia, for which they showed little enthusiasm. During a question-and-answer period there were charges against the reporter of liberal bias—but none of asking such obvious questions. They were like shooting fish in a barrel. (It's not news that soldiers don't want to go where they are sent.) It was a silly business, but it let CBS's affiliates blow off steam and may explain why CBS had less trouble with its affiliates that year than NBC had.

If NBC had also heard advance rumbling, the word did not get around. Instead, the closed (to the press) session that ended NBC's convention was one long, impassioned attack on NBC News: for lack of objectivity, for opposing the President, for favoring war protesters, for presumption, even for low integrity. What had started with Agnew's Des Moines speech was reaching a new level. There had been more than Agnew. In his message to that spring's convention of the National Association of Broadcasters, President Nixon had praised broadcasters and their stations, pointedly ignoring the networks. A month before that, the *Columbus Dispatch* had discovered a White House report calling NBC the network least fair to Nixon, CBS the most fair. NBC alone, the report added, "generates" news "to reflect unfavorably on the Administration." By the time of the NBC meeting, many of the affiliates, well-to-do businessmen whose profits depended on federal licenses, were preparing to bail out, some of them agreeing with the White House, some merely fearing it.

The general complaint was that we were one-sided in covering the war and the protest against it, that we ignored the other—that is, the President's—position. One leader of the revolt, known for right-wing views, said: "If I have a John Bircher on, I put someone on from the other side." Another owner announced that he had in his pocket a letter from his doctor complaining of NBC's slanted coverage. One said privately to a reporter hovering around the meeting's closed doors, "There are a lot of important people in my town who are very conservative, and we have to keep that in mind."

Years later, looking for more details from friends who had attended the meeting I missed, I found them remembering different things. Dick Wald remembered that the worst outbursts were about the coverage of Kent State, only the week before. But the stations had been stewing a long time; an event so recent could only have been the trigger. What seemed to anger the most was the father of one of the dead girls, a neat, well-dressed, impressive-looking man, a Republican who said he supported the war, but added, "What can my President say to me now?" It was a strong and telling piece, and the producer of every one of our news programs naturally chose to use it, which was cited as proof, if any were needed, of bias and conspiracy.

Julian Goodman remembered a different triggering issue, our coverage of Haynsworth and Carswell. The previous fall, the Senate had refused to confirm Justice Clement Haynsworth for the Supreme Court after a campaign by organized labor and civil rights leaders. In the spring, Nixon nominated G. Harrold Carswell, also an appeals court justice, for the vacancy. The Senate rejected him, too, partly for the same reasons as Haynsworth, partly for vague hints of minor shenanigans, and partly because of his reputation as a mediocre jurist, which Haynsworth by agreement was not.

(In promoting the Carswell candidacy, Senator Roman L. Hruska of Nebraska delivered an endorsement unique in the experience of the Senate when in his mellifluous basso voice he proclaimed, "Even if he were mediocre, there are a lot of mediocre judges and people and lawyers, and they are entitled to a little representation, aren't they? We can't have all Brandeises, Frankfurters, and Cardozos." The laughter greeting this endorsement drowned out any uneasiness over Hruska picking, out of the Court's long history, three Jewish names.)

The owners and managers of NBC's affiliated stations, hurling charges at the handful of executives on the bare stage in the second-largest meeting room in the New York Hilton Hotel, thus had a selection from which to choose. Goodman tried to turn away wrath with soft answers, which did not work very well. Dick Wald, in my absence the News division executive on that stage, knew that his usual posture of refusing to suffer fools gladly did not suit the occasion, and was unsure what to do. An executive sitting with him advised him to blame me since I was halfway across the world, but he demurred. I doubt it would have worked anyway. Clearly, nothing would slake their rage but action, or a sense they had acted. They voted what was in effect a motion of lack of confidence in NBC News—and in me.

The rebels moved that the officers of their affiliates' organization confront the president of NBC, Julian Goodman, with their consensus that his news division was biased, unbalanced, and unfair. The vote was 60 percent in favor of objecting to NBC News and 40 percent opposed, a stunning result, especially given the almost automatic loyalty most affiliates still displayed for their networks. I assume at least half of those who voted against the resolution agreed with it but were reluctant to be recorded as disloyal.

In Tokyo, I learned only a little bit of this. After signing the deal for the Winter Olympics, Julian and I took our wives to Expo '70 in Osaka, where we had free time for him to tell me some of what had happened. The day we got back to Tokyo, news came over the wires that Welles Hangen, our brilliant Hong Kong bureau chief whom I had visited in his home two weeks before, had been captured with his camera crew by North Vietnamese or irregular Communist forces in Cambodia. We tried through the State Department, through the Chinese embassy in Ottawa, through whatever sources we could find, but there was no further word. Pat Hangen, Welles's wife, was tireless in trying to organize support. There was a reporters' committee that Walter Cronkite agreed to head. I even wrote, in the blind—in care of the Ministry of Foreign Affairs—to my economics theory professor at the University of Toronto, who, it was said, had run off to Communist China after World War II. CBS recovered the bodies of its reporter and crew, captured and killed in Cambodia the same day, but of Welles and the two men with him, nothing useful was ever heard. I assume they were killed almost at once. I suppose I hope so.

. . .

The indelible details of the day Welles Hangen was taken and remembering the morning I learned about Kent State mark the time for me, but the days and minutes of my years as chief manager of NBC News were parceled among a complexity of obligations. In this polyglot of detail, nothing I did seemed related to what I had just done or what I was about to do, although all of it somehow had to do with putting news on television, at least indirectly. On October 31, campaigning for the 1970 off-year election, Nixon was egged and stoned in San Jose, California. The demonstrators were two thousand students from colleges in the area protesting the war. He went on television to denounce "appeasers of violence," adding, "When you permit an imbalance to exist that favors the accused over the victim, you are inviting more violence and breeding more bullies."

He had laid down an ideological challenge, even beyond the war, and the Democrats took it up as that. The networks rejected the Democrats' request for free time to reply, so Averell Harriman raised the requisite $150,000. Their spokesman was Senator Edmund Muskie of

Maine, his craggy face and honest mien a casting director's image of traditional values. He spoke quietly and calmly in his deep voice, at ease in what looked like a suburban leisure room, a brick fireplace behind him. He said nothing notable; how he said it thrust him into the lead for his party's 1972 presidential nomination.

The May 1971 NBC affiliates' meeting is recalled by some as a time of harmony between the stations and NBC News, with last year's rift healed and all recognizing their interdependence. "Divided we fall," and all that. I remember it differently. The meeting, which I attended, may have been a scene of reconciliation, harmony, and affection compared to the previous year's, the one I had missed, but I remember it as an ordeal and an imposition, when the cracks were papered over for the public but few cared to raise their voices in support.

Business was bad, money was low, and NBC chose to hold a one-day meeting in New York instead of the announced three days in Los Angeles. Part of the day was given over to a *scheduled* closed meeting, duplicating the spontaneous one of the year before, for airing complaints against News. *Variety*, in such matters invariably the repository of planted stories, called it "hardly a secret" that the stations were "nervous about attacks on TV journalism or influenced by the Government's apparent attempt to widen the chasm between networks and stations with the news issue." (The press had just quoted CBS News president Richard Salant recounting how the year before the White House had egged on members of the CBS affiliates' board to travel to New York to tell CBS's officials they objected to their war coverage and wanted to go to Vietnam to tell the reporters there. The board had been dissuaded with difficulty, he said.)

Even before our meeting, Julian Goodman had publicly asked affiliates to recognize the community of interest, to accept that a news division "cannot be operated by a committee," and that NBC News "cannot and will not shy away from reporting important news subjects." It reflects the time that such unexceptionable statements were made at all. But this year, unlike the last, NBC management was not to be surprised. NBC's allies among the affiliates, including the officers of their organization, lobbied the delegates from the two hundred stations all that morning and the evening before, and by telephone in the weeks before that. A resolution was prepared and passed opposing subpoenas of reporter's notes and newsfilm outtakes (film shot but not broadcast), a current concern after the administration's attack on the CBS News documentary *The Selling of the Pentagon*. NBC press agents, who orchestrate most of the response at these events, sold the newspapers and trade press their line that the resolution was in effect support for NBC News. Well, maybe.

At the closed session, I sat with Goodman and the others on the bare stage of the New York Hilton, where they had sat without me the year before. Goodman was to answer most questions, turning to me at times for verifying detail. The questions were not different from those the year before, as they had been described to me, although fewer. Many affiliates may have been working the floor quietly on NBC's—or, if you like, my—behalf, but exactly two stood up to be heard, Houston and Baton Rouge, both eloquent, both passionate, both the kind of allies you want in a fight, but only two. The press was told, and in turn printed, that these two men, Jack Harris of Houston and Douglas Manship of Baton Rouge, a manager and a proprietor, expressed the affiliates' general attitude, which had undergone "a remarkable change between last year and this."

If there was a hero, it was Julian Goodman, who was resolved that the previous year's atrocity not be repeated. Earlier that year he had taken the unusual step of writing all members of Congress refuting Senator Clifford Hansen's attack on how the fighting in Laos was reported, saying Hansen sought "to interfere with the free flow of information to the public." The letter may have stiffened CBS's resolve to resist Chairman Harley Staggers's subpoena of the outtakes from *The Selling of the Pentagon*, which risked CBS president Frank Stanton a citation and jail term for contempt of Congress, a citation that missed carrying the House of Representatives by the narrowest margin. Goodman's letter also stiffened NBC's affiliates' spines. Then, as the meeting grew near, he abandoned his usual consensus management and led his executives in battle. NBC News was to be supported, and to be seen to be. It worked; the written record may be less falsely rosy than I implied.

Several weeks later, the astonishing story came out about Secretary of State Henry Kissinger's secret trips to Peking (as we still called it) so President Nixon could make history by visiting China early in 1972. Both Kissinger's trip and its astonishingly successful cloak of secrecy had been made possible by the help of the military dictator of Pakistan. As conjecture, leaked hints, and official announcements tumbled over each other, the networks planned their coverage. Their representatives trudged to the White House for meetings about how many could go, who would go, how much equipment, liaison with Chinese television, pool details, the panoply of big-deal video. Nixon wanted this to be, above all, a television event. Newspaper and magazine reporters were soon complaining.

The prospect of an American President visiting China had a potent public impact. Red China, Communist China, mainland China, was for Americans the most secret, the most threatening place on earth. McCarthyism had been more about Red China than about Red Russia, with much of the inquiry centering on who had "lost" China to the Reds, the career officers of the U.S. Foreign Service or miscellaneous pinkos and other subversives. News and film from Red China were sparse, usually secondhand, coming through another Communist country or at least a neutral one. Red China had famine; Red China had The Bomb; Red China stopped our victory in Korea and helped the VC in Vietnam; Red China had a Cultural Revolution. Now, with Henry Luce safely dead, an American President, a Republican, was going there to de-fang the beast.

The impact on news organizations was at least as great, especially on television news organizations. Since the fifties, it had been the place we sought most, and succeeded least, to get film out of. Foreign television services could always find a willing American buyer for conducted film tours of mainland China. But they all showed the same steel mill, the same dam, the same collective farm, the same nursery, and children singing the same chirpy song.

Then, in 1970, an American table tennis team went to China, bringing American reporters with them. John Rich, our Tokyo correspondent, and Jack Reynolds, then Tokyo bureau chief, came with a camera crew. They filmed only a little of the Ping-Pong. Mostly they showed daily life, people in the streets of the cities, how they ate, a collective farm as neat as the one the Dutch had shown, a day-care center with children as happy as those filmed by the Hungarians, all of which fascinated the audience because these were "first films" from China. There was newspaper speculation as to whether this constituted a "thaw," and chapters in early books, footnotes in later ones, about something called "Ping-Pong diplomacy." Goodman had me bring Rich home to speak at the one-day affiliates' meeting of 1971, to buttress by his presence the case for NBC News, whose session in the ducking pond would follow lunch. After all, John Rich *of NBC News* had been to China!

That was Ping-Pong. Now NBC News was accompanying the President. Don Meaney brought me a list of four men he proposed to send on Nixon's trip to China. I insisted one be dropped to make room for a woman. But which? Pauline Frederick, our United Nations correspondent, had never worked with film on a foreign assignment; Aline Saarinen, our Paris correspondent, was seriously ill on what would be her final illness, although we did not yet know that. I put Barbara Walters on the list even though we did not always consider the *Today* cast part of NBC's news-gathering staff. The others were Chancellor, Herbert Kaplow from Washington, and Rich from Tokyo. Barbara was the only woman in the whole huge delegation of Americans broadcasting reports of the Nixon trip to China. February 21, 1971, Nixon's arrival seemed to be of more interest in the United States than in China, but in the United States there was interest indeed.

Word came one day that week that Nixon would leave Peking after nine, our time, that evening. I chose to carry it live, wiping out expensive entertainment. My wife and I dined with Aline Saarinen in her hotel suite that evening.

I interrupted dinner to watch.

There, before our cameras, with only NBC carrying it, was Air Force One on the tarmac with Chancellor describing the morning's events—it was morning in China—while in the background a squad of the People's Liberation Army, bundled in padded overcoats, marched up and down. The President was due any moment. He did not arrive. A kindly Chinese officer got the squad to march again, and again. Chancellor talked about dinners, foreign policy implications, shopping trips, and historical significance. No Nixon. One of our other reporters helped out; there were interviews that made no sense. An hour went by, an entire block of television revenue wiped out. When we signed off the President had not yet arrived.

After he returned home it came out that on his way to the airport that morning—9:00 P.M. Eastern time in the United States—he stopped to see Chairman Mao Tse-tung, a visit lasting two hours instead of the expected ten minutes, the most significant U.S.-Chinese contact of the whole trip. But I did not know that, watching in Aline's hotel suite. I knew only that I expected to be fired the next morning. An hour of prime-time television from China in which nothing happened! But I heard not a word, I am not sure why. It was not because a huge audience was turned in as NBC showed nothing at all in Peking, because that would not be known for another week.

When everybody got home, CBS's promotion specialists sent Walter Cronkite to groups of high-powered American businessmen to tell them what he found in China, the last untapped market. No similar department at NBC had the wit to suggest anything like that, but Barbara Walters did it on her own. First she got Goodman to invite her to a meeting of NBC executives to test her routine. She talked about what she saw as an American woman reporting from China. Her showstopper was a pottery doll, a recumbent female, used by (prerevolutionary) Chinese women of the higher classes to show their doctors where they ached without compromising their modesty. China was Barbara's first big step out of the herd, and we in that room watched a television star on the verge of being born.

On February 26, 1972, while Nixon was in China, Senator Edmund Muskie had lost his lead for the Democratic presidential nomination the same place he had won it, on television. He had come to stand outside the *Manchester Union-Leader* to denounce its conservative Republican editor-publisher, a famous baiter and reviler of Democrats. The newspaper had accused Muskie and his wife of using a derogatory term for French-Canadians, of whom New Hampshire has many. Muskie, shaking with anger, his voice shrill, his emotions naked, stood in the falling snow denying the report, and, as he defended his wife, seemed to be in tears. Those pictures on that night's TV news program shattered his image as the longed-for calm, reliable leader, the image he had initially won on television, sitting in front of a fireplace answering Nixon, appealing to reason. Eight weeks later Muskie withdrew his candidacy.

Try as I might to watch *NBC Nightly News* every night, I could not. In the matter of Muskie in Manchester, it was not until weeks later that I learned we were the only ones not to show film of him standing outside the *Union-Leader*, tears on his face. It seemed worth asking why. The executive producer, whom I had picked to succeed Shad Northshield because he would be a good conciliator, insisted those weren't tears; they were melting snow. We trotted up to the editing room to look again. I saw tears; he still saw melting snow. The newspapers, the wires, the other networks had seen tears where he saw melting snow. It was not his personal politics, he insisted, but his news judgment. My next question: If it was melting snow that had whipped the media to a frenzy and driven the leading candidate out of the race, why had he not reported that? It was, after all, a scoop.

It was my second disagreement with him, and I told Dick Wald it was time to start looking to replace him. The first had been when, a few months apart, the mayors of Newark and Jersey City had been

sent to jail for separate felonies. Not a word on NBC *Nightly News.*
That time I knew the problem. Not only Spiro Agnew but many in
the news business itself think of New York as a strange place, exotic,
foreign, not "the real America." This glib judgment lumps together a
tenth of the American population, the center of world communications
and finance, and the country's cultural capital.

Most national news organizations are centered in New York and
most journalists who work in them reach New York only after working
their way up from somewhere else. Few New Yorkers reach the top
at newsmagazines, wire services, networks. The others will reject as
"too New York" a story they would accept from Tupelo, Mississippi,
or Lincoln, Nebraska. When I asked why *Nightly News* did not mention the imprisonment of the mayors of the two biggest cities of the
seventh-largest state, I was told it was of no interest outside of New
York. Since I always thought of myself as first a producer, I rarely told
other producers what to do. Those I disagreed with repeatedly, or
seriously, I replaced.

In four years as president of NBC News, I became used to variety,
no two days, no two hours, no two moments alike. My time was
divided between the news floor and the executive floor, where I went
to plead for money or airtime or to bring the unwelcome word that
the President wanted to speak to his people in prime time. On the
executive floor there were a lot of meetings, long agendas with only
occasional relevance to NBC News, a few with none at all. I had come
to television in 1950; in those meetings I finally learned how it worked.

I learned that the product of commercial television is not programs.
If one thinks of making goods to sell, the viewers are not the customers,
those who buy the product. Advertisers buy the product, pay money
for it. Programs are not what they buy. What they buy, what they pay
for, is audience, people to heed their messages. The bigger the audience, the more they pay. Later, they learned it was worth paying
premiums when specified groups could be induced to watch and less
when they could not, despite others watching who were older or
younger or smarter or dumber than the objects of desire. Thus seen,
the programs are the machinery, that which makes the product. The
television tube, shaped as a proscenium arch, is less theater than
medicine show. Programs draw the motley to the pitch. But what says
the law? The law says: "Broadcasting shall be in the public interest,
convenience and necessity."

I learned to cut a budget, to report the largest possible number of dollars saved while sacrificing the smallest possible number of people. Key vacancies might go unfilled, earned promotions deferred. There was always something on the list we could do without, like the news film archives. The need for a useful archive for a growing bulk of film was becoming frantic, and techniques were improving. Every year we would include improving the archive when we planned the budget. Every year, from on high, the voice of RCA said: Cut the budget. By decree, their needs were greater than ours. Once again, I would defer improving the archive. When I left, it was in deplorable shape, most of the news film unclassified, and what files existed hopelessly old-fashioned.

Whenever a budget was to be cut, NBC's chief money officer offered his ideas on what to jettison, and I would be tempted to hit him with an inkwell, desisting because I was resolved to act, despite the evidence, as though my colleagues in high management were on my side. He was innocuous, an accountant, knowing nothing and caring little about what we did or how we did it. His devotion was to sums. Cut film editing overtime, he would say, overtime being its own line in a budget and one he understood—the amount, not the function. I would explain that if a film editor did not take a job to its end lest he incur overtime, his relief would have to start over, screen the picture, have it explained, and costs would go up, not down. He would say he understood and go to something else, but next year there he was again, suggesting I cut editing overtime.

Or he would ask, Can you trim unscheduled news? And I would say, Of course, down to zero. He would say, You don't mean it. I would insist I did. "Unscheduled news" was the budget listing for covering unforeseen events, storms, hijackings, royal weddings, even sudden presidential trips. Was I truly proposing omitting that, he would ask. Did I expect a year without surprises? Hardly. Then was I proposing they not be covered? Oh, no, I said. We could not avoid covering them. They would be covered come what may. We would merely go over budget to cover them. He would leave, muttering.

The worst budget cut of all was in 1971. That September, Robert Sarnoff, the new chairman, took RCA out of the computer business and RCA wrote off a $250 million loss—American history's largest such to that time, which the organization had to make up. Meeting followed meeting as each of us volunteered our contributions, like tuxedoed fat cats at a charity dinner. Of course, it was not enough, so we were given quotas. The process was as before, but more intense, more prolonged, as we sought pennies and, having cut fat, cut muscle; and having cut muscle attacked bone. It was during this process that I closed the NBC News bureau in Moscow.

It had become obvious that to come up with another substantial lump of money while harming news operations least I had to shut a bureau. We were past firing secretaries and copy boys and coaxing reporters to flying economy class. The Moscow bureau would be least missed. Reporting from there was still tightly censored. News from Moscow was mostly radio news so we had no resident staff cameraman. Any filming was done by hires from a local agency that charged huge fees and was said to be a KGB front. But when, as *Huntley-Brinkley* producer, I had sent Bonn reporter Frank Bourgholtzer and virtuoso cameraman Josef Oexle to Moscow with tourist visas, they got stories no resident staff dared try for. We might even be better off without staff in Moscow.

Nevertheless, I closed the Moscow bureau with regret. Early in World War II, Robert Magidoff of NBC News had been the last American broadcaster to leave Moscow, and when peace came we were the first to return. Irving Levine came with some American farmers and stayed after they went home, renewing his temporary visa as often as he could until the Foreign Office surrendered and accredited him. There was also the status factor: How could you be a big-time international news organization without a Moscow bureau? The answer: You could if you had just quit the computer business. The bureau stayed closed for several years but NBC News survived. I was told years later that the always insecure Russians felt insulted, and that in high reaches of the Foreign Ministry I was known by name as the unfriendly man at NBC who closed the Moscow bureau.

The wheel had meanwhile turned, and here was another presidential election year. The political landscape had changed since the last time, but we had not. Like generals refining our strategies to fight the war just ended, we decided to cover 1972 as though it were still 1968. Nor were we alone. Both parties would meet in Miami Beach because the few causeways connecting that sandbar to the mainland could be blocked by a few armed men. No more Chicago 1968's to mar the face of politics! Network production managers, starting their regular commuting well before Christmas or taking up residence shortly after the New Year, called first on Rocky Pomerance, the police chief of

Miami Beach. The convention hall was surrounded by a tall, sturdy, chain-link fence, ingeniously designed for easy control of entrances, of which there were not many.

With Richard Nixon's sure renomination, the Republican convention would be no more than a pageant. The Democrats would have at least a new look. Stung by how they looked in 1968, the party had appointed a commission to change how delegates were chosen. Under its chairman, Senator George McGovern of South Dakota, the commission decreed that delegations must adequately include women, the young, races, factions, and outsiders. The 1972 convention was to be a valid statistical sample of either the electorate or Democratic voters or those who bothered to be "active" in the party's business—it was never clear. When delegates thus chosen started moving on Miami Beach, McGovern would be their candidate, as had been obvious for months. By that year, moreover, the parties had started picking their candidates in primaries, merely ratifying them at conventions. In other words, there would be neither news nor surprises at either convention, but we would cover it as though Taft's and Eisenhower's ghosts were still contesting the Texas delegation, with Stevenson's still having Kefauver's to beat, and Kerr's the dark horse.

It would be my first convention without Huntley. Chancellor would join Brinkley in the anchor booth. McGee was fully engaged with *Today*, and Vanocur had gone off to write, leaving only Edwin Newman of the great Four Horsemen. It would be an imposition to ask him to undertake what I considered the most physically demanding assignment we had. We set up a "subanchor booth" just off the floor for interviewing people who might have more to offer than comments on specific details on the progress of the convention at a given moment. It turned out to be useful.

That meant choosing four new horsemen, the heart of our coverage even in a dull, newsless convention—perhaps especially in a dull, newsless convention. Tom Pettit, my first choice, had to be bullied into taking the assignment. Garrick Utley had little domestic experience but was a good, flexible reporter; Douglas Kiker was an old hand at politics, the kind of old boy Southerner who hides a lot of shrewdness behind a cornpone accent, but not as much as he thinks; alert Cassie Mackin was fresh from a Baltimore newspaper, just learning television, the first woman to work the convention floor for us. She was also golden blond, which made her easy to spot in a crowd and got her interviews denied to the others.

Both we and CBS would cover gavel-to-gavel at both conventions, as if we and our viewers might miss something if we arrived a moment late or left a moment too soon. It was not that there was no news, but what news there was did not justify the expenditure of resources implicit in gavel-to-gavel coverage. In one way, the old-fashioned approach succeeded: We won the battle for the ratings. The press saw this to mean that our "new" team had knocked off established Walter Cronkite.

As expected, the Democrats chose McGovern and the Republicans renominated Nixon, which was as inevitable as sunset. McGovern, who said he had not thought about his running mate in advance, picked a virtual unknown, Senator Thomas Eagleton of Missouri. After the convention, Eagleton became an early victim of the new political journalism, which dug into his medical history and found enough to force him to withdraw, reducing McGovern's prospects from impossible to unimaginable.

There were a few memorable moments of live television during the Democratic convention, with a feel and impact denied to other media. There was McGovern in a hotel lobby, defending himself against the onslaught of radical college students daring him to prove he was one of theirs and had not sold out. It was dispiriting but fascinating to watch, as the entire convention waited for him. Nor could anything match Chicago's mayor Richard Daley and fifty-seven other Cook County Democrats being denied seats at a Democratic National Convention and told to leave the floor, which they did, trying for dignity. Imagine it! A Democratic convention showing Dick Daley the door! Television must have been invented to record these moments as no other medium can, bringing them into every American home as they were happening. It was also sad. One has problems with the likes of Daley, but they seemed to me more aware of the needs of the people they—perhaps corruptly—represented than "activists," shrill about causes, zealots for issues remote from general concern, who reach leadership and power because most people want only to be left alone.

The Democrats struggled through endless arguments, most of them about interpreting the "McGovern rules" saying who might sit and who might not. It was impossible to follow. Delegates spent all their time caucusing and floor reporters spent theirs explaining. There was no disorder, but there was no order either. When the arguing stopped long enough for the candidate to make his acceptance speech, his access to free television time on all three networks, it was two o'clock in the morning in Miami, "prime time" only in Hawaii. Amateurishness thus persisted until the convention's last gavel.

The Republicans did nothing interesting. Their sessions were parades of speeches interspersed by organized youth in a balcony rhythmically chanting "Four more years! Four more years!" Chancellor said they reminded him of Daley's sewer workers at past Democratic conventions. A high Republican took umbrage; Julian Goodman asked me to do something. I knew I would get no revision from Chancellor, so I sent Pettit to the balcony to find a story. He found a printed schedule of those "spontaneous" demonstrations, and young people who told him of free trips to Florida so they might stand in that balcony shouting "Four more years! Four more years!" That only made it worse, but who cared?

After Eagleton withdrew, the Democrats called a Tuesday night meeting of their national committee to choose his replacement. They met in a Washington hotel ballroom, mimicking the proceedings of a real convention. I decided to cover it as such, floor reporters, anchor booth, the works. We had undertaken to cover it all, and this was part of it. CBS and ABC interrupted entertainment programs but we opted for the gesture. The meeting nominated Sargent Shriver, the Kennedys' brother-in-law, for vice president. McGovern and Shriver carried only Massachusetts and the District of Columbia. Nixon had refused to debate McGovern because a President "makes policy every time he opens his mouth." Besides, he had the votes.

Ten days before the election, Henry Kissinger and North Vietnam's Le Duc Tho agreed on withdrawing American troops and returning prisoners of war, but South Vietnam refused to go along. A month after his reelection, President Nixon resumed the bombings of North Vietnam. On December 30, it was halted, and talks began again.

Within NBC News, as the year came to an end, I sensed rhythms of work reasserting themselves over dissonances of external attack, public disillusion, and RCA interference. The organization seemed to have steadied. Even ratings improved. *Today* and *NBC Nightly News* looked vigorous and professional. There had been no budget cut in 1972. On December 7, my birthday, I asked Julian Goodman if I might go back to producing while I still knew how. We agreed that I would stay in management until February, when Dick Wald would take over.

On September 1, the *Newark Evening News*, where I got my first job, had quietly died at age eighty-eight. On December 9, *Life* magazine, which had "sponsored" NBC News's coverage of the 1948 conventions, went less quietly out of business after thirty-six years. Both times, there was much talk about television news changing American journalism. On December 31, the Gallup poll reported that for the fourth year in a row Americans respected Richard Nixon more than anyone else alive. Earlier, the general manager of the NBC affiliate in San Diego had proposed that the networks no longer cover the national political conventions gavel-to-gavel but give the Public Broadcasting System enough money to do it—for those who cared.

14

In February 1973, I went back to my trade. I stayed at it nine years, involved in all sorts of programs, but not daily news. This thrust me into the unfamiliar role of observer, only a "consumer" of news, at such watersheds as Watergate and Nixon's resignation, the evacuation of Saigon and the end of America's war in Vietnam. I was just an observer, also, of remarkable turmoil at the top of RCA, and wild changes in the leadership of NBC. I was aware and avidly interested, of course, but they did not involve my work.

Dick Wald and I had agreed I would do documentaries full time. I did exactly one. As an executive, I had come to see in documentaries a surfeit of solemnity which was eroding their welcome into the American home. Now, looking for one to do, I harked back to when I had been able to inform by seeming not to, in the *Our Man . . .* programs I had done with David Brinkley. Hiding behind Brinkley's wit and prodigious reading, those amiable travelogues were sneakily able to indict rulers for oppression and exploitation, outraging the locals in those exotic places.

To Washington, then, to see Brinkley about doing a new *Our Man. . . .* He welcomed the idea. What city did I have in mind. Zurich, because it was a facade of respectability behind which Swiss bank secrecy shielded the wealth of dictators and gangsters, because Swiss neutrality fanned bloody wars in which both sides would be better off buying bread than guns, and because a British prime minister had just accused its money establishment, "the gnomes of Zurich," of scheming to upset his government to protect their profits.

Brinkley was not interested. He was uncomfortable with economics. I insisted it was not economics. It was crookedness and hypocrisy and pretty pictures, this old city in an old country where every adult male was a reserve soldier who kept his rifle under his bed, and its biggest church boasted stained-glass windows by Chagall. Brinkley wouldn't budge. Banks and bankers were not for him.

Well, I asked, was there a city he had in mind? Yes, Riyadh. Too outdoors for me; camels and deserts and all that Book of Knowledge stuff. I said Riyadh would be worth at most ten minutes, and then only if one got more access than the Saudis usually allowed. So David and I, still friends, agreed not to do this one together. (In time he got to Riyadh, sending *NBC Nightly News* reports totaling less than ten minutes.)

That left me needing to find a reporter for a Zurich program before someone asked me to examine some noble topic he had read about in *The New York Times*. Reviewing the roster, I fixed on the Paris correspondent, Lloyd Dobyns. He had been assistant news director for the New York station, and I had come to know him well enough to move him to Chicago, as local news director and network news manager for the Midwest. There, by doing a difficult job well and surviving being yoked to the station vice president, he had earned being sent to Paris as correspondent. Also, because he was a skilled administrator, we would not have to send a separate manager to Paris, a net gain of one "head," which could be used elsewhere. Assigning Dobyns to Paris was one of my last acts as division president. He took the assignment, found an apartment, moved his wife and four children, settled in at the bureau, started reporting the news, and turned aside any attempt to have him administer, so an administrator had to be sent. I was to learn this was typical Dobyns.

Soon after Dobyns arrived, Paris became the site of "peace" meetings between Henry Kissinger, U.S. secretary of state, and Le Duc Tho, of North Vietnam's Politburo. That was Dobyns's story day after day. Nothing happened, but America cared, so each meeting was reported. I am more impressed by a reporter who is interesting when little is going on than one calling madly from a maelstrom where even little old ladies can find the news. It was his "peace talks" reporting that made me ask for Lloyd Dobyns for my Zurich program.

It was my kind of travelogue, pretty pictures and greedy people. We found an iconoclastic member of parliament who in uniquely accented English denounced his fellow-Swiss and all their institutions, their banks, their stores, their factories, even the International Red Cross. We filmed a classroom where teenage girls learned English by rapidly reciting that day's exchange rates; a banker, bald, benign, in rimless pince-nez and well-filled vest, who said, "In ze myt'ology, ze gnomes zey were very good dwarfs." Best of all, Dobyns talked about Ulrich Zwingli, Zurich's Calvin, the pastor who ushered the city into Reformation, taught it that profit was God's work, and died leading its troops in battle.

As we agonized for a title, Dobyns's wife, Patty, suggested *If That's a Gnome, This Must Be Zurich*. It harked back to a 1966 CBS documentary, *If It's Tuesday, This Must Be Belgium*, which poked fun at newly affluent middle-class Americans and their taste for guided tours of newly stable Western Europe. (Hollywood bought the title for a 1969 movie.) I disliked harking back, but playing against a remembered older title might give ours an edge, a bite, an aftertaste. Also, I could not come up with a better one.

The program did so well the Swiss parliament debated it angrily for an entire day. I was hoping for personal sanctions because anyone could be expelled from Moscow, but Switzerland . . . ? The program did so well, in fact, that I got no argument when I suggested another about a distant city, or that Dobyns and I do it together. We went off to Beirut, not yet the charnel-house it was to become, but a historic ancient metropolis full of people who hated each other. To our delight, we found a Middle Eastern Zurich, morally satisfying the needs of the immoral, providing banking to a region where the majority religion taught that usury was a capital sin, the place God-struck desert warriors could find women, whiskey, and impunity.

It may have been the best program I never got to do. When we returned to New York full of all the wonderful scenes there for the filming, Dick Wald sat me down to discuss the magazine NBC News was about to do, the first since *First Tuesday*'s life support was removed. I wanted to talk about ancient Armenians and the roots of Christianity, villages where everybody went armed, Maronites and Druse and opium, still fresh antagonisms from the days of Barbarossa and Richard the Lion-Hearted, and he wanted to talk about affiliates.

Over at CBS, nurtured and cosseted by Bill Paley and protected from intracompany jealousies, *60 Minutes* was flourishing, although not yet what it would become—the most profitable program in the history of network television. NBC's affiliates wanted to know why we did not have a program like that. Herbert Schlosser, NBC's new president, was anxious to give them what they wanted. Schlosser, a vice president in NBC's entertainment behemoth in California, had been summoned East by Bob Sarnoff to be head of Network. Bob had been feuding with Julian Goodman. Soon Goodman was moved to NBC board chairman and Schlosser to president. His years in the network's entertainment department had not prepared him for affiliates and their whims, and if a show like *60 Minutes* was what they wanted, a show like *60 Minutes* was what they would get.

It in no way detracts from Don Hewitt's achievements with *60 Minutes* to point out that it owed part of its success to its good fortune in having a "protected" time period, "protected" by an FCC dictate that networks might broadcast only news or children's programs between 7:00 and 8:00 on Sunday evenings. Thus, when *60 Minutes* finally ended up at 7:00 on Sundays, it was shielded from entertainment competition. How it got to 7:00 P.M. Sundays is part of the story.

When *First Tuesday* was kept in prime time on Tuesday evenings after its first year—as part of *Tuesday Night at the Movies*—CBS moved *60 Minutes* to 6:00 P.M. on Sundays, which the people on the program considered insulting, and rumors seeped from their corridors to ours of angry confrontations and threats of quitting. Then the Prime Time Access Rule changed American television forever.

The Prime Time Access Rule had its origins in the earliest days of television, when there had been misgivings inside the FCC about the perceived network monopoly of programs. There were discussions and hearings on mitigating the monopoly's effects. Commissioners and staff agreed that stations, not networks, should control what was on television. Stations were seen, romantically, as one with the people they dwelled among. The licensee—the station, that is, not the network—was considered part of his locality, his folks.

So, in 1970, the FCC adopted a rule limiting how much networks might fill of prime viewing time, understood as 7:00 to 11:00 each evening. Three hours each night might be the networks' but the fourth must be filled by the stations, except that a network's news half hour might appear at seven o'clock weeknights if there was local news up to 6:59. The only exception: Networks might fill 7:00 to 8:00 on Saturdays or Sundays with children's or "public affairs" programs.

From the first hint to the final rule, the debate was bathed in the Jeffersonian implication of community initiative, a showcase for the richness and variety of each American locale, so the First Baptist choir might be heard in Mozart's *Requiem* and the Little Theater's production of *The Merchant of Venice* or *A Doll's House* might be seen. What resulted was not what was expected.

Instead, the Prime Time Access Rule opened a new market to entrepreneurs known as syndicators. Even when stations were few, broadcasting few hours, not all a station's programs came from its network. (And even then there were some stations without network affiliations, "independents.") The stations' own programs leaned heavily on people talking in simple studios, demonstrating how to bake a pie, interviewing celebrities, playing a piano and singing, ending the day with a devotional word. They also rented film from syndicators, "B" movie series, which would each fill two hours but leave plenty of time for commercials, short subjects from before World War II, old newsreels dressed up as history, and the like.

The suppliers of these programs were the only ones the stations could turn to when the commission decreed they must fill some prime time themselves. But "B" movies and badly synched Japanese cartoons would no longer suffice, because the stations now had to fill hours when large numbers were watching and commercials commanded high prices. They willingly paid huge fees for programs that would attract bigger audiences than the competition's. Mozart and Shakespeare and Ibsen never had a chance.

"Access time," the half hour or hour between network news and network entertainment, became the syndicators' philosopher's stone, turning time to gold. Their number grew, as did the number of independent stations. Syndicators made so much money from "access time" that they could afford to invade all the hours of the schedule, to produce or commission every sort of program. There were talk shows whose hosts became so famous their perversities were featured on the front pages of supermarket tabloids. There were current events shows where people screamed, some of them thugs, some of them reporters for proud newspapers and magazines. There were many programs purporting to be news. What all these programs shared, besides the absence of Mozart, Ibsen, and Shakespeare, was an absence of wit, perspective, and style. For a while, they elicited a genteel outcry, but few knew to trace them to the Prime Time Access Rule.

All that lay ahead. In 1974, NBC's problem was how to use the Prime Time Access Rule to satisfy its affiliates' demand for "something like *60 Minutes*" at least cost to itself. NBC was doing very well at 7:00 on Sundays with a series provided by the Disney studios. CBS kept trying to outdo NBC at that hour with its own children's series. In 1975, after two more failures, unwilling to throw more good money after bad, almost in desperation, the rulers of CBS heeded those who advised putting "public affairs" into that time. So *60 Minutes* was moved again—and found its niche. The audience size exploded in a way that makes a salesman slaver. A star was born.

Even before that change, however, *60 Minutes* had made enough of a name, built enough of a following, to merit the ultimate television accolade—imitation, which is what the affiliates wanted. Because NBC's audiences were third largest, it paid heed to its affiliates. The top network can ignore its affiliates, knowing they are cashing in on its success, but for the last-place network the voice of its affiliates is the voice of God. NBC agreed to do a magazine, but typically gave up as little as possible. It scheduled the program for Saturdays at 7:00, thus not displacing anything NBC was already doing. That was the stations' time.

While Wald told me to arrange for an hour-long magazine on Saturday evenings to begin in the fall, two syndicators petitioned the FCC to forbid it. They were the distributors of the *Lawrence Welk Show*, a band-leader who played sweet music and showed fresh-faced couples dancing polkas, and *Hee Haw*, a showcase for rural risibilities. Each of those programs was an hour long, and with most affiliates in the bigger cities showing network news at 7:00, there was no room weekdays for syndicated programs of that length.

Unaware of these forces shaping my fate, I set off to Washington, to Los Angeles, to old collaborators in Texas and elsewhere, then to Europe, to try to describe what kind of subjects I would cover, how I should like to see them treated, what I was aiming at. I would need help in hiring cameramen and crews; as in the days when Huntley and I were doing *Outlook*, I wanted to know what stories *Nightly News* and *Today* had rejected, or underplayed, to the scorn of reporters and editors in the field. That had been a rich lode for me then, and would be again. One of my producers joined me in Amsterdam to walk through Vondel Park talking to young drug addicts, many Americans among them, and found a story worth doing. I went to London, the largest foreign bureau, whose help was more important than most. There was a message to phone Bob Mulholland in New York.

Mulholland was Wald's second in command in the division as Wald had been mine. I had first met him when I came back to bring the *Huntley-Brinkley Report* from fifteen minutes to a half hour and he was newly in charge of the Chicago desk. In time, I moved him to Washington as Brinkley's producer, and he was still there when I left producing to be a vice president. When, as president of NBC News, I needed a news director for the Los Angeles station (who would also be the network's western news chief) I bullied him into the job. There, he learned to read ratings books and cheat on budgets, and he inaugurated the first two-hour local news block on a major station, his mark on television history.

When Northshield's successor as *Nightly News* executive producer struck out, Dick Wald and I brought Mulholland to New York to do it. As I was leaving management I suggested to Wald he bring Mulholland into it because it seemed to suit him.

Now he was on the phone. "Are you sitting down," he asked. I sat down.

"Lawrence Welk and *Hee Haw* won."

That was the first I had heard that syndicators had petitioned to forbid the program I had been assigned to do.

"Well, what does that mean?"

"It means you're dead."

My immediate problem was to become undead. I had very little time. Scheduling the still untitled magazine program had been a response to the affiliates, and they might be as satisfied with the gesture as with the fact. Nor was it unthinkable that NBC had opposed the syndicators' quest for the Saturday night hour in its own interest, throwing us into the argument merely to look respectable. That battle lost, they might have no further use for us. Brooding in a hotel room, I could think of only one thing to suggest to save the program, move it from the time period before the night's entertainment programs into the time period after them.

The next morning I telephoned Dick Wald to suggest that we be put in the Johnny Carson time on Saturdays, 11:30 P.M. The time was being used for repeat showings of old Carson shows that almost nobody watched, although that did not matter because they were a device for NBC to pay Carson under his new contract. The high officers and directors of RCA, accustomed to the protocols and pay levels of semiskilled manufacturing labor, were told that NBC was getting more "product" for the added expenditure.

Wald asked was I suggesting a ninety-minute program. Yes. Every week? Yes. He would float it and call back. My hopes rested on Wald's professional interest in the project and Schlosser's awe of news. It would not have worked had I waited one more day. When Wald called back, we were approved for the Carson time beginning in October, one Saturday a month. It would be a kind of lottery; sometimes two programs might be three weeks apart, sometimes six.

By the time of our first program, Watergate was all over. The story had developed and ripened all through 1973, the hearings, the dread word *impeachment*, a President resigning. Then along came *Weekend*. I had wanted to call it, *The Midnight Sun*. Wald said Schlosser wanted *Weekend*, which seemed pallid to me, but I was too relieved to argue. For four years, on some Saturday nights, we did a ninety-minute program in the Johnny Carson period. It found an audience, young, devoted, some of whom would come up to Lloyd Dobyns or me years later still enthusing about it. Newspaper writers loved us, giving *Weekend* four years of more press attention and better notices than any other program I can remember.

In our very first year we were recognized with the most prestigious of television awards, the Peabody, for which we were nominated by the unusual initiative of the awards panel itself; the NBC department concerned with nominations had not considered us worth submitting. And *Weekend* proved to NBC that there was actually an audience at that strange time, so the next year they gave us the first Saturday each month and the rest to an experiment called *Saturday Night Live*. (In time, however, not everyone loved us. At least as many were merely annoyed to find us there when they had tuned in for *Saturday Night Live*.) Had we been able to hold to 7:00 on Saturdays, we might have done well but not that well. The exotic scheduling forced us to new ideas and untried methods, at least partly successfully. And we owed it all to the Prime Time Access Rule.

The rule was first promulgated in 1970, after years of passionate opposition by CBS and NBC, eloquently represented before commission and courts by expensive lawyers. Nor did that end with publication of the rule; it rattled on for years in courts and hearings. Only ABC, then the weakest and puniest, stayed mute, happy to be relieved of the cost of programming some hours a week, while the senior networks saw the rule as an unwarranted attack on their right to earn, a First Amendment matter if ever there was one. The year the commission promulgated Prime Time Access was the year Congress forbade cigarette advertising on television, making the ban effective the following January 2 so the networks might cash in one last time at the New Year's Day football games. Cigarette advertising then represented 10 percent of network revenue. But the rule reduced network programs, and the number of commercial minutes for sale, by 17 percent; supply of commercial time was cut 17 percent, demand 10 percent. It took no Adam Smith to see who profited. ABC benefited most, but all three came out ahead. When this finally percolated through to the managers of CBS and NBC, the attorney representing NBC was instructed to go argue *for* the rule before the FCC. A commissioner broke in: "Counselor, you have changed your position 360 degrees," to which he responded, "No, sir. Only 180."

The Prime Time Access Rule's beneficiary, *Weekend*, was not experimental in the way *Saturday Night Live* was. We had no intention of influencing others, only of doing a program "our" way. Newspaper writers invariably compare newsmagazine programs with *60 Minutes* and we were no exception despite never approaching their success. The fundamental difference was, however, always ignored. With its star journalists and crusading journalism, *60 Minutes* assumes human perfectibility, not the sort of thing Hewitt and his principals tend to acknowledge. In its own strange way, "ambush" journalism can be seen as trying to make things better—by forcing evildoers to confess in public. We were more existential than that. Even if we did not accept that crusading against wrong led to correction, we felt obliged to describe it. We took up the causes of victims without broad constituencies, like gas station owners bullied by the major companies, foreign students in American universities, fat kids in military schools. For us folly was more interesting than sin: beauty contests no one had heard of, annual conventions of pet cemetery owners, the misplaced dam on the Niobrara River.

Those same newspaper writers used "laid back" and "cool" and such words, but they were not the point. We edited *Weekend* as we would have liked to be edited for. We were committed to the narrative inherent in the picture as television's only unique capacity. Producers took their crews into the field knowing there would be enough pictures for a story but looking for others, "alert for accident," as I kept preaching, ready for the shot that is unanticipated and unplanned, the child interrupting, the phone call, the fistfight. For us all picture included some sound, like those people talking who were part of the story, or who were indeed the whole story—not experts, not interviews, not talking heads.

I inaugurated something called the "producer's footnote" in which he, or she, would face the camera on location and append a spoken paragraph. For example, at the end of a story about an American woman who disappeared, presumably kidnapped, on a Mexican vacation, the producer filmed himself describing how local police had tried to stop him at every step. Producers on newsmagazines gripe they are the real reporters, not the talking faces arriving after the work has been done, abiding their hour or two and going on to their next, laden with fame, kudos, and six- (later seven-) figure salaries. Serendipitously, "producer's footnotes" smoothed that problem for me.

The producer's principal job, however, was to get the story done, filmed in the field, back to where he would work with the film editor to assemble a coherent picture narrative, include all the best shots, make all the salient points, with images flowing from introduction to conclusion. Then and only then did Dobyns start on the script. Before each edition, Dobyns and I put in twelve-hour Saturdays and Sundays with the producers of that month's pieces. No one fussed about script more than we, but it would have been unthinkable to take a script to a film editor for pictures to be matched to words, as is now universal. (Otherwise, as said earlier, the best pictures are scrapped because they fit none of the words.) So the producer would work with the film editor, with me hovering, as Dobyns would write. Sometimes he had been on the story; more often he worked from the producer's field notes and the give and take of conversations with the producers after their return.

Weekend was remarked on, even remembered, for its funny pieces and its script, always literate, but also described as wry, sardonic, unorthodox, disrespectful, iconoclastic, and a lot of other things, some of which it really was not. We did do a piece on bad teeth in Scotland, on the Belgian army officers' mess, a NATO installation, which was the only restaurant in West Germany with two Michelin stars; on stage mothers at baton-twirling contests; and one called "I Was Nixon's Barber." But these were possible because we also paid attention to journalism, did a lot of it, and did it well.

The very first program set patterns with its stories about young people from all over Europe and America flocking to Amsterdam to kill themselves on easily available cheap heroin, the counterculture as tragic farce. We would balance a fight about textbooks between a rural Virginia school board and the local churches with Japanese bands playing American country music to large Japanese crowds, neither players nor audience understanding a word. We profiled Adnan Khashoggi, not yet known as one of the world's richest men, in Beirut, in Paris, on his yachts, on the Riviera. We did a story on movies used as tax shelters.

Our report on the Rev. Sun Myung Moon was the first worthwhile network televsion story on cults. When we showed the school Hare Krishna maintained for even the youngest children of its members, showing them deprived of sleep and food and the endless indoctrination, the Texas welfare and education departments were forced to intervene. We were often ahead of the pack: fetal alcohol syndrome, acid rain (in 1978!), a doctor trying to mitigate schizophrenia by renal dialysis, Israel's huge arms exporting industry—all basic, traditional reporting. We reported on the Sex Pistols and punk rock while they were still news to most Americans. A year after *Weekend* won its Peabody Award, producer Sy Pearlman won another, in his own name, for reporting the manipulated conviction of two not-quite-retarded North Carolina brothers for what might have been kidnapping, which they might or might not have known about. They were pardoned.

As *Weekend* hit its stride, and a sense of entity was established, producers took to trying to do film reports without "narrated" script, only the ambient sound recorded during filming and people who were part of the story telling it. (Dobyns would write an introduction, and that was all.) These reports were only, perhaps, one in five, but became such a metaphor for how we saw ourselves I had to caution them not to strain after scriptless stories or deny script to a film that needed one. It had become a sort of badge.

We told stories in different ways, twice in the form of children's books with typical illustrations, pages seen turning as the stories were being read by Irene Wicker, the famous "Singing Lady" of network radio's heyday. One of these "children's" stories was about an early comrade and collaborator of Fidel Castro who had been languishing thirty years in one of Castro's jails; the other about a Russian World War II hero, a colonel, who when peace came found all avenues closed to him by official anti-Semitism. The illustrations, Irene Wicker's voice, the script so obviously meant to be read to little children, gave a strength and polish to the irony.

In time, six of our producers were women, but only one of them appointed herself the feminist advocate. She did other stories as well, of course, like Korean influence peddler Tongsun Park and his girl-friend, Tandy Dickinson, or Mrs. Nelson Rockefeller's dismay on her first visit to what was about to be the vice president's official residence. But she also set herself to teaching me about "women's" issues. Her story on wife-beating, with real victims detailing horrors, and the shocking point about its prevalence among even the "best" people, led to one on incest, dealt with as exploitation of the women. I okayed that hesitantly.

When the piece was done, I saw that the titillation I had feared would in mere minutes be driven from the viewer's mind by the horror being perpetrated on the victims. Most of what we showed was people talking: a dozen or so victims; some fathers or stepfathers or uncles; mothers who had turned blind eyes; counselors; police—all of them added up to too many heads in shadow, too much talk and too little picture, and yet it was powerful television, social reporting at its most disturbing. I made her stretch that report to fill all ninety minutes— about seventy-five after commercials—which may have been a bit more than the story was worth but anything else in the same program would have been obliterated. A decade later, happening upon raucous talk shows mining ratings on these same topics, I could say grandly, "We did that ten years ago."

Throughout, we held to our tone, in the choice of stories, in the style of the writing. We even looked different. Our first studio set was too fussy, so we jettisoned it for what became our look, the exterior of a small neighborhood movie theater, the marquee emblazoned in three places with the "Weekend" logo and using the movable letters for any message we chose. Behind Dobyns we placed freestanding posters promoting films still to come. He sat on a red park bench a few yards in front of the theater. When the topic was too serious for this kind of playfulness, we moved the camera in on Dobyns, and the background went out of focus and disappeared.

In the five seconds most programs use to fade into commercial, or up out of it, I would put little pieces of printed text I called "verbals." One hoped for epigrams but settled for something between conceptual art and bumper stickers: "ALISTAIR COOKE IS UPWARD MOBIL" and "LABOR USED TO BE LIBERAL." I wrote (and relished) most of them: "A GOVERNMENT NOT OF LAWS BUT OF LAWYERS" and "NO OWNER WAS EVER HURT ON ARTIFICIAL TURF." The audience did not care for them, nor did most of the *Weekend* staff. Eric Sevareid once told me that for him they spoiled an enjoyable program. But they were ours and no one else's, our signature, and almost the only writing I did anymore. Keeping my mind open for them wherever I was—talking, reading, or driving—became a habit, because they surfaced unpredictably. The habit stuck: "TRAGEDY IS COMEDY WITHOUT PUNCHLINES," or "HISTORY REPEATS ITSELF, THE FIRST TIME AS FARCE."

We had other trademarks. Two bright young film animators, newly launched in business, did a pair of animations for each month's *Weekend*—a distinctive form of comment, often obvious, like Martians landing on Earth and finding no intelligent life. Soon one animation in each program was given over to a series called *Mr. Hipp Goes to Town* about a balding, sagging Lothario aching to join the sexual revolution everyone was talking about. The opening was always his shedding the somber coat and tie he worked in and putting on the jumpsuit and beads in which he went forth to make contact. Each episode had its own setting—singles' bar, dance class, yoga session— but all ended alike: He struck out.

That was it for four years, that was pictures, pictures, pictures, sunsets and cityscapes and wild animals and wrinkled faces and all the beauty and paradox and drama the attentive eye could see: rounding up feral dogs in the Bronx slums, frying omelets in deep fat for airline breakfasts, wig makers buying human hair from the poor women of Sicily, McDonald's on the Champs Elysees.

Newspaper writers took *Weekend* to their bosoms from the start—I think its attitudes tended to be their attitudes—and I exploited this by taking to the road a few days each month to visit them. Like most columnists, they had too many columns to fill, so a New York big shot coming to visit was a boon. In return for my terse evaluations of current problems of television, they spelled "Weekend" right and gave the time of broadcast. My part of the bargain was being honest and trying to be interesting. I told one columnist the obstacle in American television was commercial placement. I was not against commercials, but Britain and Europe did them better, clustering them between programs, or at most every half hour. How would Shakespeare have written *Macbeth* if he knew it had to break every six minutes for a commercial? An NBC vice president was so incensed that he wanted to stop my traveling, but it came to nothing.

And all about us the walls of the temple were tumbling. From October 1974 to June 1978, turmoil and disruption took over NBC, testing its ability to stay alive. The steady, albeit glacial, slide was not stayed by Herbert Schlosser's appointment as Network division president, or his succeeding Julian Goodman as president of NBC. In 1975, suddenly, Bob Sarnoff was dismissed as chairman by the RCA board. Inexplicably, he had kept on the board two enemies, and they, acting (they said) for the good of the company, enlisted others in the move to oust him. (As in some bad movie, his principal outrider was told to clear out his desk by five o'clock that evening.)

Ten months later, in September 1976, Sarnoff's successor, Anthony Conrad, having admitted tax problems, vanished from public view. Edgar Griffiths took over, an RCA "inside" director who might keep things going, an uncommitted, unsentimental accountant whom *Fortune* called "a bad-tempered bookkeeper." Griffiths, a stranger to broadcasting, believed in short answers. With NBC's entertainment schedule in decline, he lured from a rival network a programming executive so successful he had been heralded on the cover of *Time* as "the man with the golden gut" and certified before all as a genius. The genius, Fred Silverman, made things worse. Griffiths had made him president of NBC and Silverman, it turned out, had had no training in being president of anything. We were now at June 1978.

All that time, everything had kept changing, shifting, disappearing. At NBC News, the number of vice presidents tripled. Some old hands were promoted; some were fired; some sent to seek their fortunes elsewhere within the company. News departments of the NBC-owned stations were separated from the News division, something I had pleaded for and been denied. Now lawyers were saying it helped get the stations' licenses renewed at the FCC. The station managers were overjoyed. They could now do ratings-enhancing stunts with their news without risking the veto of the maiden aunt News division.

The 1976 political year had passed me by, and I did not mind. I had concluded in 1972 that there was no news purpose still served by networks covering conventions live, gavel-to-gavel, as even children now knew to say. In 1976, Dick Wald wanted me back in my old seat speaking into Brinkley's and Chancellor's ears, but I demurred and he resented it. He had counted on me as a friend.

Even if covering conventions had become pointless, it was the Old Man of the Sea; the networks did not know how to stop. It took courage, and they had none. So it continued, an imposition and a waste. But saying that to Dick Wald would have been unkind; he was stuck with it. I told him instead there was nothing in it for me. If things went well, it would hardly be worth noting; if not, they would tell each other, Well, he's finally lost it. So my group and I stayed inside our enclave, working hard but sealed off, aware but not involved in the big news of the world or the twists and upheavals inside NBC.

The changes engulfing television disrupted NBC first because it was structurally weakest. Of all the networks, it was the most poorly organized, the most dependent on a corporate parent, and the least fortified with reserves of money or ideas. The die was cast when ABC launched its successful run for parity with the two older networks. But as it was lived day to day, it was a drama of individuals, what happened to them, what they did to others, history as gossip; and of arithmetic, the rise and fall of ratings and of profits, the snip-snip-snipping of budgets.

The roots of NBC's decline go far back, at least to the middle sixties when someone named Monty Hall, owner of a daytime game-show hit called *The Price Is Right*, left NBC because they would not also broadcast it one night a week. ABC welcomed him. Larding its schedule with nighttime versions of daytime game shows was common at ABC. (Prime time shows give bigger prizes.) *The Price Is Right* set ABC on its way to ruling daytime, actually the most profitable broadcasting period. Also, ABC, the newcomer, owned its soap operas, which, along with game shows, made up daytime. CBS and NBC, as they had since prewar radio, merely rented time to Procter & Gamble and others who owned their own. ABC thus made its first big money in daytime, and went on from there.

Other events added to the decline, even the Soviet invasion of Afghanistan, when NBC, observing President Jimmy Carter's boycott, canceled its coverage of the 1980 Moscow Olympics, which was supposed to get the network out of the Slough of Despond. NBC's huge bid had been justified by the need for something positive when Redd Foxx, its highest-rated comedian, defected, and sloppy negotiating lost major league baseball's All-Star Game and World Series. The two baseball events had been NBC monopolies since television began, but now they had to be shared with ABC.

Neither last nor least of the contributing events was Barbara Walters leaving NBC for ABC in April 1976. She was now famous. At Frank McGee's death, she had become the dominant broadcaster on *Today* and was, in fact, the deciding voice in the choice of Jim Hartz as McGee's successor. She had begun her career in publicity, mostly show business publicity, before joining *Today* as a writer, and there were those in news whose monastic definition of journalist she did not satisfy. She nurtured contacts assiduously, became known to most of the famous and trusted by many of them. There were cabinet members and heads of state who refused all others but were available to her. It was said they felt she did not ask unfair questions. (Some think unfair questions are what public figures should be asked.) Walters, the only woman to cover Nixon in Peking, then demanded to anchor a network's evening news. Wald did not want her to anchor NBC *Nightly News* and John Chancellor would not welcome her as co-anchor.

ABC was third in evening news ratings, but its *Good Morning, America* was gaining on *Today*, which would suffer if Barbara left— or so thought Herbert Schlosser, NBC's president, who was ready to meet her demands but could not persuade Wald to move her to *Nightly News*. Fred Pierce, ABC's top operating executive, offered her one million dollars a year, half for co-anchoring the evening news, half for doing her own interview program several times a year. Schlosser was willing to match the million dollars, but Wald held fast against her anchoring. The disagreement between Schlosser and Wald was open and their mutual hostility became so. Walters left NBC for ABC.

She had crashed the million-dollar barrier in television news. The next *Weekend* opened with a still photograph of Barbara Walters before the title. After hers, photographs of those who might expect to follow through the gate she opened—Chancellor, Cronkite, Harry Reasoner, Dan Rather, Roger Mudd, Mike Wallace, Howard K. Smith, and others. Behind the pictures we played Dick Powell singing a song from one of his identical Warner Brothers musicals:

> *"Thanks a million,*
> *A million thanks to you.*
> *For everything that love can bring*
> *You brought me."*

It made history, and it was funny, to me grandly, sardonically funny. It was also sad. Television news is a group effort, and now those relationships would be forever skewed. It is American dogma that anyone earning a million dollars is smarter than someone who does not.

Barbara Walters co-anchored ABC's evening news with Harry Reasoner. The rivalry that became open enmity between her and Reasoner was at least as intense as it had been with Frank McGee, and even more public. Perhaps for that reason, perhaps because America was not yet ready to hear its news from a woman, most likely—I hope— because the news anchor is less important than how news is gathered and presented, the program languished. Soon after election day, meanwhile, Walters interviewed President-elect Jimmy Carter and his wife, Rosalynn, on her first prime-time big-name interview show. It was unexceptional—the point of big-name interviews being who is interviewed, not what they say—until the very end, when Walters said to the new President: "Be wise with us. Be good to us."

Define hubris as chutzpa and vice versa. The chorus of hoots shook towers and shattered glass. That the show's other interview was with Barbra Streisand and her producer (and hairdresser) Jon Peters, or that the third segment of the three-segment program was a filmed tour of Barbara Walters's own apartment, were nothing to what one smart, mean, male reporter called her "blessing" the new President. No future success, and there would be many, would induce the jealous, self-centered news freemasonry to accept her as one of theirs. Morley Safer wrote she had "withdrawn herself from the profession of journalism."

This was more than a raucous footnote to a time of change. Her move from NBC, where she rose to fame, to ABC, which bought that fame, was an apt symbol. Her accession to co-anchoring a network's evening news revised the definition of network anchor, not because she was a woman but because she had never reported fires or done rewrite or covered a beat. Her million-dollar salary, even though half was ABC Entertainment's payment for her interview show, made anchoring a superstardom, which altered the dynamics of television news. It brought talent raiding to news, and journalists into the purview of gossip columnists.

ABC was changing not only news but all television. This was a new ABC: aggressive, out of the poorhouse, tired of being third, disrespectful of precedent, and seeking not only revenge but to make up for all those years as the runt. In December 1976, at midseason, ABC easily led the network prime-time ratings race. Its stock had moved from $20 to almost $40 a share in only a year. Many gave credit to Fred Silverman, the programming vice president lured by Fred Pierce from CBS for $250,000 a year, then big money for that job. At the same time, *Today* began to languish. In the corridors of NBC News they wondered how long Dick Wald could last.

Early in 1977, RCA chairman Griffiths, pressing NBC for more profit, took the title of chief executive officer away from Julian Goodman and gave it to Schlosser. (During the obligatory champagne-in-the-office, Goodman, still chairman, toasted: "Herb, be wise with us . . . be good to us . . .") Interestingly, both RCA's profits and NBC's had risen smartly in 1976 over 1975, but signs of pending erosion were too strong to disregard. It was then that NBC, ignoring the usual gloomy forecasts of its risk-averse, RCA-dominated finance department, made the winning bid for the 1980 Moscow Olympics. It was the only bright ray on a gray horizon. ABC had just broken all records for size of audience and permanently changed the idea of dramatic miniseries—a single story told in many hours over several evenings—with *Roots*, tracing the American black experience from Africa through slavery to the modern ghetto. More people watched it than all opposing programs combined. The last episode became the most watched television program in history. That week, more people watched all of ABC's programs than the sum of all of CBS's and NBC's. At CBS, only *60 Minutes* managed to post a respectable figure.

That same month, February 1977, NBC News signed a five-year contract with Henry Kissinger. It was widely reported that the deal had been made by Schlosser, described in *Variety* as "a socializing friend of Kissinger's." Dick Wald, the president of NBC News, did nothing to stifle newspaper reports that he was at best cool to the deal. Journalists, some even willing to be quoted by name, found conflict of interest in hiring the architect of the eight most recent years of American foreign policy to do what amounted to news. An NBC executive who had worked closely with Schlosser during the negotiation would later recall, "It was mostly for PR, which Herb thought would be so great, and he didn't know what hit him."

In NBC's deteriorating internal atmosphere—corridor gossip about the Kissinger "deal," facts, exaggerations, fabrications, and just plain mischief—spilled into the press: The fee was reported to be seven figures, and included a New York apartment (true but hardly unusual) and a maid and butler (in fact a part-time research assistant). It was also widely repeated that ABC and CBS had turned down Kissinger's services while Schlosser was importuning Griffiths to act fast—RCA approval was necessary for sums of that order—lest Bill Paley run off with the prize. Actually, CBS seems to have made an offer for the "memoirs," although not as big as NBC's.

"NBC is fortunate that this remarkable man has agreed to participate in NBC's effort to extend its coverage and analysis of foreign affairs," began a press statement issued in Schlosser's name. It was so unlike customary press releases that several trade papers found its fulsome language worth quoting at length: ". . . unique contribution . . . first-hand knowledge . . . leading personalities . . . ability to identify and articulate the interrelated issues of foreign policy . . . invaluable . . . enlightening . . . American interests and values." (Typical NBC press releases listed Johnny Carson's guests next week, soap opera plot summaries, and how NBC broadcast an inconsequential bulletin three minutes sooner than CBS.)

The arrangement apparently included Kissinger's availability to deliver foreign affairs commentary whenever asked. After the uproar, he told reporters (in May) that he would not do "commentary" after all, restricting himself to appearing on news specials or answering reporters' questions. The "memoirs" that were so vaunted earlier became a couple of long programs presented as documentaries, one in which he chatted about history with David Brinkley against an assortment of historical backgrounds, the other a straight interview, by David Frost, ill-advisedly hired for the occasion by an NBC News executive who had not even worked there when the agreement was signed. The taping turned into a shouting match when Frost asked Kissinger baiting questions about Cambodia, sending him storming from the room. Disaster loomed because the program had been announced. The executive coaxed him back. There were arguments about how it was to be edited and both sides issued transcripts of what each claimed had been said, all in all an unsavory occurrence. The program itself was dull, but the press had a good time.

As for being interviewed by reporters, the contract specified that Kissinger would be exclusive to NBC News reporters except when he was himself legitimately the subject of news. This took adjudication every time CBS or ABC or public television or a station or foreign broadcaster called. It was awkward and vaguely demeaning. A new negotiation was called to iron out the bump. It was agreed that Henry Kissinger could talk to any reporter he cared to, and NBC would pay him a little less. There is no evidence that Henry Kissinger's association with NBC News made its foreign coverage fuller, or faster, or wiser, which had been the point of Schlosser's original press release, although there were reports he had helped convince some important but reluctant people to be interviewed.

There was talk in the press about *NBC Nightly News*, the kind of talk that is printed without attribution but everyone knows is not parthenogenetic. The hostility between Schlosser and Wald was expressing itself in, among other things, a stream of suggestions for helping NBC

News do better, be sprightlier, more contemporary, more attuned to the changing tastes of an ever-younger American public, the kind only television entertainment moguls understand. At the time, NBC News programs were doing better than entertainment programs, but the suggestions came anyway.

Some change was inevitable. Chancellor was due a new contract. Brinkley, tired of New York, wanted to move back to Washington, so the two-man anchor team would become the two-city anchor team as it had been in the glory days. (Chancellor had been paired with Brinkley after Barbara Walters left, the two of them divvying up the news in the newsroom during the afternoon, sitting side by side in the studio handing it back and forth in the evening.) But how about instead of New York and Washington it be New York and Los Angeles? What a great deal! And how about, instead of Brinkley, Tom Snyder as Chancellor's co-anchor?

Now, for the first time, leaked to the press, the people in NBC News saw the name they dreaded. Tom Snyder was a tall, large, burly, not unattractive man with a booming voice, glistening eyes, and a gladiatorial way with an interview. He was quick-witted, shallow, bright, glib, intellectually lazy, and loud in his contempt for traditional journalism. He had been a local television reporter in Los Angeles, an anchor in Philadelphia, a local anchor in Los Angeles, and then the stars fell on him.

While I was still News president, Mort Werner, then NBC's programming vice president, had asked if he might approach Gene Shalit. Mort reasoned that people watching Johnny Carson did not all go to bed when Carson ended. They would still be watching if there was anything to watch. He envisioned a low-key interview show for those not yet ready for bed, and Shalit, a central figure on *Today*, seemed to him ideal. I had hired Shalit to review movies for the New York station, and when that got good notices moved him into *Today*.

After Joe Garagiola left, Shalit took over as *Today*'s third banana, ranking below the High Communicator and the *Today* Girl. He kept reviewing his movies and interviewing stars, working his way into the "cast" of the program. Also, he was passionate about books, sometimes reviewing them, more often talking to authors and waving dust jackets at the camera. There were years when Gene Shalit sold more books than any other American . . . until someone decided books were bad for *Today*'s ratings. He even used his special pulpit to promote serious music, a unique contribution which was rarely noted.

But he would not have been my choice for Werner's show. Keeping that to myself, I told Mort I had no objection to his approaching Shalit. When Gene asked for advice I told him he had to make up his own mind. But it's so much money, he kept repeating. In the end he decided he would be uncomfortable and turned it down.

Werner turned to Tom Snyder, the Los Angeles local anchorman who was getting so much attention in the press and from executives. The resulting program was far from Werner's original idea. Snyder was aggressive, noisy, attention-grabbing. To fit with *Today* and *Tonight,* the program was called *Tomorrow.* (Schlosser then chose *Weekend* to match those.) When show business palled, Snyder decided to interview people in the news, so *Tomorrow* moved to New York. To sweeten the move, Snyder was hired at a large sum as the local station's early evening anchor, its ratings savior. Sure enough, hip critics from newsmagazines and the *Village Voice* would soon write about this herald of the McLuhan age, his persona, his power, his projection, using words like "paradigm." The audience, centrist to the end, paid too little heed, so Snyder maneuvered his way back to Los Angeles. Now sources were asking, Why not have him co-anchor with Chancellor?

Tom Snyder was the kind of news broadcaster whom entertainment executives like and news executives don't. Schlosser had been an NBC entertainment vice president in Los Angeles. Like the movie moguls and show folk he lived among, he based his views of television news largely on what he saw on the Los Angeles stations, whose local anchors swam in his social stream. Snyder co-anchoring with Chancellor was not to him unthinkable, but it was to Wald. And it was to Chancellor, who received offers from other networks and found one of them quite attractive, for which Schlosser blamed Wald and Wald blamed Schlosser. So the idea didn't fly, but it remained there, a cloud no bigger than a man's hand, Snyder's hand. He had big hands.

ABC, on its way to the most profitable season any network had ever had, also wanted parity in news. In 1977, Roone Arledge was picked to achieve it. His daring, vision, and command of television had made ABC Sports the industry's leader and goad when virtually nothing else ABC did was notable or successful. Arledge's real job was to overcome the other networks' lead of three decades. To do it, he turned news into a marketplace, bidding high not only for anchors but reporters, and producers, and directors, even field producers. Nor was money any object when it came to coverage. Mere weeks after his accession,

Moluccan nationalists hijacked a Dutch train. Arledge drew on his days covering live sports worldwide, and his checkbook, to move a television mobile unit to northern Holland, feeding live bulletins for days. Peoria, unfortunately, was bored.

It was excess, and a joke in the business, because few Americans were concerned with Moluccan nationalism, even given the exotic circumstance of a hijacked train. Tales abounded of copy boys flying by chartered plane, and three film crews appearing at even the most insignificant events. There was more notoriety the next year when co-anchor Barbara Walters made what may have been her first trip to a sitting criminal court to add her observations of the trial of New York's renowned "Son of Sam" killer, or perhaps try for an interview.

But Arledge's success is not debatable. From the moment he took over it was clear that the rules of the game were changed. He drove ABC News first to parity, then to leadership. His checkbook terrorized the other news divisions. In 1980, he would make Dan Rather an offer that CBS met by ejecting Walter Cronkite. His wooing of Tom Brokaw would make NBC likewise dethrone John Chancellor in 1982. By the time it was over, he had picked every anchorman but his own. Was there enough audience for three aggressive network news divisions? CBS seemed secure, but what might happen to NBC?

With poorly performing programs depressing profits, NBC had little money to spare for gestures in news coverage. Edgar Griffiths was frustrated in his plan to restore NBC's historic role as RCA's magic cash machine. A campaign was mounted to move *Weekend* to Saturdays at 6:00, telling the world that NBC would offer the now critically praised magazine at a time like that of *60 Minutes*. There was, however, a difference: Saturday at 6:00 was not only outside the scope of the Prime Time Access Rule, it was out of prime time altogether. It was an hour the stations used for their own cash cows, mostly local news, and they were not about to give it up to the network. Sure enough, the stations did not let commitment to public enlightenment rise above the level of lip service. "Not on our time," they told an embarrassed Schlosser. His plan to move *Weekend* quietly died.

Schlosser made Bob Mulholland president of the Network after firing Mulholland's friend and boss, Bob Howard. Asked about Dick Wald, he said, "If a decision is made, you'll know about it the same day he does," which no one mistook for an endorsement. With the new season barely begun, it was accepted that ABC would finish first; the speculation was whether NBC or CBS would end up last. Schlosser made a deal with former President Gerald Ford and a separate one with his wife, Betty Ford; those inside NBC News who might be asked to produce these programs tried to look busy.

In October 1977, Schlosser fired Dick Wald, naming Lester Crystal to succeed him. There were corridor rumors, which got into print, that Schlosser had considered making Chancellor News division president so he could bring Tom Snyder to the East Coast to anchor the *Nightly News*. Reporters were told, again without attribution, the decision to fire Wald had been made at the same time as the one to fire Howard, but Schlosser did not want both fired at once because it would look bad. Chancellor was given an announcement to read on the air which did not mention Wald's name. He rewrote it to include a short appreciation of Wald on his departure. Schlosser insisted to friends that Wald was after his job and had to be fired. More than that, he may have been making headway. Having Wald out of the way made Schlosser feel more secure.

Three months later, Griffiths fired Schlosser.

One would have expected Edgar Griffiths, RCA chairman, prototypical money man, meistersinger of the bottom line whose pure tones were undistorted by the sentimental slurring of tradition or obligation, to have done it neatly, even surgically, but in fact it was a mess. Having made clear to Schlosser, and to RCA and the world, that he was dissatisfied with NBC's inability to give him more profits, and that he understood that more profits came from more successful programs, he set about solving the problem himself. He was fed up with explanations and excuses. He believed in simple answers. He hired Fred Silverman. Schlosser was given a job at RCA.

ABC was soaring not only to ratings no network had ever achieved but to profits beyond imagining. If only Griffiths could find their magic key. He had streamlined management, lopped off dead wood, fired, early-retired, and attrited, but ABC still had what NBC did not. Columnists credited Silverman with CBS's hits in that network's heyday before he was lured to ABC to do even better. Now no programming job could seduce Silverman, not even at a million-dollar salary. He did not seek more success and recognition. He wanted respect. He wanted people to call him Fred, not Freddy, which he said "sounds like a cocker spaniel" but which everyone called him anyway. (At ABC, "Fred" was Pierce.) Griffiths gave him Schlosser's job and made him Fred. Never in charge of more than two dozen people, Silverman would be president of NBC's ten thousand employees—directors and sweepers, press agents and makeup artists, scenery movers and re- porters, engineers and salesmen, cooks and executives, represented by a dozen unions, or none, working in two dozen cities in the United States and the world. Fred indeed!

Fred Pierce, Silverman's boss at ABC, the one who had lured him from CBS, had known that Silverman was restless, hungry for status. Less than a year before, Silverman had asked to be head of ABC News and was furious when Pierce chose Arledge. (Successful entertainment people occasionally try switching to news as a sort of cleansing, like medieval kings and dukes ending lives of conquest and pillage with a few years in a monastery. Sportscaster Howard Cosell lobbied hard to be ABC News's anchor when Frank Reynolds died, and was insulted he did not get it.) It had been rumored other networks were romancing Silverman. Pierce kept asking him about them.

Silverman gave Pierce—and ABC—his assurance he would not leave for another network. This was more than satisfactory because it was his presence at another network that ABC's management feared, but his setting up as an independent producer might even be welcome. Silverman went so far as to repeat the assurance publicly, at a Los Angeles press conference, dismissing as "ridiculous" reports that he was going to NBC. Negotiations with NBC were well along as he spoke, only two weeks from fruition. Later, his lame excuse was that his promise to Pierce had been only not to go to another network as a program executive; it did not cover going to NBC as president.

Pierce was furious. Silverman told Pierce at 4:00 P.M. January 19, 1978, that he was leaving. By five, Pierce had ordered Silverman's files sealed and the locks changed on his office doors. (There truly is no business like show business.) And he invoked the ultimate sanction: Silverman would not be freed from the six months still left of his contract. Physically barred from ABC, Silverman might not yet join NBC. He took his family to Hawaii. Schlosser stayed on at NBC, a lame-duck reduced to housekeeping chores, his ordeal and indignity assuaged by the knowledge that once it was over he would move up to RCA as executive vice president in charge of videodiscs. But first, he and his programmers and administrators at NBC must carry on as before for six painful months, pretending their decisions would stand, their jobs were secure, their commitments would be honored, while throughout the trade there was this constant buzzing that off among the pineapples, Silverman was talking to this one or that one, planning changes to galvanize the industry. It was a mess.

It was into this mess that *Weekend* was launched in prime time. The idea was Mulholland's but told to me by Crystal. I tried to determine what was wanted, since I was sure that bringing the program we did from the strange hour we did it into the different arena of prime viewing time was foredoomed. As often as I said this, I got the same assurance: *Weekend* was what they wanted. *Weekend* was what the critics liked, and we had a faithful audience to build on. Even the animations? I would ask. Yes, even the animations.

I would need more producers. Fine. We also needed someone to share reporting and anchoring with Lloyd Dobyns, perhaps a pattern of alternating weeks with each program having one of them at the anchor bench while the other reported from the field. That would be my recommendation. Time for a woman. I wanted one who was as stylish a writer and as good a journalist as Dobyns. After a lot of reviewing tapes and talking to colleagues, I chose Linda Ellerbee, whom I had never met but had first seen on the air as a reporter in New York for the CBS station; she was at the time covering the Senate for the NBC News Washington bureau. We had one dinner, when I tried to explain what we would be trying to do with pictures as well as with words, and she was neither put off nor frightened by what I said, as some of the dreary ones tended to be. I told Crystal what I had decided.

Crystal urged me to consider a woman named Jessica Savitch, who was blond and attractive and hard-working. She had been a successful local reporter and anchor in Philadelphia, recruited by NBC News in bitter competition with the other news divisions, or so it was said. I watched her when I could. Her poise and appearance made her an effective broadcaster, but her writing was ordinary, and I saw nothing special about her reporting, but that is often partly accidental. A call to my old colleague Don Meaney, Washington bureau chief, arranged that the three of us would have lunch. I explained to her, too, what I liked to do with picture and words. She had never seen *Weekend* but found what I said interesting. She complimented me on the wine I chose. In a few days, she wrote asking she not be considered. She hinted at higher callings. I felt relieved.

The decision to move *Weekend* to prime time had been made before Silverman joined NBC, but the move took place after he arrived. What then happened to us may not even have been due to Silverman, but to Paul Klein, who was chief programming executive when Silverman arrived and whom he kept. Klein was a brilliant, acerbic man, trained as a statistician from which it was only a small step to ratings analyst, and then, being expert in public moods and whims, a programmer. He was neither first nor last to travel this path to the power to choose what is seen. He had little respect for the audience or for what he put on the air. He would find it illogical to withhold a program he knew would reach a large audience because he himself found it offensive. *Weekend* did not seem promising to Paul Klein.

This series, which we were told to move into prime time, and which everyone knew would have to establish itself with unshakable regularity to survive, was put, by Klein, at 10:00 P.M. Sunday, September 10, 1978—a good time. Then *Thursday*, October 12. Silverman interfered little with Klein's scheduling but was part of the decision. Silverman, so new to NBC, acted as though he had been there all his life: He gave News a crumb and told the press it was a pie. We skipped all of November but were on all five Saturdays in December. By December it was too late. He or Klein or a minion had already pointed out to the press that *Weekend* was getting lower ratings than any other series on NBC. It was duly noted and printed.

The beginning had seemed so auspicious. With mankind's first test-tube baby about to be born, we had bought American rights to a British network's exclusive, and made our story of that harbinger of revolution, the infant Louise Brown. Craig Leake talked his way into joining a team of college students recruited for the summer to sell Bibles door to door in the back hills of Tennessee, forcing on poor farmers' wives more than they could afford, or sent home for not making their quotas. Mr. Hipp sought romance again, and struck out again.

Fred Silverman called to say it was wonderful, he followed it up in writing: "*Weekend* was wonderful. Best, Fred." He added: "How would you like to produce the rest of our schedule?" The rest of his schedule was doing badly. NBC programs were yanked after a week or two. ABC was still riding high. Nor was it Silverman's schedule. It was Paul Klein's. Fred was concentrating on 1978–79 while everyone asked how long he could keep his hands off the current year. As Klein floundered, we suffered. He had faith in movies, and when it was only us, would let them run long, forcing us to cut back, so that one edition of *Weekend* ran forty minutes, one twenty-nine, and one eighteen.

The turmoil at the top accelerated. A former IBM public affairs vice president named Jane Cahill Pfeiffer, who as an RCA consultant had later been Griffiths's go-between with Silverman, became NBC chairman, moving Julian Goodman first aside then out. As chairman, she reported to Silverman as president, and sat on the RCA board, a unique, upside-down arrangement so that RCA need not publish Silverman's salary. Pfeiffer was a moralist, cutting a cruel swath through the NBC unit managers, some of whom had indeed been stealing and some of whom had kept quiet rather than lose their jobs. It was a messy situation that had gone on too long, but her handling of it broadened the definition of culprit and showed no sensitivity to a wounded organization. She discovered other transgressions for which people should be fired. Some wag dug into her past as a former religious to coin her widely used nickname: Attila the Nun.

NBC entertainment, meanwhile, held to a comfortable third.

Through all this Silverman moved in a cloud of smoke and panic, a flabby man, not as short as he seemed, the rumpled suits of ABC legend now rumpled expensive suits. Affiliates began leaving NBC, some of the best and oldest in the network, associated with NBC since the early Sarnoff days. One was KSTP-TV, Minneapolis–St. Paul. Reluctant as he was to make time for such matters, Silverman was dragooned by his affiliate relations department to fly to Minnesota to welcome the new (weaker) affiliate with a big party and a press conference. A local reporter asked about *Weekend* and Silverman said it would be on the NBC schedule forever. That was February 1979.

In March, Paul Klein was gone. Silverman had been moving in on his programs, shifting his beloved Big Events all around the schedule, going over Klein's head to his subordinates in Burbank, vetoing his decisions. Klein told the papers he quit; Silverman said he had not asked him to stay. One March week, ABC's total audience was larger than CBS's and NBC's combined—the margin itself equal to NBC's total! More affiliate defections threatened. Silverman was frantic as he tried to salvage what he could from that season's schedule and build one that would work for the following season. Anecdotes about his responses to the stress echoed around the building, about his marathon sessions with aides at Chinese restaurants absorbing vodka martinis and mountains of food, chain-smoking, talking, planning; his kicking the door when the elevator took too long; his surprise when he learned the Japanese singing sisters he had hired to star in their own series spoke no English; his hours in the boardroom that he had turned into his screening room, hour after hour into the night with tapes and films, pilots and episodes, two-hour epics and ten-second promotionals, and everywhere empty, soggy Chinese food cartons.

Newspapers had a fine time with all of this. The *New York Post* applied the sensibilities of tabloid editing as practiced in Sydney and London to the perils of *Supertrain*, the quintessential failed blockbuster, and to Silverman's inability to get a cabana at the Beverly Hills Hotel. Television stars had been good gossip since Milton Berle and Arthur Godfrey, but now television itself had become news—its executive shakeups, its ratings losers and winners, its competition, its internal squabbles. It was NBC's bad fortune to be wallowing at its nadir when this press interest reached full flower. One vice president noted plaintively that U.S. Steel's inner workings and executive changes drew less press attention, and it was true even with labor stories. Fifty broadcast technicians on a picket line get more space than shutting down an automobile plant.

By Silverman's good fortune some of that unwelcome attention was diverted by the troubles of NBC News. *NBC Nightly News* was suffering its worst ratings in years. The executive producer was replaced. Someone leaked to *Variety* that "Chancellor and Brinkley's days as co-anchors are numbered." To shore up, restore, enhance NBC News, Richard Salant, the CBS News president who like Frank Stanton had been forced to retire at sixty-five, joined NBC as vice chairman on May first. Jane Pfeiffer claimed credit for the coup. WTLV-TV, NBC's Jacksonville, Florida, affiliate for twenty-five years, switched to ABC.

All of us on *Weekend* knew the end was near. In March, I had received from Crystal a long, rambling memo that he had typed himself on yellow copy paper, no copies to anyone, saying it was his fault but *Weekend* should not have been moved intact to prime time, and could I make stories less unorthodox. I tried. We jettisoned our movie theater set for an austere abstraction in front of a large rear projection screen, which would give us the capacity for stills, maps, and graphics and lead us into and out of reports. (By consensus then current, news programs emanated from studios full of kidney shapes, like paisley ties.) We stopped using animated films.

Up top, there was talk of Tom Snyder. A *TV Guide* reporter called to ask if I was adding Snyder, or replacing Dobyns with him. I said only, "Tom Snyder and I are not in the same business." Snyder resented it.

We had not yet been canceled, so we carried on. I was in Washington to look at work of those producers—there were four or five of them, along with film editors, cameramen, a money manager, a productive little set-up that I visited at least once a week—when Crystal, also in Washington, called to suggest dinner. The Sheraton Carlton had a good steak sandwich, he said. At dinner he said, "Fred and I think that Tom Snyder might save that program."

I agreed he might, "But you will need a new executive producer."

"I expected I would," Crystal said.

I took the late plane to New York and told everyone there the next morning. I flew back to Washington and told everyone there in the afternoon. It was no longer news to them, but they were entitled to hear it from me. Our last program was in two weeks, April 22, 1979. A week earlier, Crystal had asked for help. As I knew, Schlosser had signed Gerald Ford for a lot lof money, which NBC was paying, and guarantees to show him on television, which Silverman declined to honor. Could Ellerbee or Dobyns interview him on the last program? I had sent them both to California for the interview, so they were the only ones I did not tell in person. They did the interview, then went out and got drunk. As requested, we used the interview on the last program. It was full of hot air. Few watched.

Snyder—who really said in his interview with *Hustler*'s publisher Larry Flynt, "When I say you're a pornographer I don't mean that in a bad light"—did a different version of a newsmagazine for about a year, but the ratings did not improve. Then David Brinkley was muscled into doing it, against his inclinations and judgment, by yet another president of NBC News. (Crystal had been fired in August 1979.) Brinkley brought it occasional flashes but not enough to matter. Then it was reporters doing only their own stories, the way *60 Minutes* does it, but that, too, got nowhere.

Crystal had never fit Silverman's idea of a news division president, the job he had once sought for himself. So he ordered Salant to find a president for news or he, Silverman, would make him, Salant, do it himself. Salant hired William Small, who had been a senior vice president for him at CBS News and before that his Washington bureau chief, but who had been publicly ruled out of the succession when Salant left. When Bill Leonard succeeded Salant as CBS News president, Small was sent back to Washington as CBS's lobbying vice president, having nothing to do with news, taking congressmen to Baltimore to see major league baseball games.

As CBS's Washington bureau chief, Bill Small had won the loyalty of most reporters and producers in the bureau. He had fought their battles with New York and supported them. But with others he could be harsh and arbitrary, enough to make senior correspondents lobby against his succeeding Salant. Neither he nor the people who hired him made any bones about his being brought to NBC News to "kick ass"—as one NBC executive let himself be quoted—to clean house, to instill fear and holiness. I and others suspected he was trying to prove to his former bosses they should have made him president of CBS News. Among those he got rid of by firing or heavily persuaded retirement were Gary Stindt and Eliot Frankel. He kept Crystal on as senior vice president for special programs, like convention coverage and summit meetings. His dealings with me were never less than correct, occasionally pleasant, always professional.

When Crystal was fired and Small hired, I was on vacation, smarting about what had happened to *Weekend*. After I got back, Small came to see me unannounced. We had met over the years as one does in business, and I had admired some things he wrote. I told him I appreciated his coming to see me, which saved me writing a memo. I wanted to be excused from the time remaining on my contract so I could look for work. I did not want to stay after what had happened, none of which was his doing. He asked me to defer my request, to work up some ideas for documentaries, which he wanted to bring back, and if I still felt the same after that, well, I could quit then.

We were coming to the end of 1979. I looked on Silverman's NBC as a place I did not care to be, so I prepared to look for work. Friends warned me the atmosphere was not hospitable. I wondered about cable, that growing new thing. Surely they must in time need programs to put on their channels, perhaps even news and nonfiction. Ted Turner had newly begun CNN, but that seemed no more than television's version of all-news radio, or what social scientists and MBAs call "information retrieval."

I ventured into Westchester County, north of still cable-less New York City, to meet the man in charge of almost all the cable systems in that huge, rich area. He said his company did not plan to do its own programming, that it carried CNN and something he called C-SPAN, of which I had not yet heard, mostly live coverage of important Washington events, press conferences, meetings, and the like (later, live sessions of the House of Representatives and even in time of the Canadian and British Houses of Commons). I learned that distributors of cable service to homes were not where to look.

A friend provided an introduction to the head of Warner Cable. I came at the appointed hour but had to wait. Finally he emerged, somewhat nervous, apologized for the delay, said he was in an urgent meeting, and could I call back for another appointment? I went on my way, a little miffed. The next day's papers reported the merger of Warner Cable with the systems owned by American Express to form Warner-Amex. The man I was to see had been fired. His successor was Jack Schneider, once operating head of CBS, a man I knew the way one knows people in the same industry. I called, and he came on the telephone. I said I was getting restless where I was and looking for something new, and might I come by and talk.

He said, "You're always welcome to come by, but let me tell you, I figure I have one bite left of the apple, and I'm not going to fuck it up with news." I reexamined Bill Small's offer.

I spent two weeks working up program ideas. My last proposal, an afterthought, was the decline of American industrial productivity. Small chose that one. He let me have Dobyns as writer and reporter, Clare Crawford and Ray Lockhart, two old colleagues up through the ranks, as my producers, and we set out to make of arcane economics acceptable television for a general audience. Herbert Striner, whom I had met when he was a Brookings economist and was now dean of the School of Business at American University, showed us how the Japanese had revolutionized industrial production with just-in-time parts delivery, rethought methods, and the paternalism of their large companies. Above all, he sent us to W. Edwards Deming, a statistician whose production control methods were being ignored in the United States but avidly followed by the Japanese, who gave an annual prize to the company breaking new ground in productivity and quality, calling it the Deming Prize.

Our program dealt with the obstacles to American production that were caused by government interference—a plant was cited for an ungrounded typewriter even though it was not an electric typewriter; a man trying to grow abalone by fish-farming methods was put to enormous cost to keep their body wastes out of the Pacific Ocean— we showed companies improving productivity by involving the workers themselves in production and even personnel decisions.

Most of all, we showed Dr. Deming. To this day, I do not understand what he teaches, but a prophet without honor in his own country is a classic story always worth telling. We included his home movies, showing him towering over his Japanese hosts at six-feet five, lecturing, eating, getting flowers from little girls. Part of his method is that quality improves by constant attention and careful record keeping, and it never stops; lack of quality is never the fault of workers, always of management; inspection at the end of the line is too late to catch mistakes, and too expensive. We opened with panoramas of devastated Japan in 1945, cut to factories working all out, and called the program, *If Japan Can . . . Why Can't We?*

The program created a kind of uproar. Although the audience was no more than high-average for a documentary, it had an afterlife like no other program in my experience. We got thousands of requests for transcripts; the company that sells NBC News program films and tapes for private use was swamped with orders. Major companies—Xerox, Kodak, General Motors, General Electric—bought copies. Some copied theirs by the hundreds for management training sessions. Years later, it was still being shown to management classes at graduate schools of business, Harvard, Chicago, Yale.

We made Deming a star. Into his eighties, he would get more consultancy requests than he could satisfy, and his fees became stratospheric. In the coming decade, *Fortune* or *Business Week*, writing about a major manufacturer solving its production problems, several times included the executive who saw "an NBC documentary" and called a meeting, or fired a vice president, or hired Deming. As for me, I had found myself a niche, economics—not stock tips—done for television my way: film telling a story.

While I was in my protected corner, my foxhole, Small was making changes in NBC News. He started by hiring people from CBS. The first famous one was Marvin Kalb, the State Department correspondent, and his brother Bernard. Not only did Marvin get more money than CBS News was prepared to offer, but guaranteed appearances on *NBC Nightly News*, which were rumored in the press and (falsely) denied. Some executives, one in charge of documentaries, a couple in press and promotion, were also brought over from CBS as well as some lesser-known reporters. He made a woman who had been one of his producers a vice president of NBC News as well as his assistant and the operating head of the division. He tried to hire Lesley Stahl, the CBS White House reporter. Small was telling NBC News that at CBS things were done better. He fired vice presidents, let correspondents' contracts lapse without renewing them, and refused to review Clare Crawford's.

The biggest noise he made was hiring Roger Mudd, for years CBS News's chief congressional correspondent, the presumed heir to Cronkite. Not only Mudd himself but everyone at CBS had thought he was, and he was so described publicly. It was then that Dan Rather, who had joined the *60 Minutes* troupe after making a name as CBS's White

House correspondent during the Nixon years, was wooed by Roone Arledge to be anchor of the ABC evening news program. When CBS offered the now standard seven figures, Rather insisted on anchoring the evening news. This, too, was accepted. Walter Cronkite was retired, and both he and Roger Mudd were left out in the cold.

Mudd fired his agent. He sulked in his tent. For months. Small, who had been his bureau chief and friend those many years, got him to come to NBC, to report from Washington for *Nightly News*, but he must have in writing that he would succeed Chancellor, a contract, not a mere promise. What happened at CBS must not happen again. There was a reunion in Small's apartment for which Mrs. Mudd baked a cake. The 1979–80 season was now over, with NBC still third; Silverman and Pfeiffer had quarreled publicly and she had been forced out after a lot of unseemly charges in the newspapers. Turmoil was back.

ABC, which had been using 11:30 each evening for reports on the American hostages held in the embassy in Tehran, a presumed two-week project that lasted fifteen months, cashed in on the attention it gathered to turn it into a nightly program called *Nightline*. NBC, meanwhile, was no longer doing Instant Specials in prime time, holding them until 11:30, now opposite *Nightline*. Also, by Johnny Carson's contract, his program had to begin before midnight whatever the emergency, or be junked, commercials and all. Producers of NBC News's Instant Specials learned to end at 11:56, to leave time for a station break before the tape of Carson's program rolled.

In January 1981, Edgar Griffiths and the RCA board agreed that he leave. The board had been hunting for a successor for a year, even hiring one of its members to do the search. To succeed Griffiths, he chose a fellow-director, Thornton F. Bradshaw, Jr., president of Atlantic-Richfield and a former Harvard Business School professor. One of the directors anonymously told the *Wall Street Journal* that one fault they had found with Griffiths was his making Silverman chief executive at NBC, which the director said Silverman had not asked for. But since Silverman had come to look to Griffiths for support, he now told friends his days at NBC were numbered.

At around this time, Roone Arledge offered Tom Brokaw work and money. Brokaw had been a local news anchorman in Los Angeles, then network White House correspondent during most of the Watergate story, and had since been host of *Today*. His contract was up and he was looking for bigger things—like *Nightly News*. When Small seemed unimpressed, Brokaw turned to his Los Angeles friend and tennis partner, Thornton Bradshaw, complaining Bill Small would not talk to him. Silverman was in Aspen, Colorado, at the time, on a panel examining Media and the Future of Humanity, or some such thing. During a coffee break he told an associate that NBC might lose Brokaw, and with all its other bad news this would be devastating. He, Silverman, expected to be fired soon, so he was going to Hawaii, but could the associate look into the Brokaw mess, please.

The associate went on to Los Angeles, where he instructed the entertainment division's chief negotiator to take the matter away from Bill Small and settle it. The negotiator began by booking himself next to Brokaw's agent, Ed Hookstratten, on the redeye, the overnight flight to New York. Once in New York, the agent and the negotiator met during the day. Unknown to the negotiator, the agent and Bradshaw were also discussing Brokaw's contract, at night, in the Dorset Hotel suite used by Bradshaw until he could move East. On his own, Mudd approached Bradshaw to say he would not invoke his contractual right to succeed Chancellor if Brokaw could be kept at NBC by having him and Brokaw co-anchoring. Brokaw got his seven-figure contract; Chancellor was invited to be a commentator, which his contract foresightedly guaranteed; Small announced that Brokaw and Mudd would anchor *NBC Nightly News* jointly, one in New York, one in Washington, with commentary from John Chancellor.

Bradshaw all this time was trying to find a replacement for Silverman. He found him in Grant Tinker, long ago a vice president in NBC's program department, then co-founder and president of the program producing company bearing the name of Mary Tyler Moore, and for much of that time married to her. He was cool, experienced, a Yankee, a straight arrow—Bradshaw's type. Bradshaw allowed him to continue living in Los Angeles, commuting to New York to spend three and a half days a week. (At the same time, Bradshaw was trimming down RCA by getting rid of all but its manufacturing and communications businesses. That was his plan and he stuck to it. It worked. The plan, combined with Tinker's ultimate success at NBC, restored RCA's wealth and reputation.) Tinker would be chairman and chief executive of NBC. Bob Mulholland, who was then president of the Network division, would be NBC's president.

Feelings between Mulholland and Small had never been cordial. The only time they acted in harmony was when they went together to Tinker to tell him David Brinkley wanted to leave, and were nonplussed when he did not seem disturbed. They did not know that Brinkley had earlier asked Tinker to be allowed to go quietly. Brinkley saw nothing at NBC for him to do. His departure was a damaging public black eye for NBC. When Roone Arledge approached him with a Sunday morning "public affairs" show that would be more rounded, more sophisticated, more complex, and better produced than the relics hanging on by inertia, Brinkley found a new career—at ABC.

What else occurred between Mulholland and Small I do not know. Nor do I really know why Mulholland wanted to fire Small, how he got Tinker to agree, or why he turned to me to take over, three separate questions. On January 27, *Variety* said it had talked to the managers of seven NBC affiliates whose consensus favored Bill Small and exhorted "the NBC brass . . . to finally start doing something about the rumor control offices on the fifth floor [NBC News] of Thirty Rock where word keeps leaking out that Small is out."

Mulholland and I had lunch. He had called once in September, but I could not make it, and then he could not make it and then he had to travel as network executives do and it was February 1 before we were both free. We spent no more than five minutes talking about the old days before he got to the point: Would I be willing to replace Small as president of NBC News? Tom Pettit, a skilled reporter and an old friend and colleague of both of ours, would be my executive vice president, and we would run the division together. I sensed that he wanted me to train Pettit, and also that had I said no Pettit would have been his choice, but Mulholland did not say either of those things. What he said was that he wanted me to be president of NBC News. I said I needed time to think about it.

15

It took me a month to agree to be president of NBC News again. My misgivings were many, but obvious: I was getting too old for that kind of tension; I would not be in editing rooms and other places I enjoyed; above all, there was nothing in it for me, not money, not prestige, nothing but the prospect of doing less well than last time while heads shook sadly. On the other hand, it was a challenge; I felt obliged; documentaries were becoming unexciting. If nothing else, I thought, it would be easier than last time because now I was a known quantity. This time, what I stood for must have been what they wanted or they should not have asked me. I had not changed. I, who had once been known as a pain in the ass, was now seen to represent the good old days.

I insisted Mulholland arrange that Pettit and I hear what Grant Tinker thought. Tinker was the boss, and he must talk to us as least once. To escape prying eyes, the four of us—Tinker, Mulholland, Pettit, and I—met for dinner in the University Club, in its exquisite dining room, where gentlemen did not discuss business. When I asked Tinker what he expected of his News division, he was vague, apparently never having thought of it that way. I got the sense that firing Small had been Mulholland's idea, even that Tinker might be less than completely happy with it. Also, I learned later that when he allowed Mulholland to get rid of Small he had his own candidate to succeed him. As to my question, he would venture only that he would like to see NBC News back where it used to be, with morale repaired. News was important to NBC. He wished us well.

I truly expected to be left alone to do what I thought I had been recruited for—reprofessionalize the division, restore morale, attend to basics. Despite all the talk, news is a simpleton's business, its rules easily expressed and understood. The press was friendly, with *Variety* noting in surprise that NBC had finally kept a secret; not a word had leaked out in the month since Mulholland's first approach. Former senator Abraham Ribicoff, whom I had met once—in Vanocur's house—wrote me a warm note saying he had been in our Washington bureau when the announcement was made and there was dancing in the corridors. It made pleasant reading although I knew the dancing was for Small's departure, not my arrival. Marvin Kalb and others Small had brought over from CBS later admitted fearing for their physical safety that day. They felt they had witnessed a coup.

Only days later, the NBC affiliates' board of delegates came to New York for their regular meeting with Tinker and the other managers. Dinner was in a private room at "21," first exotic appetizers, as we stood amid the Remington statuary, followed by bloody steaks and costly wines. One of the owners of "21" said I had been missed; it was my fourth time in his building. What the affiliates thought of my appointment I was never to know, but the one beside me, from the Sunbelt, enjoying the wine more than the steak, slapped my back all evening repeating that I was a winner because I talked like a winner and thought like a winner. "A winner," he kept muttering, "a winner." He was concerned about the *Today* ratings.

And what concerned affiliates is what concerned NBC management. While Tinker was occupied with fixing prime time, aided by his young programming chief, Brandon Tartikoff, and a staff that swelled by mitosis—vice president of Monday comedies, vice president of Wednesday tragedies, vice president of neither long nor short series— those administrators I dealt with had more complex problems. As daunting as finding television hits may appear, it is terra firma compared to the quicksands of holding affiliates against competitors' wiles, getting them to clear low-rated series when Billy Graham will pay a relative fortune for showing him, having enough stations carry a program to retain advertisers. Keeping affiliates for NBC had become the first priority of the NBC News division president.

While Mulholland was scheming to get rid of Small and I was brooding about his offer, Ted Turner upset my plans and set my agenda for at least a year. Weeks before I took over, Turner, tycoon of the established but not yet profitable Cable News Network (CNN), had invited station managers to Atlanta to see how CNN gathered news, news they could buy as programs or incorporate into their own news shows. Turner needed income urgently and would sell to anyone.

Only a few bought, but dozens of NBC's affiliates called Bob Mulholland or the president of the Network division, Ray Timothy, with teasing tales of how this could free them from network news and perhaps of networks altogether, of how rich they would become buying and scheduling for themselves. Timothy insisted it was up to me to do something, and do it right away.

And here I had thought the problems I had been sought out to solve were those of *NBC Nightly News* and *Today* and the morale and performance of the only staff within NBC—or at any network—that produced its own programs. (Sports no less than Entertainment buys or rents what it shows.) *Nightly News* was headed into uncharted waters. In a month, John Chancellor was to hand over the anchor chair to Tom Brokaw and Roger Mudd, not because of any shortcoming on Chancellor's part but because Small had seduced Mudd from CBS with the promise of an anchor chair and Brokaw had been snatched back from defecting to ABC with the same promise.

As for *Today*, not only had it lost its morning monopoly, but ABC's program, *Good Morning, America*, softer, more down market, full of "news you can use," was comfortably ahead in the ratings and had been for some time. Small's stratagem, auditioning Brokaw's many possible successors on the air, which had taken months, had decimated the audience. The morning audience watches with half an eye, listens with one ear, and only wants to know what's going on and is it going to rain. The final result was a three-headed anchor, Chris Wallace, a feisty reporter, Small's choice; Bryant Gumbel, a skilled network sports broadcaster, Mulholland's candidate; and Jane Pauley, who, in her own way, had occupied the Barbara Walters chair when Brokaw was anchor. They alternated reading the news from day to day, and rotated asking questions of the day's "big" interview.

I had thought my other problems would be the reporting staff, grown sullen about too much direction and second guessing from New York, and the relaxation of its standards of writing. These problems must have been why Mulholland and Tinker had turned to me, because they were the kinds of problems I had handled pretty well last time. But they were not to be my first concern. The marching orders I had so vainly sought while debating whether to accept the job came in full flood the moment I entered it: keep the affiliates happy and fight off Ted Turner.

Despite its unenviable position as the third-ranked network with the most to lose, NBC was last into this battle. CBS was already planning a news-cum-talk show to occupy the empty hours between 2:00 and 5:00 A.M. ABC was reported planning a newscast to go before *Good Morning, America*, which would, in the minds of schedulers, hold an audience for the program itself and give it an even greater edge over *Today*. And what were Pettit and I, not even knowing yet what our budget was, going to do about it? (I savored the implied recognition that only news can hold affiliates because only news defines networks. But it would not help us when we needed it. "For it's Tommy this, and Tommy that, and Tommy go away. But it's 'Thank you, Mister Atkins' when the band begins to play.")

What we did about it was to organize as fast as we could some news to precede *Today* plus a late night news program and to expand the news picture package we distributed to affiliated stations. That package had begun in the early fifties, when ABC network television news was still of little consequence and CBS still bought its newsfilm from an outside supplier. An NBC executive began making a daily newsreel out of newsfilm ignored as secondary or excessive by the *News Caravan*, what print people call "overset." This he sold to what were still a mere handful of stations who produced newscasts of their own and had it delivered by the U.S. mails, rarely in good time.

In time, this accommodation to affiliates grew, flourished, and was copied by the other networks. Since the cable and microwave links that in those days formed the physical network stayed connected around the clock, whether programs were being fed out or not, we started sending these syndicated newsfilms during network down time. It was never a major effort, assigned serious resources, or involving our best people. (In fact, it was a good place to park those who could not be fired.) The stations, however, grew to like it and depend on it, even to make demands. More sports, they would say, or more personality stories, and, invariably, less of that there foreign news. From the beginning, the Network would not let us make back our costs, so what they got was virtually free. Then we took to supplying bulletins when major stories broke in time for their eleven o'clock local news. When they asked that we do it every night whether news was worth a bulletin or not, we did.

In 1973, when I handed over to Dick Wald, I advised him not to devote too much to the syndication service but never let it go. Perish the thought, but it might in time be all that was left of NBC News. Now, nine years later, I was beefing it up, assigning good people to it, allowing it access to pictures that would be important to that night's *Nightly News*, ordering correspondents to report for it, adding a second feed of stories each day, expanding the eleven o'clock bulletin, anything to keep affiliates from deserting us for Turner.

The budget I had inherited from Bill Small, the budget I had not yet even seen, went immediately into deficit. I asked Ray Timothy to increase the stations' subscription fee, but he considered that unwise. I complained that this large unanticipated expense had nothing to do with sudden news, where unanticipated expenses are anticipated. He gave me a subvention of half a million dollars from his division's funds. This is all, of course, moving internal charges around, mere accounting, "funny" or "Chinese" money, but from time immemorial managers were instructed to take it as seriously as cash, and reputations might be made and broken by it. RCA, characteristically, could never tell the difference. With the first signs of success, Ray Timothy told the affiliates NBC would cut their compensation (for carrying network programs with commercials in them) to balance "enhanced news costs" but they raised such a howl he added a thirty-second commercial to *Nightly News* instead. Nor was I warned the time for news on my key news program was being reduced.

The newscast to precede *Today* was simpler to do. I told Steve Friedman, the executive producer, his responsibilities had expanded and left him to it. Gumbel and Pauley would alternate coming in early to do a half-hour newscast that would begin at 6:00 in the morning—and be played on tape at 6:30 to some stations. We omitted Wallace to save the overtime cost of opening the Washington studio an hour earlier; New York was cost enough. Gumbel and Pauley hated the hours, and it showed. Friedman complained that it detracted from their more important work. We called the new newscast *Early Today*.

ABC was making vague noises about a talk and interview program to follow *Nightline*, and CBS had already announced it would do something called *Nightwatch* for three predawn hours, and what were we going to do about it? Pettit and I had just arrived. We were still in the planning stage on our news programs and luckily I already knew my way to the bathroom or I should not have had time to look for it. I wanted a real program, not just another headline wrap-up or still another package of good news material given gratis to disloyal and hypocritical affiliates so they could use our reporters and our pictures before we did.

So my late-night entry in the crack-the-whip game of network news expansion would be a news program as I understood the term. But I had no budget for a news program. Nor would anyone give me any to pay for professionalism, authority, or style. That was not what the affiliates threatened to get from Turner, so that was not what was wanted from us. Nor would there be a nickel for special coverage or for anything other than the material in the flow coming out of NBC News every hour of every day as it went about its business around the world, as the people we worked for thought of it.

I assigned Lloyd Dobyns and Linda Ellerbee, who were already under contract to NBC News and so involved no extra cost. As producer, I assigned Herb Dudnick, who had climbed all the steps and been through the mill of a basic news organization but had emerged with his iconoclasm still intact. I announced that any pictures we got could be taped by affiliates for later use. This got me some money for a studio to broadcast from, and a little more for staff. Dudnick recruited beginners and out-of-favor oldsters. We were assigned no office space, so Dudnick turned half the studio into a newsroom where Dobyns and Ellerbee and the rest worked. They broadcast at their desks. The studio's dressing rooms became such private offices as were needed. After an hour of Johnny Carson and an hour of David Letterman would come *Overnight*.

Its mandates were: to be cheap—for its entire short career it was the cheapest program on the NBC network, at whatever hour, even when it was canceled for costing too much; to be a news program; to be well written; to be interesting. From 1:30 to 2:30 A.M., nursing mothers and insomniacs would get the best and best-written review of the day's news in all of American television. (Shortly after it was canceled it received the Alfred DuPont–Columbia University Award for just those reasons. A program getting a big award after it is canceled is a television cliché.)

Without money, Dudnick enlisted NBC News's bureaus and affiliate newsrooms for their best material, the most ingenious, the most telling. When a plane crashed in New Orleans, he switched to the New Orleans station reporting to the New Orleans audience, and stayed with them. Who better? From Canada, France, West Germany, the rest of Europe, East and West, he got, by traditional exchange arrangements or the pleading of our bureaus, tapes of their major stories, which he ran in their languages with English subtitles. In affiliate station editing rooms reporters and film editors stayed up late cutting for *Overnight*, competing to be on it. The writing was civilized, the reporting thorough, the attitude detached, the wit never too far submerged. The spirit of *Weekend* lived—in the low-rent district in the middle of the night. Again, newspaper writers clutched it to their thin bosoms. And I, who had also to watch *Today* and *Early Today* as part of my work, could only tape it to view in the morning, beaming like a proud parent.

The expanded syndicated service started almost immediately in April. We announced the beginning of *Early Today* and *Overnight* for Monday, July 5. CBS and ABC, who had not announced dates, struggled to catch up. Television's "news explosion" became a hot-weather story in the newspapers. Less than a year and a half later, as 1983 was ending, I was summoned to a meeting. Among those present was the adder, adding. He said *Overnight* was not making money and projected that it would never make money. By that time, I had replaced Dobyns so I could assign him to a revived newsmagazine; Herb Dudnick had begged off because of what the hours were doing to his life, and I gave him a new assignment; Ellerbee had warned me she would not do it much longer. The replacements worked well, but I had no heart for a fight. With Mulholland at my side, I delivered the coup de grace in person to the *Overnight* staff.

NBC Nightly News had other problems. Less than a month after I replaced Small, his arrangement for Brokaw and Mudd to become the joint anchors took effect with Chancellor shunted aside. Chancellor's contract, which did not protect him from summary treatment, did ensure that he would continue on the program as a commentator— three or four times a week *on his initiative*, with virtually no say from the editorial hierarchy of the program.

The organization ground out the news satisfactorily enough, but as the weeks went by I began to get misgivings about how the program "worked," an inadequate term that frustrated the principals and the executive producer when I used it. But I was a producer by trade, and to my taste the components of the program did not add up. Why was

Mudd in Washington and Brokaw in New York if, the way stories fell, Mudd might well report on what was happening in Asia and Brokaw on that day's doings in the Senate—"report" meaning introducing another reporter's words and pictures. I thought I felt a slavish mechanical equality—or perhaps I knew too much—of the executive producer's care in alternating the lead story between them from one day to the next, even ensuring that each was seen and heard no longer than the other, and if one day provided an imbalance to make it up the next.

On the surface things seemed to be working well. Brokaw, always the boy scout, tried to be interested in everything; Mudd, in contrast, stuck to his work and dealt minimally with all those around him. I first thought this was due to the shock to his system when CBS, where he had been heir apparent to Walter Cronkite for a decade, dumped him at the last minute and enthroned Dan Rather. Soon I would be hearing about people who did not want to work with him. But I found no fault with what I saw, and he wrote well.

The first big story of the new program was the British-Argentine war over the Falkland Islands when Margaret Thatcher and the British general staff combined to shut out the press. Soon after, timed to disrupt an economic summit meeting, the Israelis invaded Lebanon. As their troops moved farther north, crossing the Litani River, their stated objective, and clearly aimed at total victory, it grew more and more difficult for reporters to keep up, and the pictures made Israel look bad. Bombing military targets in cities can never avoid civilian casualties, which we showed, among other things. The Israelis' own confusion and debate over their war aims were necessarily echoed in our reporting.

Israel's powerful and experienced American friends rose up in wrath against the media, especially television, and most especially NBC. Chancellor, seated on a pile of rubble in Beirut referring in his commentary to "imperial Israel . . . not the Israel we knew," remained for years a special target. Israel's supporters, who once to brilliant effect promoted to American journalism a country that was different, ethical, and democratic, now berated us for our "double standard." A *Jerusalem Post* reporter came by to ask me if I was a self-hating Jew; in Rockefeller Plaza pickets denounced me by name, their leaflets saying my father would have been horrified; the head of NBC's little security force offered to escort me out a back door so I could go to lunch.

If the Israelis had applied the rules Mrs. Thatcher had in the Falklands, and Reagan established in Grenada, their troubles, and so their friends' anger, would have been less. The undeniable fact was that for four years there had been, in all news media, too little reporting of what had gone before, of the Palestine Liberation Organization's sub-suming Lebanon like a parasitic growth, sucking dry its institutions and destroying its internal order, quite apart from threatening Israel. The answer to such criticism always sounds feeble, worse if the subject is important: Journalism's dirty big secret is it cannot cover where it is denied access.

That noted, we did well on most big stories—on the Falklands, on the invasion of Lebanon. We got the news, reported it, got it on the air. Although this is the indispensable basis, it is never enough. There is little difference among network news programs in the news they report, certainly in the major news. It is how they differ that attracts, or loses, viewers. It is easy to preach against "ratings-driven" news programs, but even critics talk about communications, which means communicating to *somebody*. Who would broadcast the perfect news program if convinced nobody would be watching? I felt *Nightly News* was not working as a program. I could not explain it; I just felt it.

Affiliates, who had welcomed the pairing of Mudd and Brokaw, began to grow restive, and for NBC, lower ratings meant less money. Mulholland would call on the executive intercom each morning. It would be buzzing as I arrived at my desk, conditioning my stomach to ache when I heard it. I once asked Mulholland why he never spoke to me in English, only in numbers—how much over budget, how far behind in the ratings. But I was as frustrated as he.

Pettit rented a meeting room in a hotel in the Berkshires, between Brokaw's weekend place and my more modest one, where I invited him and Mudd and the executive producer, Paul Greenberg, to talk about what was wrong. Mudd saw no problem; the others were not sure what I was driving at, even Pettit. Mudd said we gave the news better than anyone else. I kept saying, "But it's not a program." It was a strained session. We broke up in the dusk of a July Saturday, shaking hands all around, Mudd complaining he had to drive back to New York, then fly to Washington. Someone told the *Washington Post*, which reported it as some sort of cabal.

By the spring of 1983, with the pairing a year old, I felt I had to do something: Not for the ratings, because it is my belief that a good news program will find its audience in time, and not for the affiliates, who had taken to offering advice about a pairing that "didn't jell" and why didn't I put both in the same studio so they could chat and banter the way they did on their local news? My best conclusion was that pairing these two powerful anchors, both strong broadcasters and journalists, was not working because it made no sense. I could find no other reason. So, one of them had to go.

That was the easy decision. The difficult one was, which one? Mudd wrote and spoke better but did not ad lib well; Brokaw was at his best without a script, covering events live, the world falling down around him. Since it was now traditional that whoever anchored the network's evening news would anchor convention and election coverage—and that was next year!—the decision made itself. But the contract Small had given Mudd specified that he would anchor NBC's evening news program when Chancellor stopped. I took my problem to NBC's general counsel who turned to NBC's high-powered outside law firm. I brought other contracts that annoyed me, in which more than terms of agreement and compensation were dealt with, contracts which specified that journalists would be guaranteed they would appear on television whether or not they had any news.

Jessica Savitch was guaranteed she would anchor the Saturday news. Marvin Kalb, the State Department correspondent, had been lured from CBS by Small with not only more money but a guarantee he would be on *Meet the Press* every week, become its moderator when the current one left, and, last and most burdensome, appear on *NBC Nightly News* three times a week, on any topic he liked. (Greenberg would call and say, "I'm not using Marvin tonight. He doesn't have anything. It's just some rehashed thumb-sucker. He'll call you." Then Marvin would call: "I don't like reminding you that my contract specifies . . ." Sometimes I mollified him; when I didn't I had to call Greenberg and tell him to throw out a story and use Kalb.) Also John Chancellor's contract, which provided that commentary was his decision alone. There were others. I considered guaranteeing time on the air an outrage, and whoever had agreed to it wickedly irresponsible. It left an executive producer arriving in the morning with half his show committed before he knew what the news was, and as for me, president of the division, I could not make decisons I judged in the division's interest without breaching somebody's contract.

When I returned to the NBC chief lawyer's office, the "outside" lawyers were there, one old and small, one young and large. I not only outlined the facts; I pleaded, as though before a judge, to be allowed to make changes in the News division in the exercise of my responsibility. We assembled again in two weeks. The verdict was in my favor: pay or play. I did not have to put anyone on television, only pay them—except for Chancellor, whose contract was so written he could comment away with no one gainsaying him. I took the news to Mulholland and Tinker, whom I had kept informed all along, and said I would drop Mudd from the program. Again, I sensed that Tinker did not wholly approve, but again he did not say so.

The next step was to talk to Mudd's agent, Ralph Mann, who was also my agent, when I had an agent, and whom I fired each time I entered management. Mudd had turned to Mann when he blamed his former agent, a man named Cooper, for losing the Cronkite inheritance, something beyond any agent's capacity. Mann had then negotiated a fat contract for Mudd with a willing Bill Small, and now I was proposing to breach it. I told him I had been informed I was not in breach. He wanted to know by whom, hinted vaguely as suing. That was his right, I said, but I was sure enough to go to the next step, informing Mudd. Don't you tell Mudd, Mann insisted. I'll tell him. Although I boast of not shirking unpleasant duties, I do not enjoy them. Mann volunteered; I let Mann tell him.

Mudd's reaction was shock and anger. "This is some kind of monstrous joke," he kept saying. He was wounded at what he saw as a repetition of what CBS had done to him, although they were not really similar events. To him, this was his second humiliation.

I had gone to Washington to testify, along with the other networks, before a House subcommittee investigating exit polling, the growing practice of sampling voters as they left the polls. Results were being projected with astonishing accuracy while voting was still going on, and many congressmen wanted it stopped. They were chiefly upset at television's declaring the winner of the last presidential election with polls still open in the West, to which they attributed defeat of friends lower down on the ticket. The chairman, Congressman (later Senator) Tim Wirth of Colorado, a Ph.D. and a management consultant, gave us a hard time, as did Congressman Al Swift of Washington, a former TV station editorial reader. No one ever proved anything, but Bill Small, at the last hearing, had used the term anecdotal to describe some testimony. Swift thought Small was accusing him of telling jokes, and I was Small's successor.

I don't like what advancing technology has done to election nights; it has made them uninteresting. But there is no way to stop it. I told Wirth not to ask us to withhold any information we judged reliable.

I said we were unschooled in withholding information. If they had to do something, they could pass a law. We obeyed laws. Otherwise, we would keep on using exit polls. My successor reneged on that, apparently finding some higher good than the free flow of information. One always needs friends in Congress.

After that, instead of lunch, I met Roger Mudd in a room borrowed from the NBC lobbying office. He asked for "some kind of explanation" for what had been done to him. I told him it was no reflection on his work or professional competence but, rather, my subjective feeling that the program would benefit from the change, and that the program was my first responsibility. We would be happy to find other projects for him and consider any he suggested. He answered angrily that he had volunteered to share with Brokaw, that he had told Bradshaw he was willing to do that if it would keep Brokaw. I said I understood that, and had not decided lightly, but I could not put even that consideration before what I saw as the good of the program. He later told reporters I had said my decision was "subjective," which was duly printed as a pejorative term, and that he thought I was "shortsighted." He insisted he had done nothing wrong.

One can understand his distress, but it made no difference that he had done nothing wrong. They always fall back on that to be judged on, this small, select group who are paid like basketball stars or stock manipulators but, when adversity strikes, complain, Have I not arms, eyes, organs, dimensions? as though that were the argument. Once they have reached that level of money, they forget how unusual it is, and ignore what they are getting it for. A fraction pays for their competence and unique talents, and for doing "nothing wrong." The rest, inescapably, is paid because the network expects to get it back—many times. It is an investment.

We concluded our meeting by his telling me that one of his sons had called, a marine captain, he said proudly, and at the end of the call had said to him, "Tell them to go fuck themselves." And that is how Roger Mudd told me to go fuck myself. We shook hands and parted. I flew back not knowing what he would do: refuse to work as he had for months after CBS had announced Rather would succeed Cronkite; or pick a role he might enjoy in the coming presidential year; or ask to be paid off or to do documentaries. These were only a few of the possibilities as I made my way to New York. Back in my office, I told Pettit and then Brokaw, who promised I would never regret the trust I was showing in him. Then I asked my secretary to order me a sandwich and an iced tea. I felt sorry for myself.

The ratings went down and then up and then down, and then wavered, so that it was after I had handed over to my successor that they reached their high point and sustained it for a while, but it was clear to me that it had become a better program. The news was no different, obviously, but how it was presented made more sense. Quite probably, the program would also have been better if it had been Mudd doing it alone. But that would have meant Mudd anchoring the primaries about to descend on us, and the conventions and election night to follow, a chance I could not take.

The program was better because it was simpler. The problem I tried to solve on *Nightly News* was thus no different from the problem I had to solve on *Today*. The way the work was distributed made no sense; add to that, in the case of *Today*, a feeling of no one in charge, which consensus holds vitally important on that sort of program. Also, if *Nightly News* had gone through deterioration, *Today* had lived through melodrama. First, at about the time Nixon resigned, Barbara Walters had defected to ABC. That set in motion a complete set of changes: Tom Brokaw, the White House correspondent during Watergate, was brought to New York to be the *Today* anchor to replace Jim Hartz, and then Jane Pauley was promoted from Chicago local anchor to work with Brokaw. At first, the program foundered in the ratings, as all do when there is a change, especially the morning programs.

Next, Silverman succeeded Schlosser as president of NBC; Small succeeded Crystal who had succeeded Wald as president of NBC News; and the *Today* executive producer, who was feuding with Brokaw, was succeeded by someone from management who did not know how to produce. Everyone named in the preceding sentence had his own idea of how *Today* should be done. Finally, there arrived a new executive producer, Steve Friedman, *Today*'s brash regional producer in Los Angeles. No sooner had he got the ratings up than Brokaw left.

Brokaw was then succeeded by three people—because Small wanted Wallace, Mulholland and Friedman wanted Gumbel, and the third, Jane Pauley, could not be slighted without offending feminist sensibilities. Politically, three was the perfect solution. As television it was awful, disconcerting, pointless. It also was disastrous in the ratings. When I later asked Friedman how he, with his feel for television, had allowed it to happen, he said, "I didn't know Small was going to be fired." Again, the ratings were trouble enough, but even if they were better I was struck by what bad television the program had become. There was a leadenness to the way things were presented, a sense of artificial, arithmetical balance.

The affiliates at their spring 1983 convention applauded Pettit and me for all the things we told them we were doing and would do for them, without charge, but were disturbed by *Today*'s ratings. (One issue I had not anticipated was what would I do about Jane Pauley's hair. She has a round face, full lips, a small nose, and wore her thick dark-blond hair long, so that she looked like a doll peeping out of a haystack. By the time of the meeting, she had cut her hair, but I was still asked, as Small had been, to do something. A decade before, inspired by Spiro Agnew, affiliates had howled to rid NBC News of subversive influences and me. Now, they wanted something done about Jane Pauley's hair.)

With *Today* as with *Nightly News*, the obvious solution involved unpleasant confrontation. Friedman, who wanted it to happen, was sure I would chicken out of it, or be talked out of it, or be ordered not to. I informed Tinker and Mulholland, making it clear I was not asking for permission. I had lunch with Gumbel, told him what I intended, and asked him to keep it to himself. I booked a suite in a Washington hotel—normally I find one room adequate for a night's sleep—and asked the NBC News Washington vice president, Bob McFarland, to join me for breakfast. Also, would he please make appointments with some members of his staff?

Chris Wallace was first. I told him I was changing *Today* and it was my feeling he would be better used elsewhere. I offered him chief White House correspondent. He said something like, "You can't do that." I told him to think about it before refusing.

I told Judy Woodruff she would move from being a White House correspondent to *Today* Washington editor, doing most, but not all, of the reporting and interviewing from there. Then I told the chief White House correspondent, John Palmer, that I wanted him to move to New York and do the newscasts every hour and half hour. It was the way *Today* used to be done, and I wanted to go back to it.

Back to New York to tell Jane Pauley that Bryant Gumbel was sole host of *Today* because the other way did not work. She made it clear she did not like the decision, but that was all.

My romantic sense of the organization I grew up in and then headed was that it could survive any defection, if it came to that. I was prepared to have Chris Wallace quit, although I considered him a good and useful reporter. Gumbel or Brokaw might be a problem once they were in their jobs, but the possibility must always be faced. In any event, no one quit. But I used to keep a mental list of whom I would use to replace each key broadcaster and also some of the producers and executives. After all, they might not only be lured away by Roone Arledge, they might be hit by a truck. I would sometimes discuss the list with Pettit, but no one else.

Early in 1983, Connie Chung's agent approached the faithful and long-suffering manager who handled these matters for me. Connie, one of television's few beautiful women, grew up in suburban Washington when her father had served on Nationalist China's purchasing mission, attended the University of Maryland, learned some Yiddish from the family next door, and landed a job as a beginning reporter at CBS News where, during Watergate, she made a name by her persistence in stakeouts. She then went to CBS's Los Angeles station to anchor the late evening news. After several years of this, where she became well known but not dramatically successful, she hankered to come back to network news. She approached all three networks.

At first, I had no interest because we had no vacancies. Then it became obvious that the half-hour news preceding *Today* was becoming a burden to Bryant Gumbel and Jane Pauley and making them surly. We would have to do that one over again despite its success attracting viewers and advertisers. Jessica Savitch turned down doing it; she was exhausted, her agent told us, and would like to reduce her already minimal workload by half. I agreed on condition that her compensation also be cut by half, and this was accepted. I mentioned to Mulholland and Tinker that Connie Chung was looking for a network assignment. Tinker was especially enthusiastic. He lived in Los Angeles, and she was his local news anchor. I made the point that I would not match what her agent said the Los Angeles station was paying her, $700,000 a year.

After several months of negotiation, my surrogate in these matters sent me a memo I cherish for how it illustrates the looniness we had come to. Connie's agent still expected, besides the *Early Today* assignment, these "contractual commitments":

- Anchor either Saturday night or Sunday night *Weekend Nightly News*
- Weekday general reporting duties covering stories in the New York area that would hopefully air on *Nightly News*
- An unspecified number of News Digests
- General political campaign reporting assignments in conjunction with the 1984 national presidential election campaign
- Presence at both the Democratic and Republican conventions in 1984 as a floor reporter, although an assignment of comparable responsibility might be negotiable.
- Substitution as vacation relief co-anchor on *Today* (both Pauley and Gumbel), *Nightly News*, Monday through Friday (both Brokaw and Mudd), and *Weekend Nightly News*.
- One or two documentaries per year.

All this to be spelled out and committed to in a contract, even though we had said at the outset that what she was paid by KNXT in Los Angeles was irrelevant, and we would not guarantee broadcast appearances in a contract. The agent seems not to have believed me, because no one talked like that anymore. I told Tinker and Mulholland a deal was unlikely, unless she struck out at the other two places, and we must start looking elsewhere.

In my two years as division president, while Mulholland called me almost every day, Tinker called me perhaps a dozen times. Half of them were about Connie Chung. To Grant Tinker, Connie Chung was a star, and although it was not his management style to tell a division president he was not pushing hard enough, he clearly felt so. He offered to go see her, if it would do any good.

"Do you know her?" I asked.

"No, but she lives not far away."

I said I would feel more comfortable sticking to the conditions we had set down at the beginning. In April, the ice floe cracked. Conscious of Tinker's interest, I had agreed to fatten our original offer, but it was still substantially lower than what her agent said KNXT was paying her. Soon there was a signing. And a press lunch at "21" with all the trappings. The name of *Early Today* was changed to NBC News *at Sunrise* and it got its own producer. In time I told Chung she would be a floor reporter but she must first use some of her astonishing energy to travel around the states of the Northeast getting to know principal politicians, delegation chairmen, and the like. I would see that she got the time it would take. Her efforts were perfunctory. I admit I was disappointed.

The News Digests she was assigned to—a perfectly sound assignment but, like floor reporting, not what one puts in contracts—found her faithfully at work despite the length of her working day. What Pettit and I had dubbed "digests" and others called updates or newsbriefs or some other term of incompletion were a disgusting little form first suggested during my previous time as an executive. The idea was born in the mind of some advertising thinker looking to create an extra prime-time commercial spot without breaching the voluntary code still being observed. NBC resisted such blandishments for years. As it did so often, CBS broke first.

Thus, at a minute before nine each evening, the audience gets forty-two seconds of news, the program of that hour having been trimmed to make room. It was no surprise it was the highest rated daily news program of the division, a fact that Mulholland thought worth teasing me with. In professional terms, these minutes are an insult. But people watch them—willy-nilly. In the early days of *Weekend*, Dick Wald had given Lloyd Dobyns one a week as a way of fattening his pay. A writer with Dobyns's skill gave the minute more class than it deserved, but he was removed by Wald's underlings as unacceptably flip because he would open with, "Here's some news." For Connie Chung, Digests were a quick way to fame, or at least recognition, quicker than *NBC News at Sunrise*, so twice a week there she was, still reading headlines, if that is what they were, at the end of a working day that had begun while it was still dark.

I had some other interesting experiences with the prevailing atmosphere of raid and counterraid, with correspondents (and their agents). Both newspapers and affiliates got uncommonly worked up over the "investigative" team of Brian Ross and Ira Silverman. Atypically, they went as an entry, reporter and producer paid equally and almost equally well known. Their biggest moment had been their exclusive access to the Abscam tapes, in the case that shook Congress and further degraded Americans' views of government. As their contract approached its term, I had been led to believe negotiations were going well when, suddenly, they announced they were going to CBS, apparently through the personal involvement of Dan Rather himself. Then, just as suddenly, they let it be known they were not jumping to CBS but to ABC. It was ideal trade gossip.

Pettit had been closer to the negotiation than I, dealing with them personally—a mistake—and felt double-crossed. At his insistence, I issued a statement, but kept it mild, expressing disappointment and surprise, since we had been talking in good faith. Mulholland was upset because affiliates were upset, and their annual convention was looming. They knew Ross and Silverman by name; Small had paraded them before an earlier convention as the stars of Abscam.

I held to my offer. At the convention, affiliates asked questions about Ross and Silverman by name, as if these were stars upon whom ratings depended. My negotiator called from New York to say they were veering back to us and might even sign before the convention ended. Ray Timothy hoped for my sake that it was true and prepared to announce it to the hall. Another telephone call; it was not true. We went into the meeting and were duly and unrelievedly beat up on— the *Today* ratings, the decline in *Nightly News* ratings, the magazine program they didn't like, and Ross and Silverman. I remembered history, but I was still condemned to repeat it.

Soon after the convention, Ross and Silverman signed the contract we had offered all those weeks before. ABC News, which had given them a raucous "welcome aboard" party and even arranged a loan to tide them over between networks, reacted sourly. "Reuven Frank was right in the first place," said a vice president. "He's welcome to them." What had changed their minds? Silverman said it was Pettit and me. I am not sure. Perhaps they were overcourted and felt dizzy. Like so many newspeople, they are at bottom simple folk.

Hindsight tells me that all this time my position with Grant Tinker was eroding. I reported to Bob Mulholland, but Tinker was the boss. He had not been enthusiastic about replacing Bill Small, with me or anyone else, and found the attendant noise distasteful. It is not that he treated me badly. I got bonuses at bonus time and was addressed with courtesy and personal warmth when we were together. But what I said needed doing was rarely done, and what I was charged with was not a prime concern. When I pointed out that NBC's New York FM radio station had a bigger advertising and promotion budget than the network news division, I got sympathy but no help. When I asked for time for documentaries, when I said our people were still not ready to respond quickly—competitively—to the kind of disaster that had twice made NBC News look like bumblers and amateurs (and may have led to Small's dismissal), when I tried to start a new newsmagazine, I had no handhold. As president of the division the first time, I was custodian of a commonly revered icon. This time I was on my own, outgunned by those who did not share my scale of values, without enough help from the top to be effective.

Tinker was trying to bring NBC back from where it had been driven—low in ratings, in profits, in the esteem of peers. His early attempts did no better than the worst of Silverman's, but Thornton F. Bradshaw, Jr., the new RCA chairman, had promised to leave him alone to make it work, and he did. It was a hard road. Tinker favored quality entertainment, but such programs take longest to get an audience. *Variety* talked in its false-knowledgeable way of NBC not earning enough to finance new programs, speculating that RCA might sell it. Tinker was embarrassed that his first hit, really Tartikoff's, was *The A-Team*, a crude shoot-'em-up bordering on camp. It took him years to bring NBC around, but when it finally came around its success was enormous, its profits unprecedented. As for us, to someone for whom news always merely existed, we had no claim on finite resources, not money, not airtime. First things first.

His opinion of his news division worsened, I think, when NBC scheduled for broadcast in March 1983 a two-hour drama postulating a nuclear disaster. It was called *Special Bulletin* and came from the production company of one Don Ohlmeyer, formerly a vice president of NBC Sports and a close colleague of Brandon Tartikoff, NBC's entertainment president. The program had antinuclear zealots threatening to blow up Charleston harbor with a nuclear device if the government did not destroy a thousand nuclear detonators. The program used the forms and clichés of a live news special report, opening by seeming to interrupt a network program, switching back and forth between an anchor in New York and reporters on the scene and in Washington, making well-rehearsed technical errors, even keeping picture quality poor to look more like news and less like slickly produced drama.

Orson Welles had used the same method on CBS radio in 1939, in his history-making dramatization of H. G. Wells's *War of the orlds*, causing panic, hysteria, and injury in the entire Eastern seaboard. I was old enough to remember the Welles broadcast; few others were, perhaps not Tinker, certainly not Tartikoff. Someone else who was old enough, a vice president in Tartikoff's department, said quietly to Pettit, "You fellows [in News] should look at that." News still had the right to stop anything that so resembled news broadcasting as to confuse someone watching. Pettit and I screened the tape with Tinker. The program undeniably was intended to look like live coverage. Any viewer tuning in after the first minute would think it was a live broadcast, a "special bulletin."

Pettit was loud with disdain, Tinker defensive, and I mediating between them. "A Dramatization" was superimposed every five minutes. The week before broadcast the producers denounced me on talk shows as a censor and conservative toady. I was willing to concede, had anyone asked, that times were different, that what had happened with Orson Welles was not likely to happen again. But if there might not be mass hysteria, some people were sure to be misled. (Phone calls to stations confirmed that.) *Special Bulletin* was junk, and did poorly in the ratings, but it conformed to the Hollywood hunger for leftish *gravitas*. I was outraged when it was given a Humanitas Award and would have returned mine but I couldn't find it.

My campaign to try once again for an NBC News magazine program—there had been four failures since *Weekend* was suffocated, all using the best audience research on what people would watch and no thought to the obligation or the fun of just being in the news business—did not sway Tinker until one day he asked me why I wanted to do a magazine. Was it only because I was a "good soldier"? (He seemed to mean it as a compliment.)

"We should do it because we are a network," I told him.

To Grant Tinker that was reason enough, and as frustrating as those times were, I cherish his response and must not deny it. I went ahead with yet another NBC newsmagazine. We called it *Monitor*, an NBC program name not being used. I took Dobyns off *Overnight* to do it. Sy Pearlman would be executive producer, other *Weekend* almuni were scattered through the producing staff. But it was not to be *Weekend*, which we had learned would not work in prime time. The reports would be built as much around reporters as around pictures, turning only rarely to the whimsical and outrageous.

The time we got was Saturday evening, not as good as Tuesday evening for that kind of program, but good enough. Dobyns wrote his own stuff, as he always did, skillfully, but his natural skepticism had been distorted into an unattractive cynicism by years of knocks and insults. His comments were still biting but no longer witty. They cast a pall. Reports and reporting were still first rate, but there was too little variety, too much concentration on social ills, too few stories with vistas. And yet they included the first good television report on Alzheimer's disease, and a scary one on hospitals failing the poor. Ratings were low; many affiliates choosing not to carry the program drove them even lower. They would not carry a show with so small a rating. They ignored the paradox. Mulholland called on a spring Saturday as I sat on my porch in upstate New York looking across a valley at the wooded hills of Massachusetts. I had better come to the city the next morning or "my" program would die. It would be a casualty of the following season's schedule, being made up as we spoke. He had argued as much as he could; it was now up to me to save it. I left Sunday morning at dawn, arriving in Tinker's sixth-floor conference room before ten: two dozen men in golf shirts, a couple of women, cigarette smoke, yellow pads, coffee dregs in polyurethane cups. With Tinker in the chair, Tartikoff explained the alternatives and justified the choices as Bill Rubens, grand vice president of statistics, used past performances to predict which programs would soar and which crash.

As in a Rembrandt canvas, all eyes were fixed on a large felt board on an easel, marked up by a grid representing the prime-time hours of the seven days, on which pieces of cardboard with the names of programs were moved on and off, into this time slot or that one. By the time I got there, most of the decisions had been made, including the magazine, whose life had been spared. There were two conditions. One was that it was to go opposite *60 Minutes*, which everyone interested in that kind of program had been devotedly watching for years. The other was that, during football season, the program would adjust so that the eight o'clock program, about a young man who pursued the wicked aided by an automobile that talked, would start on time. In solemn, accusing tones I was told, *"Knight Rider* starts at eight!"

Contracts with the National Football League oblige a network carrying its games on Sunday afternoons to televise all the games in its conference, showing them on several regional networks, and especially to the home cities of the away teams. This meant breaking down NBC, for example, into a half dozen networks, a couple with later (West Coast) games, and all games inevitably ending at different times. CBS started *60 Minutes* after the last game ended. If that meant starting after seven o'clock, it and all CBS programs on that night's schedule would play in their entirety, pushing the end of prime time that many minutes past eleven. We were not to do it that way. We would have to tailor for several networks, jumping in as each game ended, jettisoning a few minutes on this one, perhaps twenty on that one. A nightmare.

A producer would sit in a master control room deciding how much of each Sunday's program would go to each of several partial networks, his reflexes in overdrive, his stomach churning, his sense of professional fitness violated. Any story that might show on one network and be dumped from three or four others would represent two or three months' work, a story worth watching, even exciting, but the stupid football won't end! With five minutes to go, the decision to dump it. Could it be saved for next week? No, it had already played on the four stations that carried the Cleveland game. Shitshitshit. Dump it.

Were I the executive producer, I would have refused. But I was division president, choosing between a magazine under these conditions and no magazine at all. If I said no, people would be fired, and new ones found when inevitably we started all over. I had no right to say no. NBC had to broadcast something on Sundays at 7:00; news was elected. A magazine was, after all, my idea. In return, I would be called on for something to tell the press and palliate the affiliates about how the new magazine would be a major improvement over the old, which no one in the room liked except me. So we gave it a new title, *First Camera*, and said big name reporters like Marvin Kalb and Jack Perkins would contribute from time to time. When I told Pearlman what he faced, he sighed and said he would try. If they could hang on through football, January would bring whole hours every week—until Tartikoff suggested, in an unrelated discussion, that if I was serious about time for more documentaries, I could preempt my own magazine since it really wasn't very good anyway, was it?

The affiliates thought putting *First Camera* against *60 Minutes* was stupid, and said so, privately, publicly, and through surrogates in the press. But when I announced, as part of my few minutes in the parade of division presidents before them that *Knight Rider* would start on time, they applauded. It was the only applause I got. It was not that they had special affection for young men who talked to cars, or even cars which (who?) talked back. What I was saying to them, what they heard, was that they would not have to delay their eleven o'clock local news during football season, almost one-third of the year.

What the affiliates were most concerned about was *Today*, whose fortunes so directly affected their incomes because it had commercial blanks for local station sale. I told them I had stood before them the year before with promises, to double syndicated news service, to upgrade news material given to them virtually free, to add network news programs early in the morning and late at night, and those promises had been kept. Now we had made our changes on *Today* and I could promise those ratings would improve but they must give us time. It didn't sell. They were outraged.

A station manager, asking that his name not be used, told *Variety*: "I think Reuven Frank should be fired. He's a man of the 1950s." This was slander. I was at worst a man of the sixties.

Another told *Broadcasting*, "Frank is from the old school and as such is too preoccupied with covering the news in a substantive manner." (I am considering that for my headstone.)

The changes did work. The *Today* ratings did turn around. But it took time, and the waiting was difficult, and in May 1983 I still had little to show. They were within their rights to chafe. Mulholland and Tinker also chafed, but only in private, when we had our weekly sessions, and Mulholland and I would talk and Tinker would listen, no matter how hard I tried to lure him into the conversation. Mulholland asked if Connie Chung could be paired with Bryant Gumbel, replacing Jane Pauley. Somehow, that idea had been shared before it got to me, even floated past some of the affiliates. The feedback included snickers about a "third world" program, the only time I heard this kind of mean reference to Gumbel's being black.

In late summer, with the *Today* ratings still slipping, speculation about changes moved from the trade press to the newspapers, first the tabloids, then the *Washington Post* and the *Chicago Tribune*, and, finally, even *The New York Times*. I called Tinker to suggest that a public expression of support and confidence in the *Today* gang might be useful. Morale was becoming a problem, I said. It was the only such request I ever made of him. He said only that he would think about it. I was disappointed. It was the kind of problem he understood better than others, and he had not expressed dissatisfaction with the people involved, only with the ratings. I must assume he was distracted by other worries.

The problems of *Today* were not only the lead *Good Morning, America* had in the ratings. A full-fledged *CBS Morning News* had suddenly emerged. Since *Today* sprang from Pat Weaver's brain to commercial success in the fifties, CBS's attempts to compete had all failed, in part because there was something in the CBS corporate soul blinding it to the difference between a show in the morning and the Holy Grail kind of news they espoused. Whatever they tried was self-conscious, all the gears showing, Walter Cronkite making small talk with a hand puppet, the search for their own blonde (Sally Quinn), and other instances of painting by numbers. An even bigger obstacle was CBS's historic commitment to children's programming. Mornings at 8:00, Captain Kangaroo spoke to little children, he and his friends telling stories and dispensing advice. Captain Kangaroo obstructed CBS News in the morning the way Johnny Carson obstructed NBC News at night. But, with the years, the institutional need for a morning program grew and Captain Kangaroo was moved back an hour to make room. When that was not enough, he was shunted to 6:30. The rush to ever earlier news programs doomed that, and he was moved to weekends, and to do specials, television's equivalent of "Go in peace, good and faithful servant." A true *Morning News* was ready to be born.

To us, that made catching up with *Good Morning, America* secondary to staving off being passed by CBS, which would drop *Today* to third. The *Morning News* combination of a Chicago anchor named Bill Kurtis and ex-Junior Miss and Nixon White House assistant Diane Sawyer started to work, edging past *Today* for one dreadful week. To the staff's deserved celebratory Friday lunch the president of CBS News sent champagne, a nice gesture, or so wrote the many newspaper reporters who had been let in on it. My intercom buzzed with fellow executives asking, Had I read . . . ? I insisted to Mulholland and Tinker that I had made the necessary and logical changes; I had confidence in the executive producer; the rest must take time. The suspicion grew on the executive floor that, whatever my virtues, I was too impractical for this business.

Steve Friedman, *Today*'s executive producer, made his changes, copying what he thought he saw in the old Garroway tapes, that the permanent members were a family. His had Gumbel in charge, Jane Pauley as the young mommy, Gene Shalit and weatherman Willard Scott the goofy uncles. I took his word for it. I had to; it was not my language and I felt insecure. In this framework, he wanted news and more news, but he wanted news seen live. To him, that's what television is about, hitting news hard. When NBC News was not somewhere he wanted them to be, he staged a tantrum. He demanded people be fired when his needs were not met. The head of the technicians' union came to my office to complain.

But he got his interview with Qaddafi, the tour of the earthquake ruins, openings, aftermaths. One of his tantrums was about Bhopal, which no one from any medium reached for a couple of days. He was enjoying himself hugely, at last. As for the program's "guests," he insisted on exclusives, especially from entertainers. As his ratings improved, he used them as weapons: "You don't want to talk to those guys; they have no audience. And the others get only old people. They don't buy records. Remember, if you go across the street, forget about

being on our show." Or, "Okay, if we're first. Not the same day. First."

And as a throwback to earlier times, he took *Today* traveling—to South America, to Rome. All three network shows would go to London for, say, the wedding of the Prince of Wales, the ultimate supermarket tabloid fantasy, but that was to cover an event. This was travel for the sake of travel. In the early days it was difficult; in 1983 and 1984 it was merely complicated. It was also refreshing. Then the others did it, too; as technology moved, anyone could do it, even stations. By then, *Today* had its audience lead, a fat one.

Friedman had predicted it. When Jane Pauley came back from maternity leave, he promised me, the ratings would go up. She came back early in 1984, and the ratings, as he had foreseen, started to go up and never stopped. By then, I had informed Tinker of my wish to do other work, and my successor had been named.

In late 1983, I had gone to Maui for NBC's executives' winter meeting with the "delegates" of its affiliated stations. NBC was still a season away from what would become a crushing dominance, but the signs were positive; the bad days were over. NBC was making money, its owned stations were making money, its affiliates were making money. The most important discussion would be the satellite system NBC had chosen for program distribution now that broadcasting was no longer dependent on AT&T for intercity transmission. It would be dull.

Executives in slacks huddled around coffee urns, gummy pastries in their hands, ready for another soporific session, when Grant Tinker asked me to walk with him a little. It was the only discussion with me he initiated in the twenty-two months since dinner at the University Club. It was to tell me he had picked my successor. I had recently written to him and Mulholland saying I was now past the midpoint of my three-year contract. Because it was a difficult job to fill, and to make filling it in an orderly and considered way possible for once, I was advising them that I preferred not to be asked to continue after March 1985. Any help I might be was theirs for the asking, and I hoped sixteen months' notice would give them the luxury of time to consider what kind of news division they wanted as well as what kind of person they wanted running it.

What Tinker was saying to me, in effect, was, "Wonderful. Can you leave tomorrow?"

Lawrence Grossman, his choice, had been at NBC many years before. I had known him when I was a producer and he vice president for advertising. He had gone on to become president of the Public

Broadcasting System, and we had once talked about my producing
political convention coverage for them, but Bill Small would not give
me a leave of absence. (We later agreed it would not have worked
anyway. The two anchormen he had would not have shut up long
enough for floor reporters to report.) I wondered about someone without news experience taking over the job, but from the little I knew he
seemed a decent and bright man and presumably had good instincts.
Getting out of PBS would be complicated, Tinker told me, and Grossman would not join until February. This would give him and me
several months to "work together" until I handed over in May. I was
to tell no one. Did Mulholland know? Yes, he knew.

We went back to the meeting. Afterward, I pulled Mulholland aside
to ask what he knew. Not much. He had disagreed but Grant would
not listen. In fact, did I know that back when he got approval to fire
Small, Tinker had wanted then to give the job to Grossman? No, I
didn't. I wished he had told me earlier. I said it might work out well
after all. Mulholland did not think so.

Three weeks later it was announced, and I could make my own
announcement to my staff. I told them I thought it was a good idea.
I asked all to help Larry Grossman as he spent his months preparing.
During those months, I told them, I did not expect to be a lame duck.
Tinker called me on the executive intercom for the last time. He
congratulated me on the "classy" way I was handling the transition.
(What had he expected?) He told me it was a great arrangement and
how lucky Grossman was to have me—as he put it, "a Reuven
Frank"—to ask questions of, to look to for guidance. We were by then
into 1984's primary season, with little time to stop and think. Grossman
traveled the country and the world seeing how things worked, deciding
how he would change them.

On a Wednesday morning after one of the primaries, I was awakened
by the ringing of the telephone in the hotel room where I had gone
after we finally got off the air. It was my secretary; Mr. Tinker would
like me at a meeting in his office in half an hour. Grossman was there.
So was Ray Timothy, the adder, and some others from the Network,
but strangely, not Mulholland. The adder said the magazine would
not make it. It was guillotined. That was it, ten minutes. As we left,
Grossman asked if things were always so rough. In those five months,
it was the only question he ever asked me. I went to see Mulholland
in his office. "Grant fired me," he said. "Last Monday. He called me
in, said it wasn't working, and that was it." I was not surprised. They

were neither alike nor complementary, and I believe Grant Tinker did not like Bob Mulholland before he knew he did not like Bob Mulholland.

Also, I learned later, Grossman had asked that he report to Tinker, not to Mulholland. That might have swayed Tinker's decision, added a feather to the balance. From the start, Grossman enjoyed Tinker's confidence in a way I never had. Like any executive, like me, for that matter, Tinker was more easily persuaded by those with whom he was comfortable. Grossman agreed with Tinker on how the procedures in the News division should resemble those of entertainment, with pilot programs, audience research, hiring program "consultants" to boost ratings, even asking them to recommend what news should be covered and how.

Within a year, NBC executives were saying that Larry Grossman was Grant Tinker's chosen successor, one of them telling me long afterward that Tinker had recommended Grossman to the General Electric Company, the new proprietors. If so, it was only a gesture. By that time, Grossman and his bosses were in public conflict; GE's penury, inept public relations, and single-minded managerial cynicism granting him the luxury of standing before the world as the white knight of journalistic purity. News sets no entrance exams.

Grossman stayed in the job four years, during which he remolded things to his heart's desire, like sending Dobyns to Tokyo and finding new assignments for Ellerbee, but in the end showing them both the door. I agreed to sit in my old chair for the 1984 conventions, with coverage cut to three hours a night, and those hard to fill because there was no news. Twice nightly, Roger Mudd reported from the convention platform, once a key spot but never when there was no news. Or this news: Mario Cuomo and Jesse Jackson rousing the Democrats; Walter Mondale naming Geraldine Ferraro to his ticket before his convention began, terminating the only suspense; Ronald Reagan, his back to the audience, waving at a screen showing an immense live picture of Nancy in a hotel room, and she waving back, or was it the other way around?

My closer associates were weeded out, new people brought in, some top jobs filled from outside. Pettit was among the last to get it, and was rehired as a reporter. Grossman was quoted in print about how he had improved morale, what a mess he had found on arrival. But he did not say specifically I had made the mess. We were cordial when we spoke, and he let me do some programs I enjoyed. Earlier, in the spring, I was paged as I landed in San Francisco with Ray Lockhart to plan how to cover the Democratic convention. Pettit was calling from New York to say Gary Stindt had died in Berlin.

Conventions with no news were only one way my world had changed. In the nine years between my turning over the division to Dick Wald and my taking it back from Bill Small, network news had become something else, something I foolishly tried to fight, because, even more foolishly, I thought it was for that I had been picked, I and not someone else.

The three biggest changes grew from new machines, but they were institutional and cultural, changing not only how things were done but what was being done. Otherwise, the new machines would have made no difference, solutions without problems. The first change was the end of the network monopoly on world news. No longer were the networks the only source of the full range of news material. The Prime Time Access Rule had fertilized the growth of strong, rich stations that could now support their own independent organizations for the distribution of news pictures, cooperatives to make stations' regional news reciprocally available to each other, and specialized purveyors of fillers and features or Washington and foreign material covered to order. Videotape replacing film, progressively easier and cheaper satellite transmission, tape cameras indulgent daddies could afford and even FBI agents operate—each played a part in ending our monopoly.

Then cable television exploded the number of sources reaching the home. Homes reached by four channels could be opened to more than a hundred. One was an all-news channel, with its own worldwide organization, built at first around eager young people working for low wages and then meeting early financial troubles with a campaign to sell material to any buyer, any station. It then split itself into two all-news channels, one concise, the other detailed.

The 1984 conventions were covered live not by three networks but by five. The other two provided true gavel-to-gavel coverage regardless of what we fogies did. They were CNN and C-SPAN, cable's consortium for live coverage of Congress, the House of Commons, and symposium after symposium. (Cable does not have to worry about *time* for news; it has channels to spare.) From the floor of the 1984 conventions *more than seventy* local station reporters sent their reports by satellite to their newsrooms—and even more in 1988. We had come far from Mayor Daley's limiting each network to two floor reporters, the rest making do with messengers' passes.

The end of monopoly meant the executive producer of an evening news program had to assume that, by the time he went on the air, local news programs preceding his had reported the world and national news he was about to give, often with the same pictures, the ones we so jealously guarded in my days as a producer. (I even had the right to withhold New York news pictures from New York local news programs if I meant to use them on *Huntley-Brinkley*.) The producer's problem became making his news different. He could not rely on the public accepting his people as better, smarter, and more informed—which they usually were—or that even with their new capabilities, stations upstaged his news only for the very biggest events and without background. (Instead, the networks themselves gave up forewarning, so that developments now came as surprises.) His competitive weapon became his anchorman, his million-dollar baby in his (increasingly) five-and-ten-cents store, above all the anchorman live wherever the news was. As for the anchormen, they relished their progress from "I am Sir Oracle," to "History begins when I get there."

The networks used the live presence of the live anchorman in the live place as a way of spicing up public interest—that is, boosting ratings. The anchormen, demanding and getting ever larger, and more exclusionary, roles in the running of the programs, saw it as competition among themselves, bursting out of the confines of studios to chase the news. Or hoping it would so appear. I tried keeping the worst of this down during my two years in charge with appeals to logic, never a popular course, and good taste, which was even worse. Anchors went to conventions, of course, and to economic summits, athough the latter was only customary. But if an anchor is an editor, he should be at the point of publication, not at the event.

My successor believed none of this, seizing instead on the ability of Anchorman on Location to get written about, a major preoccupation. He took both *Today* and *Nightly News* to Moscow in a trumpeted effort to advance understanding, always a questionable undertaking for journalists; it gets in the way of looking for news. He got a scoop anyway. The Soviet defense minister was scheduled to be Bryant Gumbel's Big Interview the morning an internal upheaval displaced him. The Soviet state had advanced far enough by then that the new man showed up for the interview instead. That was how the world learned the name of the new Soviet defense minister. He and Gumbel were the front-page picture on the *International Herald Tribune*.

This was, however, too Kremlinological to help the ratings. And I wondered during the subsequent all-hands trip to China how much it helped the ratings for someone in Des Moines to see Brokaw in front of the Gate of Heavenly Peace reporting how many died in mudslides in Latin America, with pictures shown from New York.

It could get sillier. Brokaw was the only network anchorman in New York during one of those foreign news outbursts that capture American attention: the ouster of Philippine dictator Ferdinand Marcos. Dan Rather, in ratings trouble, was touring the farm belt, and on the night of the overthrow gave an extraordinary nine minutes to its problem, ninety seconds to the Marcoses. Peter Jennings, who had achieved fame by trotting the globe pronouncing foreign names, was in Moscow for the first meeting of the All-Soviet Central Committee since Gorbachev's rise to general secretary, an event of crucial importance at Columbia and Georgetown universities, but not the sort of thing you program against reruns of M*A*S*H.

All this had been foreshadowed for me on Maui in November 1983 when the affiliates' board had chided me because, however good our reporting, Brokaw was not in the anchor chair when the marine barracks in Beirut were blown up. If it was that big a story, where was Brokaw? Soon the President of the United States, and then the President of the Soviet Union, could not cross a border without attracting three American anchormen—and, in time, Japanese, West Germans, and others whose television news followed American modes. Gorbachev, it will be recalled, was in the United States when disaster struck the nuclear power plant in Chernobyl, in the Ukraine. He hurried home, deferring a side trip to visit Fidel Castro in Havana. A few years later, as a matter of form, he eked out a visit to Castro, his henchmen informing all who heard that nothing would happen. The three anchormen, and the support staffs they needed for live reporting from a foreign capital, went anyway, and indeed found no news. All this at a time when new proprietorships at all three networks were insisting on cutting costs, especially in news.

Thus burned, two of the four—CNN must now be included—opted to bypass Gorbachev's trip to Beijing to formalize the new warming between the two big Communist powers. CBS's Dan Rather and CNN's Bernard Shaw were there; ABC's Peter Jennings and NBC's Tom Brokaw were not (though both were represented by good reporters and skilled camera crews). The hand shaking was no news and not much picture. But what seethed beneath the surface of Chinese society picked that occasion to bubble up, as young urban Chinese protested totalitarian control. Gorbachev's proximity was not the cause but an encouragement. An even greater one was the presence of television cameras from the United States and other Western countries. The anchormen did not make history; the presence of live cameras did. That confusion will distort accounts and memories, perhaps forever.

For a time, misgivings about how the overwhelming anchor was distorting news presentation centered on CBS's Dan Rather, because he did things that got into the papers. In September 1987, he left his anchor desk fuming that a tennis match was not ending in time for his news program, so when his telecast started it opened with seven minutes of blank screen. During the 1988 primary season, like all anchormen enraptured by himself interviewing news persons live, even though that meant making the least possible news in the given time, he invited George Bush on to talk about his candidacy. In a strategy crafted by Roger Ailes, Bush's handler, when Rather asked the vice president what he had known about Iran-Contra, they got into a shouting match. The vice president asked the anchorman how would he like being asked about seven minutes of blank screen.

The incident is credited with changing Bush's "wimp" image and may have won him the nomination and the election. *Time* magazine ordered a poll, which reported most people thought Bush had won. Presidents can be defined by their antagonists—Roosevelt by Hitler, Kennedy by Khrushchev, Reagan by Qaddafi. Bush by Rather?

Soon all the network news programs were using live interviews, necessarily short ones to fit in with their total of twenty-two minutes for all the news of all the world, rarely productive because any public figure is primarily adept at not answering unwelcome questions. Live interviews, longer ones to be sure, used to be the province of the morning programs because they fill time so well and cost so little to produce. Add to that picking topics for better ratings, the way most station news had come to do, and what I found when I returned to management was the localization of network news and the morning-ization of evening news. It was not heartening.

Also, along with the end of the network monopoly and the emergence of the dominating anchorman I found a third fundamental change when I came back to management: There was no photojournalism in television news. The word people had won. I used to boast of being the only producer left who assembled pictures first and then had the scripts written, but I did not know what it meant in a larger

sense until I resumed responsibility for the work of others. Except for
live coverage—a very large exception, but that's another matter—
words were decided and then pictures were put to them. Perhaps it
could not have been prevented, but it denied television news its one
unique capacity, showing things happening.

All the people who mattered were on the side of words. Anchormen
are word people; an anchorman is seen only when he is speaking.
Managers were increasingly word people, usually former reporters and
writers, sometimes lawyers, who are a special class of readers. (A lawyer
thinks a television program is the same as its transcript.) From Pat
Weaver on, those who ran networks understood words better than
pictures, judging the news by the words spoken. Sometimes, a cameraman was promoted to field producer or a film editor to director,
but none I know of has become an executive.

Besides what might be termed this class interest, there was a certain
logic. When television news accepted that its mandate was to be a
primary news source rather than the complementary one it had been
when it began, it was obliged to report important stories that were not
available to the human eye or the camera lens: negotiations, tax in-
creases, the clash of beliefs, economic trends—the list is infinite. In
the time of film, such topics were covered by anchormen or other
reporters seen talking, sometimes helped by graphic illustration, but
that was never satisfactory. All this was revolutionized by the advent
of videotape because it is immediately and infinitely reproducible.

All news reports, even on arcane subjects, became all-picture, yet
rarely using pictures of the event reported. Even the smallest news
organization has its "archive" of videotapes of events, scenes, and
things. After words are written, pictures are matched to them, relevant
or irrelevant, that day's or last year's, but pictures. In editing rooms
they're called "wallpaper" or even today's TV "eyewash," but news
could not function without them. A reporter going out on a story,
down the block or across an ocean, will carry a box of tape snippets
from the archives and may use no other pictures in his report. (The
real thing may not illustrate it as well.) As Congress debates price
supports, script will be spoken against farms being auctioned five years
ago, corn pouring into a freighter—any old freighter will do—tractors,
seamed faces. The viewer has not seen anything happen. He does not
learn from the pictures; only from the words. Network news writers
have even taken to calling their news tape archives with completed

scripts asking for the pictures to match for use on the "news" that night.

Pictures of real events are never used only once. The DC-10 cart-wheeling down the Sioux City airport runway in perhaps the most unforgettable domestic picture of 1989 was a chilling sight, a news picture in the purest sense. Then, every day for the weeks of subsequent inquiry, every report on every station and every network, morning and evening, used the same picture of the DC-10 cartwheeling down the runway. Months later, whenever aviation reporters did pieces on safety, or on DC-10s, we saw old cartwheel again. Jack Ruby shooting Lee Harvey Oswald before live cameras was not replayed one tenth as often as that cartwheeling DC-10, although Ruby is the favored citation of those denigrating television as the index of our degraded civilization.

Television is referred to by reflex as a "visual medium," a phrase repeated as though it had meaning. Print is no less a visual medium; eyes read it. What matters is that television is best as a narrative medium, worst as an expository medium. It nevertheless must report all the news, what it reports well and what it reports clumsily. It may not ignore what it is not good at. A stock market crash, a telegram declaring war, may not be omitted as not good picture, not things seen happening. But they are not photojournalism, nor, finally, is television news. Otherwise why, in forty years, has it produced no Capas, no Margaret Bourke-Whites, no David Douglas Duncans, no Larry Burrows? Photojournalism on television had become a possibility forever lost.

What ultimately robbed television news of stature and cachet was how cheap it is. Factual presentation—using forms and techniques we old settlers had developed over forty years ago—cost half as much as entertainment programs. If subject matter could be liberated from our dusty rules, prime-time entertainment might ensue. It did. Old crime scenes revisited, aging victims recounting horrors in salacious detail, anchormen from central casting, fleeing felons brought to justice by exposure on the tube, these easily held their own against formula comedies and dramas about not very nice rich people. It was a matter of texture, that which tells you in seconds whether your car radio push-button has reached baroque or rap. Shows were made to look and sound and feel like news—without the rules.

The syndicators did even better, proclaiming openly, even proudly, their debt to supermarket tabloids. Their way was pointed by the enormous success of *Entertainment Tonight*, which reported news about show business and its people, but broke few rules except relevance. That led the way to tales of lust and mayhem, perhaps true, perhaps exaggerated, perhaps prevaricated. Soon there was hardly a station in the country that did not have one of these programs in "access" time, legacy of the Prime Time Access Rule.

By day, there were interviews by Famous Interviewers—Phil Donahue, Oprah Winfrey, Geraldo Rivera, Sally Jessy Raphael—who asked guests and audiences questions about important social issues and mutual orgasm and education and psychiatrists who rape patients and diet and sex change operations. Even CNN, moving from All News to Almost All News, found Sonya, its own Famous Interviewer of the Famous. The lines blurred and vanished between reality and deception, news and pseudo-news, nonfiction televison and trash television. As the imitators became more interesting than the news, producers of news jazzed it up to keep pace. All this might be regretted, but not deplored, because the common man, as an FCC commissioner once said, has a right to be common.

Some of this developed while I was in management, trying to keep news presentation going. The rest grew after I had gone back to producing, enjoying documentaries while they lasted. My lame-duck period as division president was to have lasted through May 1984, but both Grossman and I grew tired of the charade and ended it in April. I took time off after the conventions to attend to medical problems, as I always seemed to do when between jobs, and then went back to work. I put together a small group to do an hour on the growth of pension funds to where they would soon devour the equity markets and give big headaches to policymakers. We called it *The Biggest Lump of Money in the World* and introduced viewers to still unknown and mysterious figures like Ivan Boesky and Carl Icahn and broached issues the U.S. Senate would debate five years later. A good and seasoned reporter named Steve Delaney interviewed well and gave us a fine script, informing while fascinating. It was a good start.

I then went to Tokyo with a couple of producers, old colleagues, to work with Lloyd Dobyns on the parts of the Japanese miracle that the business pages missed, the ridiculous land prices, the two-thirds of the work force that had no job security, the well-to-do living without indoor plumbing, the bullying of small suppliers, the inferior role of women. Everything being said about Japanese production—its quality, its efficiency, its competitive power—was true, but measured by purchasing power—that it, by living standard—the Japanese were poorly paid and one of their international economic advantages was, in fact, cheap labor. Just before he died, Theodore H. White wrote to say it was the best thing on Japan he had seen. Delaney and I did the next one on why nuclear power was such a success in France while it was such a botch in the United States.

Grossman chose not to renew Dobyns's contract, then Delaney's. Cost-cutting had set in. The networks feared shrinking revenues, and, even before the two years during which all three were taken over by new proprietors, started picking who and what to throw off the back of the sled. (Although their share of the money spent on broadcast advertising shrank as more independent stations and cable channels claimed portions, the aggregate kept rising. The top of the curve would not be reached for a while.) Cost-cutting also enhanced each network's price when it came time for sale.

From the inside, each network seemed different, not only in what has come to be known as its "corporate culture" but in the specifics of its problems. To the outside, which, in the context of waning twentieth-century America, means securities analysts, they all looked the same: bloated, slow to move, and outpaced in an expanding and increasingly competitive marketplace. The analysts advised the chief executives that a crisis threatened them. The trimming of budgets began, that of news divisions neither most nor least but by far most widely reported. Bradshaw began cutting costs at RCA, Tinker at NBC. Grossman named a committee for NBC News.

In the manner of committees, by the time it reported, all three networks had been taken over by the new proprietors. To those who deal in money, whose product is paper and not goods, there really was no difference. It had come time for all three to submit to the American economic reality of the 1980s, the one that created a new thirty-year-old Wall Street billionaire every day while conceding world economic leadership to the Japanese and West Germans because there is no money in it for me. The first, in 1985, was when Leonard Goldenson sold ABC to Capital Cities, a company that owned stations and publications. The last was in 1986 when the CBS management group, which had shunted William Paley aside, succumbed to Laurence Tisch, a billionaire investor in theaters and hotels. In between went NBC. Riding an unprecedented crest of ratings and income, NBC might have seemed least vulnerable, but it was, however successful, only a subsidiary of RCA, and RCA was vulnerable indeed.

In December 1985, without any warning from the rumor mill, it was announced that General Electric had bought RCA. Surprisingly little has been written about that sizable transaction. At least a dozen reporters started out probing and delving but there were few results. The deal was a harsh one, cash only for RCA stock, no swapping for GE's stock or other choices. This caused grumbling, but that was all. Thornton Bradshaw drove the deal through RCA's board with one dissenting vote, and shareholders were told it was an irreversible deal. Felix Rohatyn, the financier who conducted the arrangements, told a friend we have in common that it had not been his initiative; it was Bradshaw who had approached him. GE's cold-eyed chairman, Jack Welch, went on NBC's closed circuit TV to address his new employees. Little he said was memorable except that he had bought RCA primarily for NBC, because NBC had no foreign competition.

Tinker stayed on for a year, then chose to return to Hollywood. He was succeeded by Robert Wright, a rising GE executive who had once run a cable company in Atlanta. Wright, whom people found personable and approachable, was a GE manager first. The usual clumsy mistakes were made and duly noted by the newspapers. Wright wanted NBC executives, including those in NBC News, to contribute to a political action committee to lobby congressmen for the special interests of broadcasting. That brought forth a mighty howl, as if it had never been done before, although I remembered a chairman of the NBC affiliates' organization saying at a meeting two years earlier that we should get together behind something or other of importance to broadcasters—the National Association of Broadcasters was also behind it—and in due course I got a request in the mail. I sent $100 and told no one. I did not feel compromised, only blackmailed.

Welch, visiting *Today* while it was being broadcast, observed that book authors being interviewed should pay commercial rates. That, too, was reported and chortled over. What got most newspaper space, of course, was Grossman's budget cutting. Each of the three network news divisions was in some stage of a plan to reduce costs, all pounced on by newspaper writers who trumpeted them as betrayals and warned of dire consequences. It seemed hardly fair, however, for them to blame it all on GE. Bradshaw and Tinker were no less responsible. GE had yet to demand major cuts, but soon would. Bradshaw, however much good he had done at RCA, was no tower of support for NBC News in his new role on GE's board of directors.

There was no denying that Bradshaw had turned RCA around and enabled Tinker to turn NBC around. After what was euphemistically referred to as the merger, he complained that GE rarely asked his advice and never took it. I visited him on the fifty-third floor, once the RCA executive floor, where now his was the only office occupied. We chatted. He told me how busy he was, about running the MacArthur Foundation, about seminars and conferences. A few months before, in a *Los Angeles Times* interview, he had supported the cuts made by GE, especially in NBC News. For thirty-five years now I had been hearing executives wonder why we needed so many reporters. "There's no reason that all three networks need to have people sitting around in Zimbabwe," said Bradshaw in his turn.

The quotation jumped off the page at me. I had never known him to sneer, but this was denigrating, supercilious sneering. Nor had he earned the right. He did not know the reporters he so airily dismissed as "sitting around in Zimbabwe." He knew anchormen and commentators, vice presidents and political science professors. He did not know erudite Welles Hangen, dead in Cambodia while reporting for NBC News. He did not know George Clay, who by himself defined reporting from Africa for the "winds of change" decade, picked off in Katanga in a nighttime convoy because he insisted on riding up front where he could record better sound. (Clay was among the few who heeded the plea not to forget radio when on a story.) Nor had he known fearless Ted Yates, cut down in the Six-Day War by Jordanian troops on a hill who thought the long lens on his camera down below was a weapon.

Thornton Bradshaw, a gentle man, who promoted noble conferences in Colorado resorts about the responsibilities of the media and their influence on the national soul, had turned out to be just another of the high-minded dilettantes who thought news gathered itself. They looked to television to show them famous correspondents interviewing well-known faces, including each others', about the significance of events described in *The New York Times* that morning.

I meant to bring it up when I visited him in his lavish office on that dramatically empty floor, but he seemed so tired and disappointed. We had very little to talk about, but he did not want me to leave. Over and over, he told me how busy he was. He gave me an opening when he asked me what I thought of what was going on, but I answered only that I was happy I no longer had to deal with those problems. It is worth noting, nevertheless, that in all the cost cutting imposed by the new proprietors at all three networks, most of the cuts came out of getting the news and almost none from the costs of presenting it. News bureaus were closed as anchormen's salaries rose; cameramen were laid off while stage settings became more elaborate and graphics devices more complicated and expensive.

All, of course, under the eager and watchful eye of the newspapers. When Grossman fired me, they had a picnic, although they were wrong to blame GE and Bob Wright. But that was their mood at the moment. Myself, I never doubted it was Grossman's idea. The two-year contract to do documentaries I had signed after being division president was now in turn about to end. In December 1986, Grossman took me to lunch at a three-star restaurant and told me he could not afford a new contract for me although he hoped I would keep thinking of ideas for programs and submitting them and he would look forward to picking a good one so I could produce it for NBC News.

I thought he was trying to lighten the conversation with parody. But he meant it, which made it funnier, because what he said to me is what we tell people who annoy us at parties.

I had quit twice, but this was my first time being fired. I looked on it as a learning experience.

Someone told someone and the next day my name was in a headline in *The New York Times*. The newspapers and wire services picked it up, and I was on the telephone for days. I was called "immortal" and "legendary" and was privileged to read my obituary while still alive, not once but dozens of times. Reporters solicited quotations—the "sound bites" of print—from Brinkley, Vanocur, and Chancellor, who made appropriate eulogious noises.

Ralph Mann asked if I wanted him to get involved. No, I said, this is too much fun. He went ahead anyway. In a few days, he called to say a contract was possible calling for two documentaries, no time specified, at so much each, after which we would see. I had no better prospects so I did them.

And then it ended. Just like that. Chancellor had me and four or five to lunch, Brokaw gave a small dinner. My files were packed in boxes, and I left, thirty-eight years and some weeks after I arrived. The last two documentaries had gone well enough. The 1988 political conventions had come and gone and I had hardly noticed, nor did most Americans. Larry Grossman was in Atlanta for the Democrats' convention when he was fired. After a long search, the principals at General Electric had given up looking for his successor in broadcasting and turned to a newspaper man, Michael Gartner, an editor and publisher in the Gannett organization, first in Des Moines, then in Washington. He claimed to know everything about news and nothing about television, a position he has since adhered to.

Like the others, he cut costs claiming to be cutting fat. Anyone in the trade more than ten years became an old-timer, a grumpy old-timer. Like all American companies and later than most, broadcasting had moved from supplying customers to maximizing stock prices, and their managers' bonuses. Journalists had told how it happened to others but were unprepared for it happening to them.

When we started network news, we assumed those who watched already knew the news. So we gave them news they already knew in a different dimension. We *showed* it to them. We transmuted into experience what had been information. Now, as I left, network news programs were again produced in the awareness that those who watched already knew the news—but now they had also seen the pictures. Why should anyone watch? What role was left for network news? The old role, our way, had served a long time. Never had Americans known so much about the world as in those years. It would be enough to be remembered by.

The end of the network news monopoly was not heroic enough to be a Götterdämmerung or sad enough for tears. But I found it sad enough. Whether what replaced it was an improvement was in the eye of the beholder, but like the Roman Empire, it did not fall; it petered out. The causes, as noted, were suddenly cheap equipment, the ease of live satellite transmission, feisty independent stations, co-operatives and private ventures offering all who wished reports from Washington or around the world, and finally, but only finally, cable TV and the Cable News Network. It was no wonder that the New Proprietors objected to paying so much money for so little gain.

All three news divisions were planning staff and budget cuts once again when Iraq marched into Kuwait in August 1990. By January, when it became the Persian Gulf War, covering it had become an open wound in their treasuries. The networks reported well, with praise enough to go around, but CNN took the laurels on the first day of the war itself and the news divisions never caught up, not in reputation, not in the regard of their owners. When the war ended, interest in television news receded, and CNN would in the end gain less than the network news divisions lost.

Until then, there was much talk of live coverage, of Vietnam, the "living room war," being succeeded by the instant war, war seen as it happened. Academics had been predicting this since Saigon fell, and now they saw it appear before them. They knew they would, so they did, war as a video game. But although "Live" was inserted over almost every TV report, little was seen as it happened except for generals in the act of describing today what had taken place yesterday, reporters in "standupper" locations introducing pictures taped earlier, and experts whose predictions were wrong even more often than the laws of probability justify.

There were also live pictures from where Scud missiles had hit, but not of missiles hitting; of reporters putting on gas masks, of reporters being the news they reported. That was all. But to the human eye, tape, unlike film, is identical to live television, so viewers believed they saw the war being fought, just as they had seen Jack Ruby shoot Lee Harvey Oswald. It will be so noted in editorial pages, then in history books. It fact, the military had seen to it there were few pictures, live or tape, of war being fought. Until the Defense Department releases its own, Americans will not know what the Gulf War looked like.

With CNN reporting around the clock, starting with its exclusive (sound only) reports of the bombing of Baghdad, the networks scrambled to keep up. It cost each of them tens of millions of dollars in direct costs, in commercials lost when entertainment programs were canceled for special reports, and in the reluctance of advertisers to put their messages in those special reports, although this last was overplayed by newspaper writers who enjoyed the irony. And when it was over, the network owners had little for their money. Furthermore, thenceforward television news coverage of very important events would involve the added expense of instantaneous coverage, or the possibly greater expense of the illusion of instantaneity.

The networks' news audiences had indeed increased during the Gulf War, but that was to be expected with news of such importance and interest, and each network's audience increased about equally. No competitive advantage there. As for acclaim, most of it had gone to CNN. (Nor, strangely, did acclaim seem as important as it used to be.) As for affiliates, some sent their own reporters to Dhahran and Riyadh, something anyone could do, since once there he could ask foolish questions at the briefings along with everybody and get his copy of pool pictures, along with everybody.

Furthermore, many stations, some independents but some affiliates of the networks, arranged to carry CNN's reports whenever they wanted war news, by the hour in the early days, by the minute in later ones. In war as in peace, a viewer tuning in to a network news broadcast knew most of the news he was about to get, and had seen the best of the pictures. The high quality of reporting and presentation by the network news staffs did nothing to halt the further erosion of network news. It may have accelerated it. How much was there left to go? The end would not be abrupt, but it had now come very close.

At the time I was leaving NBC, my granddaughter, not yet three, was going through the stage of pretending she was someone in the television cartoons she watched, someone different each day.

"And who are you today?" I once asked her.

"I am two persons," she replied.

"Which two persons?"

"Hinckley and Beastley."

"Who are they?"

"The bad guys."

Her brother assured me that there was indeed a TV cartoon whose mandatory bad guys were named Hinckley and Beastley.

It seemed better than leaving no footprint at all.

ACKNOWLEDGMENTS

Many friends and colleagues kindly shared their recollections with me, some even their files. Who they are is in most cases clear from the text, but these should be mentioned: John Agoglia, Lester Bernstein, David M. Brinkley, John W. Chancellor, Charles H. Colledge, Jr., Kenneth Cox, Esq., Robert C. Doyle, Douglas Edwards, Jerome L. Fenigen, Eliot Frankel, Julian B. Goodman, James Greenfield, Andrew R. Heiskell, Don Hewitt, Martin Hoade, Edwin James, Sidney L. James, Robert D. Kasmire, David Levy, Ralph Mann, Robert J. Manning, Howard Monderer, Esq., Robert Northshield, Jack Reynolds, Irwin Segelstein, Dr. Frank Stanton, Ron Steinman, Harry Thoess, Patrick Trese, Sander Vanocur, and Richard C. Wald. I hasten to add that mistakes are my fault, not theirs.

My own records survived the decades because of the care they got from Lois Marino, Joan Gifford, Lydia Houghtelling, and Carol L. Aerenson. I was allowed to mine the treasures of NBC's program logs by Betty Jane Reid and Leona Malone and the resources of the NBC reference library by Vera Mayer and her staff. Jerome Feniger provided me with a place to operate from in the big city, which made the work easier. I am indebted to Esther Newberg of ICM, who took my suggestion into the marketplace; and to my editors, Alice Mayhew, who thought there might indeed be a book there, Jenny Cox, whose sharp eye for a redundancy limited its heft, and Ari Hoogenboom, who tried to restrain my excessive quirkiness.

Finally, this book would not have been written at all had I not had the benefit of a senior fellowship at the Gannett Foundation Media Center. I am beholden to its director, Dr. Everette E. Dennis, and to his staff for practical assistance, guidance, and support and for the center's special atmosphere of professional collegiality.

I tried, with middling success, not to overburden the book with opinions and conclusions. The ones expressed are my own and not necessarily those of the National Broadcasting Company, its past or present shareholders or proprietors, sponsors or employees, or the ghosts who walk its corridors.

INDEX

ABOUT THE AUTHOR

Besides seven Emmys, including Program of the Year, Reuven Frank received the Peabody, George Polk, DuPont-Columbia, and Ohio State awards. He and his wife live in New Jersey.